ISLAMIC ECONOMICS

This book is a comprehensive study, which provides informed knowledge within the field of Islamic economics. The authors lay down the principal philosophical foundation of a unique and universal theory of Islamic economics by contrasting it with the perspectives of mainstream economics. The methodological part of the theory of Islamic economics arises from the ethical foundations of the *Qur'an* and the *Sunnah* (tradition of the Prophet) along with learned exegeses in an epistemological derivation of the postulates and formalism of Islamic economics. This foundational methodology will be contrasted with the contemporary approaches of the random use of mainstream economic theory in Islamic economics.

The book establishes the methodological foundation as the primal and most fundamental premise of the study leading to scientific formalism and the prospect of its application. By way of its Islamic epistemological explanation (philosophical premise) in the form of logical formalism and the use of simple real-world examples, the authors show the reader that the scientific nature of economics in general and Islamic economics in particular rests on the conception of the scientific worldview.

With its uniquely comparative approach to mainstream economics, this book facilitates a greater understanding of Islamic economic concepts. Senior undergraduate and graduate students will gain exposure to Islamic perspectives of micro- and macroeconomics, money, public finance, and development economics. Additionally, this book will be useful to practitioners seeking a greater comprehension of the nature of Islamic economics. It will also enable policymakers to better understand the mechanism of converting institutions, such as public and social policy perspectives.

Abul Hassan is a Research Scientist II/Associate Professor in Finance and Economics at the CRE-IBF, Research Institute, King Fahd University of Petroleum and Minerals, Dhahran, Saudi Arabia.

M.A. Choudhury is a Professor in Economics at the Department of Shariah and Economics, Academy of Islamic Studies, University of Malay, Malaysia.

ISLAMIC ECONOMICS

Theory and Practice

Abul Hassan and M.A. Choudhury

Routledge
Taylor & Francis Group

LONDON AND NEW YORK

First published 2019
by Routledge
2 Park Square, Milton Park, Abingdon, Oxon OX14 4RN

and by Routledge
52 Vanderbilt Avenue, New York, NY 10017

Routledge is an imprint of the Taylor & Francis Group, an informa business

British Library Cataloguing-in-Publication Data
A catalogue record for this book is available from the British Library

Library of Congress Cataloging-in-Publication Data
A catalog record has been requested for this book

ISBN: 978-1-138-36241-3 (hbk)
ISBN: 978-1-138-36243-7 (pbk)
ISBN: 978-0-429-43208-8 (ebk)

Typeset in Bembo
by Newgen Publishing UK

CONTENTS

FIGURES

TABLES

PREFACE

Islamic economics as a distinct discipline has emerged since 1983 (AD), and the subject is now offered in many universities as part of the Economics curriculum at undergraduate and post-graduate level. Thousands of students have pursued a PhD in the area of Islamic economics and finance at different universities around the world, including the USA and Europe. Although a few introductions to Islamic economics and finance are available in the market, this book, *Islamic Economics: Theory and Practice*, is the first of its kind. It has been written as a serious and rigorous book in Islamic economics as a discipline and its methodology, its formalism, and its applications. The approach is comparative in nature with modern mainstream economic theory. The centrepiece of the book is Islamic methodology as the universal and unique foundation of the Islamic socio-scientific project, contrasted with all those incomplete systems based on perceptions rather than reality that are immersed in the project of both capitalistic and socialistic materialism.[1] The unique and contrasting basis of Islamic economics, as opposed to those based on capitalistic and socialistic materialism, is its foundation in the concept of *Tawhid*. *Tawhid* literally means the "oneness of God" (*Allah*). It is also understood as the concept of the unity of knowledge of the divine law. This book also refers to the curriculum on epistemology covered in the International Baccalaureate program, but from a firmly Islamic perspective and methodological worldview.

Islam is one of the monotheistic religions, along with Judaism and Christianity, which encompasses a worldview that centres the study and organization of the details of the world-system within the episteme of divine law. Academic exploration of the Islamic worldview offers complex learning and conceptualization, which offers bright new potential in an academic world that is constantly seeking new socio-scientific epistemologies. Heterodoxy in the disciplines is in the air.

This book has been written under the text book project of the "Deanship of Scientific Research of the King Fahd University of Petroleum and Minerals,

Dhahran, Saudi Arabia." Although it is intended for university freshmen in Economics departments, this book ought to be considered as a course in Islamic economics only after the students have gone through a thorough training in mainstream economic theory. This legitimates a critical and methodological study. These students should have completed courses to the level of both intermediate microeconomics and intermediate macroeconomics. At this level, the students should have an adequate grounding in mathematics. Besides these areas of preparation, the student is also expected to use the *Qur'an* and *hadith* for exegeses of topics in Islamic socio-scientific methodology, analytics, and examples. Indeed, a thorough course in Islamic economics may claim to be covering a distinctive original field of erudition and learning, as Islamic economics is substantive and rigorously epistemological in nature, being based on the true Islamic methodological foundation of *Tawhid*. As we know, *Tawhid* means not only oneness of God (*Allah*) but also the unity (consilience) of divine law in its combination of conception, formalism, and applications.

There are distinct features belonging to Islamic economics that characterize this heterodox discipline of knowledge. These features must be understood at the outset of this study as the pertinent direction to the study of all socio-scientific systems. Most notable among these is the study of economics in respect of its wide field of valuation incorporating ethics with the transaction of exchange. This causes the meaning of exchange to be understood more widely, including material exchange as well as exchange of services, which includes caring and well-being, morality and ethics, and social and behavioural norms.

The following are particular characteristics of Islamic economics as based on *Tawhid*:

1. The central episteme is that of unity of knowledge as the core concept, leading to concepts, formalism and applications regarding economic relations as a system and a cybernetic approach into the study of organic interconnected reality. This arises from the primal ontology of *Tawhid* as the law of the *Qur'an*. This is also the domain of the divine law of God (*Allah*) whose signs are of unity of being and becoming proof of God's greatness. (These essential ontological facts are further explicated by the teachings of the Prophet Muhammad, called the *Sunnah*.)
2. Further to the first characteristic there is the important essence of continuous participation (complementarity) as discourse (*shura*) carried out between self, other and society, mind and matter at large concerning the implications and choices emanating from the fundamental episteme of unity of knowledge based on *Tawhid* and the generality and specifics of the particulars under inquiry (*tasbih*). The *Qur'an* refers to these phenomena as *shura* with *tasbih*.
3. The ethics of exchange and transactions in its widest conception and applications are embedded in the conscious interrelations between the variables in the area of Islamic economics. Such relations may be tested on the basis of inter-system and inter-variable organic interrelations.

4. The domains of inter-variable relations encompass choices of the good things of life as mandated by the *Qur'an* and explicated by the purpose and meaning of the *Shari'ah*, termed *maqasid al-shari'ah* (objectivity of Islamic law). These may be fully understood by continuously visiting renewed discourse with consciousness through the method of *fiqh al-Qur'an* as based on *Shari'ah* law.

5. The ontological, epistemological, and applied parts of the comprehensive model of the Islamic methodological worldview together form Islamic phenomenology. Phenomenology is the scientific way of explaining and revealing the degree of consciousness in mind and matter interrelations (Husserl, 1964).

6. The theory of Islamic economics arising from the Islamic methodological worldview forms a continuous evolutionary learning system in unity of knowledge across the dimensions of knowledge, space, and time.

7. The Islamic epistemology of unity of knowledge infers that Islamic economics should be and is everywhere and in everything.

8. Islamic economics is also methodologically distinct from the conventional form of economics.

9. The formal model of Islamic economics is vastly applicable to the entire genre of socio-scientific problems. This embodies extensive empirical depth giving rise to inferential inferences on the morality and ethics of the episteme of unity of knowledge and its reformative consequences.

10. The universality and uniqueness of the methodology in Islamic economics is proved by its application to mainstream economic phenomena with opposite conceptions, meanings, applications, inferences, and implications.

Throughout this book the logical development of ideas in reference to the exegesis of the *Qur'an* establish the fact that, indeed, in the description of all of creation between the heavens and the earth, from these worldly transactions to those of the Hereafter, the organic relations explained to exist between these are of the nature of perpetual exchange. Such exchange can be financial, in terms of goods and services, and in terms of morality and ethicality. This universal meaning of transaction exists for both the good choices and otherwise. Hence the idea of exchange and equivalent transactions premised in the concept of total valuation is of a continuous and extensive system encompassing the endless domain of knowledge, space, and time, prevailing from the beginning to the end, and between the heavens and the earth in the form of seven heavens of dimensions.[2]

Basic explanations

There are some basic definitions that need to be understood in the study of this book from the outset. First, the definition of ethics means the organic unification between the good things of life according to the *Qur'an* and *Sunnah*, as contained in the purpose and objective of the *Shari'ah* referred to as *maqasid al-shari'ah*, to avoid the catchword and deceptive terminology of '*Shari'ah* compliance'. The invoking of the unity of knowledge and its induced systems of relations arises from the nature of the law of *Tawhid* in the *Qur'an* and the *Sunnah*.

From the *Qur'anic* explanation of the organic unity of relational unity arise the many attributes of the good things of life regarding which the *Qur'an* (Chapter 55: *Ar-Rahman*) declares, "There is no end to these." Hence this book addresses the derivation and formalism of the general theory of truth versus falsehood. From the general theory, particular issues and problems are addressed relevant to Islamic economics. The *Qur'an* (31:28) declares regarding this endless generality of goodness within which all good and truth are endowed:

> And if all the trees on earth were pens and the ocean (were ink), with seven oceans behind it to add to its (supply), yet would not the words of God be exhausted (in the writing): for God is Exalted in Power, full of Wisdom.

This book thus makes the argument that there is no need to pick out especial attributes, such as justice, fairness, charity, etc. to explain *Qur'anic* total evaluation. These are simply incomplete examples and not the worldview. For instance, above justice, prayer, *zakah* (mandatory spending for alleviation of hardship), *riba* (financial interest) and the like is the general *Qur'anic* worldview of submission to God as the pinnacle of the divine truth and purpose against falsehood and evil. Within the general theory, the issues of justice as balance (*mizan*), fairness as distributive justice (*iqhlas*), prayer as divine communication etc. are especial cases of surrendering to the *Tawhid*-based law. Thus the episteme of unity of knowledge in *Tawhid* is primal while all specifics are particulars. Everything ensues from *Tawhid*. Nothing ensues from these others to *Tawhid* if *Tawhid* was not invoked as the quiddity in the first instance. The *Qur'an* (13:39) declares in this regard: "God effaces and confirms what He wishes. With/By Him is the mother of the book."

It is because of this type of reference to particulars as selected attributes, rather than starting from the generality of the Islamic worldview and then addressing particulars, that Islamic thought contains gaps in otherwise profound erudition. Among these kinds of intellectual gaps is the quest for the theory of justice according to the *Qur'an*. There has not been any profound work in Islamic thought that has addressed the principle of justice from the basis of a "general theory of justice" according to the Islamic worldview. There have only been, admittedly laudable, treatment of attributes that are partly explained as arising from the principle of justice (Kamali 1991).

This book has shown that as a result of this type of intellectual gap there have remained limitations in the understanding of the wider, generalized meaning of *maqasid as-shari'ah*. The *Qur'anic* cosmic understanding of balance (*mizan*) could not be interconnected with the well-being of the physical combined with the social world-systems to convey the comprehensive meaning of the principle and choices according to the *maqasid as-shari'ah* (Choudhury 2015).

The wide understanding of the particular in unity of relationship with the total reality, the general, has been succinctly explained by Whitehead (1979). With respect to the learning and unifying nature of the universe, he says:

The creative action is the universe always becoming one in a particular unity of self-experience, and thereby adding to the multiplicity which is the universe as many. This insistent concrescence into unity is the outcome of the ultimate self-identity of each entity. No entity – be it "universal" or "particular" – can play disjoined roles. Self-identity requires that every entity has one conjoined, self-consistent function, whatever be the complexity of that function.[3]

Whitehead 1979, p. 57

The primacy of *Tawhid* over all creation in mind, matter and the hidden (*ghayb*) implies the cardinal function of jurisprudential interpretation (*fiqh*) is pertinent only through its continuous revisiting of the *Qur'an*, leading thereby through the *Sunnah* to learned discourse as *usul al-fiqh al-Qur'an*. Contrarily, *fiqh* and *Shari'ah*, in the absence of ontological and epistemological references, have become a sorrowfully exclusive human preference restricted to sects (*madhabs*). This book has avoided this concoction of belief and turned to the continuity of discourse based on the *Qur'an* and the *Sunnah*; these are then brought back to human understanding to develop continuity of *usul al-fiqh al-Qur'an*. A clear distinction must be upheld between the idea of the evolution of species (Darwin 1936) and evolution as the dynamics of increasing (or decreasing) learning in regards to the principle of consilience, and Islamic episteme of unity of knowledge. The *Qur'an* and *Sunnah* abhor the species context of physical evolution. In this regard, the *Qur'an* (95:4) declares: "We have indeed created humankind in the best of moulds." Humankind comprises those who treat *Tawhid* as the primal source of knowledge. The *Qur'an* (95:5) further declares for the contrary category of humankind: "Then We return him to the lowest of the low." These are the ones who deny *Tawhid* and instead, invoke their own failed experiences of modernism. The verse (*Qur'an*, 95:6) then continues to strengthen its promise of knowledge to the believers, that is, those who uphold *Tawhid* as the ultimate source of knowledge and nothing else:[4] "Except for those who believe and do righteous deeds, for they will have a reward uninterrupted."

This book invokes this latter definition throughout. It is also referred to as the *Qur'anic* dialectics of rising towards (or falling from) heightened understanding of the Islamic episteme of unity of knowledge in continuous phases of evolutionary learning. 'Knowledge' throughout this book means 'knowledge of *Tawhid*'. The other kinds of knowing that do not invoke the *Tawhid* law of unity of knowledge are equated with rationalism.

The expression that knowledge is endowed in nature is a static idea. To discover knowledge in its meaning, quiddity, and application in the framework of Islamic unity as law brings out the dynamics of a functioning world-system in such a framework of total reality, encompassing truth and falsehood, right and wrong. In this regard the *Qur'an* (25:1) writes: "Blessed is He who sent down the Criterion upon His Servant that he may be to the worlds a warner." Furthermore, in respect of the final origin of true knowledge, it rests on the *Qur'an*, that is *Tawhid* as law that explains 'everything'. In this regard the *Qur'an* (13:31) declares:

If there were a *Qur'an* with which mountains were moved, or the earth were cloven asunder, or the dead were made to speak (this would be the one!). But, truly, the command is with God in all things! Do not the Believers know that, had God (so) willed, He could have guided all mankind (to the right)? But the Unbelievers, never will disaster cease to seize them for their (ill) deeds, or to settle close to their homes, until the promise of God come to pass, for, verily, God will not fail in His promise.

For this reason – that the ultimate and only source of knowledge rests in *Tawhid* (*Qur'an*) – this book also enquires into the nature of universality and uniqueness in the nature of the Islamic methodological worldview and its particularization of the vastness of the theme of exchange transaction that is studied in terms of its total valuation in Islamic economics.

Rationale of this book

The need for a standard textbook that covers necessary topics of Islamic economics, in a comprehensive manner, in the light of the Islamic epistemology of unity of knowledge, has been felt for a long time. As part of the book project, the Dean of Scientific Research, the King Fahd University of Petroleum and Minerals, Dhahran, Saudi Arabia is privileged to present this book to fulfil the need. Indeed, there is real concern to enlighten stakeholders in the discipline of Islamic economics, whether students, academics, Universities and general readers, about both teaching and learning Islamic economics. Further, those particularly interested are students of business and economics, who intend to study Islamic economics. While the stakeholders would be able to understand more from this book about the ethical foundation of Islamic economics, on the other hand, the young and reflective scholarly minds will get orientation as to the rigorous study of Islamic methodology, and will then be able to conceptually understand and apply it to more comprehensive issues, particularly problems of economics and world-systems. The Islamic methodological perspective will thus be a real contribution to the world of learning.

The book is designed for senior undergraduate and postgraduate students of Islamic economics and finance who have already studied intermediate-level or advanced courses in micro- and macroeconomics. Since the conventional theory is also discussed critically under the relevant topics, these may be attractive and useful for students in other areas of social sciences, like political science, sociology, Islamic political economy, commerce and advanced Islamic studies related to *muamalat* (socio-economic affairs).

Organization of the book

The book is a contribution to the conceptual realm of Islamic economics where the divine law (the law of *Tawhid*) functions in formal, analytical, and applied methods of epistemology of unity of knowledge and unity of the knowledge-induced world-system. This book consists of sixteen chapters, explaining the philosophy, concept and theory of Islamic economics (both micro- and macro-economics), as well as economic policy (monetary, fiscal and developmental) in light of Islamic epistemology.

Chapter 1 provokes thought about and reflects critically on diverse ways of knowing and on areas of knowledge; it prompts students to be aware of Islamic economics in the light of the epistemology of *Tawhid* and encourages them to become better acquainted with the complexity of the knowledge contained in this subject.

Chapter 2 concentrates on the inter-relationships between economics and ethics in Islam. The main point is that ethics establish essential values in Islamic economics. In Islam, economic behaviours and commercial dealings cannot be detached from values and ethics. Islamic values are intended to rule, direct and govern human beings' conduct in their day-to-day economic lives.

Chapters 3 and 4 develop the foundational epistemological (methodological) worldview. On this basis, the keystone of *Tawhid* as moral law, and its dynamic in the evolutionary learning system of inter-causal relations between the 'good things' of life can be studied. The methodical derivation from these foundations, known as circular causation, and the interactive, integrative, and evolutionary properties of this method derived from Islamic foundational methodology, become universal applications in economic problems.

Chapter 5 explains several important concepts that emanate from the formal model of Islamic economics and treats the essence of the Islamic instruments within this model, which is what differentiates the Islamic methodological worldview.

Chapter 6 shows the institutional possibility of integrative financing instruments in trade and development according to the Islamic theory of unity-of-knowledge and unity (*Tawhid*), focusing on the specific case of the participatory instrument.

Chapter 7 focuses on Islamic economics as contrasted with mainstream theory. Consumer and market behaviour are explained with reference to the fundamental Islamic model of unity of knowledge.

Chapter 8 provides detailed explanations of the theories of the firm, consumer behaviour, imperfect competition, and general equilibrium, in reference to the fundamental Islamic model of unity of knowledge.

Chapter 9 is devoted to the concept of macroeconomic theory in mainstream and Islamic economic perspectives, with particular reference to the fundamental Islamic model of unity of knowledge.

Chapter 10 focuses on monetary, financial and real economy issues in Islamic economics and comparative perspectives. It explains in detail the necessary and sufficient conditions of economic and social bliss that are reached by the endogenous interaction between money, finance and the real economy.

Chapter 11 contains some guiding principles of fiscal policy in Islamic economy with special reference to *zakah* by emphasizing the issues of eradicating unemployment, distribution of wealth, economic stability and economic growth.

Chapter 12 attempts to show the justification of taxation in Islam; it looks at the objectives and structural design of the taxation system from an Islamic perspective.

Chapter 13 provides an overview of the resources mobilization for economic development in Islamic perspectives. It covers the issues of the availability and mobilization of both financial resources and human resources for economic development.

Chapter 14 elaborates on the resources mobilization for economic development in Islamic perspectives. It covers the issues pertaining to the availability and mobilization of both financial resources and human resources for economic development.

Chapter 15 looks at the Islamic model of development goals and strategies as a dynamic one. Having discussed the conceptual issues relating to economic development, this chapter attempts to elaborate on the development goals and strategies from an Islamic perspective with reference to distributive justice in Islam.

Chapter 16 discusses the essence of evolutionary learning in Islamic economics as an academic discipline from the perspective of the Islamic methodological worldview of unity of knowledge, from the angle of analytical universality. It also critically discusses mainstream economic reasoning and concludes with a summary of the differences between Islamic economics and conventional economics.

Summary

This book, while emphasizing the origin of every epistemological methodology in the birth of the revolutionary meta-scientific worldview, differentiates in meaning and application between the terms 'methodology' and 'method'. For example, although all of mathematics is a method, methodology impacts upon the *choice* of method, selecting according to the appropriate methods to be used in response to the logical implications of the Islamic methodological worldview. Thus while optimization is a mathematical method, such a method is untenable in studying the method of evolutionary learning properties of *Tawhid* formalism and applications, except for purposes of creating a study of critical realism (Whitehead & Russell 1910–1913).

This is a rigorous book on Islamic economics for students and scholars at all levels, and also across the multidisciplinary areas that combine the studies of ontology, epistemology, and phenomenology of conceptual systems and their applications. The particular emphasis is on the Islamic methodological worldview in respect of *Tawhid as law* arising from the exegeses of the *Qur'an*, the *Sunnah*, and human discourse which is called *ijtihad*. Yet its broadest methodological worldview is of unity of knowledge in a highly realist context. Indeed such has always been the quest of all the sciences.[5]

Some may have the impression that this book is overly philosophical and thus an epistemological treatise. The ontological, epistemological, and phenomenological contents of the building blocks of Islamic economics and the generalized theory of the Islamic methodological worldview cannot be denied in the development of the rigorous foundations of what is truly Islamic in terms of the *Qur'an* and the *Sunnah*. Yet this book does not have a speculative containment in philosophy. Its objective in fact is to use philosophical terms and explanations because of the analytical thoughts that emanate from the *Qur'an* and the *Sunnah*. Such emergent intellection must be encapsulated in the building blocks of any revolutionary theory of meta-science.[6] The theory of Islamic economics is in the particular case out of the general analytical case.

The teaching of the book first requires good understanding of the subject by the teacher. The teacher may then like to tailor the content of this book as necessary in order to teach good critical learning and with both a conceptual and an applied perspective, extracting sections of this book according to the needs of the students at various levels. Ideally, students should be required to have already studied at least introductory and, preferably, intermediate economic theory. The students should also have reached a sound level of mathematical understanding of economic theory. Ideally, they would also have been prepared in introductory epistemology at the level of the International Baccalaureate (IB).[7]

One way to apply this book in a three-credit course is the following lecture structure:

1. One month of lectures should be devoted to the study of Islamic methodology, in particular the essential features of Islamic economics in critical contrast to mainstream economic theory and its different methodology. Exegeses of the *Qur'an* and the *Sunnah* would be used to delineate the critical foundation of Islamic economics. Examples and exercises will build understanding of the relevant area of methodology.
2. The next month should be devoted to the study of the contrast between Islamic and mainstream/neoclassical microeconomics, again referring throughout to relevant methodology through examples and exercises.
3. The last month of lectures should be devoted to the study of the contrast between Islamic and mainstream macroeconomics, still using practical solutions to examples and exercises to focus on the development of the relevant methodology. The lecturer should encourage visual thinking and diagrams to explain the logical differences between these two schools of thought.
4. The lecturer may draw together notebooks for their students from this book, creating parallel handbooks or exercise books suitable for the level at which they need to teach their particular group of students.

It was mentioned earlier that this book is formed of three interrelated parts. First, there is a substantive part on the distinctive methodology of *Tawhid* as *Qur'anic* law, looking at the derivation of this worldview of meta-science from the *Qur'an* and the *Sunnah* (*usul al-Qur'an*). Second, there is a section on the emergent theory of Islamic economics as distinctly different from mainstream economics. Third, there are applications of the theory by way of examples and exercises. More can be formulated. The conscientious and erudite scholar can further develop and innovate in these specific areas and beyond; each specific instructor, group of scholars, and well-informed practitioners can also formulate their local issues and problems in the light of the total valuation concept of Islamic economics.

It is hoped that this work in the authentic Islamic methodological worldview of Islamic law (*Shari'ah*) and its applications will substantively widen the knowledge available on this subject to the academic world. It should not be restricted to use purely by Muslim students and scholars. Through its publication and dissemination we hope that this book will become one of the vital reference works on the subject around the world. This book is a study on Islamic economics which stands for socio-moral justice and efficiency to be achieved through growth and employment creation. It is very much concerned with equitable distribution of income and wealth and reduction of inequality. The rise of Islamic economics as a discipline as an alternative to the global economy could very well serve as an aid to the ills of the capitalistic system.

Both teachers and students would like to have a comprehensive text that covers all the areas of economics. However, sorting out every essential topic from a vast body of literature and accommodating them in a small text of limited scope is really a tedious and cumbersome task. Moreover Islamic economics is a new but growing discipline. More work need to be done in the area of Islamic economics and we hope that some young Islamic economists will come forward to produce more textbooks on the subject. Due to the breadth and complexity of the task at hand, some inconsistencies and shortcomings are inevitable. No human effort in this world can be complete in coverage and perfect in attaining its objectives. The contributors have attempted to do some justice to the objectives of their project, but never claim perfection. Time will reveal the true successes and failures of this work.

Last but not least – God – the Almighty deserves all the gratitude and praise, Who has bestowed upon us the wealth of *iman* (faith and belief) and an understanding of *ilm* (the field of knowledge).

On behalf of the Textbook Project, *Islamic Economics: Principles and Practice*,

Abul Hassan,
(Principal Investigator)
King Fahd University of Petroleum and Minerals
Dhahran, Saudi Arabia
November 26, 2018.

Notes

1 In regards to the worldview of the *Qur'an*, that is of *Tawhid*, Nasr *et al.* (2015, p. xxvi) writes: "No sacred scripture of which we have knowledge speaks more about the cosmos and the world of nature than does the *Qur'an*, where one finds extensive teachings about cosmogenesis, cosmic history, eschatological events marking the end of the cosmic order as it now exists, and the phenomena of nature as revealing Divine Wisdom. In fact, the *Qur'an* refers to these phenomena as *ayat*" (signs of *Allah*).
2 *Qur'an* (65:12): "It is God (*Allah*) Who has created seven heavens and of the earth the like thereof. His Command descends between them (heavens and earth), that you may know

that God has power over all things, and that God surrounds (comprehends) all things in (His) Knowledge."

3 The term 'concrescence' means unity between the entities of learning processes.

4 Chittick (1989) translates Ibn Arabi who wrote: "Two ways lead to the knowledge of God… The first way is the way of unveiling… The second way is the way of reflection and reasoning (*istidlal*) through rational demonstration (*burhan aqli*). This way is lower than the first way, since he who bases his consideration upon proof can be visited by obfuscations which detract from his proof, and only with difficulty can he remove them" [slightly edited by author].

5 Whitehead (1938, p. 205): "The doctrine that I am maintaining is that neither physical nature nor life can be understood unless we fuse them together as essential factors in the composition of 'really real' things whose interconnections and individual characters constitute the universe."

6 The meaning of a revolutionary methodological worldview is borrowed from Kuhn (1970). Kuhn remarked regarding the emergence of scientific revolution beyond normal science and paradigm shift: "… scientific revolutions are here taken to be those non-cumulative developmental episodes in which an older paradigm is replaced in whole or in part by an incompatible new one" (1970, p. 154).

7 IB Theory of Knowledge Program: http://ibo.org/en/programmes/diploma-programme/

References

Chittick, W.C. (1989). *Sufi Path of Knowledge*, Albany, NY: State University of New York.

Choudhury, M.A. (2015). *Res extensa et res cogitans de maqasid as-shari'ah, International Journal of Law and Management*, 57(6): 662–693.

Darwin, C. (1936). *Descent of Man* (or *Origin of Species*), New York, NY: Modern Library.

Husserl, E. (1964). *The Idea of Phenomenology*, trans. Alston, W.P. & Nakhnikian, G., The Hague, Netherlands: Martin Nijhoff.

Kamali, M.H. (1991). *Principles of Islamic Jurisprudence*, Cambridge, England: Islamic Texts Society.

Kuhn, T.S. (1970). *The Structure of Scientific Revolution*, Chicago, IL: University of Chicago Press.

Nasr, S.H. *et al.*, eds. (2015), *The Study Qur'an*, New York: Harper Collins.

Whitehead, A.N. (1938). Nature Alive, Lecture 8 in his *Modes of Thought*, New York: Macmillan.

Whitehead, A.N. (1979). Fact and form, in *Process and Reality*, eds. Griffin, D.R. & Sherburne, D.W., New York: The Free Press.

Whitehead, A.N. & Russell, B. (1910–13). *Principia Mathematica*, New York: Cambridge University Press.

ACKNOWLEDGEMENTS

The book project titled *Islamic Economics: Theory and Practice* has been sponsored by the Deanship of Scientific Research, King Fahd University of Petroleum and Minerals, Dhahran, Saudi Arabia under the scheme of the KFUPM internal research grants (Vide DSR Approved Project No. IN131050, Start Date: 01/6/2014). The authors of this book would record their appreciation and gratitude to the Dean and the staff of the DSR for entrusting us the task of writing this manuscript.

We also record our gratitude to Professor M. A. Choudhury for playing the role of International Consultant in the design and development of the scheme of the book project.

GLOSSARY OF ARABIC TERMS

A glossary of the principal Arabic terms used in this book is provided below.

A'dal	justice
a'lameen	universe or world
ayat	verse or proof
Ayat Allah	Word of God
Akhirah	Hereafter
baitul mal	Islamic public treasury
burhan àqli	rational demonstration
bay muajjal	leasing according to the Islamic law
fardh	obligatory
fiqh al-Qur'an	jurisprudence of *Qur'an*
fitrat	habit
fuqaha	the interpreter of *ahakam* (rules) derived from Islamic law
futuhat	etymology/history
haqq	entitlement
huquq al Allah	duty to God
huquq al ibadah	duty to the world through one's belief in God
halalan tayyiban	permission of consumption in Islamic way
ijara	rental
ijma	social consensus
ijtihad	discourse on Islamic issues for developing *ahakam* (rules) for reaching consensus
iqhlas	purity
Khalaq	creation or natural order
maqasid al-shari'ah	objectivity of *Shari'ah*
maslaha	public interest

mizan	balance
muamalat	socio-economic order
mudarabah	profit-sharing contract under Islamic laws
mujtahid	most learned scholar in *Shari'ah*
murabaha	mark-up pricing
musharakah	equity participation in business under Islamic laws
qard-e-hasanah	interest-free loan
qiyas	Islamic analogy for developing social consensus
Qur'an	holy book for believers
riba	interest
Shari'ah law	Islamic law
shura	Islamic consultative institution
sirat al-mustaqim	straight but richly complex
Sunnah	sayings and traditions of Prophet Muhammad
Sunnat Allah	Sign of God
tasbih	repetitive utterance of short sentences to glorification of God
Tawhid	Oneness of God
usul	epistemology, foundation
waqf	endowment
zakah	compulsory wealth tax (2.5 per cent) in Islam

1

HOW TO STUDY ISLAMIC ECONOMICS AS SCIENCE IN REFERENCE TO THE *QUR'AN* AND THE *SUNNAH*

LEARNING OBJECTIVES

This chapter aims to:

- highlight the concept of high morality and ethics in the light of the *Qur'an* in the development of the foundation of theory of Islamic economics
- pinpoint fundamental values necessary for economics behaviour and the sole axiom of Islamic economics studies
- emphasize the formalization of the Islamic methodological worldview in the rise of the corresponding economic and socio-scientific reasoning with a brief critique of conventional economic theory and practice
- rationalize the need for an alternative economic paradigm.

Islamic economics as a field of study began in the 1950s with the works of some Indian scholars in the field. The King Abdulaziz University's Islamic Economics Research Institute, in Jeddah, Saudi Arabia records the origin of the contemporary approach to the study of Islamic economics to be about forty years after that. The works of the great Islamic scholars, the *mujtahids*, such as Imam Ghazali, Ibn Taimiyya, Imam Shatibi, Ibn Qayyim, and Ibn Khaldun recorded the study of Islamic economic and social problems either in reference to the *Qur'an* and prophetic teaching, the *Sunnah*; or independently of those as ideas were based on economic thought in the light of *ijtihad* (Islamic scholarships). The latter examples are of Ibn Khaldun (Rozenthal 1958), and the Muslim philosopher, Al-Farabi (Waltzer 1985). The use of the terminology 'Islamic economics' reflects the classification of educational disciplines given to us by the Western world.

While classification of the disciplines carried with it the specialization and independence of the areas of learning as separable activities, Islamic economics, by its contemporary term, became one of the emergent ways of such thinking.

It is fact that a lot of work has been done by Islamic economists regarding the conceptual understanding of the reasons why conventional theory is not relevant to Islamic analysis of economic behaviour. Even some non-Muslim economists have roundly criticized conventional economics and have called for the development of an Islamic ethical approach in order to understand economic behaviour in general. However, most of the scholars writing on Islamic economics have confined their research within the framework of neo-classical economics – a framework that is being increasingly recognised, even by mainstream conventional economists, to be inadequate to explain the economic behaviour of man. This marks the point of departure of the Islamic methodological worldview and its potentiality to contribute to and sustain Islamic originality, erudition, epistemology, and consequential analytics in the wider academic world. Islamic economics entered the scene of the classified disciplines in a tragic state, depicted critically by Mahomedy (2013). Nonetheless, great potential remains for Islamic economics as a discipline of meta-science that should be grounded on truly Islamic epistemological foundations.

Growing dissatisfaction with conventional economics requires the derivation of Islamic economics from the teachings of the *Qur'an* and the *Sunnah*. It needs to develop as an alternative framework of analysis so that the edifice of Islamic economics is not constructed on wrong foundations (Khan 2013). This alternative framework has to be such that it can accommodate the knowledge of the *Qur'an* about human nature and behaviour. The *Qur'an* is the revealed book of guidance for those who seek guidance.[1] It thereby provides guidance for all issues of mind and matter, and thus of science economics in its meta-perspective of morality and ethics embedded in materiality. The methods and models of Islamic economics have to be universal in application and realistic in making assumptions and axioms based on Islamic morals and ethics. It should be noted that the concept of science in the *Qur'an* and *Sunnah* is not limited to positive knowledge that is consistent with reality only, but also includes proponent presumptions. For this reason, Muslim jurists are in agreement in calling *fiqh* a science, although many of its rules are based upon presumptive evidence (Zarka 2003). Therefore, the science of Islamic values must be attached to the notion of Islamic economics.[2]

The present state of the study of economics

The Royal Economic Society points out that, since 1999, smaller universities in the United Kingdom have abandoned exclusive focus on economics. Yet the larger universities in the UK, by virtue of their advanced ideas in economic reasoning and by integrating related disciplines, have flourished. One such area that has arisen in the larger universities is heterodox economic theory. According to orthodox economic theory, to which neoclassical economics belongs, the principal attribute of rational choice-making in goods and services is 'marginal rate of substitution' between competing goods and services for the command over scarce resource allocation between such competing ends. We will also refer to this neoclassical premise as 'marginalism'. Islamic economics immersed in mainstream orthodox economics could not belong to the holistic sociological economic school.

Since then, Islamic economics is in its heyday in the Muslim world. It by and large has been encouraged by the now stylized caption of Islamic finance. The example is the present failing of Islamic banks. They raise large equity values from investors in the market. Unfortunately, Islamic banking and finance is then clearly directed towards a profit-oriented entity rather than a social-based entity, which has not been given attention when the objectives of Islamic economics have been discussed (Mohammad and Shahwan 2013). The major problem of Islamic economics, like Islamic finance, Islamic banking, and other Islamic socio-scientific ventures, is that it has no articulated epistemological foundation. On the other hand, any science, social or natural in category, ought to be based in solid epistemological foundation. Such an orientation gives shape, form, axioms, assumptions, and methodological formalism to the entire body of theory and application. Einstein (Bohr 1985) said that science without epistemology remains muddle-headed. This being the case, the axioms, assumptions, nature, methodology, and applications at the core of Islamic economic reasoning, namely morality and ethics, must be included in the developing framework of Islamic economics.

The rise of heterodox economics in recent times is of a deeply ontological and epistemological type. Even neoclassical economics is epistemological in nature according to its own axiom of economic rationality. Classical economics is thoroughly epistemological, in reference to the *Theory of Moral Sentiments* as Adam Smith's first great epistemological contribution to economic reasoning. The basic paradigm of science as we have inherited it rests on the epistemology of heteronomy. Heteronomy conveys the nature of dualism between *a priori* and *a posteriori* domains of reasoning. We will discuss these issues in subsequent chapters, to bring out the distinctive difference between the rationalism of the Western theory of science and the episteme of unity of knowledge of the Islamic methodological worldview.

Contrary to all such epistemological moorings, current Islamic economics, and likewise, all other Islamic socio-scientific fields in recent times have not been able to formalize and contribute to the internal dynamics and functioning of the primal axiom of the entire Islamic methodological worldview upon which a meta-science can be established. This is the ineluctable axiom of *Tawhid* as the monotheistic law of unity of knowledge. It exists not simply in words. Rather, as Imam Ghazali said (Karim, n.d.), the understanding of *Tawhid* as a methodological worldview has sixty stages with increasing depth. Islamic economics has casually adopted a surface attitude towards declaring *Tawhid* (belief) without mentioning its world-system dynamics and axiomatic character in the building of socio-scientific thought, meta-science, and applications (Naqvi 2003).

The Islamic methodological worldview is the universal and unique foundation of all Islamic intellection. It is formal in nature if properly utilized for the construction of the cognitive and material world-system and its specifics. Such a formal intellection with its methodology, methods, and application is equally applicable to the building of meta-science as well as economics as discipline in the world of learning. On the indispensability of the Islamic methodological worldview in the mundane world-system, Ibn Arabi wrote in his *Futuhat* (trans. Chittick 1989):

> The first way is by way of unveiling. It is an incontrovertible knowledge which is actualized through unveiling and which man finds in him. He receives no obfuscation along with it and is not able to repel it....The second way is the way of reflection and reasoning (*istidlal*) through rational demonstration (*burhan `aqli*). This way is lower than the first way, since he who bases his consideration upon proof can be visited by obfuscations which detract from his proof, and only with difficulty can he remove them.

The surface approach to Islamic economics, which only utters *Tawhid* at the beginning and at the roots, rather than throughout the concept, is unable to formalize the monotheistic meaning as a methodology, formalism, and application.

As a consequence, in Islamic economics the Kantian *problematique* of heteronomy between the moral imperative of the *a priori* domain and the practical reasoning of the *a posteriori* domain has entered Islamic socio-scientific thought in general and Islamic economics and finance in particular in a most surreptitious way. Heteronomy, like rationalism, causes a dichotomy between the moral law (*Tawhid = a priori*) and the world-system (*a posteriori*). Contrarily, the *Qur'an* presents the moral and cognitive world-systems as being one of a unified and indivisible holism. It has its endogenous dynamics of organic unity of being and becoming concerning mind and matter. The Islamic methodological worldview is thus indispensable, in order to give the universal and uniquely original, revolutionary, essential Islamic foundation to finance, science and society (Choudhury 2015).

As was mentioned above, Islamic socio-scientific intellection in general and Islamic economics and finance in particular have not been able to stop the emergence of a field of heterodox economics. Heterodox economics by itself is a deeply ontological and epistemological inquiry (Lawson 2003). If the ontological and epistemological foundations of the *Qur'an* and *Sunnah* are missed out, then the constructive dynamics of the Islamic foundation cannot be understood. This is equivalent to uttering but not knowing how to cognize and apply the methodology of *Tawhid* in the building of meta-science for rendering to the world of learning. Will it stay this way? Have not the *Qur'an* and *Sunnah* given the challenge to raise the world-system to the pinnacle of knowledge for global well-being? This possibility is not to be found in the present state of Islamic economic thought, by missing out the episteme of *Tawhid*. Yet substantive effort and contributions in this direction abide.

The nature of Islamic economics according to the Islamic episteme

This book elaborates on the epistemological methodology of *Tawhid* based on the groundwork of a heterodox Islamic economics and finance. The resultant Islamic methodology is rigorously analytical, invoking science, formalism, and analytical depth as well as universal application to particular issues and problems. It is a mistake and a complete denial of scholarly knowledge to say that *Tawhid* is purely philosophical and that its necessity in Islamic economics is not understood.

The fundamental attributes of Islamic economics in the light of Islamic methodology begin from the exegesis of the principle of 'pairing' in the *Qur'an*.[3] Pairing conveys the organic unity between the good things of life as well as the association of the bad things of life, in accordance with the *Qur'an*. The good things are to be accepted; the bad things shunned. Pairing as organic unity of knowledge conveys the universal meaning of God's creation and purpose. It is a reflection of the unity of being and becoming along the dynamics of forming complementarities between the good and recommended things of life. The good things of life participate and complement each other in a unified inter-causal relationship. The bad things compete and marginalize each other. There is no scope of unifying for purposive unity, except to marginalize each other by association and differentiation.

This book will explain how the nature of Islamic methodology is intrinsically related, by circular cause and effect, to a deep knowledge of economics. According to the *Qur'an*, *Tawhid* is the bedrock of complete and absolute knowledge. God is the fullness of knowledge that is embodied in the monotheistic law as the primal ontology, meaning theory of being and existence. The world-system (*a'lameen*) is described and is spanned by the signs of monotheistic unity of knowledge in the good things of life, and its opposite in the bad things of life, by association and differentiation. These are both the Signs of God (*ayath Allah*). They together explain the natures of the paired and the differentiated universes. They provide the ways of moral construction by consciousness of unity of knowledge in the details of the conscious universe. Thus the nature of Islamic economics is axiomatically premised on the Islamic methodology of unity of knowledge functioning as an organic relationship of being and becoming. The result is the continuous nature of evolutionary learning emerging from inter-causality between the participatory and complementary good things of life. This presents the sure sign of paired unity of knowledge acting upon diversity of things. The world-system that is constructed by the Islamic episteme is a continuously simulated universe of unity of knowledge. The process of participatory and complementary organic relations never ceases. It simply closes in the Hereafter (*Akhirah*).

According to the Islamic episteme of unity of knowledge and the methodology applied to Islamic economics this book will prove that almost all orthodox and mainstream economic thought in its critical components is untenable in Islamic economics. Continuous evolutionary learning in unity of knowledge results in annulment of steady-state equilibriums, optimization models, formal functionals of maximization, and almost all of the economic postulates of rationality. Only evolutionary learning models abide. This theory is substantively explained throughout this book.

Critique of axioms and assumptions of Islamic economics borrowed from mainstream economics

The use of Islamic methodology of unity of knowledge and the world-system causes almost all of the postulates of mainstream and orthodox economic theory to be ineffective in Islamic economics. They are replaced by the holistic, knowledge-induced, evolutionary learning economic reasoning.

Scarcity: The core mainstream orthodox economic axiom is scarcity of resources. This assumption is unacceptable in the *Qur'anic* worldview of abundance. This is true both in the absolute and relative meanings of resource scarcity. Scarcity does not exist in absolute terms by virtue of the principle of abundance in the *Qur'an*, except when resources are spoiled by human acts. Even these states of scarcity are recoverable ones, in a move towards reviving abundance. That is, moral reconstruction is always the goal and a possibility of the Islamic evolutionary worldview that increases resources continuously. Scarcity of resources does not exist relatively because in the state of mutual learning and endogenous role of ethics and technology in resources – learning as by complementarities in the pairing universe of the *Qur'an* – continuously increases resources. Resources are thus endogenized continuously by knowledge.

Opportunity cost and marginal rate of substitution (marginalism): Because of the continuously endogenous effect of interaction, integration, and evolutionary learning as properties of the pairing – i.e. a complementary or participatory universe – there is no steady-state equilibrium point, and no optimal resource surface exists. In this way, neither the consumer indifference curve nor the production possibility curve takes shape and form.

Objective functions of mainstream and orthodox economics: The non-existence of smoothly concave to the origin indifference curves and production isoquants, and a smooth convex production possibility curve, imply that the well-behaved types of utility function and production function in substitutes do not exist. Besides, substitutes cannot exist in continuous evolutionary learning by pairing the complementarities of goods, services, and productive inputs. Ethically speaking too, in the first order condition of relationship between goods and productive inputs the economic expansion path remains positively sloped. In the second order condition of allocation of resources it is possible that one of the goods and services receive differentially less than the other. But both gain along the positive economic expansion path.

Relative prices of goods, services, and productive factors: The non-existence of smooth indifference curves, production isoquants, and production possibility surfaces cannot allow for well-determined relative prices.

Market prices: In the absence of well-determined relative prices, consumer demand curves and market demand curves cannot exist. This happens also due to the absence of a simple price–quantity relationship for a specific good in demand and supply. Rather, other critical factors militate. Examples of such systemic interferences are dynamic preferences of choice, and endogenously related variations on other characteristics, e.g. continuously variable relative prices, incomes, and resources in the demand and supply functions (not curves).

Marginal cost pricing: Marginal cost of variable factors cannot exist because of knowledge-induced learning cost curves and production functions. Besides, under the effect of increasing returns to scale the total cost curve, average cost curve, and the productivity curve of output remain continuously evolutionary and downward shifting with endogenous learning.

Marginal productivities of productive factors: The absence of substitution and its replacement by pervasive complementarities between goods, services, and productive inputs cannot allow for marginal productivities of inputs, goods, and services. All other characteristics of non-existing steady-state equilibrium and optimal points cannot allow for marginal productivities to exist.

Dynamic preferences and technological change: The evolutionary learning properties of utility curve (therefore consumer indifference curve) and production function (therefore production isoquants) are causally related with dynamic preferences and tastes. Consequently, all the properties of rational choice theory are annulled in the presence of evolutionary learning and pervasive organic complementarities caused by the Islamic axiom of unity of knowledge and its effect on the evolutionary learning (pairing) universe.

The same kind of result is true of **technology**. Unlike the exogenous nature of technology in mainstream orthodox economic theory, technology is endogenously determined by continuous evolutionary learning. This phenomenon present in unity of knowledge affects resources, preferences, and choices by their mutual interaction and integration followed by continuous evolution. These substantive characteristics of the evolutionary learning in Islamic economics will be explained in detail in the course of this book.

Economic rationality: This is a mainstream and orthodox economic axiom based on full-information and pre-ordering of given preferences as datum, so as to establish internal consistency of the neoclassical theory in problem solving. Yet in Islamic economic theory according to the Islamic methodological worldview, the postulate of full-information is untenable. The God-centric universe to which we are exposed by cognition and experience under evolutionary learning in unity of knowledge can never allow for discontinuity of knowledge (and thereby differentiation oppositely in the states of non-learning). Besides, dynamic preferences and endogenous technological change under the impact of evolutionary learning in unity of knowledge cannot be pre-ordered. Problem solving is done not by any assumption of consistency. Rather, the formal results and experiences of emergent economic and social models cause the need for addressing the problems at hand in pertinent ways. McCloskey (1985) promoted such an idea of addressing the nature of the state "as is", rather than by theoretical prediction of economic theory.

Optimization and equilibrium consequences of absence of economic rationality: The absence of economic rationality in the Islamic methodological worldview (of continuous evolutionary learning in unity of knowledge and unity of the knowledge-induced world-system) results in the complete absence of optimal states and steady-state equilibrium. While mainstream economics allow for exogenously induced changes in pareto-optimal steady-state equilibriums, the

Islamic methodological worldview has only endogenous resource augmentation and changes of organization under the impact of unity of knowledge. The result then is a continuously endogenous change in resource allocations, technological change, preferences, and every other participatory variable. Consequently, all points on the economic surfaces are continuously perturbed by continuous change along non-optimal directions. Likewise, steady-state equilibrium points are changes into evolutionary learning points without convergence into attained states.

Economic systems: The concepts of perfectly competitive markets (economy), imperfect competition, and monopolistic competition are all rendered untenable in the midst of the continuously evolutionary learning methodology of Islamic unity of knowledge. The reason for this is that the existence of optimality and steady-state equilibrium makes all genres of economic systems untenable. The attenuating cost and production functions do not preserve their smooth structures to all for calculus of differentiation. Only learning curves in cost and output exist, causing non-existence of the marginal cost curve and marginal productivity measures. This was pointed out above. From the Islamic perspective of continuous evolutionary learning with inter-causal participation and complementarities, the competition and methodological individualism concepts of self-interest cannot exist, as otherwise found in mainstream and orthodox economics.

Behavioural perspectives: Morality and ethics remain exogenous to mainstream and orthodox economic theory. Knowledge borne out of the monotheistic law of unity of knowledge is centrally poised in morality and ethics. Thus for example, social justice and materiality – likewise, social capital and private capital ownership – are competing opposites for substitutes in mainstream economic theory of opportunity cost and scarcity of resources, (except as exogenous ethical impacts change behaviour, though not continuously). Such resource injection occurs exogenously by external imposition. On the other hand, in the case of the endogenous nature of knowledge, learning, and thereby the continuity of moral and ethical consciousness, social and economic choices are treated as complementary, participatory, and continuously evolutionary by learning in unity of knowledge. Islamic behavioural attributes are primarily based on the consciousness of *Tawhid* as Oneness of God and the unity of the monotheistic law. This in turn needs the extraction of ontological knowledge (theory of existence of being) from the *Qur'an* through the medium of the *Sunnah* (teachings of the Prophet Muhammad) and discourse among the learned ones in the Islamic nature of a purposive world-system.

God, morality, ethics, and the world-system: The oneness of God as belief, which is projected in the episteme of unity of knowledge in God's law, is the sole exogenous ontology of the Islamic world-system. All other variables in the Islamic world-system (*a'lameen*) are paired by endogenous interrelations, and circular causality of complementary relations (organic 'pairing' as in the *Qur'an*). Thus, unlike the exogenous nature of morality and ethics in mainstream and orthodox economic theory, and then too the notion of ethics emerging from the *a posteriori* world of mind–matter, Islamic methodology sets the emergence of ethics and morality in the monotheistic law of unity of knowledge; and points out the opposite of differenti-ation. The extraction of such morality and ethics proceeds from the *Qur'an* via the *Sunnah* in order to induce the paired causality of the world-system. The ontology of God's law is then rendered to human discourse vis-à-vis the generality and details of diverse world-systems. These comprise the mind–matter dynamics, formalism, application, and context.

The study of the moral and ethical induction of Islamic behaviour in economics and its representative inter-causal variables in the light of the Islamic methodology of unity of knowledge invokes mathematical methods mostly of the topological type. Topology is the only branch of advanced mathematics that studies relations between non-dimensional categories. Differential calculus is sparingly used in rela-tion to knowledge variables. Time in the tuple – comprising knowledge, space, and time dimensions of functional categories – remains simply a recorder, not creator of anything. Knowledge remains the sole creator of events and change over the dimensions of knowledge, space, and time.

Islamic economics (and its applications as studied in this work) can be defined as follows: "Islamic economics is a scientific study of issues of economics in concert with all possible related fields that together interact to form an organic influence on economic issues and events and vice-versa." Such an encompassing scientific worldview of Islamic economics is particularized in the meta-science of the prin-cipal and sole axiom of all Islamic socio-scientific studies – that of the monotheistic law of unity of knowledge in the good choices of life, which are choices derived from the purpose and objective of the *Qur'anic* law – *maqasid al-shari'ah*. The same law rejects the bad choices of life. The two categories of goods and services are deciphered from evolutionary learning according to the monotheistic law of unity of knowledge (*Tawhid*) and the induced economic world-system with its moral, ethical, and systemic congeries.

This contrariety exists between the nature of mainstream economics and the Islamic methodology applied to the generality and particular of human cognition and experience on the other hand. An example of the particular is the emergence of the *Qur'anic* study of the economic issues of man and the universe. This book will formalize the Islamic methodological worldview in the rise of the corresponding economic and socio-scientific reasoning. Examples will be provided to illustrate this contrariety between these opposing worldviews of science, society, and the economic world-system; and of morality, ethics, and the world-system with its par-ticularity in economics.

An example here is of the problem of Islamic economics replicating from orthodox and mainstream economic learning. The example is shown by the acceptance of marginal rate of substitution or the opportunity cost idea in existing idea of Islamic economics. Such marginalized ideas lead to the replacement of social justice with economic efficiency as a substitute. Both of these are dear to epistemo-logical reasoning. They are internalized in endogenous choice behaviour in social preferences and their technological implications. In the Islamic methodological worldview, morality and ethics are endogenously embedded in human inclinations by consciousness. They are not determined exogenously by costly external imposition, as by government and policing by the state. The *Shari'ah* (Islamic law) is naturally accepted by humankind for the common good and general well-being (*maslaha*) and purpose (*maqasid al-shari'ah*). The *maqasid al-shari'ah* is not coerced law, as the *Qur'an* declares (10:32–33): "Such is God your real Cherisher and Sustainer: Apart from Truth, what (remains) but error? Thus, is the Word of thy Lord proved true against those who rebel: Verily they will not believe."

For whom is this book appropriate?

This book is meant for students entering a rigorous course of Islamic economics as science and with critical thinking. Indeed, Islamic economics studied in the light of its epistemological foundations and as a scientific discipline should only be taken up after the student has completed at least an introductory economics course, or better yet, has studied economics at an intermediate level. Indeed, the study of economics in the light of its epistemological issues is taught to International Baccalaureate students as a general mandatory course.

The internet version of the International Baccalaureate (IB) Theory of Knowledge course states the significance of the theory of knowledge: "Theory of knowledge ... asks students to reflect on the nature of knowledge, and on how we know what we claim to know. Theory of Knowledge is part of the International Baccalaureate (IB) Diploma Programme (DP) core and is mandatory for all students." For a more detailed introduction to the theme of epistemology as scientific methodology, please see Martin (2010). Theory of Knowledge aims to make students aware of the interpretative nature of knowledge, including personal ideological biases – whether these biases are retained, revised or rejected. It offers the students and their teachers an opportunity to:

- reflect critically on diverse ways of knowing and on areas of knowledge
- consider the role and nature of knowledge in their own culture, in the cultures of others and in the wider world.

In addition, Theory of Knowledge prompts students to:

- be aware of themselves as thinkers, encouraging them to become more acquainted with the complexity of knowledge
- recognize the need to act responsibly in an increasingly interconnected but uncertain world.

Theory of Knowledge also provides coherence for the student, by linking academic subject areas as well as transcending them. It therefore demonstrates the ways in which the student can apply their knowledge with greater awareness and credibility.

Conclusion: How should this book be used?

This book covers five distinctive areas under the Islamic methodology of unity of knowledge. These are (i) methodology; (ii) analytical formalism of the imminent theory of Islamic economics; (iii) its application to the important field of Islamic financial instruments in the light of Islamic economics; (iv) analytical applications arising from the theory of Islamic economics; (v) supporting exercises and working examples encompassing all these areas.

The first three chapters are devoted to the study of ethics and Islamic economics and the Islamic methodology of unity of knowledge used for the nature of Islamic economics in view of the *Qur'an*, the *Sunnah*, and comparative intellectual discourse. The remaining chapters are a combination of theoretical and applied work in the light of a comparative study of the first three chapters. Given below is the distribution of contents in this book in reference to the Islamic methodological worldview of this book in comparison and contrast to the mainstream and orthodox economic theory. The topics pointed out below comprise those that are contained in this book, and which the student must learn.

It should be noted that, because this book carries some rigorous and advanced treatment of the subject matter of Islamic economics, it uses terms that are at an advanced level as well. These terminologies and concepts may arise from mainstream economics, as studied in introductory and intermediate-level economics courses. They may also arise from epistemological terminologies in establishing the Islamic analytical methodology, derived methods, formalism, and applications. It would therefore be necessary for the teacher to explain such terms where they appear in the text. Besides this, the teacher ought to select specific topics of his/her choice in Islamic economics to focus on with the students. As the book does, so should these lectures use PowerPoint, diagrams, simple mathematical formalism, exercises and examples towards delivering a comprehensive course of Islamic economics.

Topics to be covered

Introduction

The foundational issues

1. ethics in Islamic economics
2. Islamic economic methodology
3. the scope of Islamic economics
4. the formulation of the Islamic economic model
5. Islamic participatory instruments and their ethical dimensions

Contrasting Islamic and mainstream theoretical issues: microeconomics

6. Islamic economics *contra* mainstream consumer theory
7. Islamic economics *contra* mainstream theory of the firm

8. Islamic economics *contra* mainstream imperfect competition
9. Islamic economics *contra* mainstream general equilibrium theory

Contrasting Islamic and mainstream theoretical issues: macroeconomics

10. Islamic economics *contra* mainstream generation of outputs and macroeconomic variables
11. policy and institutional issues: money, finance and real economy and general ethico-economic equilibrium

Public finance in Islam

12. fiscal policy in Islamic economy
13. taxation in Islamic economy
14. mobilization of resources for Islamic economic development
15. Islamic model of development goals and strategies

Students' preparation

- undergraduate courses in microeconomics and macroeconomics
- undergraduate mathematics: set theory, calculus, statistics
- exegesis of the *Qur'an* and the *Sunnah*.

A number of exercises are given in each chapter. Some examples are presented within the chapters on pertinent issues studied in those chapters.

The teacher of this course should focus on a selected number of topics while leaving the more detailed and rigorous ones for later treatment, according to the maturity of the students. There is no need to overwhelm the students with difficult concepts at the beginning, even though this book is a substantively rigorous and thorough exploration of Islamic economics as the explication and application of the Islamic epistemic core of the truly Islamic methodological worldview *contra* mainstream economics and Islamic economics.

It will help the teacher and students to have a critical approach to the study of mainstream and neoclassical economics. There is no good reason to teach any good course in Islamic economics at sub-standard levels. Any such course includes a sound basis of methodology – therefore, epistemology and ontology – and the corresponding analytical understanding of what the true Islamic orientation in economics and the socio-scientific project is, as a meta-scientific worldview. Such are the holistic contents contained in this book on Islamic economics.

Notes

1 *Qur'an* (2:2): "This is the Book about which there is no doubt, a guidance for those conscious of God."

2 *Qur'an* (30:7): "They know but the outer (things) in the life of this world; but of the End of things they are heedless."
3 *Qur'an* (36:36): "Glory to God, Who created in pairs all things that the earth produces, as well as their own (human) kind and other things of which they have no knowledge."

References

Bohr, N. (1985). Discussions with Einstein on epistemological issues, in *The Philosophy of Niels Bohr: The Framework of Complementarity*, Folse, H., Amsterdam, The Netherlands: North Holland Physics Publishing.

Choudhury, M.A. (2015). *Res extensa et res cogitans de maqasid as-shari'ah*, International Journal of Law and Management, 57(6): 662–693.

Karim, F. (n.d.). *Imam Ghazzali's Ihya Ulum-Id-Din*, Lahore, Pakistan: Shah Muhammad Ashraf.

Khan, M.F. (2013). Theorizing Islamic economics: Search for a framework for Islamic economic analysis, *Journal of KAU: Islamic Economics*, 26(1): 209–242.

Lawson, T. (2003). An evolutionary economics? in *Reorienting Economics*, London: Routledge, pp. 110–140.

Mahomedy, A.C. (2013). Islamic economics: Still in search of an identity, *International Journal of Social Economics*, 40(6): 556–578.

Martin, R.M. (2010). *Epistemology: A Beginner's Guide*, London: Oneworld Publications.

McCloskey, D.N. (1985). *The Rhetoric of Economics*, Wisconsin, MN: The University of Wisconsin Press, pp. 36–61.

Mohammad, M.O. & Shahwan, S. (2013). The objective of Islamic Economics and Islamic banking in light of *Maqasid Al-Shariah*: A critical review, *Middle-East Journal of Scientific Research*, 13: 74–84.

Naqvi, S.N.H. (2003). *Perspectives on Morality and Human Well-being*, Leicester, UK: The Islamic Foundation.

Rozenthal, F. (1958). *Muqaddimah: An Introduction to History*, in 3 volumes, London: Routledge & Kegan Paul.

Waltzer, R. (trans.) (1985). *Al-Farabi on the Perfect State*, Oxford, UK: Clarendon Press.

Zarka, M.A. (2003). Islamization of economics: The concept and methodology, *Journal of KAU: Islamic Economics*, 16(1): 3–42.

2

ETHICS IN ISLAMIC ECONOMICS

LEARNING OBJECTIVES

This chapter carries forward the issues initiated in the previous chapter to:

- discuss the Islamic ethical system, which lays down a standard of values and ideals in all facets of human life including that of economic activity, in the light of the *Qur'an* and the *Sunnah* (tradition of the Prophet Muhammad)
- enable the students to understand the difference between Islamic and secular ethical viewpoints
- discuss different strategies advocated by Islam to achieve the intended moral and ethical goals like social equity, social security, mutual cooperation, economic life, moderation in all walks of life, ethical banking and financial aspects, wider circulation of wealth and distributive justice, etc.

Introduction

This chapter is devoted to the inter-relationships between economics and ethics in Islam. In summary, it states that ethics establish endogenous portents in Islamic economics. In Islam, economic behaviours and commercial dealings cannot be detached from values and ethics as Islamic values are intended to rule, direct and govern human beings' conducts in their day-to-day economic lives. They are intended to guide people to differentiate between bad and good things while performing economic actions. The ethical values in Islamic economics are based on the two key texts of Islam, namely the *Qur'an* (the Divine book of Islam) and the *Sunnah* (the behaviours and teachings of the Prophet Muhammad, peace be upon him). Both represent the main pillars of *Shari'ah* (Islamic ethical guidelines and laws), which is understood by Muslims as the appropriate way to contentment not only in economic life but also all facets of life. Consequently, ethics is a fundamental aspect of Islamic economics. The principles of divinity, justice, cooperation, trust and humanity are all contained within the parameters of Islamic economics. This chapter also discusses why we should study Islamic economics.

Background

Ethics is defined as moral, etiquette, morals, norms, rules of conscience, courtesy, manners, values, and so on. Etymologically, it is a discipline that describes good or bad, duty or moral obligation, or a set of principles or moral values (Frankena 1988). It derives from the Greek word *ethos*, in the plural form (*ta etha*), which means custom or habit. In this case, it is related to values, a good way or rule of life, and all the habits adopted and passed on from one person to another or from one generation to another. In a firmer meaning, it is a systematic study of the nature of the concept of value, good, bad, right, wrong and so forth and of general principles that justify its application. Ethics, according to Naqvi (1981), is a science that describes the meaning of good and bad, explains what a person should do to another, states the purpose of life addressed by humans in their actions and points which way they should take. Frankena (1988) understands ethics to be a science which explains what to do, or as knowledge about local customs. In summary, it can be defined in three ways: (i) it is used in terms of value and moral norms which control the behaviour of a person or a group; (ii) a set of principles or moral values or code of ethics; (iii) the science of good and bad (Harahap 2011).

The study of ethics covers all fields including economics. Ethics and economics share a close relationship concerning norms or legal/illegal actions in economic activities. According to Naqvi (1981), economics means the same in terms of a science or an activity. The only difference between one economics system and another is its economic ethics. It means economics and economic practices are essentially the same although they are in different settings, but differ because of the focus of the moral values on which they are founded. The economic ethics in Islam will be different from the economic ethics found in other religions (Naqvi 1981). This difference is rooted in the source and methodology of the ethics itself. According to Frankena (1988), economic ethics is thought or reflection about morality in economics. Morality means behaviour, whether good or bad, commendable or reprehensible, and therefore which behaviour is or is not allowed under the moral system in place. It is always present in what humans choose to do, and this includes economic activities. Economic ethics has become a matter of serious study in various parts of the world. The traditional methods of positivistic economic study as they stand are no longer adequate to nor capable of responding the challenges of today's global economic issues. As a result, economics cannot separate itself from the ethics at play (Haron 1997).

The ethics of economics

The ethics of economics need to be studied, bearing in mind that economic development tends to ignore this aspect. Criticism of current economics has been levelled by many parties. The current paradigm ruling economics is unable to create the desired welfare and justice in society. Paradoxically, it brings poverty and widens the gap between the poor and the rich. Such circumstances happen as a result of an economy which ignores the ethical aspect. In this regard, economic ethics is important to learn for three reasons (Frankena 1988):

1. to embed or increase awareness of the ethical dimension in economics and business
2. to introduce moral arguments, especially in the fields of economics and business, and supporting players in these fields to maintain proper moral arguments
3. to support economic and business players to determine the proper moral attitude of their professions.

Islam is a religion that is focused on a single powerful God who has pronounced his word through the *Qur'an*, a book considered by Muslims to be the exact word of God (*Allah*) and through the wisdoms and normative model (the *Sunnah* and the collected *Hadith*) of the Prophet Muhammad (peace be upon him) (570–632 AD), the final Prophet of God. Muslims have faith that God is the unique sovereign Master of the universe; that the aim of existence is to adore God; and that Islam is the universal and complete form of a primordial belief that has been revealed previously several times in various places in the world, including particularly through Adam, Abraham, Noah, Moses and Jesus, all of whom are considered prophets of Islam. Further, Muslims uphold that the preceding revelations and messages have been partly altered and misinterpreted over time, but believe that the *Qur'an* to be unaltered and the last revelation of God. Spiritual practices and concepts are based on the five pillars of Islam. These are basic concepts and mandatory acts of worship, and *Shari'ah* (law of Islam) is woven through virtually each facet of society and life, giving guidance on diverse areas from welfare and banking, to warfare and the environment.

Ethics establishes the keystone of Islamic economics. The wisdoms of Islam aim to enable ethical values in all facets of human life, including economic activity. As a religion, Islam is not limited to worship – fasting and praying – but rather includes the whole human life. Therefore, Islam is understood as a comprehensive method of life, recognizing both the spiritual and the secular. In contrast to conventional economics systems, Islamic economics bases its philosophy on faith: the principle of balance in meeting worldly and religious needs, not in focusing on mere pleasure; the principle of wealth distribution; and supporting the poor by creating jobs (Khan 1995). In addition, it is considered as divine, moral, humanitarian and middle class-based economics (Al-Qardhawi 1980). In this regard, the ethics of divinity, humanity, cooperation and justice are an important part of the foundation of Islamic economics (Naqvi 1981). Islamic economics maintains a balance between individual and social interests, between this world and the hereafter, and between wealth and charity. As a result, this ethical and moral foundation is what makes

Islamic economics distinctive from other systems. Unlike the capitalist, socialist, or welfare-based state economic systems which abstain from morality, the Islamic economics system offers religious ethics. Naqvi (1981) believes that this ethics-based economics system becomes the main character of Islamic economics.

What is Islamic economics?

Economics is usually defined as the theory of human behaviour relating to the production, consumption and distribution of goods and services. Modified to suit the tenets of Islamic ethics, Mannan (1970) has given a simple but very useful definition for Islamic economics: "a societal science which studies the economic problem of the individuals instilled with the morals of Islam" (p. 131). Ahmad (1992) has defined Islamic economics as "organized efforts to try to comprehend the economic problem and men's behavior in linking to that problem from an Islamic perspective" (p. 19). It may be pointed out that Islam is not merely a religion but a complete code of life and that human behaviour, or more precisely, human economic behaviour, is a subset of the Islamic ethical code. In this light Islamic economics can be defined as that part of Islamic ethical code which studies the process of economic, social and moral human behaviour in an integrated manner in relation to the production, distribution and consumption of goods and services. We can draw four facts from this explanation:

1. Islamic economics deals with only part of the Islamic ethical code, which is defined primarily in terms of the *Qur'an* and the *Sunnah* (tradition of the Prophet), through *ijma* (Muslim juristic consensus), and *ijtihad* (an Islamic lawful term denoting an independent reasoning or the comprehensive efforts of a jurist's intellectual faculty in finding an Islamic explanation for a legal inquiry).
2. Islamic economics is a process which refers to the study of behaviour of producers and consumers. This aspect of Islamic economics becomes particularly relevant when we consider the case of economic development from an Islamic perspective.
3. It presumes that economic values cannot be separated from either social or moral values, as they are in the case of capitalistic and socialist economics.
4. It studies human behaviour with particular reference to production, distribution and consumption of goods and services (Mannan 1984).

Features of Islamic economics

It is very important to know the main features on which the whole Islamic economics structure depends, in order to demonstrate the necessity and credibility of studying Islamic economics as a distinct area of social science in the contemporary world. Islamic economics is considered by its own structures, which make it different from any other form of economics (Boutayeba *et al.* 2014). The important features of Islamic economics are:

Divine-based discipline: Islamic economics is ultimately based on belief and morality, because its guidelines and values represent the teachings of Islam, and because Muslims follow the divine guidelines when dealing with economic issues; i.e. they obey God wherever and whenever they exercise any type of economic action.

Ethical: Islamic economics is mainly based on morals and ethics. Consistent with Islamic ethics, economics should not be detached from ethics. This matter is a vital element of the Islamic philosophy of life, because Islam is largely a structure of ethical guidelines from God to humans. The Prophet Muhammad (peace be upon him) stated: "I have been guided just to complete the moral values" (*Hadith*, from Boutayeba *et al.* 2014). The relationship between economics and Islamic ethics should reflect clearly in different economic activity, such as manufacture, consumption, distribution and so on. For example, Muslims cannot consume or produce what is prohibited, like alcohol or drugs, since they may harm their health.

Humanistic: Islamic economics is based on heavenly guidance, as pointed out previously, but is equally concerned for human values and welfare. There is no ambiguity between these dual features, although Islamic economics are essentially based on the *Qur'an* and the *Sunnah*. Their wisdom is *a priori* addressed to a person who is both their means and their end. The devotion to humanities characteristic of Islamic economics is signified in a set of ethics which can be summarized as brotherhood, justice, freedom, compassion, cooperation, dignity and private ownership.

Modest: The essence of Islamic economics is the values of equilibrium and moderation. While, for instance, capitalism places an excessive importance on the individual rather than society, and socialism reverses these priorities, the goal of Islam is to create a balance between society and the individual. It permits both public and private ownership.

The ethical dimensions of Islamic economics

Islamic economics rests on faith and values. Muslims perform their economic actions following the guidelines and instructions recommended by Islam. Muslims follow Islam because they strongly believe that God helps them to differentiate correctly between bad and good; between what is forbidden and what is allowed. Freedom, Justice, Brotherhood, Moderation, and Compassion are among the principles that help Islam root itself in the day-to-day life of Muslims in their own society as well as the wider world. In order to do that, Islamic economics provides a number of alternative tools that can help to accomplish those values. For example, Muslims give regular charity and *zakah* to destitute orphans and people; they must shun *israf* (widespread use of resources through luxury); *riba* (interest) and *iktinez* (hoarding of wealth).

In fact, ethical values are an endogenous factor of Islamic economics because they characterize the essential pillars on which Islam stands. In contrast to other economic systems, the Islamic economic structure depends on the spiritual teachings that establish an everlasting ethical structure. Consequently, it is frequently labelled as an ethic–economic structure. The Islamic economic system is possibly the only recognized social directive that has robust features of moral endogeneity. This is because it has unique principles and goals and gifted strategy and instruments for achieving these objectives (Choudhury 1990). Nienhaus (2000, p. 86) notes:

> While Western economists have inclined to suppress value judgments and have only initiated to reoccurrence to the behavior of normative queries in the past few years, Islamic economics, in disparity, has always established itself as a science which creates unequivocal value judgments and associated them to the outcomes of positive economics.

Figure 2.1 exemplifies a synthesized opinion of the close relationship between financial instruments and Islamic ethical principles in an Islamic economy. The main Islamic values are specifically: belief in the Hereafter, the Unity of God, and God's sovereignty over the universe. Then, for financial tools, Islamic teachings comprise several of them. One-fifth of *Qur'anic* verses are dedicated to commercial dealings or transactions (Boutayeba *et al.* 2014). Further Figure 2.1 shows how ethical standards work within an Islamic economic scheme. It may be noted that the principle of faith establishes the basis for Islamic economic activity. Spiritual faith is a powerful force in a Muslim's day-to-day life in general, and in their economic activities in particular. Therefore, Muslims have faith that God is the only God, and that He is the creator of all creations and sovereign Master of the universe, so it is obligatory to follow what the creator, God, has commanded them to do.

In an Islamic system, all the guiding principles and commands aim to establish a healthier life that is based on ethics and morals. The human race cannot live in true

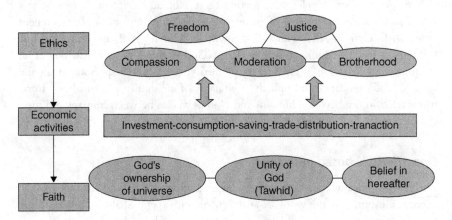

FIGURE 2.1 Ethical dimensions in Islamic economics

happiness in this world without divine wisdom. In this connection, every Muslim should understand that there will be a Hereafter (life after death) where they will be questioned and judged. Should they neglect the divine commands in their life, they will be penalized. This spurs them on to behave properly in their economic actions in this world according to the Islamic plan. They will commit to do only what is virtuous.

The objective (*maqasid*) of Islamic economics

According to Mohammad and Shahwan (2013), the purposes of Islamic economics should be the guiding principles behind Islamic banking and finance. However, Chapra (1979) underlined four important goals of Islamic economics in order for the values and all-inclusive purpose of the Islamic economic system to prevail. These four goals are: to attain economic welfare within the paradigm of the ethical norms of Islam; to maintain justice and universal brotherhood; to achieve equitable circulation of income; and to attain freedom of the individual within the framework of social well-being (Mohammad and Shahwan 2013). Scholars define the objective of Islamic economics in various terms. For example, some use the term 'objective' (*maqasid*) and some others use the word 'feature', 'principle', 'axiom' and philosophically based objectives as well as operationally based objectives. We describe briefly below the meaning of these two kinds of objectives.

Philosophically based objectives

The philosophically based objectives are those that relate to the internal features of Islamic economics in general and particularly how to focus these features toward its ultimate goals. By familiarizing the aims of Islamic economics, Ahmad (1986) divides the philosophically based objectives into four themes: *Khilafa* (steward), *Tawhid* (oneness of God), *Rububiyyah* (God as provider and sustainer), and *Tazkiyah al Nafs* (purification of self). Interpreting these, Ahmad (1986) further elaborates that *Khilafa* means the matter of accountability of humanity as God's viceregent or steward; *Tawhid* is the acknowledgement by humanity of the unity of God; *Rububiyyah* refers to human awareness that God is provider and sustainer of all creations; and *Tazkiyah al Nafs* refers to purifying of human personality in the light of God's guidance through the *Qur'an*. All four signify a vertical and horizontal relationship between humans and God as well as between humans and their complete lives.

Operationally based objectives

The philosophically based objective generally appears in a vertical-type association, as illustrated by the word "*al-falah*" (Mohammad and Shahwan 2013). In the contemporary literature on Islamic economics, *al-falah* has been the operational objective of Islamic economics (Khan 1984; Choudhry 1999). It covers the sphere of human activities for the sake of God and may also be accomplished through fulfilment of the operationally based objectives. These objectives therefore need a tangible valuation process to ensure their effectiveness and accomplishment. As a result, Muslim scholars have also explored different methods of determining the goals of Islamic economics. Basically, operational objectives are those object-ives which have measurable, testable outcomes and are directly related to human worldly activities (Mohammad and Shahwan 2013). Grounded in the literature of Islamic economics, ethically the operationally based objectives may be divided into six kinds: social-based objectives, economic-based objectives, justice-based objectives, enjoying good and forbidding evil (*nahianil munkar wa amr bilmaruf*) based objectives, self-based (inner-self) objectives, and state participation object-ives. Khan (1994), Chapra (1979) and Zaman (2008) have revealed that economic goals and societal aim are the key components in an operationally based intent. The remaining objectives are similarly significant, and include justice (Chapra 1979; Choudhry 1999), inner-self (Khan 1984; Chapra 1979); enjoying good and forbidding evil (Khan 1992; Maududi 1984) and social participation in the order of the state (Khan 1994).

EXAMPLES

1. A distinctive example adapted from the study of Mohammad and Shahwan (2013) who have shown a significant correlation in the implementation of the objectives (*maqasid*) framework in determining the aims of Islamic economics and Islamic banks. Specific attention is given to guard the dignity (*al-muru'ah*), and the safety of mind (*al-aqal*), as well as pro-tection of wealth (*al-mal*). Mohammad and Shahwan (2013) show that this outcome is central to the aim of Islamic banking, as depicted by the Association of Islamic Banking Institutions Malaysia (AIBIM) in directing Islamic banking towards socio-economic justice. They concluded that each objective of Islamic economics and Islamic banking gives due attention to the study of humanity or to the stakeholder's behaviour. It can be reasoned from this finding that Islamic economics was seldom associated with human welfare, while the stakeholders are the main group of actors in the events.

2. In respect of the association with and disparity of the objectives of Islamic economics and Islamic banking, this study rests all objectives of Islamic economics and Islamic banks on both God-related objectives and human-related objectives. Almighty God as the one and only Creator of the cosmos is considered as a significant element in establishing the root of these two fields. This connection is also seconded by a range of literature that places our return to God as the final goal of human beings, in other words, life after death (Ahmad 1984; Khan 1994).

Why Islamic economics?

Given the present state of conventional economics and its failure to deal with the socio-economic problems facing the contemporary world, particularly as regards the Third World, the study and the development of Islamic economics has become more important than ever before. The study of Islamic economics is important not only for its own sake but also for the sake of bridging the missing link of the modern economics itself. As a result, there is a need for an independent discipline of Islamic economics for the whole of mankind for the following reasons:

1. **Bridging the missing link**: Contemporary economic system has evolved in purely materialist Western developed societies. As the spiritual, cultural, social and political set-up in Islamic society is dissimilar to Western society, it follows therefore that a Western-style economic analysis should not fit every society. Because contemporary capitalistic economic system is value neutral. Ahmad (1992, p. 21) states that:

    > During the pre-18th century phase, the economic problem, economic analysis and its relation with ethical values and norms are intertwined. They were merged into each other. It is in the post-18th century developments, despite its moral origins that economics seems to have grown into self-contained discipline.

    Further, Sen (1987) has rightly emphasized that "moral taking of rights (particularly rights that supported and valued and not just appreciated in the shape of constraints) may consider for systematic departure from selfishness behavior" (p. 29). Sen went on to add, "Even a limited and partial selfishness in conduct can tremble the behavioral foundation of normal economics theory" (p. 30). Therefore, the study of Islamic economics is expected to establish a link between economic values and socio-moral values. This integration between economic and socio-moral values implies, among other things, equitable distribution of income and resources among all human beings and also among all living creatures.

2. **Resolving the economic crisis**: Third World countries, particularly Muslim countries, are facing economic crisis and conflicts in their development and modernization process. It is widely believed that the current international order, which is in a state of crisis, is incapable of explaining and influencing the course of current events and that only Islam can provide viable solutions to these problems. Herein lies the importance of interpreting society's socio-economic problems from an Islamic perspective, and hence the importance of Islamic economics (Chapra 2000).

3. **Meeting Islamic responsibilities**: Muslims are under obligation to comply with the *Shari'ah* ethics of the *Qur'an* and *Sunnah*, such as helping the poor and the needy, or paying *zakah* and *sadaqa*. It is here that the Islamic economists should come forward, identify the relevant socio-economic prescriptions from

an Islamic perspective, and make use of them in creating Islamic economics as a scientific discipline. This explains why the study and development of Islamic economics is so vitally important.

4. In the conventional economics framework, economics is a positive science; it scientifically analyses and examines the causes of a problem. It has no concern about ethics and norms. Contemporary conventional economists are concerned only about the analysis of procedures as they take place, contrary to Islamic economics. Islamic economics has a normative feature, which is as important as the positive feature. An Islamic economist critically analyses the observable economic fact, makes a statement about its consequences, and then suggests ways and means that these should conform to *Shari'ah* (Chapra 2000).

5. Conventional economics carries out studies on human behaviour in the context of the 'market'. In economic modelling some economic factors have been incorporated which may be qualified, but did not include an account of the relevant social system, and made a sharp division between non-market and market variables. Conversely, Islam considers life as a unity where economics is only a sub-system of the complete Islamic code of conduct. Several variables, which are considered as exogenous variables in conventional economics, are considered as endogenous variables in the case of Islamic economic system. The Islamic economic models also include socio-cultural variables; for instance, the rewards in the hereafter have been incorporated. It provides Islamic economics a broader range of study in comparison to the scope of study of contemporary mainstream economics. The study of Islamic economics must be regarded as crucial for translating the various principles of Islamic economics into action.

Conclusion

At the conceptual level, the Islamic economics is seeking an ideal system. The economics is built on the principles of *Shari'ah* (at the philosophical level) – which are distinguished from secular conventional economics – and on the economic behaviour of Muslim communities at the level of practice (positivistic). In fact, the development of Islamic economic norms is dominated by Islamic jurisprudence (legal formal). The rulings of *Shari'ah* as the single standard of Islamic economics is characterized by *halal–haram*, acceptable–unacceptable and legal–illegal in responding to economic activities. It considers the ethics of Islamic economics, where ethics is a fundamental aspect of economics. Consequently, the principles of divinity, justice, cooperation, trust and humanity remain within parameters of Islamic economics.

Islamic economics is designed to realize the ideals of Islamic teaching, which is to meet the objectives of *Shari'ah* (*maqasid al-shari'ah*). The purpose of *Shari'ah* is the achievement of welfare and protection based on five core principles. These five principles include protection for religion, life, intelligence, lineage and wealth. To realize these principles, scholars have formulated the foundation of Islamic economics, which consist of four aspects: to attain economic welfare within the context of the moral standards of Islam; to maintain cooperation, justice and brotherhood;

to accomplish just allocation of earnings; and to achieve freedom of the individual within the framework of social justice and well-being.

References

Ahmad, A. (1992). Macro-consumption function in an Islamic framework: A survey of current literature, in Lecturers in Islamic Economics, eds. Ahmad, A. & Awan, K.R., Jeddah: IRTI-IDB.

Ahmad, K. (1984). *Studies in Islamic Economics: Selected Papers Presented at the First International Conference in Islamic Economics, held in Makkah in 1983*, Delhi: Amar Prakashan.

Ahmad, K. (1986). Keynote address, in *Fiscal Policy and Resource Allocation in Islam*, eds. Ahmad, Z., Iqbal, M., & Khan, M.F., Islamabad: IPS.

Al-Qardhawi, Y. (1980). *Dawr al-Qiyamwa al-Akhlâq fi al-Iqtisâd al-Islâmy*, Cairo: Maktabah Wahbah.

Boutayeba, F. Benhamida, M., & Souad, G. (2014). Ethics in Islamic economics, *Annales: Ethics in Economic Life*, 17(4): 111–121.

Chapra, M.U. (1979). *Objectives of the Islamic Economic Order*, Leicester, UK: The Islamic Foundation.

Chapra, M.U. (2000). *The Future of Economics: An Islamic Perspective*, Markfield, UK: Islamic Foundation.

Choudhury, M.A. (1990). The humanomic structure of Islamic economic theory: A critical review of literature in normative and positive economics, *Islamic Economics*, 2: 52.

Choudhury, M.A. (1999). *Comparative Economic Theory: Occidental and Islamic Perspectives*, Norwell, MA: Kluwer Academic.

Frankena, W.K. (1988). *Ethics*, 2nd Edition, Harlow, UK: Pearson.

Harahap, S. (2011). *Ethics in Islam and Business*, Jakarta: Salemba Empat.

Haron, S. (1997). *Islamic Banking: Rules and Regulations*, Kuala Lumpur: Lemur Publications.

Khan, M.F. (1984). Macro-consumption function in an Islamic framework, *Journal of Research in Islamic Economics*, 1(2): 34–44.

Khan, M.F. (1992). *Human Resources Mobilization through the Profit Loss Sharing Financial System*, Jeddah: IRTI-IDB.

Khan, M.F. (1994). Comparative economics of some Islamic finance techniques, *Islamic Economic Studies*, 2(1): 42–89.

Khan, M.F. (1995). *Essays in Islamic Economics*, Markfield, UK: The Islamic Foundation.

Mannan, M.A. (1970). *Islamic Economics: Theory and Practices*, Lahore: Sh. Mohammad Ashraf.

Mannan, M.A. (1984). *The Making of Islamic Economic Society: Islamic Dimension of Economic Analysis*, Cairo: International Association of Islamic Banks.

Maududi, S.A.A. (1984). *Fundamentals of Islamic Economics*, Lahore: Islamic Publications.

Mohammad, M.O. & Shahwan, S. (2013). The objective of Islamic economics and Islamic banking in light of *maqasid al-shariah*: A critical review, *Middle-East Journal of Scientific Research*, 13: 74–84.

Naqvi, N.H. (1981). *Ethics and Economics: An Islamic Synthesis*, Leicester: The Islamic Foundation, UK.

Nienhaus, V. (2000). Islamic economics: Dogma or science, in *The Islamic World and the West*, ed. Hafez, K., trans. Kenny, M.A., Leiden: Brill.

Sen, A. (1987). *The Standard of Living*, Cambridge: Cambridge University Press.

Zaman, A. (2008). *Islamic Economics: Survey of the Literature*. Religions and Development Research Programme, Birmingham: University of Birmingham.

3

ISLAMIC ECONOMIC METHODOLOGY

LEARNING OBJECTIVES

This chapter widens the discussion of certain fundamental concepts like:

- a meaningful foundation is created for an Islamic methodological worldview of economics; through this, a generalized foundational worldview of Islamic socio-scientific field is explained
- a comparative approach is followed to understand the subject matter and the goals of Islamic economics vis-à-vis conventional mainstream economics
- the positive and normative aspects of Islamic economics where theory and policy are in complete harmony and objective is overall human welfare to fulfil the goals of *maqasid al-shari'ah*.

What is the meaning of socio-scientific methodology in its broader sense? How is economic methodology derived from such a broad meaning of socio-scientific methodology? What is the relevance of Islamic epistemology in this broad concept of methodology?

These are fundamental questions that must be first inquired into before a meaningful foundation of an Islamic methodological worldview of economics can be created, and through this, a generalized foundational worldview of any Islamic socio-scientific field can be explained. It is through such foundational inquiry that the substantive difference between Islamic economic and mainstream economic ideas, conception, formalism, and applications can be established.

On methodology in Western thought

Methodology is fundamentally an epistemological matter (Pheby 1988). The term 'epistemology' means theory of knowledge (Bartley *et al.* 1988). It also explains the most reduced premise of knowledge as a generalized way of studying our real conceptions of the nature of the world and its problems. Epistemology also includes the area of formulation of knowledge towards investigating the problems under study. It also gives the expectations that can be derived from the particular form of theory of knowledge used for the study of problems under investigation.

All theories of knowledge assume that reason and rationality and its substantive overarching domain of rationalism are the foundation of the theory of knowledge (Descartes 1954). Yet epistemology as the core of methodology remains substantively divergent in its understanding between different cultures, theories, worldviews, and religions. The critically debated issue is based on how the meanings of reason, rationality and of rationalism are derived (Smart 2000). These are substantive terms in the construction of the worldview of socio-scientific conceptual and applied dimensions. Thereby, we ask the question by the epistemic core of methodology: How can the broadest theory of scientific inquiry be defined for all areas of inquiry? Karl Popper (2004) referred to this selection criterion for the truly scientific nature of inquiry as the problem of demarcation. It means the separation of science from pseudo-science.[1]

The broader question that emerges is this: Does science, as we have inherited it, by its characterization in the realm of analytics and applications present a complete theory of science? Or are such theories simply a temporary and incomplete vision for studying reality, which is formally conceptualized and examined experimentally, merely in the light of how the world is observed and interpreted by the inquirer? In other words, such a pursuit of the scientific enterprise in every area of knowledge is defined by the rationalist worldview leading to a reasoned space of concept and action as understood by the inquirers, their models, and the instruments of investigation? These approaches then lead to further abstraction that generates more of the same in diversity *ad infinitum* (Popper 1998).

Examples: Bringing out the meaning of methodology in Western thought

Example 1: Water is chemically H_2O – two atoms of hydrogen and one atom of oxygen. Yet if we are to conceive of the humanly useful meaning of water with all its minerals, the chemical definition does not complete the human well-being function of water. Instead of the H_2O definition of water for human well-being, the example may be used of *Zamzam* (water fetched from the well located in the *Masjid al Haram* in Makkah). *Zamzam* is believed by Muslims to continue to offer spiritual and health benefits to humankind until the end of time.

Example 2: Rational choices by human will are not necessarily tied to moral conscience. In the Western epistemological sense, rational choices are determined simply by free will as decreed by individual and collective social affirmation. Thus an open field of choices to accept, to reject, and to choose again appear in the global markets, carrying human preferences linked with such rational choices. No moral conscience is necessarily needed.

Such are the ethically defeating markets, choices and preferences that the *Qur'an* and the *Sunnah* overrule as a result of the concept of good choices. In the Western world, there are no consciously governing market choices in rational choice theory other than the individual and collective free will. In this sense of individualism, the human claim on free will becomes contrary to the injunctions and the purpose and objective of the *Shari'ah* – the *maqasid al-shari'ah* relating to individual, collective, and social choices for the common good.

In this respect, the recent business clamour regarding good corporate governance and corporate social responsibility are merely carried through within the so-called industrial democratic institutional environment. The institutional collective preference on choice is once again governed by the collectivity of individual preferences based on methodological individualism. This in turn is subsumed by the free will of the maker of the rational choice. The free will of rational choice in turn arises from the totality of socio-scientific rationalism.

In the above examples we note that, the overarching presence of rationalism in free will determines rational choices. Such choices reflect the perceptions and decisions of individually determined categories. The underlying notion of abstraction based on methodological individualism does not establish a set worldview. Consequently, socio-scientific inquiry ends up in random conceptions of reality. A plethora of rationalist thought concerning free will is named as the problem of over-determination in the literature of political economy (Resnick & Wolff 1987). Popper (1998) refers to such a situation of preferences, choice, and abstraction of thought in the venue of methodological individualism as un-decidability in epistemologies. Un-decidability is the permanent feature of the theory of knowledge in occidental socio-scientific worldview.

Analytical definition of methodology in Western thought and Islamic rebuttal

The idea of rationalism that underlies the Western understanding of reason, rationality, and rational choice needs to be explained. In the Western model of epistemology such randomness of free will arises from theories like those of Kant (1949) and Hume (1988).

Kant divided his theory of knowledge into reasoning that is differentiated between the *a priori* domain comprising the moral imperative; and the worldly, reasoned *a posteriori* domain of sensate forms and schemes. There is independence between these pure and practical ways of reasoning. The dichotomy referred to as antinomy is shown in Figure 3.1.

Islamic rebuttal of Kantian idea of rationalism

Figure 3.1 points out that the divine law as the law of monotheism is not subsumed in free will. It resides in the *a priori* domain independently of free will, which resides independently in the choices of the *a posteriori* domain. Thus in Kantian

A	C	B
A priori domain Of pure reason Abode of God Religion, and Morals	antinomy	*a posteriori* domain of Practical reason: Abode of sensate materiality

FIGURE 3.1 Rationalism as free will: independence of the formal law of moral determination from the worldly law

socio-scientific methodology (Choudhury 2015) of independence between *a priori* and *a posteriori* domains of pure and practical reasoning, respectively, the rational process commences in the B-domain independently of the A-domain. Thus all worldly rational matter has its emergence in the *a posteriori* domain.

On this delineation of the origin of knowledge of two independent kinds, Kant wrote (1949, p. 25):

> This, then, is a question which at least calls for closer examination, and does not permit any off-hand answer: whether there is any knowledge that is thus independent of experience and even of all impressions of the senses. Such knowledge is entitled *a priori*, and is distinguished from the empirical, which has its sources *a posteriori*, that is, in experience. ... In what follows, therefore, we shall understand by *a priori* knowledge, no knowledge independent of this or that experience, but knowledge absolutely independent of all experience. Opposed to it is empirical knowledge, which is knowledge possible only *a posteriori*, that is through experience.

These explanations regarding the nature of Western socio-scientific thought thus point out the subjective nature of a disconnected methodology that separates God from the experimental domain. This is the meaning of antinomy. Contrarily, in Islamic socio-scientific thought, God by His law of monotheism is integral to the experimental domain of reality. This law unifies the A-domain with B-domain and renders the C-domain null and void. Islamic knowledge ingrained in the mono-theistic law and functioning in the socio-scientific order is thus the law of unity of knowledge. Such a functional unity between the A-domain and B-domain is made possible pervasively in 'everything' by the Islamic epistemic methodology of the *Qur'anic* law of unity of being and becoming; and by the *Sunnah* that carries the *Qur'an* into our practical domain of human action.

An important reflection arising from the framework of unity of knowledge in Islamic socio-scientific methodology is the fact that, by the annulment of anti-nomy in the C-domain, Islamic methodology premised on monotheism and com-pleteness absorbs 'everything' within it. This is possible in Islam by making the

A-domain and the B-domain analytically continuous within its methodological framework of monotheistic unity of knowledge. Such an analytical continuity of interrelationships between *a priori* and *a posteriori* domains of reasoning also explains the organic relational unity between the divine law and the world-system. Western socio-scientific methodology is unable to realize such a socio-scientific continuity and completeness. That is because of the independence of A-domain and the B-domain by the intervening gap of antinomy (C-domain).

The impossibility of obtaining unity of knowledge as the methodological core of scientific holism

The opposite understanding of scientific thinking as methodology in Kant was given by David Hume (1988). In Kant's methodology, which predominantly governs all of Western scientific theory and reasoning, the moral imperative is primal but is separated from the experimental and sensate world-system. Hence, the inability of integrating the *a priori* and the *a posteriori* domains in Kant's methodology led to surrendering to the free will in the *a posteriori* domain. The moral law was indeed primal above all. It is the basis of the thought and actions of the world-system. But there is no analytical function to integrate the two domains by any permanent law. The idea of rationalism in Kant is thus the idea of integrating the moral impera-tive of the *a priori* domain with the *a posteriori* domain of experimental and sensate actions. But there is no original law in place; and no command by law and guidance that would cause the two domains to become integrated and blended in the con-tinuous sense. Such integration is referred to as an endogenous functional rela-tionship between interrelating domains; that is between the *a priori* and *a posteriori* domains, each reinforcing the other by cause and effect. In Kant, this kind of unifi-cation of knowledge of the two domains in a continuous interactive and integrated way is not possible. So the Kantian (Western) methodology of rationalism made the moral law rest on the free will of the individual and collectivity in the *a priori* sense. But the *a posteriori* domain does not establish an analytic and endogenous interrela-tionship with the *a priori* moral imperative.

The endogenous (interactively combined into an integrated system) and con-tinuous nature of the inter-system cause–effect feedback relationship (circularity) is otherwise essential in understanding the role of the theory of unity of knowledge and its induction of the generality and details of the world-system in which the sciences are founded. Indeed, for a long time now the methodologists of the his-tory of economic thought have argued on opposite sides whether economics is a science or not in the sense of whether economics has an extensive experimental possibility over human affairs and rational behaviour (Schumpeter 1968; Blaug 1968). The matter is disputed at the methodological level of questioning regarding inter-convertibility of reversible relations between multiple domains, or systems, or between variables representing these systems. Examples are emergent *a priori* and *a posteriori* domains across sequences of abstractions. Each of these abstractions stands for a perception under rationalist scientific theory.

The gap between *a priori* and *a posteriori* domains means that certain domains, e.g. the Kantian antinomy, cannot be explained by *any* law. The result then renders the continuity and the inter-system endogenous relations to be null and void. Kant wrote in regard to the dualism in rationalist reasoning:

> In what follows, therefore, we shall understand by *a priori* knowledge, no knowledge independent of this or that experience, but knowledge absolutely independent of all experience. Opposed to it is empirical knowledge, which is knowledge possible only *a posteriori*, that is, through experience. *A priori* modes of knowledge are entitled pure when there is no admixture of anything empirical.

We note thereby that Kant's epistemology fails to provide a unity of knowledge at the origin of thought pertaining to science, its entities or variables, forms, their mathematical relations, abstractions, applications and explanations.

The properties of continuity and an inter-convertible analytic functional relationship are essential to understand the methodology of unity of knowledge and its opposite, the property of antinomy as shown in Figure 3.1. This point of the difference between endogenous interrelations and its opposite as exogenous mono-causal relationship is essential in understanding the substantive differences between Western methodology of rationalism, rationality, and reason and the Islamic methodological worldview of unity of knowledge. The *Qur'an* refers to this grand design of the universe in terms of the law of *Tawhid*. The overarching field of the term stands for the strictest monotheism, of the divine law, as well as the teleological precept of God as the Absolute One.

Endogeneity, multi-causality, and unity of knowledge in scientific methodology

At this early point of this book this substantive difference between Western and Islamic epistemic methodology is explained by Figure 3.2 in regards to multi-causality, organic interrelations of unity of knowledge, endogenous circular causation relations, continuity and reversibility. These properties are not universal in Western socio-scientific thought. Thereby, the methodological implications of the Western socio-scientific thought and of the Islamic methodological worldview in science are not identical. Despite this, there are details of phenomena that can be equivalent, as far as reason and logical formalism of unity of knowledge establishes or rejects acceptance of facts.

An example of the Western and Islamic methodological contrasts of socio-scientific meaning

A salient example of acceptance of scientific domain is co-planar mathematics in mono-causal reasoning, and rejection of Cartesian formulations in multidimensional

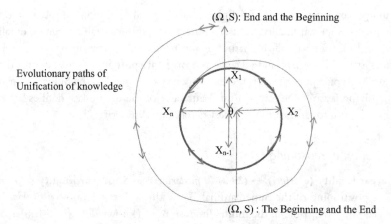

FIGURE 3.2 The Islamic methodology of unity of knowledge: from the beginning to the end; definitions: rationalism, mono-causality, multi-causality, organic relations, unity of knowledge, circular causation relations, continuity, reversibility

ethically induced formal analytical complexes. The opposing scientific views are of those of monotheistic Islamic epistemology, and Western free will. Consider the issue of pre-determinism of the divine law in Islamic creation methodology. Contrarily, there is the anthropological belief of creation in terms of Western-style free will.

The term rationalism was explained in reference to Figure 3.1. From the concept of rationalism vis-à-vis free will, inter-system differentiation, and antinomy there arises the derivation of the concept of reason and rationality. We explain the latter attributes now, as derived from the overarching concept of rationalism in the Western methodology of science.

Reason via rationalism

By the nature of rationalism, according to the Western methodology of scientific belief as was explained in terms of Figure 3.1 and by Kantianism, reason by free will is the intrinsic quality of humankind and the consciousness; nature can be, in the sense that nature does not preclude freedom precisely because it is consistent with the kind of causation from intelligible characters which is causation according to freedom. For example, (2+2) does not equal anything other than 4, whatever way the system of addition is defined. Yet this is an *a posteriori* truth as so observed and materially reasoned. On the side of the *a priori* domain, consider the addition of (2+2) for God. This is impossible according to the monotheistic law in Islam, for God (*Allah*) is not incarnate in any shape and form.[2] Yet God has given laws and has ordained shape, form, and balance.

Therefore, the implication of the Supercardinal Being bearing no conception and dimension for the attributes of God[3] in the *a priori* domain of reasoning must be the unique explanatory root of defining mathematical operations in the *a posteriori* domain. Yet Supercardinality by itself remains the immeasurable large cardinality (Rucker 1983). The implication then is reversible authentication by the material world-system to confirm and advance the original epistemology of Supercardinal Being.[4] The concept of (2+2) is then imminently contained in the Supercardinality of the divine law. Yet the Supercardinal attribute of the divine law defines 'reason' (2+2) as logical formalism in the *a posteriori domain*. We write:

Completion of reasoning

Supercardinality (*a priori*) → **(2+2)** (*a posteriori*) → **Supercardinality** (*a priori*)

The positioning of the Supercardinal Being through the monotheistic law has now become extendable in the multi-dimensions of (knowledge ($\{\theta\} \in (\Omega, S)$, space $\{X(\theta)\}$, time $(t(\theta)) \equiv Z(\theta)$. The methodology of and by reasoning in socio-scientific details takes place through the continuity of evolutionary learning in the event domain $(E(.))$ across (knowledge, space, time). Thus, reasoning in Islam pervades the continuity of the *a priori* and the *a posteriori* domains by the logical annulment of 'antinomy' in Figure 3.1 and its replacement by the continuous multi-causal circular organic relations between entities, variables, and systems (see Figure 3.2). Each point of the path of events, $E(Z(\theta))$, is a coordinate point interrelating God, man and universe in a unified consciousness that is determined and continued across history by the emergent events.

In Kantian domain, and thereby Western socio-scientific thought, $E(Z(\theta))$ is dichotomous between *a priori* reasoning $\equiv E_1(Z_1(\theta_1))$, all symbols belonging to the *a priori* domain and *a priori* reasoning. $E_2(Z_2(\theta_2))$ denotes the presence of antinomy. $E_3(Z_3(\theta_3))$ denotes the *a posteriori* domain. In Islamic epistemological reasoning (methodology), $E(Z(\theta))$ is unified, continuous, and organically interrelated by circular causation across systems from the beginning to the end.[5]

Rationality via reasoning and rationalism

Rationality in scientific terms comprises the reasoned attitude governed by rationalism to make choices of everything that underlies such *maqasid*-choices, be they of individual preferences or institutional, national, and collective preferences. Being based on choices governed by reason via rationalism, the scientific meaning of rationality becomes a convenience attained by assigning convenient attributes to solve problems. The implication then is this: Individual, institutional, national, and global preference arrangements are formed such that they can solve impending problems implicit in these choices, in the interest of the decision-making groups.

Rationality derived from rationalism

How is rationality in the methodological sense derived from reason via rationalism? We consider here three kinds of rationality as attributes of individual and collective preferences on decision-making. These are moral rationality, procedural rationality, and consequentialist rationality (Etzioni 1988).

Moral rationality in terms of Kantian *a priori* reasoning is a differentiated ethical concept of humanism as opposed to the existence and application of the moral law. An example is the moral imperative of the competing concept of freedom in choices that substitute between social justice and economic efficiency (economic growth). In the *a priori* sense of the Kantian moral imperative, social justice substitutes for economic efficiency and economic growth. This is also the approach of Rawls (1971). The predominance of the moral imperative is an altruistic view of moral rationality that was once practiced by the Soviet Union and proved to be to the utter disadvantage of their economic goals. Yet the possibility of integrating social justice and economic growth (efficiency) remains unexplained as a methodological fact.

On the other hand, the neoclassical approach to rational choices results in the substitution of social justice with economic choices based on self-interest and personal gains under given amount of resources and the freely competing will of the decision-maker. This is the approach of Nozick (2001) to the topic of taxation, property rights, and what he refers to as the moral abhorrence of market government intervention.

The integration between the goals of social justice and economic growth cannot be possible in the case of an endogenous and continuously complementary interrelationship. Exogenously, governments may opt for external injection of funds and technological advancement coming out of taxation. The endogenous nature of production relations and resource distribution is abandoned. Consequentially, social participation and continuity of resource development and resource mobilization are lost.

Procedural rationality

This is the form of rationality arising from convenience and social pressure to accomplish tasks. Such an attitude towards problem solving is also driven by the goal of self-interest, to optimize certain so-called objective goals. Procedural rationality is also a form of mismatch between *a priori* and *a posteriori* reasoning based on the optimal use of limited resources of opportunity to otherwise make more discursively oriented mutual benefit available to all parties in discourse and in the context of continuous opportunities to share knowledge-induced resources at all levels. An example in this case is to confront a common enemy by befriending old enemies, which is the case of procedural rationality caused by the absence of a discursive social behaviour overall. Many global wars and conflicts continue because of belligerent attitudes and the absence of participatory behaviour that can generate understanding (Choudhury 1996).

Consequentialist rationality

This concept carries an empirical meaning. That is, rational behaviour relating to either material acquisitions or political acquisitions, which become self-interest material considerations, are weighed in terms of quantitative benefits and costs (net benefits) to determine the decision to act or not to act on a specific course of decision-making. Game-theory method is used to determine the optimal payoff for strategies. In every single such approach of evaluating the effects of the consequentialist rational decision-maker there is no methodological explanation to endogenously interrelate the *a priori* reason of the transcendental ego and the *a posteriori* reason of empiricism. Walsh (1985) forcefully writes:

> He saw no possible intermediary form of intellectual activity between that of an intuitive intelligence, creating its objective, and that of an informing intelligence, imposing intelligible forms on sensed objects. He (Kant) completely overlooked and ignored the possibility of abstracting intelligence. Thus, in the Kantian "reconstruction" of knowledge, the value and function attributed to the objective datum is so reduced that the weight of reconstruction must be borne almost exclusively by the activity of the knowing subject.

An example of consequentialist rationality is the quantitative cost–benefit evaluation of an investment project upon which an acceptance or rejection of the project is decided. However, not simply by the question of non-acceptability of this method based on consequentialist rationality, but also by the absence of endogenous ethical quantification of cash-flows and exogenously felt moral appropriateness of the projects, the methodology of the moral imperative remains uncertain, undetermined, and thus void.

By taking the above three kinds of rationality concepts we can premise the rationality concept on the rationalist, and consequentially reason according to the Kantian calculus of dichotomy and moral differentiation, his antinomy. This problem of differentiation between *a priori* and *a posteriori* components of reasoning rather than establishing their organic unity of being at the level of the ontological truth (Oneness of God) is referred to as heteronomy.

The following conditions for rational economic behaviour are categorized in respect of mainstream economic arguments:

1. Economic resources remain fixed and given for preferred decision-making unless these are exogenously changed by injection of resources and technological change.
2. The objective criterion is optimized by means of scarce resources that are allocated between competing ends.
3. Steady-state equilibrium is the result of allocating scarce resources between competing ends.
4. Self-interest rather than sharing prevails. Consequently, preferences remain datum.
5. Freedom of property rights prevails.
6. The combination of the above-mentioned properties of allocation of scarce resources among competing ends leads to marginal substitution of one choice by another.[6]

7. All agents are predicted to abide by the above-mentioned rules as internally consistent behaviour in optimal decision-making.
8. The combination of the above-mentioned properties of economic rationality establishes transitivity of choices and preferences for economically rational agents, e.g. consumers, producers, and other agents.[7]

The postulates of mainstream economic rationality contra knowledge-induced theory

The entirety of mainstream economics, especially that explained by neoclassical microeconomics and neoclassical macroeconomics, upholds the above generalization of the postulates of economic rationality. In turn, as explained above, such postulates are derived from the concept of rationalism and reason and different concepts of rationality in the framework of the Kantian type methodology of the *a priori* opposing *a posteriori* reasoning.

Consequently, in the event-plane of learning denoted by $\{\theta\}$, ethical choices denoted by $\{\mathbf{X}(\theta)\}$ – which includes technological change, innovation, and policies and strategies – preferences of all kinds by agents, denoted by $\{\wp(\theta)\}$ over time $t(\theta)$ must necessarily generate endogenous interrelations. Such an event-domain is not possible in the case of economic rationality of the mainstream genre. Consequently, the induction by the endogenous learning effect of $\{\theta\}$ causes continuous changes across all the elements of the rationalist-based reason and economic rationality. Only the presence of exogenously enforced new forms of change can cause shifts. But such shifts are not endogenously automated in the system of analysis that is driven by continuous learning interrelationships between diverse entities, variables, and systems. Consequently, the role of endogenous induction of knowledge arises from the unity of relations of *a priori* and *a posteriori* domains.

David Hume's *a posteriori* materialism in socio-scientific methodology

Contrary to the moral imperative foundation of Kantian thought, though disabled by the problem of antinomy persisting throughout, there is the epistemological thought of David Hume. Hume's epistemological thought has also profoundly influenced Western socio-scientific methodology in the domain of empiricism and the experimental foundation of scientific knowledge. Hume, contrary to Kant, argued that the epistemological origin of science lies in the sensate world of forms and relations and their interactions.

To Hume the origin of knowledge is derived from the cognition of memory, impression, imagination, relations, modes and substances. Thus, through these elements of human possibility to attain reason and to construct a methodological order, Hume took the mind–matter relationship purely at the level of human free will. This was reason determined at the sensate origin of meanings by interrelations. Human imagination, memory and the continuity of forms and relations in space–time domains were the building blocks of Hume's characterization of scientific methodology. The divine law, which is the *a priori* domain, was thus divorced from Hume's *a posteriori* reasoning. The latter alone was in Hume's methodological development of scientific thought.

Thus, while Kantian approach to methodology was of the deductive type, Hume's methodology is premised on logical positivism and induction. Hume wrote (quoted in 1992, p. 1):

> All the perceptions of the human mind resolve themselves into two distinct kinds, which I shall call Impressions and Ideas … Those perceptions, which enter with most force and violence, we may name impressions; and under this name I comprehend all our sensations, passions and emotions, as they make their first appearance in the soul. By ideas I mean the faint images of these in thinking and reasoning.

On his extended methodological premise Hume wrote (1992, p. xvi):

> And as the science of man is the only solid foundation for the other sciences, so the only solid foundation we can give to this science itself must be laid on experience and observation.

Furthermore he wrote (1992, p. xvii):

> For me it seems evident, that the essence of the mind being equally unknown to us with that of external bodies, it must be equally impossible to form any notion of its powers and qualities otherwise than from careful and exact experiments, and the observation of those particular effects, which result from its different circumstances and situations. And tho' we must endeavour to render all our principles as universal as possible, by tracing up our experiments to the utmost, and explaining all effects from the simplest and fewest causes, 'tis still certain we cannot go beyond experience; and any hypothesis, that pretends to discover the ultimate original qualities of human nature, ought at first to be rejected as presumptuous and chimerical.

The above narration clearly establishes the ultimate source of scientific phenomena to which Hume assigned the roots of knowledge. It is also clear that the source of the divine unity of knowledge remained beyond the realm of Hume's idea of rationalism. The divine law could not be incorporated in Hume's extension of the relational order of impressions, forms, imagination, and memory, to the deductive and the inductive knowledge-induced domains organically unified with each other by inter-causality. This is the essence of the episteme of unity of knowledge integrating the *a priori* with the *a posteriori*; the deductive with the inductive; divine knowledge with the knowledge-induced world-system taken in generality and details.

Hume's relational order is categorized as being from simple to complex. His complex form is simply a causal assemblage of simple forms. Hence, in the language of linearly separable forms and the meaning of causality between interacting forms, these are not substantively integrated in forming complex forms. There is only a lateral aggregation of simple forms to cause complex forms to arise.

Hume wrote in regards to his concept of causally determined complex forms in relation to simple forms (1992, p. 13):

> Amongst the effects of this union or association of ideas, there are none more remarkable, than those complex ideas, which are the common subjects of our thoughts and reasoning, and generally arise from some principle of union among our simple ideas. These complex ideas may be divided into Relations, Modes, and Substances.

Hume's concepts of modes and substances in themselves are also a collection of simple ideas. He wrote (1992, p. 16):

> The idea of a substance as well as that of a mode, is nothing but a collection of simple ideas, that are united by the imagination, and have a particular name assigned them, by which we are able to recall, either to ourselves or others, that collection.

Hume's concept of 'relation' exists in association with the infinite divisibility of space and time. His universe reflects unity within which every part is infinitely reducible. A relation in such an infinitely divisible order is a linear concept of interconnectedness by means of contiguity and continuity purely in the *a posteriori* domain.

Summary of Western methodology in reference to Kant and Hume

The dichotomous nature of epistemological reasoning is thus firmly established in Western scientific methodology. The consequentialist nature of the world is devoid of unity of knowledge in the framework, as signified by unification between deductive reasoning and inductive reasoning. This is the same as the differentiation between *a priori* reasoning and *a posteriori* reasoning, and between Kant and Hume. Yet each and every one of these perspectives of reasoning is barred from the analytic nature of endogenous continuity and logical formalism of the law of monotheism (unity of knowledge).

Summarizing Kant and Hume's rationalist thought

The Kantian impossibility of deriving complex forms for the quantitative forms of the world-system was discussed earlier and carried over into a footnote.

Consider a numerical example: Hume's *a posteriori* reasoning assigns the numerical value to the sequence $\{n^{\theta}, (n+1)^{\theta}, \ldots\} \rightarrow \infty^{\infty}$, with $n = 1, 2, \ldots \infty$; $\theta = 1, 2, \ldots \infty$. This is an undefined result in the *a posteriori* domain of empirical relations. Hence such a sequence cannot explain the *a priori* result in terms of the precept of Supercardinal Being (Ω), which cannot be taken as infinity because of the non-numerical nature of Supercardinality. Rather, Ω denotes the topological entirety of the divine law: immeasurable, but generating causal relations ($\leftrightarrow$) between the divine law and the experiential world-system through the mapping by the *Sunnah*. These dynamics were explained earlier.

Another example is this: Hume's inductive reasoning independently of the divine law implies that the postulate of economic rationality cannot have a time measure explained by $t(\theta)$. This would otherwise mean the determination of events recorded in time but under induction of unity of knowledge. Contrarily, in the explanation of the postulate of economic rationality, time, preference, and technology are data. Knowledge as learning is terminally benign at the optimal and steady-state points of fixed resource allocation. Economics is non-processual science. If knowledge-flows are endogenously continuous then resources are continuously reproduced and distributed in society at large under the impact of inter-variable causality and continuity of knowledge-flows recorded over time.[8]

Let us consider: If it is the case that a household budget, production function, and social choice individually or together sets up their resource allocation by way of economic and social participation, then such participation generates inter-causal knowledge continued by knowledge induction of the interrelating variables. At any given point of time by continuous regeneration of knowledge via participation the knowledge-flows induce the continuous and endogenous participatory relationships between the variables. Thereby, the following inter-causality occurs: $t(\theta) \leftrightarrow \{\theta\} \leftrightarrow R(\mathbf{X}(\theta))$. In such a case, the postulates of economic rationality are altered towards a knowledge-induced study of reason and rationality that annuls every trace of neoclassicism and its full mainstream methodological effect.

Figure 3.3 depicts the knowledge-induced resource allocation path with some details.

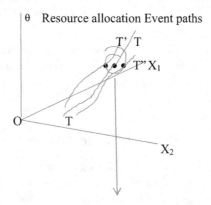

FIGURE 3.3 Historical paths with spheres of evolutionary neighbourhoods of events: $E(\theta, X(\theta), t(\theta))$[9]

Rationalism, reason, and economic rationality: summary

On the methodological scale of socio-scientific characterization, the attributes of reason and economic rationality are derived from the domain of rationalism. According to the nature of deductive and inductive thought and the postulates and models built on them, contesting methodological worldviews arise. Scientific doctrines and methodologies are thereby demarcated between these contesting epistemologies.

The postulates of economic rationality have no endogenous ethics in them. There is therefore no *a priori* context in these postulates. Ethical endogeneity belongs to the *a posteriori* domain of humanism in every case. Endogenous ethics means an inter-system causality of relations determined by the episteme of unity of knowledge. In Western socio-scientific methodology, ethics acquires the role of human free will in choices, decision-making, and individual, institutional, and social behaviour even though sub-optimal and non-steady state conditions are conveyed by the simulation idea of satisficing. Satisficing conveys the postulate of bounded rationality (Simon 1957).

The postulates of economic rationality in particular and in the socio-scientific domain in general have remained barren of ethics as a consciousness defining the endogenous interrelations. Morality and ethics everywhere and in every part of scientific investigation has remained an exogenous practice. It is precisely in the area of developing a sound and applicable theory of endogenous ethics and moral consciousness along with the experiential world-system, as of economics and the natural sciences, where possibility lies (Wilson 1998). This challenge of methodology belongs most profoundly and clearly to the Islamic methodological worldview of the monotheistic unity of knowledge as derived from the *Qur'an* combined with the *Sunnah* (tradition of the Prophet) and a discursive learned society.

Other definitions

Unity of knowledge

The foundational epistemological precept of unity of knowledge conveys the meaning of unity by multi-intercausal relations between all components of the *a priori* and the *a posteriori* domains. This invokes the nature of the law that drives reason and rationality as an endogenously integrated reality in human preferences constructed individually and collectively. Islamic understanding of reason and rationality also means the integration between deductive reasoning and inductive reasoning to reveal the reality of unity of knowledge and the consequential relational unity of the knowledge-induced world-system.

The episteme of unity of knowledge as the epistemological origin of intellectual thought also conveys the meaning of organic pairing by relationship between entities, variables, and diverse systems. Organic pairing conveys the idea of participative shared relations. This involves learning gained by participation and complementarity, which present a form of systemic unity of knowledge between

unifying knowledge-induced verities. The organic relationship of inter-causal unity by pairing all around is caused by interaction leading to integration, and thereby followed by the further potential for evolutionary learning arising by the confirmation of mutual well-being of the participants gained from the total learning processes.

Circular causation

Figure 3.2 explains that every selected variable, whether it is an ethical choice or otherwise, has reverse multi-causal relationships with the remaining vector of variables to display the degree of positive complementarities or negative relations signifying substitutions that exist inter-variably. This kind of a multi-regression equation model conveys several properties of learning systems:

1. Unity of knowledge between the selected variables is conveyed by their endogenous inter-causality.
2. Such a meaning of unity of knowledge conveys organic relational unity by pairing.
3. The evaluation of the multi-equations system is done at two stages. First, the use of actual observations in the variables leads to 'estimation' of the system. The results represent the positivistic state of circular causation inter-causal relations.

   The normative picture is conveyed by improvement of positive complementarities between the ethically chosen variables. This is the normative case-study. It follows in the light of possible allocation of resources between the selected variables and their entities. The change from the positive (estimated) to the normative (simulated) change is done by selecting the coefficients of the inter-variable relations to make them more complementary by a positive-signed change or less negative-signed coefficients as plausible. These are technical methods that will be explained further in this book.

   Negative coefficients imply marginal rates of substitution, and thereby, an end to learning between the variables (or a 'de-learning' state). Positive coefficients imply complementarities that are inter-variable, and thereby enhancement of learning.
4. From such results the total well-being conveyed by the interaction, integration and participatory learning between the selected variables can be quantitatively evaluated.
5. Policies and strategies can be generated by means of the 'estimation' and 'simulation' of the circular causation equations and the quantitative form of the well-being function also as endogenously related variables with the rest.
6. The 'estimation' and 'simulation' equations are further used to generate predictors of the circular causation variables.
7. Inter-process evolution by means of the simulated results can be developed (Figure 3.3).

Continuity and reversibility

In what has preceded by way of explaining the endogenous inter-causal circular causation interrelationship between the diverse *a priori* and *a posteriori* domains, reversibility and continuity was implied by the interrelationship as of the circular causation equations (Figure 3.2). Such interrelations are symbolized by (↔). The interrelationships lead to the annulment of antinomy in Figure 3.1.[10] The idea underlying the ultimate dependence of everything in Figure 3.3 on knowledge-flows to describe a continuously changing system is that knowledge is instrumental in change, whereby no consequences ever remain still in the midst of a participatory, complementary, and discursive medium. On the contrary, events in time in the absence of a methodology of knowledge embedding imperceptibly may not create change. Thus the revolutionary change that had occurred in the modern world-system is due to the endogenous nature of technological change (Romer 1986).

EXERCISE

As a revision exercise, read the given extract and answer the following questions:

1. Identify the following properties: unity of differentiation of knowledge; organic relationship; mono-causality; multi-causality; endogenous interrelations; *a priori* domain; *a posteriori* domain; institutional discourse via preference formation.
2. Construct a system-wide diagram (like the one given in Figure 3.4) with these answers.

Palan (2002, p. 215) writes in regard to the axiomatic nature of neoclassicism and its prototypes vis-à-vis prescribed preferences and their enforcement by corporate and political governance versus the discursive worldview:

> Modern institutionalist thought in particular is united in rejecting rationalist, progressivist and crude-materialist explanations of social processes and practices. Rather than adopt simple ideas versus practice type of theory, they view "the materiality of social institutions and their dynamics (as product) of evolving interrelated systems of institutions and discourse rather than as grounded in externalised and objective social realities."
>
> *Cameron and Palan 1999*

To economic neoclassicism, the externally imposed and institutionally enforced 'objective external realities' are its axioms of choices premised on the assumption of economic rationality. To other paradigms, the premise is one of assumed conflict and engagement between opposing sides in development paradigms. Such conflicts are construed as a form of marginal substitution appearing on the social versus economic planes with the intervening medium of institutions and polity. Even when discourse is promoted, it centres on one or the other form of such contending epistemologies of the development debate.

The Islamic monotheistic law as the methodological worldview contrasting with Western thought

The central keynote and the substantively contrary methodology of Islamic world-system in everything, and thus in Islamic economics as a specifically methodology-driven scientific enterprise, is its principal epistemology of monotheism (*Tawhid*). Thus the label we use in this book is Islamic economics. In terms of the methodology of unity of knowledge the representation of monotheism (*Tawhid*) is cast as follows.

The domain of monotheism overarches the Supercardinal Being of the divine law. From the divine law is derived the precept of unity of knowledge as the phenomenon of multi-causality between the good things of life.[11] Such multi-causality in the embedded field of continuously regenerated knowledge derived and returned to the divine law is the manifest universal law of pairing in the *Qur'an*.[12] Pairing is unravelled by the properties of interaction, which is discourse by reflection and participation as established by the *Qur'anic* principles of consultation (*shura*) with conscious reflection on the issues under discourse. Interaction is followed by integration as consensus formation in decision-making. Interaction together with integration describes the dynamic induction of preferences with the episteme of the monotheistic principle of unity of knowledge. Finally, out of the sequences of interaction (discourse) leading to integration (consensus), arises the circular causation relations between the knowledge-induced variables by way of evaluation followed by continuity of learning, as shown in Figure 3.4. This stage of the methodology of the monotheistic law is referred to as re-origination, and thus continuity of the new stages of knowledge reproduction and rediscovery regarding the generality and details of the world-system taken up in diversity. Such evolutionary learning processes continue through over the dimensions of knowledge, space, and time.[13] The monotheistic law thus transcends the sheer space–time structure on epistemological grounds (Bohr 1985) to the widest limit of human intellection, responses from creation as inherent consciousness (*fitra*), and cognition, application, and empirical work throughout.

The monotheistic law as the completion of the divine law being in 'everything' as the law of organic unifying interrelationship arising from the divine unity of knowledge, it performs two important tasks to establish its uniqueness and universality. The monotheistic overarching worldview brings out the nature, search, and discovery of the inter-causal holism of the world-systems (*a'lameen*) in terms of the monotheistic, that is *Tawhidi*, meaning of unity of knowledge and unification of the world-system by organic pairing in and of 'everything' (Barrow 1991).

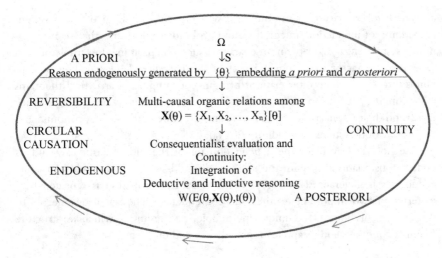

FIGURE 3.4 Interconnection between various properties of the learning relations: unity of knowledge

The uniqueness and universality of the monotheistic epistemological methodology is also manifest in the parallel formalism and application of the method and methodology of all disciplines of thoughts and distinctively by their organic combinations. All such studies are derived from the monotheistic law (*Tawhid* as law) (Choudhury 2003, 2006). The methodology followed by the conformable method and modelling applies to the case of differentiation of the forbidden and non-recommended things of life, and also to the unification of the good things of life. Thus the methodology of unity of knowledge corresponding to the monotheistic law explains both the phenomenon of unity of knowledge and the phenomenon of heteronomous differentiation of knowledge and reasoning between the *a priori* and the *a posteriori* domains. The latter reflects the consequences of the rationalist free will that is devoid of God and the divine law reflected by monotheism at its analytics.

The analytics of the monotheistic methodology in the development of circular causation model and its implications concerning continuity, organic pairing of relations, and institutional policy and strategy development by focusing on participation and complementarities as endogenously interrelated dynamics of being and becoming, altogether embrace the good and recommended choices. The methodologies of the unity of knowledge and its opposite in differentiated logic, as of the mainstream postulates of economic rationality *à la* neoclassical economics, are both contained and explained by the Islamic methodological worldview in its analytical form.

The monotheistic methodology also points out the legal framework of the good choices made individually and socially; and the rejection and impermissibility of certain choices according to the legal framework of the *Shari'ah*. This comprises the domain of the purpose and objective of the *Shari'ah*. It is referred to as *maqasid al-shari'ah (objectivity of monotheistic law).* In such a meshing of multi-system embedding of interaction, integration, and evolutionary learning, the Islamic economic system engages deeply in inseparable issues. The prominent example of such an embedded factor is the Great Event of the Hereafter (*Akhirah*). This precept builds into the organic interrelations bringing out important analytical theorems and properties of the inter-systemic evolutionary learning systems (Choudhury 2012) and their implications in the nature and structure of the social, economic, and scientific world-systems (Choudhury 2014a).

The holistic feature of the *a priori* domain of the monotheistic law and its endogenous relationship with the *a posteriori* world-system in the field of Islamic economics is generalized in Figure 3.4. The same explanation is repeated here in terms of two important features and consequences. These will be referred to throughout this book as the unique methodology according to which we structure Islamic economics and its applications – theory and practice.

Methodological formulation of socio-scientific relations according to Islamic analytics

These methodological formulations of monotheism analytics are explained as follows:

1. The induction of knowledge into socio-scientific variables in the form $\{X_1, X_2, \ldots, X_n\}[\theta]$, with $\theta \in (\Omega, S)$, subject to circular causation in continuity and reversibility of inter-variable and multi-causal relations like, $X_i(\theta) = f_i(\mathbf{X}_j(\theta))^{14}$, $i, j = 1, 2, \ldots, n$. Because of the trace of unity of knowledge $\{\theta\} \in (\Omega, S)$ in the knowledge-flows and their induction of the $\mathbf{X}(\theta)$-vector of variables, the nature of moral reconstruction of the interacting composition of the world-system also reflects the unity of knowledge. This marks the all-comprehending unity of multi-causal circular causal interrelationships between the *a priori* and the *a posteriori* domains of reasoning that emanates from the monotheistic understanding of unity of knowledge.

2. All the postulates of the concept of economic rationality mentioned earlier for the case of mainstream economics are rejected and changed for those that are induced by $\{\theta\}$ in Islamic economics along with the complete change in the concept of reason and rationality. The underlying explanations were presented earlier. The consequences are utterly damaging for the postulates leading to the permanent *problematique* of the entire mainstream economic theory.

For instance, consider the interrelated event-coordinate, $E(\theta, X(\theta), t(\theta); \wp(\theta))$, on any economic surface or in the bundle of social choices, be these of a microeconomic nature (Walras 1954) or of macroeconomics (Solow 1980). Because each of the entries in E(.) is interactive with the rest by way of continuity, reversibility, organic unity of knowledge, and circular causation, therefore, the learning neighbourhood around $\{\theta\}$ will sensitize all the other entries.

The result as shown in Figure 3.3 will be perturbation of the geometrical coordinates on the economic surfaces, and thereby perturbations of the historical path of evolutionary learning events. The economic optimal surfaces with steady-state equilibriums explained by marginal rates of substitutions create perturbations all around in neighbourhoods. As well as the economic expansion path as shown in Figure 3.3, the effect of a continuously endogenous increase in resources, compounds to create perturbations everywhere. Now the only way to regulate such perturbations is to study the inter-causal relations between the variables 'nearest' to their point of occurrence (Choudhury 2014b). Such points are denoted by (·) in Figure 3.3. Such extensive inter-variable complementarities by means of participation and discourse describe the entire socio-scientific analytical surface.

With these kinds of analytical consequences, the underlying neoclassical method – of marginal rate of substitution to measure relative prices between substitutes and choices of inputs and goods – fails to function. The end result is a completely corrugated destruction of the smooth type of surfaces yielding choices of goods and productive inputs, and relative prices of goods and inputs. Such perturbations, leading to an impossibility of estimating relative prices and marginal rate of substitution either by the methodology of unity of knowledge or by the dialectical process-oriented evolutionary economics (Georgescu-Roegen 1981), cannot be determined by the methods of stochastic surfaces in expected values or by the method of Data Envelopment Analysis (DEA) for determining efficient consequences of resource allocation. The resulting simulations from the evolutionary learning method of circular causation as indicated by the evolutionary neighbourhoods of event points in Figure 3.3 will cause shifting and changing evolutionary event paths. This will defy the measurement of efficiency ratios by using the stochastic surface analysis.

Instead of taking recourse to these analytical methods, the method of circular causation yields an approach that is primarily derived from the monotheistic foundations of Islamic epistemology. Thereafter, by the choice of any of many appropriate statistical methods, mathematical specification of the circular causation model, and the use of simulation methods for normative reconstruction of the model-coefficients, the multi-causally related variables yield their explanations and values. More on this will follow in subsequent chapters.

The meaning of economic value in the Islamic methodological sense and its derivation from Islamic epistemological roots yields the evaluation criterion of social well-being (*maslaha*). The measurement of social well-being is carried out discursively from the perspective of a life-fulfilment regime of sustainable development. This in turn is explained by degrees of complementarity between the inter-causal variables of the circular causation system of equations. The degree of inter-variable complementarity represents the quantitative sign of the degree of unity of knowledge between the variables included in the well-being objective criterion function. The evolutionary learning path of such inter-causal relations between the variables conveys the meaning of sustainability.

The estimation and simulation of (relative) prices of inputs and outputs, quantities of goods and productive inputs, finance and money, physical and technological resources – in fact, the whole gamut of variables as required for the investigative study at hand – arise from the evaluation of circular causation equations. The concept of embedded economic value is the rate of change in the quantitative form of the social well-being function in terms of its component variables. Such numerical changes are taken for a given process or time. These are then summed. Thus there is no reliance on marginal rates (e.g. of utility, production, inputs, social welfare alternatives, etc.) for the meaning of value. That is because the marginal rate as a mathematical formula cannot be quantitatively computed on a permanently corrugated surface caused by evolutionary learning under the epistemology of unity of knowledge and thereby with embedded moral and ethical forces.

The well-being function in the Islamic monotheism knowledge plane

We note the unified relationship between the goals of the well-being function in the light of the core of Islamic epistemology as Islamic methodology. Inter-causal relations in unity of knowledge explained, estimated, and simulated in terms of econometric predictors by the circular causation equations lead to the study of degrees of inter-variable complementarities. Such estimated and simulated predictor values of variables explain the degree of sustainability in the system. The predictor values of the estimated and simulated variables feed into the social well-being function. This end result of the social well-being function is called *maslaha* in Islamic terminology. It is the evaluative function of the purpose and objective of the *Shari'ah* (*maqasid al-shari'ah*) on conceptual and practical issues.

Methodology and method

Scientific methodology and method should be understood as different concepts. Method represents analytical instruments and models that carry the epistemology inherent in methodology. The methods so chosen for scientific analysis must therefore be consistent with the scientific implications of the methodology. The conclusion is that methods which are conformable to the methodology can be selected from all available categories in respect of the appropriate choice of methods.

An example here is the circular causation model. Inherent in it are the methods of estimation, simulation, and evolutionary learning by deductive–inductive dialectical method of unison of causes and effects. All these cogently feed into the social well-being function to study the Islamic concept of value and the life-sustaining criteria of socio-economic development. Yet it is perfectly acceptable to use all *forms* of regression and simulation methods, mathematical forms, or otherwise denoting the system and cybernetic approach. Such methods are Ordinary Least Square Method; Maximum Likelihood Method; Structural Equations Method; Variance Autoregression Method, Co-integration, Spatial Domain Analysis Method, etc. In the same way, various kinds of software for testing the circular causation system of equations by different acceptable methods can be used.

Contrarily, optimization and a steady-state equilibrium situation cannot exist in the entire case of circular causation relations and evolutionary learning behaviour across neighbourhoods and expansionary historical paths. Therefore, mathematical methods like Lagrangian, construction of production possibility surface, linear programming, and others can only be studied in respect of their critical evaluation. They cannot be used for the purposes of modelling and evaluating circular causation systems under the episteme of unity of knowledge.

As well, the dialectical method of evaluating conflict and competition scenarios as in evolutionary economic theory can be done by the use of the circular causation model to evaluate inter-variable and inter-causal differentiations. Yet the results to be expected will be for those dialectical situations that would not present the scenarios of unity of knowledge as fundamentally defined by the epistemological origin of $(\Omega,S) \to \{\theta\}$. Rather, the results will represent systemic and inter-variable differentiations as by choices arising from rationalist background and neoclassical substitutions.

The same is the case for studying optimal and steady-state mathematical systems, as in mainstream economics. The inter-variable signs of coefficients in the estimated circular causation system, if found to be negative, imply marginal rates of substitution (marginalism). This indeed is a consequence of resource scarcity and competition. The postulate of marginal rate of substitution between competing alternatives returns in this case of negative inter-variable relations. The inference then is of the semblance of mainstream economic theory, especially of the neoclassical axiom of economic rationality regarding marginalism.

What then is the nature of economic rationality, if any, for Islamic economics and socio-scientific reasoning? Any entrepreneurial and academic system that is defined on the epistemic basis of unity of knowledge, which is derived from the monotheistic law and agrees with the extended nature of *maqasid al-shari'ah* (Choudhury 2016), establishes the very different meaning of rationality as *fitra* in Islamic epistemology. Economics being an embedded academic enterprise with other multi-systemic disciplines reflects unity of knowledge by the positively complementary inter-variable coefficients of the circular causation system. Figure 3.4 summarizes the relational epistemology of the Islamic methodological worldview. The entirety of evolutionary learning holism in such a case explains the meaning of Islamic rationality in economics and other socio-scientific areas.

Identification of the postulates of Islamic socio-scientific (economic) rationality

The following postulates establish the meaning of Islamic socio-scientific (economic) rationality:

1. There exists a functional concept of the *a priori* domain with the world, the *a posteriori* domain: unity of knowledge, $[(\Omega,S) \ni \{\theta; \wp(\theta)\}] \to \{(\theta, \mathbf{X}(\theta); \wp(\theta))\}$.

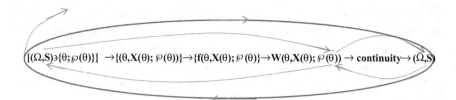

$$[(\Omega,S)\ni\{\theta;\wp(\theta)\}] \rightarrow \{(\theta,\mathbf{X}(\theta);\wp(\theta))\} \rightarrow \{f(\theta,\mathbf{X}(\theta);\wp(\theta)\} \rightarrow W(\theta,\mathbf{X}(\theta);\wp(\theta)) \rightarrow \text{continuity} \rightarrow (\Omega,S)$$

FIGURE 3.5 The continuous evolutionary learning field along the *sirat al-mustaqim* (straight but richly complex) path of *Tawhid* to world-system to *Tawhid* in the Hereafter and the induction of this to the continuous learning experience in the dimensions of knowledge, space, and time[15]

2. The knowledge-induced vector, $\{(\theta,\mathbf{X}(\theta);\wp(\theta)\}$, evaluates the *maslaha* choices from *maqasid al-shari'ah*: Evaluation of $W(\theta,\mathbf{X}(\theta);\wp(\theta))$, subject to circular causation inter-variable relations denoted by $\{f(\theta,\mathbf{X}(\theta);\wp(\theta)\}$ for examining inter-variable complementarities or lack of these.
3. The continuity axiom of events in knowledge, space, time holds (see Figure 3.5).

Figure 3.5 summarizes all the attributes of the continuously learning world-system in terms of the Islamic episteme of unity of knowledge. This is the major attribute of the participatory and complementary nature of evolutionary learning dynamics presented by the Islamic methodological worldview. It applies universally and uniquely to all Islamic socio-scientific thought, formalism, and application. In the particular case of the general methodological worldview, the same method-ology and its emergent formalism and methods apply to Islamic economics.

This explanation gives the summary definition of the Islamic rationality axiom of structure and behaviour. It is the opposite prototype of the combined axiom of transitivity in rational choice in mainstream economics (see exercise given below).

EXERCISE

With three (and multiple) choices, say, A, B, C:
If A is preferred to B; and if B is preferred to C; then A is preferred to C.
If A is preferred to B and also B is preferred to A, then A and B are mutually indifferent in choice.

Answer the following questions:

1. If A, B, C are knowledge-induced, can they be pre-ordered by preferences as in the case of the postulate of rational economic choice in mainstream economics?
2. Can strict reversibility of choices hold true with knowledge-induction as in the case of 'indifference of preferences' in the axiom of rational economic choice?

3. Why did Amartya Sen (1977) refer to the axiom of rational choice as the axiom of 'rational fools'?
4. Draw an indifference curve to show that knowledge-induction of preferences cannot lie on a smooth and convex to the origin surface. Consequently, the consumer utility function cannot be well defined in such a case.

Conclusion

Epistemology as methodology is the soul of scientific thought. Epistemology deepens in socio-scientific discovery, as new intellection, and new problems and issues bring about fresh challenges to think far beyond normal science and paradigm shifts. The next domain of fresh epistemology colouring science is of the nature of "scientific revolution" as Thomas Kuhn (1970) called it. Yet despite the great threshold of knowledge that scientific thought and application have contributed in the modern age, a large number of questions that are intertwined remain unresolved and unanswered. These are fundamental questions, the answers to which are essential to qualify the true purpose and goal of all of science – meta-science.

The problem in this sphere of a profound lack of understanding of the meta-scientific enterprise arises from methodological inability to answer certain great questions: First, although much of humankind looks up to a divine origin of life and upholds an ultimate reliance on this profound origin, yet the methodology of socio-scientific thought, and thereby the applications thereof, have failed to embed the divine law as a functional ontology in scientific methodology, methods, and thereby towards understanding the overarching true reality.

The words of Edward Wilson (1998, p. 264) are profoundly reflective on this topic:

> Looked at in proper perspective, God subsumes science; science does not subsume God. Scientific research in particular is not designed to explore all of the wondrous varieties of human experience. The idea of God, in contrast, has the capacity to explain everything, not just measurable phenomena, but phenomena personally felt and sublimely sensed, including revelation that can be communicated solely through spiritual channels.

The post-modern age is one of a search for that overarching scientific methodology that can embed religion with science. This would lead to the discovery of the methodology of meta-science. It is in such a challenging methodological discovery that Islamic monotheism strides in with much to offer. The future of meta-science with monotheistic law embedded in it can offer a methodology that can be blended and analytically used for conceptual and practical applications by conformable methods of the monotheistic methodology as the final epistemology of the realm of meta-science.

The Islamic epistemology derived from the *Qur'an*, the *Sunnah*, and through enlightened socio-scientific discourse, thus unifying the *a priori* domain with the *a posteriori* domain of holistic reasoning, is full of analytical wealth. This describes and embeds all world-systems, and thereby economics with morality, ethics, and materiality in a unique and universal methodology having substantive depth and details that cut across the most advanced nature of new scientific search, discovery, and applications. The nature of analytics of the monotheistic embedding in meta-science is mathematical in nature. Its application is the totality of the *a posteriori* domain by the instrumental forces of the discursive understanding interrelating God, men, intellect and machines through learning models of unity of knowledge and its induction of socio-scientific generality and details. This is where epistem-ology and methods blend in their multi-inter-causal organic pairing. Such will be the rendering of the Islamic monotheistic episteme of unity of knowledge and its moral construction of the unified world-system taken up in its generality and particulars. One such particular system is the field of Islamic economics.

This book will overarch across a comparative study of the embedded economic phenomena by the contrasting methodology between the Islamic methodological worldview and Western approaches. We have already introduced the contrasting perspectives between these two methodologies in this chapter. Much remains to cover in the subsequent chapters.

Chapter summary: the foundational issues

1. introduction
2. Islamic economic methodology in comparative perspectives
3. the scope of Islamic economics
4. the nature of the Islamic economic introductory model
5. exercises and examples for establishing applications of Islamic economics.

Notes

1 The *Qur'an* rejects the field of rationalism because of its vagaries in understanding truth as a holistic unity. The *Qur'an* (28:50) declares: "But if they hearken not to thee, know that they only follow their own lusts: and who is more astray than one who follows his own lusts, devoid of guidance from God? For God guides not people given to wrong-doing."
2 *Qur'an* (*Iqlas*, 112:1–4).
3 *Qur'an* (87:1).
4 Supercardinality (Ω) is the abstract mathematical topology (non-dimensional mathem-atical function) that establishes the following continuous functionals: (i) $S \subset \Omega$ by way of the reversible relational functional, $\Omega \leftrightarrow S$; (ii) $S \leftrightarrow X$; and thus, $\Omega \leftrightarrow S \leftrightarrow X$. Therefore, the example of the organically unified domains of *a priori* and *a posteriori* multi-causal reversible relations are defined by knowledge-flows according to unity of knowledge and denoted by $\{\theta\} \subset \{X\} \in (\Omega, S)$ by the relationship $(\Omega, S) \leftrightarrow \{X\} \leftrightarrow \{\theta\}$. In the example of mathem-atical operation $\{X\} \leftrightarrow \{\theta\} \Leftrightarrow \{\mathbf{X}(\theta)\}$; (Ω, S) as the epistemology; thereby, say, $(2+2) \leftrightarrow 2^{\theta} . 2^{\theta} = 2^{2\theta}$ and higher analytic forms of 2^{θ}. In the end, since $\{\theta\} \in (\Omega, S)$, therefore, the

functional $\{2^{\theta}, 2^{2\theta}, \ldots\} \equiv$ divine law in one case (*sunnat Allah*) $\in (\Omega, S)$, the totality mapped by the advancing understanding and application of the *Sunnah* as ontological mapping of the supercardinal domain of *sunnat Allah*, denoted by S. Hence a numerical equivalence is established between the supercardinal domain of *sunnat Allah* through the *Sunnah* and the experimental world-system. All functions are interrelations ($\leftrightarrow$). Such interrelations are inter-convertible by reversibility of knowledge production and continuity involving simply the corporeal function and extension of the reading, understanding, and applying of the monotheistic law (unity of knowledge) in the order of world-system in all shapes and forms (extendability across systems and their organic relations, meaning complementary multi-causal reversible relations. The property of multi-causal reversibility through these organic interrelations is that of continuity in knowledge, space, and time.

5 *Qur'an* (57:3; 92:13).

6 Marginal rates of substitution between goods, inputs of production, and social choices are the logical derivation from the condition of optimal allocation of resources between competing ends.

7 Preferences thus remain datum and are devoid of the endogenous learning behaviour and technological induction.

8 Let $R(\theta)$ denote resources as a function of inputs, $\mathbf{X}(\theta) = \{X_1, X_2, \ldots, X_n\}[\theta]$. Thus $R(\theta) = R(\mathbf{X}(\theta))$. Thereby, by continuous knowledge-induction, $dR(\mathbf{X}(\theta))/d\theta = \Sigma_{i=1}^{n}(\partial R/\partial X_i).(dX_i/d\theta) \geq 0$ because of each $(\partial R/\partial X_i) \geq 0$; $(dX_i/d\theta) \geq 0$.

But contrarily, $dR(\mathbf{X}(t))/dt = \Sigma_{i=1}^{n}(\partial R/\partial X_i).(dX_i/dt) = 0$, where the optimum and steady-state equilibrium points are attained as on the production possibility curve, the indifference curve, and production isoquants. In such a situation, $t(\theta) = t$ is independent of knowledge induction. If exogenous shocks ($\varepsilon(t)$, $t = T_0, T_1, \ldots$) are introduced, then $R(t) = R(X(t)) + \varepsilon(T_i), I = 1, 2, \ldots$ At the resource optimal point, $R(T_i) = R(X(T_i)) + \varepsilon(T_i)$; $dR(\mathbf{X}(t))/dt = \Sigma_{i=1}^{n}(\partial R/\partial X_i).(dX_i/dt) + \Sigma_{i=1}^{m}\partial\varepsilon(T_i)/\partial t = 0$. Hence the exogenous effect of resource injection dies away at a subsequent optimal and steady-state point. The nature of the theory of resource allocation in mainstream economics thus remains intact even following resource injunction. In endogenous resource allocation the addition $\varepsilon(T_i)$ is unnecessary.

9 By characterizing the event-path as a functional transform we note the following result: $dE/d\theta = \Sigma_{i=1}^{n}(\partial E/\partial X_i)\star(dX_i/d\theta) \geq 0$, with $\text{plim}\{\theta_i\}_{t(\theta i)} = \theta_t$, hence a convergent path TT derived from multiple paths T', T" etc. as shown.

10 $dE(\theta, \mathbf{X}(\theta), t(\theta))/d\theta = \Sigma_{\mathbf{X}}(\partial E/\partial \mathbf{X}).(d\mathbf{X}/d\theta) + (\partial E/\partial t).(dt(\theta))/d\theta > 0$ for every $\{\theta\}$ $\in (\Omega, S)$ in the sense of multi-causal relations denoted by ($\leftrightarrow$). This means that the knowledge of the monotheistic law Ω and its transmission via S increases from the proofs of the experienced world-system.

On the other hand, if change is not functionally based on $\{\theta\}$, then t is independent of θ. Consequently, $dE(\mathbf{X}(t))/dt = \Sigma_{\mathbf{X}}(\partial E/\partial \mathbf{X}).(d\mathbf{X}/dt) = 0$, when optimum in $\mathbf{X}(t)$-values are attained.

11 *Qur'an* on the good things of life, *hallal at-tayyabah*. See also *Qur'an* (14:24, 25).

12 *Qur'an* (36:36).

13 *Qur'an* re-origination (27:64).

14 More extensively this expression is written as $X_i(\theta) = f_i(\theta, \mathbf{X}_j(\theta))$, where $\mathbf{X}_j(\theta)$ denotes the vector of variables (see Figure 3.4) without the variable $X_i(\theta)$, thus i,j = 1,2,...; i≠j.

15 The role of the mapping by the teachings of the Prophet was from the *Qur'an* as the chapter *an-Najm* (53:5) declares: "Nor does he speak of (his own) desire. It is only an Inspiration that is inspired. He has been taught (this *Qur'an*) by one mighty in power [Gabriel]." The role of the mapping 'S' along with the extent of the *Tawhidi* law is essential to map the *Qur'an* onto life and to carry the cumulative experiences of life to the

Hereafter, which is identical with the great Closure (Great Event) of *Tawhid*. Sayyid Muhammad al-Hasani (2013) writes, taking from Al-Bukhari and Muslim sources of *ahadith*: "He is the most knowledgeable of God's creation and the most well-acquainted of them with God…"

References

Al-Hasani, Sayyid Muhammad Ibn 'Alawi al-Maliki (2013). *Muhammad (SWA) the Perfect Man*, trans. Williams, K., UK: Visions of Reality Books.

Barrow, J.D. (1991). *Theories of Everything: The Quest for Ultimate Explanation*, Oxford, UK: Oxford University Press.

Bartley, W.W. (1988). Theories of rationality, in *Evolutionary Epistemology, Rationality, and the Sociology of Knowledge*, eds. Radnitzky, G. & Bartley, III, W.W., pp. 205–213, LaSalle, IL: Open Court.

Blaug, M. (1968). *Economic Theory in Retrospect*, Homewood, IL: Richard D. Irwin.

Bohr, N. (1985). Discussion with Einstein on epistemological issues, in *The Philosophy of Niels Bohr: The Framework of Complementarity*, ed. Folse, H., Amsterdam: North Holland Physics Publications.

Cameron, A. & Palan, R. (1999). The imagined economy: mapping transformations in the contemporary state, *Millennium*, (28)2: 267–89.

Choudhury, M.A. (1996). Economic integration in the Sextet Region and the Middle East Peace Accord, *International Journal of World Peace*, 13(2): 67–78.

Choudhury, M.A. (2003). *Explaining the Qur'an: A Socio-Scientific Inquiry*, 2 volumes, Lewiston, NY: Edwin Mellen Press.

Choudhury, M.A. (2006). *Science and Epistemology in the Qur'an*, 5 volumes (different volume titles), Lewiston, NY: The Edwin Mellen Press.

Choudhury, M.A. (2012). On the existence of learning equilibriums, *Journal for Science*, 16(2): 49 – 62, [2011 issue appeared in 2012].

Choudhury, M.A. (2014a). *Tawhidi Epistemology and Its Applications in Economics, Finance, Science, and Society*, Cambridge, UK: Cambridge Scholars Publishing.

Choudhury, M.A. (2014b). *The Socio-Cybernetic Study of God and the World-System*, Philadelphia, PA: Ideas Group Inc. Global.

Choudhury, M.A. (2015). *Res extensa et res cogitans de maqasid as-shari'ah*, *International Journal of Law and Management*, 57(6): 662–693.

Choudhury, M.A. (2016). Religion and economics, *International Journal of Social Economics*, 43(2): 134–160.

Descartes, R. (1954). Discourse on method, in *The Philosophers of Science*, eds. Commins, S. & Linscott, R.N., New York: The Pocket Library.

Etzioni, A. (1988). What is rational? in his *The Moral Dimension, Towards a New Economics*, New York: The Free Press.

Georgescu-Roegen, N. (1981). *The Entropy Law and the Economic Process*, Cambridge, MA: Harvard University Press.

Hume, D. (1988). *An Enquiry Concerning Human Understanding*, Buffalo, NY: Prometheus Books.

Hume, D. (1992). Of the understanding, in his *Treatise of Human Nature*, Buffalo, NY: Prometheus Books.

Kant, I. (1949). *The Philosophy of Kant*, trans. Friedrich, C.J., New York: Modern Library.

Kant, I. (1977). Religion with the limits of reason alone, *The Philosophy of Kant*, trans. C.J. Friedrich, New York: The Modern Library.

Kuhn, T.S. (1970). *The Structure of Scientific Revolution*, Chicago, IL: University of Chicago Press.

Nozick, R. (2001). *Invariances: The Structure of the Objective World*, Cambridge, MA: The Belknap Press of the Harvard University Press.

Palan, R. (2002). The constructivist underpinnings of the new international political economy, in *Global Political Economy: Contemporary Theories*, ed. Palan, R., pp. 215–228, London: Routledge.

Pheby, J. (1988). *Methodology and Economics: A Critical Introduction*, London: Macmillan.

Popper, K. (1998). *Conjectures and Refutations: The Growth of Scientific Knowledge*, London: Routledge & Kegan Paul.

Popper, K. (2004). *The Logic of Scientific Discovery*, London: Routledge.

Rawls, J. (1971). *A Theory of Justice*, Cambridge, MA: Harvard University Press.

Resnick, S.A. & Wolff, R.D. (1987). *Knowledge and Class: A Marxian Critique of Political Economy*, Chicago, IL: The University of Chicago Press.

Romer, P.M. (1986). Increasing returns and long-run growth, *Journal of Political Economy*, 94: 1002–1037.

Rucker, R. (1983). *Infinity and the Mind*, New York: Bantam New Books.

Schumpeter, J.S. (1968). *History of Economic Analysis*, New York: Oxford University Press.

Sen, A. (1977). Rational fools: A critique of the behavioural foundations of economic theory, *Philosophy and Public Affairs*, 6.

Simon, H. (1957). *Models of Man*, New York: John Wiley & Sons.

Smart, N. (2000). *Worldviews*, Upper Saddle River, NJ: Prentice Hall.

Solow, R. (1980). *Growth Theory: An Exposition*, Oxford: Oxford University Press.

Walras, L. (1954). *Elements of Pure Economics*, trans. Jaffe, W., Homewood, IL: Richard D. Irwin.

Walsh, M.J. (1985). *A History of Philosophy*, London: Geoffrey Chapman.

Wilson, E.O. (1998). *Consilience: The Unity of Knowledge*, New York: Vantage Books.

4

THE SCOPE OF ISLAMIC ECONOMICS

LEARNING OBJECTIVES

This chapter intends to provide the students with:

- a clear idea within the scope of Islamic economics that there is a large class of economically relevant social and moral behaviour between the firms and the households
- an explanation and detailed analytical meaning of consumption and investment functions without involving *riba* (interest/usury), *mysir* (gambling) and *gharar* (uncertainty) which come under the heading of Islamic economics
- a comprehensive basic understanding that the subject of Islamic economics is not restricted to Islamic society only but also includes all economic behaviour where the central embedded role of *Tawhid* as law pervades the socio-scientific domain of 'everything'.

The general epistemological methodology of scientific investigation from the contrasting Western and Islamic perspectives that was formalized in Chapters 1, 2 and 3 is now brought forth to establish the nature and scope of Islamic economics. The starting point is to note that in comparative methodological perspectives, like all other disciplines of study, economics has also been cast in the framework of its own differentiated specialization (Holton 1992). Thereby, in the name of disciplinary specialization, mainstream economics has been deprived of its embedded methodological worldview along with the important human elements of concern. These elements are morality, ethics, and the crosscurrents of issues with other disciplines, whether by way of a unique methodology and methodical study, or by way of formalizing economics as a generalized human science (Boulding 1968). Yet quite evidently, the various disciplines lack the methodology and the attenuating method to blend morality and ethics with the material forms and considerations regarding this embedding. Even more damaging has been the fact that no methodical discovery has been made that can analytically study morality and ethics as neural system studies, and thereby draw policies, strategies and institutional forms that can present a wider field of endogenous learning phenomena (Choudhury 2014b).

In previous chapters, we explained why the estrangement of morality and ethics from socio-scientific studies occurred in respect of the differentiated worldview that was moulded by the peculiar meanings given to rationalism and reason, and also constructed the conforming meanings of reason and economic rationality. Chapters 1, 2 and 3 also pointed out the opposing meanings given to these methodological terms in Islamic scientific perspectives that are erected upon monotheism as the episteme of unity of knowledge, and according to it of the unity of the world-system. Accordingly, economics as a sub-system of the wider ensemble of embedded systems has been deprived of what it used to be during the Greek World and which tapered off in Adam Smith's *Wealth of Nations* (1976). Neither could it survive in the works of Walras (quoted in Blaug 1986) despite the ethical views of human sciences that he upheld.

One example, beyond the different methodological ways of understanding and methodically applying the meanings of rational economic choice with and without ethics, was given previously. We give another example here. This shows how an endogenous blending between ethics and economics, as with any other branch of science, cannot be attained in the existing theoretical structure. The intertemporal theory of resource allocation is necessarily between the real economy yielding rates of return and the financial economy yielding interest rates. By the neoclassical postulate of marginal rate of substitution, which forms the core of economic theory treating resources as scarce, there always exists the inherent opportunity cost between real rates of return and interest rates; and between the real economy and the financial economy.

There is no ethical treatment in such an allocation of scarce resources over time to link up the financial sector with interest, and the real sector with real rates of return on spending. One of the prime reasons for this impossibility in using organic relational coherence between the two possibilities is caused by the permanent prevalence of interest rate in individual and collective behaviour and preferences. The intertemporal allocation of resources cannot be endogenously induced except by being ethically and morally induced with exogenous economic and social policies and regulations. When such exogenous actions are introduced into economic theory, market failures are argued to arise in terms of allocation of quantities of resources and prices via the incidence of tax rates.

The nature of morality and ethics in economic theory

The nature of morality and ethics arises from the rationalist background of taxation and charity. In Milton Friedman's case of subsidy for guaranteed income supplementation, every dollar so received, while increasing the household income, brings this nearer to the graduated taxation bracket. This kind of income distribution caused by subsidy as charity is known as 'negative taxation'. The moral and ethical implications of subsidy as charity dissipate with the impact of negative taxation on household income.

In the case of a tax levy, the incidence of taxation and subsidy creates price distortion in the dented area of the production possibility curve caused by the tax/subsidy (inner point). Likewise, the market demand and supply curves shift due to the impact of the tax levy. Now the net change in consumer and producer surplus is shared between the consumer and producer. The result is an inequitable impact of the tax levy either on the consumer or the producer. In the end, the tax instrument does not yield the ethical change that is expected.

The problem of the inequitable impact of government policies to correct market failures is a consequence of method. The result of inequity points out that correction of market failures by non-market policy and regulatory instruments is a departure from the endogenous realization of ethical consequences in fair market dealing and instead is the exogenous imposition of government intervention. In the latter case, the legal tenets play an important role in determining the direction and extent of intervention. The question is whether governments should raise taxes and apply fiscal expenditure directly affecting consumers, producers, and collective groups, or whether these general revenues should be spent in raising social consciousness to allow markets to correct themselves.

The above question is similar to the following:

1. Should governments and charities promote food stamps to address the problem of hungry and poor households? Or should government tax revenues and charities raised for ameliorating the poor and hungry be given to the needy to spend on their own needs? The approach for market-driven adjustment would promote the latter case.
2. Would a lump sum of charity be preferred to a tax-adjusted household budget improvement? The answer is to opt for the first approach.

Similar considerations are functions of the social and legal perspective as to how these view the welfare context of taxation versus market-driven allocation.

Because the rationalist methodological approach is based primarily on government interventions in the case of market failures, the corresponding exogenous nature of policy intervention will necessarily cause market distortions. On the other hand, if spending is used as an instrument towards market adjustment as an endogenous action, then a different economic attitude towards market orientation is cogently effective. We will dwell on this point between mainstream economics and Islamic economics to bring out the meaning of systemic ethics and what enables it as an endogenous force of social and economic actions.

Some necessary definitions

Morals and ethics

Morality is always the source of ethics, but ethics is not the same as morality. Ethics by and large is equated with humanism, which is derived from the rationalist roots of individual and collective free will. Consequently, as explained in Chapters 1, 2 and 3, the derived meanings of reason and rationality under the canopy of rationalism in the Western epistemology as methodology also pursue economic differentiation and methodological individualism (Buchanan 1999).

Yet again, ethics necessarily arise from moral law, which transcends rationalist doctrinaire. When such equivalence occurs, ethics becomes an instrument carrying the moral law into experience. Consequently, ethics cannot subsume moral law. The epistemological foundation of Islamic economics is found in moral law. Ethics is a sign of good conduct according to the details of the moral law as textually provided and discursively extended. Yet ethics that is revisionary of the moral law is unacceptable as the moral origin of ethics. Likewise, ethics that arises from the rationalist epistemic roots is unacceptable by the moral law. These conditions imply strongly that ethics is neither of a primal epistemic nature nor is it foundational in the realm of methodology.

A few examples will bring out the nature of essentiality of the moral law surpassing ethics in economic behaviour and actions. Islamic charity like *zakah* (obligatory form of giving) is said in the *Qur'an* to be a claim of the poor on the wealth of the rich. Yet the meaning of *zakah* goes into its literal meaning of purging and increasing wealth. Through it, the spirit and practice of the moral law yields amelioration of the needy in their productive transformation, in business and socio-economic development, and in proper choices of the good things of life. These and their like choices define the criterion of well-being. The attainment of well-being in turn establishes progress along the life-fulfilling regime of ameliorative socio-economic development.

How is the choice of the good things of life determined in the moral law? This is a matter of discerning the choice according to the precept of the monotheistic law of unity of knowledge by its intrinsic property of organic relational oneness by 'pairing'. This topic was covered in Chapters 1 and 3. We will return to this topic in greater depth later on. It is sufficient to point out at this time the following role of morality and ethics in the moral law: The *Shari'ah* is the moral law of 'everything'. Its practice is discursively established in the details of life, experience, and applications of the moral law in and by the purpose and objective of the moral law – *maqasid al-shari'ah*. This field of intellection, application, and practices arises out of specific and social details by keeping focus on the *Shari'ah*. The monotheistic law as the moral law is permanently assigned.[1] It is carried by the *Sunnah* of the Prophet Muhammad and the learned discourse of the community, to determine the appropriateness of choices of goods and services, institutions and the criterion of well-being by the ethics of the moral law. The extent of ethics in such a domain of choices in accordance with the monotheistic law comprises *maqasid al-shari'ah*. Thus, while the monotheistic law comprises the primal moral law, which is the indispensable epistemology of unity of knowledge, the *maqasid al-shari'ah* forms the ethical domain of the moral law. The monotheistic law is established and unchangeable. The *maqasid al-shari'ah* is extendible (Mustapha 2006; Choudhury 2016).

In reference to the moral law that subsumes *zakah* and its ethics as found in *maqasid as-shari'ah*, there is the critical element of the moral law as the principle of unity. It is signified by the joining of the hearts of the rich and poor to attain mutual (participated as unity) well-being. On the other hand, the ways of social distribution and usage of *zakah* in productive, sustainable, and extended ways of bringing about organic functioning of possibilities to enable the recipient and the donor in the grand social context is the ethical manifestation of *zakah*. Ethics is thus behaviour and action that realizes on the relational plane based on the foundational epistemology of the moral law. The organization of *zakah* is of the nature of relational epistemology by constructing organic unity of knowledge between diverse possibilities for realizing sustainability of the common good contributed by *zakah*.

EXERCISE 4.1

Those who devour usury will not stand except as stands one whom the Evil One by his touch has driven to madness. That is because they say: "Trade is like usury. But God has permitted trade and forbidden usury...."

Qur'an 2:275

Identify some ethics as examples of relational epistemology that can be derived as ways of relating trade with the inversion (abolition) of *riba*. (Hint: consider the various relational ways that relate trade (X_1, X_2) to the inversion of *riba* (R) as $(1/R) = f(X_1, X_2, \theta)$; X_1 denotes national income; X_2 denotes value of total international trade as (Export + Import). $\{\theta\}$ is knowledge derived as relational epistemology based on *Tawhid* as the law of unity of knowledge.)[2]

Many similar specific examples can be derived to prove that underlying the precept of the moral law is its permanence in governing over the order of things as the primal law.[3] But ethics is derived from moral acts as the ways, instrumentation, and application of the moral law on all issues under study. Islam happens to be the only worldview wherein the moral law is codified. This enables the moral law and the derived ethics from it to co-exist without contradiction in purpose and objective of the common well-being of all. This fact is proved by the uniqueness and universality of the monotheistic law as the ultimate law that governs all specifics (see Chapter 2). Contrarily, in the case of the rationalist methodology the theory of over-determination of epistemologies prevails. This renders any law based on rationalism random and conflicting in nature. Consequently, the domain of ethics derived from such random over-determined laws remains undetermined as a moral edict of life, thought, experience, practicality, and application.

An example of the nature of over-determination in rationalist moral law and the idea of ethics can be traced down to the definition of interest in this case. Mainstream economic theory of interest is strewn with many forms of interest rates. Among them are nominal rate of interest, real rate of interest, simple rate of interest, compound rate of interest, term structure of interest rates, effective rate of interest, own rate of interest, marginal efficiency of capital as interest rate, and so on. Many Muslim economists argue that the real rate of interest, the own rate of interest, the marginal efficiency of capital, and simple against compound rates of interest, are permissible in the presence of inflation. The argument is also launched on the permissibility of less as against usurious rate of interest. Such ideas float around because of the absence of any legal edict that would unequivocally and conclusively rule on the moral theory of trade versus interest, and then leave this to human discourse under the ethics of understanding and applying the moral law via various ways of studying the truth of the *Qur'anic* verse (mentioned above) relating to trade and *riba*.

Interaction and integration

The other attribute of evolutionary economics and Islamic economics is the property of interaction and integration. These properties are understood and applied in different ways in these two economic theories. However, neoclassical economics is not based on and therefore cannot explain the process nature of occurrence of economic events. For instance, optimization of the neoclassical 'objective' function is a terminal condition of the first-order maximization of the Lagrangian resulting from the mathematical operation of constrained maximization. The terminal point of occurrence of the optimal state has no process dynamics to explain change as to how such optimal states are attained. It is simply that the first-order conditions of optimization happen as a mathematical necessity of a selected approach to problem solving, namely the Lagrangian. Yet underlying such necessity of optimization and the steady-state equilibrium there remains the governing axiom of economic rationality. The underlying inter-relationships between rationalism, rationality, and reason in scientific problem-solving were explained in Chapters 1 and 3.

The evolutionary learning world of processes and multi-causal organic relations as in the case of an embedded idea of economic theory – and likewise, of the entropy and evolutionary theory of economics rendered by Shackle (1972), Georgescu–Roegen (1981), Boulding (1981) and others – have not found their way into neoclassical economic theory. Where the process-orientation was forced into neoclassical economics, the result remained of the optimization character in the preferences of agents in public choice, and rational expectation (Nelson & Winter 1982). The axioms of scarcity, competition, and full-information remained unchanged. Consequently, the concept of optimality and steady-state equilibrium remained as conditions of datum of preferences and economic rationality in all such neoclassical economic innovations.

Yet the evolutionary learning perspective of organic unity of knowledge across multi-causal fields of entities, variables, relations, and systems is the natural result of the Islamic economic (socio-scientific) worldview. See Figures 3.3 and 3.4 (Chapter 3) in this regard. The consequences of resource allocation are thereby permanently probabilistic in nature. The consequences across knowledge-induced fields of actions and responses on given issues and problems to study, remained evolutionary learning points that converge towards but never attain what is referred to as the 'nearest' points of the evolutionary learning equilibriums in the framework

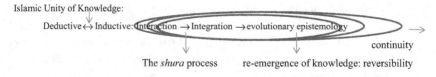

Islamic Unity of Knowledge:

Deductive ↔ Inductive: Interaction → Integration → evolutionary epistemology   →

continuity

The *shura* process   re-emergence of knowledge: reversibility

FIGURE 4.1 Co-evolutionary convolutions of the IIE-learning universe

of a probabilistic idea of neighbourhood of nearness. The continuity of the evolutionary learning phenomenon, as explained in Chapter 3 regarding the concept of continuity and reversibility (Figure 3.4), denies attainment of the evolutionary equilibrium points and the optimal point where novelty of learning and innovation as endogenous forces die, unless such points are applied as exogenous shocks.

In Western economic and political economy theory, the evolutionary learning context of the underlying methodology of over-determination, conflict, and undecidability in terminal decision-making militate to establish the permanent conjecture without convergence. The moral law of unity of knowledge does not apply. Consequently, a permanent scenario of disequilibrium prevails. Such a socio-economic scenario was the rendering in Marxist political economy (Mandel 1971; Cole 1966).

At the end of this definitional sojourn we note that abstraction *qua* abstraction *ad infinitum* does result in consensus by discourse. There remains always the randomness of discourse between contending epistemological thought and academe. Integration as consensus or convergence of views resulting from the interactive pattern of a discursive milieu, governed by epistemic unity of knowledge and leading to ever more of the same pattern of discursive actions and responses, is not to be found in the disequilibrium theory of political economy. Consequently, evolutionary learning though true, yet Western epistemic thought cannot yield an interactive leading to integrative, followed by co-evolutionary, learning in the framework of unity of knowledge.

In the Islamic methodological framework (Chapter 2) the *Qur'anic* exegeses on universal 'pairing'; convergence by means of consultation (discursive) – *shura* dynamics (Choudhury 2011); and re-origination of the world-system in the light of divine law (*khalq in-jadid* = moral consciousness), together establish the continuous interrelationship in the Interactive, Integrative, and Evolutionary (IIE) Learning framework of the scope of Islamic economics and diversely embedded world-systems.

EXERCISE 4.2

How are market prices set in the following three cases?

1. The theory of market equilibrium;
2. Non-convergent evolutionary dynamics (dialectics);
3. IIE learning dynamics leading to co-evolutionary equilibriums.

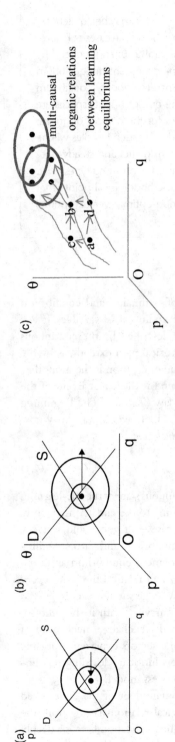

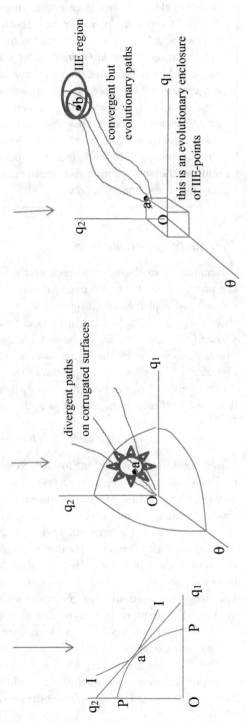

FIGURE 4.2 (a) Steady-state market equilibrium; (b) Non-convergence evolutionary disequilibrium; (c) Convergence with evolutionary learning equilibrium in unity of knowledge

FIGURE 4.3 Contrasting forms of equilibriums and non-existence of optimality

We denote by 'p' prices of goods, services, inputs as the case may be; 'q' denotes quantities of goods, services, or inputs as the case may be. In the cases of Figures 4.2a, 4.2b and 4.2c, 'p' and 'q' are respectively, neutral to θ; and induced by θ-values of different kinds – in Figure 4.2b for non-convergent disequilibrium dialectical model; and in Figure 4.2c for convergent evolutionary equilibrium model of Islamic epistemic unity of knowledge. The output (input) spaces are also shown in these three cases: q_1, q_2 are quantities for the choices of goods, services, inputs 1, 2. In the case of Figures 4.3b and 4.3c, such bundles will be an increasing category. In these two figures, optimum points and steady-state points cannot exist. Only evolutionary learning points of contrasting types exist. The student needs to describe all the underlying methodological points that underlie the above contrasting equilibrium and non-optimal versus optimal conditions of economic theory.

Optimality and equilibrium

Continuing from the previous section, the study of optimality and equilibrium can now be extended to the intertemporal case with multi-causal variables. It was defined and explained in Chapter 3 that history is described by the continuous sequencing of events. In the Islamic case such a historical path extends, as by the *Qur'an*, from the beginning to the end. The beginning of creation is the monotheistic law of creation by the divine command.[4] The end is the Great Event of the Hereafter (*Akhirah*) as the completion of the divine law (*Tawhid*).[5] The Beginning is thus equivalent to the End and conversely as well. The universal trajectory now described by *Tawhid* is the straight path, the *sirat al-mustaqim*:

$$Tawhid \rightarrow \text{World-System} \rightarrow Tawhid \tag{4.1}$$

This expression (4.1) is true both for the smallest continuous state of the IIE-learning processes and for the very large process of the beginning to the end. Consequently, as an example, the exchange equilibrium in every case – of goods and services, productive inputs, monetary equilibrium, general equilibrium and partial equilibrium, computational general equilibrium, full-employment equilibrium and such like entities – are all within the above-mentioned grand relationship. Thus every one of these equilibrium states is induced by the knowledge variable that is derived from the epistemic origin of the monotheistic law carrying with it the unity of knowledge and unification of goods and services in the exchange mechanism of markets.[6] Furthermore, by the fact that all systems and sectors experience organic multi-causal relationship between them, therefore, evolutionary learning equilibriums characterize all the multi-systems in the IIE-process model.

Therefore this relationship (4.1) is the grand containment of the generalized system of IIE-processes as evolutionary epistemological relations lasting from the beginning to the end of the history of the universe. The implication here is a deeply analytical and conclusive one. The universe of 'everything' (Hawking & Mlodinow 2010)[7] is structured in the framework of multi-causal and multi-dimensional unity of probabilistic relational epistemology. This indeed is the grand design conveyed by the relational and learning universe of the *Qur'an*. The *Qur'an* originally explains that such 'pairing' also remains inherent between the false things of life, but in the context of their ultimate dissociation. In the midst of the IIE-process explanation of the multi-dimensional and multi-causal relationships between diverse systems, the only true depiction of the conscious universe is that of evolutionary learning from *Tawhid* to *Tawhid* through the processes of the intervening world-system. The universe with its diversely unifying systems realizes itself in the midst of evolutionary equilibrium denying steady-state equilibrium and all semblances of optimality.[8]

Take an example in the small-scale sub-universe of expression (4.1). Consider an investor driven by economic rationality allowing perfect information predicting an increasing price level and net capital gains. His cash-flows are expected to increase over time because he assumes perfect or expected values of intertemporal cash-flows to be known. This generates perfect information either by deterministic knowledge or probabilistic knowledge. So the rational investor has to know his cash-flows fully in these two cases at every point of time, standing in the here and now with a financial telescope peering out into the future.

Then comes the storm by the will of God that breaks down his garden of expectation, wealth, and prospects, of the overweening man who stood above God.[9] All this occurs because the investor's rational behaviour made him forget the various calamities that could come about if he did not include consciousness of *Tawhid* in his calculations of prospects and expectations. One such calamity that always happens is the depressive fluctuation of stock prices in the financial market where assets survive, continue, or die by unknown contingencies all the time.

So now, how will you predict or expect cash-flows to behave? The conscious social system induces the cash-flow by the epistemic knowledge arising from the monotheistic roots. How can cash-flows be evaluated in this case? This is where the praises of God is raised at the 'nearest' point of occurrence of an event, which is always knowledge-induced including those events that occur at any given point of time.[10] Yet 'time' is simply a recorder, not the cause of events. Only knowledge creates events and change by the will of God in the order and scheme of everything.[11] The student can explain the footnote formula and shown how to calculate it with assumed values of the variables with and without θ-values.

Utility and welfare

According to our explanation of ethics as an instrument carrying with it either the moral law or rationalist behaviour that yields the axiom of economic rationality, the criterion of the consumer utility function thus conveys satisfaction gained from the individualistic (household) or group enjoyment of a bundle of consumption goods. It is an ordinal psychological measurement of individualist consumption satisfaction. The ethics of utility function as a way of exercising individualistic preferences on the rational choices of a bundle of goods has no moral implications in as far as economic rationality permanently pits these choices in competition with each other as marginal substitutes.

Although the idea of complements is invoked in neoclassical economic theory by way of determining the final satisfaction derived from the consumption of the bundle of goods, the theorem goes that in any three consumption goods or produced goods, two are substitutes. Or in any n-number of goods, there will always be some choices that are complements for attaining the final utility from the choices.

This is a flaw of understanding in terms of the principle of pervasive complementarities contrary to selected complements for the short-run. The reason is that, in an economic system with embedded system-phenomena with multi-causality and unity of knowledge as interrelationships between them, long-run substitution to engender social well-being cannot exist as we have defined it.

Take an example. Say that tea and coffee are gross substitutes of each other, and sugar and milk are complements of these beverages. In this case, depending upon the size of the population as tea drinkers versus coffee drinkers, the increasing population of tea drinkers will draw on the stock of sugar and milk from the market. This would consequentially cause substitution between the sugar and milk for tea, and the sugar and milk for coffee. Such a substitution will be more pronounced by the long-term substitution effect on demand. What happens to the supply of tea and coffee and the stocks of sugar and milk? Answers here remain the same *ceteris paribus*.

The utility function is thus a criterion towards happiness and satisfaction by way of substitution. However, we have argued that it is the complementing characteristic of resource allocation, which is found to sustain life-sustaining well-being. The markets for the corresponding kinds of goods in the dynamic kinds of life-sustaining regimes of development and the market process therein stabilize prices and expand quantities with an attenuating increase in population size. The implication for the demographic state is that the population remains young, to generate and sustain the innovative and dynamic life-fulfilment regime of development and market processes.[12]

In the case of pervasively complementary relations between the elements of well-being function replacing the utility function, both the individual and the social well-being function, as defined earlier, rejects substitution altogether. The result of pervasive complementarities is the reversible rejection of marginal rate of substitution (see endnote 12 again). Consequently, relative prices or equivalent opportunity cost of the variables cannot be written off by the notion of marginal utility function of substitutes. As a result, the concept of value changes from that of marginal utility to complementary effect on well-being by the complementary variables in consumption and production. At the end, as explained in Figures 3.2 and 3.3, relative prices cannot be determined by anything like the smooth convex-to-the origin surface.

The above result holds true for welfare function just as for utility function, because the welfare function is simply a map of the collection of consumer utility functions of individual citizens or households. Now the same kind of explanation as above can be transferred to the case of substitution and competition between differentiated utility indexes as the variables of the welfare function.[13]

EXERCISE 4.3

As in Figure 4.2 and Figure 4.3, a higher-level analysis can be repeated for the relationship between allocation of goods by the utility function and evolutionary objective functions, and the utility allocation by the welfare function in the three cases as shown. The student can complete the formal steps for these three cases using Figure 4.4.

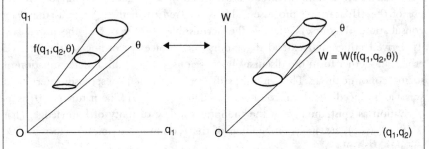

FIGURE 4.4 Well-being distribution of evolutionary learning choices

Well-being function (maslaha)

To reiterate, well-being is the functional explanation followed by its transformation of organic unity of relations between its component variables according to *maqasid*-choices. The well-being function, while being primarily conceptual, also assumes a measurable form in determining the degree of organic complementarities that exist between the variables. Such variables of choice in the well-being function represent the good things of life determined by the moral law, its derived ethics, and by the social discursive rule. In such a definition, the well-being function assumes the place of the *maslaha* objective arising from *maqasid as-shari'ah* and complying with Imam Shatibi's "basket of goods" in consumption and production. These are necessaries (*dhuruiyarh*), comforts (*hajiyath*), and refinements (*tahsaniyath*). Altogether these categories of goods and services comprise the dynamic life-fulfilment regimes of development. They are dynamic by virtue of sustainability across dynamic regimes of development.

The well-being function is evaluated in terms of the circular causation relations between the *maqasid*-variables of the well-being function. In case of a deficiency in inter-variable complementarities signified by the negative sign of the inter-variable coefficients, the well-being function is simulated by changing these negative coefficients into either plausible positive ones or less negative ones, in a particular process of moral transformation, to be progressed onwards. The change in these values accords with the possibility of available resources; over all expected change that arises from the simulated choices; and by technical discourse on the appropriateness of the choices of complementary or less negative coefficients is in the nature of the Islamic consultation process called the *shura*.

So as explained in Chapter 3, the estimation and simulation of the well-being function, $(W(\mathbf{x}(\theta))$ with all the variables explained, and taken in its conceptual and quantitative forms, is represented in the following way. We use the term 'evaluation' to mean both 'estimation' and 'simulation' performed sequentially in the quantitative model of well-being subject to circular causation relations:

$$\text{Evaluate } W = W(\mathbf{x}(\theta)); \mathbf{x}(\theta) = \{x_1, x_2, \ldots, x_n\}[\theta] \tag{4.2}$$

All variables are commonly induced by θ-knowledge-value; $\theta = \text{plim}\{\theta_i\}$ by the use of the IIE learning processes. This is referred to in the *Qur'an* as the *shura* consultation (discourse). Thereby, the permissible choices out of the moral law, its derived ethics, and extended discourse on choices according to the derived ethics, altogether form the discursively conscious basis of ethical determination of socio-economic things. The symbol $\{\mathbf{x}(\theta)\}$ represents such consciously determined variables induced by ethical consciousness denoted by $\{\theta\}$. The nature of $\{\theta\}$ is its derivation as epistemology of the monotheistic law of unity of knowledge. That is $\{\theta\} \in (\Omega, S)$, etc. in its embedding of the economic variables (socio-scientific variables) $\{\mathbf{x}(\theta)\}$.

The evaluation of the well-being functional criterion (*maslaha*) is done by evaluating the circular causation relations in the $\{\mathbf{x}(\theta)\}$-variables. The circular causation equations are:

$$x_i = f_i(\theta, x_j(\theta)), (i,j) = 1,2,3,\ldots,n; i \neq j. \tag{4.3}$$

Expression (4.3) comprises n-number of equations in n-number of variables. Finally there is the θ-equation:

$$\theta = F(\mathbf{x}(\theta)). \tag{4.4}$$

Clearly expressions (4.2) and (4.4) are 'similar' functions (same type of functional forms). Hence both are expressions of the well-being function. While expression (4.2) is the conceptual form explaining the substantive meaning underlying the theoretical properties of the well-being function, expression (4.4) is the empirical form in the actual measurement of the well-being function. Therefore, we can write $F(\mathbf{x}(\theta))$ as a positive function of expression (4.2).[14] More on the empirical computation of the system of $(n+1)$ equations comprising expressions (4.3) and (4.4) will be formalized later on in this book.

The socially embedded economic problem

Process-oriented and epistemological-driven economic and social thinkers, as well as the Islamic epistemological approach, are no longer restricted to narrow areas that exclude the great moral and ethical issues. Such a comprehensive search and discovery interrelates diverse systems by interaction, integration, and continued co-evolutionary epistemology – IIE-learning processes.

In mainstream socio-economics a type of social embedding is studied (Holton 1992; Parsons 1964) as being contrary to a differentiated system. Also a specific kind of embedded system can be derived from the neoclassical criticism by Sraffa (1960), by virtue of the fact that, in every given year of circular production of commodities by commodities, the output at the beginning of a time-period is distributed to factors of production. The output so distributed to productive factors forms a new chain of output production, and so on. Pasinetti (2001) writes on Sraffa's circulation of output as a criticism of neoclassical economics in the following words:

> Four themes that appear as poison-arrows in Sraffa's critique of economic theory (are): (i) The marginalist theory of production and distribution; (ii) the theory of value (which the marginalists call price theory; (iii) the theory of marginal utility; (iv) the theory of interest, when interest is presented as a reward for abstinence.

EXERCISE 4.4

This version, shown in Figure 4.5, of Piero Sraffa's famous contribution to the circular causation idea underlying his *Production of Commodities by Means of*

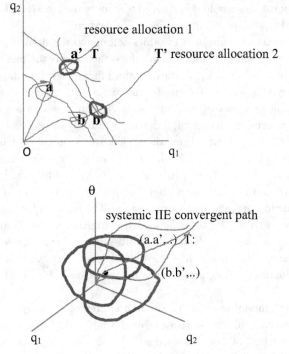

FIGURE 4.5 Nature of social embedding of the economic space

Commodities is extracted from Dorfman, Samuelson, and Solow (1958). The student/reader is asked to formalize the following questions embodied in the model presented:

1. Explain the nature of Sraffa's model in the perspective of circular causation idea of endogenous output and input relationships in a model of economic resource allocation/distribution.
2. Incorporate in this model a diverse-system outlook for the study of inter-active system-relations as the theory underlying embedded systems.
3. How does Sraffa's model negate the neoclassical marginalist hypothesis in production and consumer choice theory as depicted in Figure 4.4 with fuzzy points on the production possibility curve and the consumer indifference curves?

Relational epistemology concept of ethics

The entire sequence of selected definitions of terms given above can now be summarized to explain the nature of Islamic economics in comparison and contrast to mainstream economic thought. The central methodological worldview comprises the substantive meaning of morality. From this core of the divine law, ethics as relational epistemology is derived to convey the core meaning of unity of monotheistic knowledge and the unified world-system.

Thus the substantive meaning of ethics belongs to the domain of the world-system that is depicted in Figure 4.1, in which there exists the interplay between the ontological (primal) order of unity of monotheistic law and the details of the constructive world-systems. The underlying interactive, integrative, and evolutionary learning processes of the embedded economic system are explained by means of the internal epistemological dynamics of unity of knowledge.

Thereby, ethics as derived from the moral law is neither an implement of humanism nor is it independent of the moral law. It is not the primal individual and collective preference of a rationalist design of civil conduct and its institutions. Instead, ethics is equivalent to the relational epistemological belief and its expression in the construction of embedded world-systems. The methodology of the resulting explanatory worldview of unity of knowledge together manifests the nature and design of the monotheistic believing world-system. The systemic endogenous nature of ethics in Islam, which is also invoked by some heterodox economists (Sen 1992; Boulding 1968), presents the theory of embedded study of ethics in economics.

The total methodology, which is Islamic epistemology in essence, is referred to as the episteme of the system-oriented study of Islamic economics. This reflects the totality of the knowledge-induced worldview. It comprises the knowledge-dimension of reality. But beyond this realization, the embedding of the knowledge-dimension with the dimensions of space and time comprises the study of phenomena as events occurring in these three dimensions. This comprehensive use of ethical dynamics in the totality of study of the unified world-system is referred to as phenomenology. In the Islamic epistemic context, phenomenology represents the combination of consciousness with the discursive investigation of the world-system (*shura*) to know reality in general, and issues, problems, and events in particular. Taken together, the experience of the phenomenology of consciousness in the ethics–economics interrelations is thus causally related with consciousness-*shura* (Choudhury & Zaman 2006). In the Islamic epistemic theory of Islamic economics, the entire field of phenomenology is unravelled and applied in the mould of participation and complementarities between diverse entities, variables, relations, and systems, deductive and inductive reasoning, and *a priori* and *a posteriori* frame of mind and matter. Thereby, ethics implies the relational conception of unity of knowledge derived from the moral law.

Introducing Islamic epistemology in developing the theory of financial economics

Initially defined, financial economics in mainstream terms marks the study of the interplay of conceptual and applied relationship between economic and financial theories. In such a definition, no academic demand is made regarding the interactive, integrative, and creative study of the multidisciplinary and multidimensional phenomenon of systemic interrelations caused by inter-causality between the representative variables. Thereby, for example, the study of social justice is considered as an exogenous (external) factor of social consideration. Such an ethical factor is at best influenced by government action, institutions, and policies and by sheer human choices of the good ones in society at large. There is no scope in such exogenous treatment of the theme of social justice and ethics to inculcate in society at large a reaction towards consciousness caused by interaction between self, human preferences, and conscious experiences that together can automatically generate inter-causality between ethical character, actions, responses, belief, mind and matter.

The embedding of knowledge with the generality and specifics of the world-system, as in the case of financial economics, also conveys the idea of phenomenology. Phenomenology is the study of consciousness through the organic interrelationship between deontological (duty-bound) characteristics of self with its preferences and the creative actions and responses generated by relational experiences. The resulting attribute of ethics thus formed is explained as an endogenous actualization as opposed to ethics as exogenous behaviour in mainstream financial economics.

An example of the meaning of ethics is based on the formation of preferences regarding ecological consciousness on matters needing ethical preferences as a natural reaction. Such an attitude is contrary to being enforced by institutional policies. There is no conflicting enforcement in the interrelationship between action and response in a conscious framework of endogenous ethics. The conscious self in concert with the world-system generates and sustains integrity between self, individual and collective preferences, and the sustainable ecological experience in our example. The result of endogenous ethical behaviour is the generating of a system of interaction, integration, and evolutionary learning in the domain of unity of knowledge as episteme and its induction of the issues under study. In our study, such issues belong to the field of financial economics.

Conclusion: on the epistemological nature of Islamic economics

Having clearly shown these initial contrasting features of mainstream and Islamic epistemological worldviews in financial economics, we can now introduce the nature of Islamic economics. This is the foundational methodological worldview of Islamic economics that will be used throughout this book in terms of theoretical perspectives of economic issues, examples, and the imminent applications leading to inferences. Thus the outlook of this book is thoroughly methodological as well as applied, in the context of the Islamic methodology that has been discussed thus far and that will be developed and explained throughout this book. This foundational methodological worldview establishes the bedrock of the revolutionary field of Islamic economics and socio-scientific world-system studies.

Yet as we proceed on through various fields of economic reasoning, the approach of this book will be rigorously comparative, with mainstream economics taken up in original reference to the Islamic epistemological worldview. This approach will allow both mainstream and Islamic economic reasoning to be examined and analytically tested to study specific economic problems through analytical formalism as they arise from the epistemic roots. In undertaking these directions of research the methods of (as opposed to methodological, which is universal) mathematical and empirical models will be invoked.

What is Islamic economics?

From our methodological formalism revolving around the episteme of monotheistic unity of knowledge, which is equivalent to *Tawhid* as divine law projected in its complete phenomenology, we derived the distinctive nature of what is termed as the Islamic *unity* of knowledge functioning in the world-system. Indeed, the extensive interpretation of the monotheistic law by its function of organic unity of knowledge and the induced diversity of things can be read in many verses of the *Qur'an*.[15]

The central embedded role of *Tawhid* as law pervades the socio-scientific domain of 'everything'. Within this vast domain is the field of economics as an embedded socio-scientific study. The meaning of 'everything' is that of the universal and unique nature of the immanent methodology that arises from the Islamic epistemology for all and every issue and problem. This is a fact despite variations in the diversity of issues, problems, theories, and applications in various disciplinary focuses (Choudhury & Hoque 2012).

Islamic epistemology arises from its independent and substantive origin that is distinctive in the following three core contexts: First, the monotheistic law is established irrevocably in the *Qur'an*. Second, there is the guidance of the Prophet Muhammad in his teachings, called the *Sunnah*. The third essential component of Islamic epistemology is the guidance of the learned ones based on the *Qur'an* and the *Sunnah*. These three components taken together ground the true nature of Islamic methodology and the desired methods of analytical and applied formalism that are consistent with the nature of the methodology. Such methodical relevance arises from the nature of organic unity in the process of being and becoming underlying the problems under investigation. The methodological implication is very strong in the understanding and application of the Islamic worldview. In fact, there cannot be any thought, conception, inquiry, applications, and inferences without the conscious understanding of the Islamic methodological worldview. The *Qur'an* details these implications.[16,17]

Thus the Islamic methodological worldview as the primal and foundational Islamic epistemology of 'everything' rests upon three irrevocable perspectives. Firstly, the Islamic episteme explains the organic unity of knowledge of the 'paired' universe. Second, the singular Islamic precept of unity of knowledge constructs the world of unity of being and becoming. Third, such things belong to the life-fulfilment needs. The universe of these divine and worldly attributes of the good things of life exists perpetually in the dimensions of knowledge, space, and time. They form the choices according to the *maqasid al-shari'ah* – the *maqasid*-choices (Choudhury 2014a).

The truly epistemological study of Islamic economics like all other worldly fields of study is embedded in the monotheistic nature and design of the embedding universe within the dimensions of knowledge, space, and time. The market is sensitized by endogenous ethics across interrelating systems. The institution is the body framework for the study and implementation of ethics and economic behaviour with consciousness as a learned endogenous experience (*tarbiah*). Human economy and financial activity are entrenched in moral and ethical consciousness. The objectivity of purpose and objectivity conceptualized and quantified by the well-being criterion of *maslaha* is in everything and is everywhere.

Understanding the dimensions of knowledge, space, and time through the permanence of monotheistic law[18]

Yet it is not possible to know the three attributes of reality in knowledge, space, and time conclusively by disclosed manifestation. That is because the hidden reality (*ghayb*) is not manifest according to the meaning of knowledge in the *Qur'an* (3:190–191). The *Qur'an* declares regarding the unseen:

> Behold! In the creation of the heavens and the earth, and the alternation of Night and Day, there are indeed Signs for men of understanding, men who celebrate the praises of God, standing, sitting, and lying down on their sides, and contemplate the (wonders of) creation in the heavens and the earth,

(with the thought): "Our Lord! Not for naught have You created (all) this! Glory be to You! Give us salvation from the Penalty of the Fire."

An exegesis of these verses is as follows: The monotheistic law in its manifest-ation and explication of the universe comprehends 'everything' ("Creation of the heavens and the earth"). This enables us to see but not understand the impossible divine attributes. Rather they are the cognitive and material unravelling of these attributes in things that are manifesting ("Behold!").

The extensive meaning of "Night and Day" embodies in it the meaning of the differentiation, the discernment of falsehood as darkness and truth as day. In such a way, between truth and darkness, the human comprehension of total reality advances. Such realization exists in a seamless and continuous way, across continuums of 'everything'. There lie the evidences as 'Signs of God'. The signs manifest the proofs arising from the primal ontology (moral law) and epistemology of the monotheistic law and its deep explications (Choudhury 2012).

In such a structure of creation the monotheistic law is reflected by its purpose and meaning: "Our Lord! Not for naught have You created (all this)." Such an encompassing universe, as far as human comprehension proceeds, is defined by the temporal and the final 'Closure' in processes of evolutionary equilibrium trajec-tories that enclose the open evolutionary learning universe. We present this idea in Figure 4.5.

The nature of evolutionary equilibriums to be studied in monotheistic Islamic financial economy through the *Tawhid*

Closure: $(\Omega,S) \leftrightarrow$ World-System$(\theta,\mathbf{X}(\theta),t(\theta)) \leftrightarrow$ *Tawhid: Akhirah*
Open Universe (learning universe): World-System $(\theta,\mathbf{X}(\theta),t(\theta))$

(Ω,S) denotes the primal ontology of *Tawhid* (Ω: symbolically to represent the supercardinal (Chapter 3) topology of the *Qur'an*) mapped in degrees by the *Sunnah* of Prophet Muhammad (S).

$\{\theta\}$ denotes worldly knowledge-flows derived from the epistemology of (Ω,S).

$\mathbf{X}(\theta)$ denotes the mathematical ensemble of knowledge-induced variables.

$E(\theta,\mathbf{X}(\theta),t(\theta))$ denotes an event (E(.)) represented by the multi-systemic coordinate in knowledge (θ), space ($\mathbf{X}(\theta)$), time ($t(\theta)$).

Time, $t(\theta)$, is induced by knowledge because it is knowledge not time, that causes an event to occur. Time reads the event and its systemic relations.[19]

The Closure encompassing the Open Universe is a necessary and sufficient condi-tion for the existence of a meaningful evolutionary equilibrium. The existence of equilibrium is established by the Fixed Point Theorem (Brouwer 1910; Kakutani 1941; Nikaido 1987). The evolutionary nature of such equilibrium is established

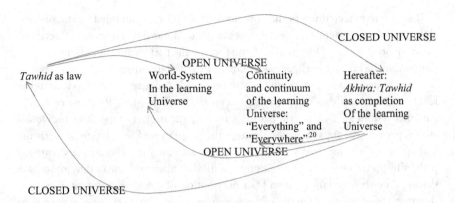

CLOSED UNIVERSE

OPEN UNIVERSE

Tawhid as law

World-System
In the learning
Universe

Continuity
and continuum
of the learning
Universe:
"Everything" and
"Everywhere"[20]

Hereafter:
Akhira: Tawhid
as completion
Of the learning
Universe

OPEN UNIVERSE

CLOSED UNIVERSE

FIGURE 4.6 Closure of the complete universe of Signs of God in the order of "everything", "everywhere"

by neighbourhoods around equilibrium points within the Fixed Point Closure (Choudhury, Zaman, & Sofyan 2007). In the monotheistic epistemological formulation of Islamic financial economy, all equilibriums are evolutionary equilibriums within the purposeful Closure. Steady-state equilibriums are denied any relevance. They can be explained by the degenerate case of neoclassical economics and full-information assumption.

In Chapter 3, we defined Event as $E(\theta,\mathbf{X}(\theta),t(\theta))$. Our worldly categories of events are diverse across systems and experiences. In regards to the study of economic issues and problems, the *Qur'an* points out several of these, from which the world can derive lessons for diverse human ends. Here are three specific cases on which the study of economics rests. These cases are events $E(.)$. Then there is the vector $\mathbf{X}(\theta)$ comprising consumption bundles along with consumer behaviour; production along with production function and production diversification, and production, distribution, and ownership relations; wealth, money, and spending, and many more. Over all such categories is the defining place of the conscious purpose, objectivity, and meaning (see Masud 1994) on Shatibi's theory of meaning).

The functional understanding of consciousness (θ) induced in consumption and production comprises the phenomenological study of the *Qur'an* in relation with the world-system. Examples of such conscious behaviour are moderation and balance for enjoying a happy self, the family, the community, and society.[20] On the theme of ownership, and distribution the *Qur'an* has declared fairness and equity.[21] The *Qur'an* has nonetheless left this equality not in terms of measure but in terms of justice. The theme of justice and spending is connected with abundance and sharing.[22] The matter of money is connected with resource mobilization.[23] All these activities of sustainability and the social economy are treated in an interconnected way of organic pairing and inter-causality. The extent of such interconnectivity is widely inter-systemic.[24]

The interconnectedness of the conscious attributes is exemplified by the sustainability of life-fulfilment regimes of development. Along this trajectory of development we note the complementarities, and thereby the participative functions over the dimensions of knowledge, space, and time, of the organic inter-causal relationships between consumption and production and the underlying agential behaviour in the reality of the ethically induced market process and market system. Preferences in such a market system are dynamic in nature, caused by the impact of θ-values. Individual ethical preferences are aggregated through the properties of interaction, integration, and creative evolution under innovation occurring along the evolutionary learning path of history. Every point of continuity of life-fulfilment regime of development is sustained by the equitable, just and fair distribution of wealth, property, and ownership that a life-fulfilment regime of development ensues. This is because of the nature of needs and the stable prices and wages and returns on spending. These cause stable forms of the price-output relationship, the nature of appropriate technology, and returns on these activities to profit-sharing, wages, and rates of return. Now when monetary expansion occurs along the life-fulfilment regimes of development, the continuous relationship between money and the real economy replaces interest rate with trade. The abundant rewards in the life-fulfilment regime of development come about. The social well-being function (*maslaha*) is then simulated to higher levels by the force of continuous resource regeneration and its equitable ownership by all. Thus by the impact of evolutionary learning in unity of knowledge as episteme the nature of life-fulfilment regime of development becomes of the dynamic type. We refer to such a regime of change as the dynamic life-fulfilment regime of sustainability, or the dynamic basic-needs regime of participatory development.

The meaning of moral consciousness in Islamic economics and science

In reference to the previous definition of phenomenology and consciousness that results from the interrelationship between the monotheistic law of unity of knowledge and the unifying world-system we can give it an analytical meaning. This is explained in Figure 4.7.

When studying this chapter, it is important to keep the following areas of Islamic economics in mind:

1.   Islamic economic methodology
2.   the scope of Islamic economics
3.   the formulation of the Islamic economic model.

Conclusion

Conventional classical and neo-classical economics as a discipline have developed to their present state over the last 600 years, whereas Islamic economic thinking is newly developing. It started taking shape only after the first international conference

True Reality $\quad$ Worldly Causation $\quad$ Continuity $\quad$ True Reality

$$[(\Omega \to_s) \equiv (\Omega,S)] \;\to\; \{\theta^*\} \to \{\theta\} \;\to\; W(E(\theta,\mathbf{X}(\theta),t(\theta))) \;\to\; dW/d\theta > 0 \ldots \to \;(\Omega,S)$$

The Primal Origin Of God and His Divine Law (*Sunnat Allah*)			
Consciousness as indestructible Transcendental Realism in God-Man-Creation Transmitted by Circular Relations:[26] Unity of knowledge	Conscious World-System endowed by unity of knowledge	Sustainability: Continuity across systemic Continuums: Unity of knowledge	Consciousness: Transcendental Realism in God-Man-Creation: Circular Relations: Unity of Knowledge

the functional Ontology of the Prophet Muhammad's Teaching, Guidance (*Sunnah*):[27] Unitary Epistemology

FIGURE 4.7 The analytical meaning of Islamic consciousness or phenomenology in the world-system

on Islamic economics held in Mecca in 1983. At this stage, Islamic economic literature has been poor in elaborating the nature and scope of Islamic economics. Islamic economics is a social science. Mannan (1984, p. 8) discusses Islamic economics as a "composite social science" which implies that the study of Islamic economics is concerned with the social, economic and moral consequences of production, distribution and consumption in an integrated manner. Islamic economics is neither fully positive nor fully negative. Positive statements concern *what is, was or will be* whilst normative statements concern *what ought to be*. Separation of positive from normative statements is not at all allowed in Islamic economics. The *Qur'an* and *Sunnah*, which serve as the basis of Islamic economics, contain both positive and normative injunctions (Zarkah 1992, p. 50).

Islamic economics studies the behaviour of economic variables but in a comprehensive and integrated manner. It includes absorbing the Islamic values of social responsibility in respect of obligatory sharing of wealth and income of the rich with the poor. In conventional economics, economic problems arise because of the parsimony of nature. It assumes that man has unlimited wants to be fulfilled but that the resources for their fulfilment is limited. So there is a supply constraint. In Islamic economics, it is maintained that God has provided sufficient means for the fulfilment of all human needs. It assumes that economic problems arise because of lack of effort on the part of individuals and society on the one hand, and uncontrolled human wants on the other.

The scope of Islamic economics is, by definition, wider than that of conventional economics. There is a large class of economically relevant social and moral behaviour shared between firms and households. The study of consumption and investment without involving interest (*riba*), and looking after poor neighbours and people regardless of their race, colour and religion, come under the scope of Islamic economics (Mannan 1984, p. 56). Furthermore, the subject of Islamic economics is not restricted to Islamic society but also includes all economic behaviour whether according to or contrary to Islam (Zarkah 1992, pp. 55–57).

Notes

1 *Qur'an* (48:23).
2 We write this as $R\star$, that is, $f(X_1, X_2, \theta)$ = constant. This implies that a percentage increase in *riba* decreases trade by the sum-total of elasticity coefficients of X_1, X_2, and θ-variable. Contrarily, a 1 per cent decrease in *riba* increases trade by the sum-total of elasticity coefficients of X_1, X_2, and θ-variable. The induction of the X-variables by θ-value will cause greater degrees of changes either of the two ways. θ-value thus introduces X-efficiency in the inter-variable relations (Liebenstein 1966).
3 *Qur'an* (2:117): "To Him is due the primal origin."
4 *Qur'an* (2:117).
5 *Qur'an* (6:75): "So also did We show Abraham the power and the laws of the heavens and the earth, that he might (with understanding) have certitude."
6 The *Qur'an* exemplifies the entire universe of mind and matter as created and governed by the divine law to be a fully established order of exchange. In this complete domain the signs of God (*Allah*) are displayed and explained by *Tawhid* as the episteme of unity

of knowledge both for the good choices as ordained; the bad choices that are forbidden; and the undetermined choices that need to be sorted out between the good and the bad ones. There is exchange and forms of equilibrium in everything that God has created by virtue of the synergistic model of unity of knowledge inter-connecting *haqq ul-yaqin* (*Tawhid* as law), *ilm ul-yaqin* (knowledge of *Tawhid* as law), and *ayan ul-yaqin* (observations and reflection or *burhan aqli*). Consider the many verses of the *Qur'an* regarding the central function of exchange as learning dynamics in everything from end to end of the universe of the *Qur'an*, mind, and matter. Of particular note is the following (62:11): "Say: The (blessing) from the Presence of God is better than any amusement or bargain! And *Allah* is the best to provide for all (for all needs)." The universal persistence of trade and transactions by exchange in every matter concerning God, existence, mind, and matter and the contrariness of misguidance from the true path is found in the following verse (2:16): "They have traded guidance for error, but their bargain has had no profit and they have missed the true guidance."

7 Hawking & Mlodinow (2010, p. 80) write about similar learning (probabilistic general system) histories: "…for a general system, the probability of any observation is constructed from all the possible histories that could have led to that observation. Because of that (t)his method is called the 'sum over histories' or alternative histories' formulation of quantum physics."

8 In respect of the pervasively probabilistic nature of events in the universe Hawking & Mlodinow (2010, p. 72) write: "According to quantum physics, no matter how much information we obtain or how powerful our computing abilities, the outcomes of physical processes cannot be predicted with certainty because they are not determined with certainty."

9 *Qur'an* (3:117); *Qur'an* (18:32–44).

10 Value of asset = $W(\mathbf{x}(\theta)) = \prod_{t=1}^{n}\text{Prob.}[(1+r_t(\theta))^t]\star\mathbf{x}(\theta)_{t=0}$; subject to each $\{r_t(\theta)\}$ and $\{\mathbf{x}(\theta)_{t=0}\}$ being evaluated by the IIE-process model over the time-period for $\{r_t(\theta)\}$ over the vector of $\{\mathbf{x}(\theta)_{t=0}\}$. This is done by a special method called circular causation. In Chapter 1 we explained the idea of circular causation. We will deal with it more later on. The continuity of the conscious social and economic system conveys the meaning of consciousness and sustainability that arises from the ethics of the moral law.

11 *Qur'an* (45:24): "And they say: 'What is there but our life in this world? We shall die and we live, and nothing but time can destroy us.' But of that they have no knowledge: they merely conjecture."

12 In a dynamic basic-needs caused by the incidence of θ-values we note for well-being replacing the utility function, $W(\theta) = W(Q,p,P)[\theta]$. Q denotes output. p denotes prices of basic needs. P denotes population size. The stable population increase is characterized by a young population. Thereby,

$$\overset{+}{} \qquad \overset{+}{} \qquad \overset{+}{} \qquad \overset{\pm}{} \qquad \overset{\pm}{} \qquad \overset{+}{} \qquad \overset{+}{} \qquad \overset{+}{}$$
$$dW/d\theta = (\partial W/\partial Q).(dQ/d\theta) + (\partial W/\partial p).(dp/d\theta) + (\partial W/\partial P) \star (dP/d\theta) + \partial W / \partial\theta$$

Note that the $\pm$ signs remain correspondingly paired – positive for positive; negative for negative. $(\partial W/\partial P)$ and $(dP/d\theta)$ are each positive in the life-fulfillment regime of development and by the fact that $W(\theta)$ and θ are monotonic transformations of each other in the sense of well-being.

Hence, $dW/d\theta > 0$ identically in the presence of complementary relations between the variables of $W(.)$. The result is the sustaining of the dynamic life-fulfillment regime of development and basic-needs markets in it.

In the case of substitution, say between X=(Q,p) and P, there is no presence of θ-values. The well-being function reverts to the utility function as $U=U(X,P)$; $\partial X/\partial P < 0$, contrary to $W=W(X,P)$, $(\partial W/\partial P)/(\partial W/\partial X) > 0$.

13 In the case of welfare WL maximization the result yields $(\partial WL/\partial U_1)/(\partial WL/\partial U_2) = -dU_2/dU_1 > 0$, implying that dU_1 and dU_2 are oppositely related, thus the case of marginal rate of utility substitution.

14 Say that $W=W(\mathbf{x}(\theta)) = f(\theta) = \theta^a$. Then $\theta = {}^a\sqrt{W(\mathbf{x}(\theta))}$, which is a transform of the well-being function. It is therefore a well-being function itself. Hence, W and θ are transforms of each other.

15 *Qur'an* (10:22): "He it is who enables you to traverse through land and sea; so that ye even board ships; – they sail with them with a favourable wind, and they rejoice thereat; then comes a stormy wind and the waves come to them from all sides, and they think they are being overwhelmed: They cry unto God, sincerely offering (their) duty unto Him, saying, 'If Thou do deliver us from this, we shall truly show our gratitude!'"

16 *Qur'an* (41:53): "Soon will We show them Our Signs in the (furthest) regions (of the earth), and in their own souls, until it becomes manifest to them that this is the Truth. Is it not enough that your Lord does witness all things?"

17 *Qur'an* (96:3–5): "Proclaim! And your Lord is Most Bountiful, – He Who taught (the use of) the Pen, – Taught man that which he knew not."

18 *Qur'an* (33:62): "(Such was) the practice (approved) of *Allah* among those who lived aforetime: No change wilt thou find in the practice (approved) of *Allah*." This practice is the divine manifestation of *Tawhid* as law from the beginning to the end of the knowledge, space, and time dimensions – the total reality.

19 *Qur'an* (76:1): "Has there not been over man a long period of Time, when he was nothing – (not even) spoken?" Thus 'time' was dysfunctional until functional knowledge dawned with the creation of man.

20 *Qur'an* (6:141–142), on production: "It is He who produces gardens, with trellises and without, and dates, and tilth with produce of all kinds, and olives and pomegranates, similar (in kind) and different (in variety): Eat of their fruit in their season, but render the dues that are proper on the day that the harvest is gathered. But waste not by excess: for God loves not the wasters." (141)

On consumption and good things of life: "Of the cattle are some for burden and some for meat: Eat what God has provided for you, and follow not the footsteps of Satan: For he is to you and avowed enemy." (142)

21 *Qur'an* (4:161): "That they took usury, though they were forbidden; and that they devoured men's substance wrongfully; – We have prepared for those among them who reject Faith a grievously penalty."

22 *Qur'an* (2:261): "The parable of those who spend their substance in the way of God is that of a grain of corn: it grows seven ears, and each ear has a hundred grains. God gives manifold increase to whom He pleases: and God cares for all and He knows all things."

23 *Qur'an* (18:19): "Now send ye then one of you with the money of yours to the town: let him find out which is the best food (to be had) and bring some to you, that (you may) satisfy your hunger therewith: and let him behave with care and courtesy, and let him not inform any one about you."

24 *Qur'an* (13:3): "And fruit of every kind he made in pairs, two and two: He draws the Night as a veil Over the Day. Behold verily in these things there are Signs for those who consider!"

References

Blaug, M. (1986). *Great Economists before Keynes*, Atlantic Highlands, NJ: Humanities Press International.

Boulding, K.E. (1968). *Beyond Economics: Essays on Society, Religion, and Ethics*, Ann Arbor, MI: The University of Michigan Press.

Boulding, K.E. (1981). *Evolutionary Economics*, New York: Russell Sage.

Brouwer, L.E.J. (1910). Uber un eindeutige, stetige Transformationen von Flachen in sich, *Mathematische Annalen*, 69.

Buchanan, J.M. (1999). The domain of constitutional economics, in his *The Logical Foundations of Constitutional Liberty*, Indianapolis, IN: Liberty Fund.

Choudhury, M.A. (2011). Dynamics of the *Shari'ah* and the Islamic world-system, *King Abdulaziz University Journals: Islamic Economics*, 23:1.

Choudhury, M.A. (2012). *Islamic Economics and Finance: An Epistemological Inquiry*, Bingley, UK: Emerald Publications.

Choudhury, M.A. (2014a). *Tawhidi Epistemology and Its Applications (Economics, Finance, Science, and Society)*, Cambridge, UK: Cambridge Scholars Publishing.

Choudhury, M.A. (2014b). *The Socio-Cybernetic Study of God and the World-System*, Philadelphia, PA: Ideas Group Inc. Global.

Choudhury, M.A. (2016). *Res extensa et res cogitans de maqasid as-shari'ah*, *International Journal of Law and Management*, 58:3.

Choudhury, M.A. & Hoque, M.Z. (2012). *An Advanced Exposition of Islamic Economics and Finance*, Lewiston, NY: Edwin Mellen Press.

Choudhury, M.A. & Zaman, S.I. (2006). Learning sets and topologies, *Kybernetes: International Journal of Systems and Cybernetics*, 35:7.

Choudhury, M.A., Zaman, S.I., & Harahap, S.S. (2007). An evolutionary topological theory of participatory socio-economic development, *World Futures: Journal of General Evolutionary Systems*, 63:8.

Cole, G.D.H. (1966). *The Meaning of Marxism*, Ann Arbor, MI: The University of Michigan Press.

Dorfman, R., Samuelson, P., & Solow, R. (1958). *Linear Programming and Economic Analysis*, New York, NY: McGraw-Hill.

Georgescu-Roegen, N. (1981). *The Entropy Law and the Economic Process*, Cambridge, MA: Harvard University Press.

Hawking, S.W. & Mlodinow, L. (2010). Alternative histories, in *The Grand Design*, London: Transworld Publishers.

Holton, R.L. (1992). *Economy and Society*, London: Routledge.

Kakutani, S. (1941). A generalization of Brouwer's Fixed Point Theorem, *Duke Mathematical Journal*, 8(3).

Liebenstein, H. (1966). Allocative efficiency vs. X-efficiency, *American Economic Review*, 56(3): 392–415.

Mandel, E. (1971). *The Formation of the Economic Thought of Karl Marx, 1843 to Capital*, trans. B. Pearce, New York: Monthly Review Press.

Mannan, M.A. (1984). *The Making of Islamic Economic Society: Islamic Dimensions of Islamic Economic Society*, Cairo: International Association of Islamic Banks.

Masud, M.K. (1994). *Shatibi's Theory of Meaning*, Islamabad, Pakistan: Islamic Research Institute, International Islamic University.

Mustafa, O.M. (2006). Objectives of Islamic banking: *Maqasid* approach. *International Conference on Jurisprudence*, August 8–10, IIUM.

Nelson, R.R. & Winter, S.G. (1982). *An Evolutionary Theory of Economic Change*, Harvard: Harvard University Press.

Nikaido, H. (1987). Fixed point theorems, in *The New Palgrave: General Equilibrium*, eds. Eatwell, J., Milgate, M., & Newman, P., pp. 139–44, New York: W.W. Norton.

Parsons, T. (1964). *The Structure of Social Actions*, New York: The Free Press of Glencoe.

Pasinetti, L.I. (2001). Continuity and change in Sraffa's thought, in *Piero Sraffa's Political Economy*, eds. Cozzi, T. & Marchionatti, R., pp. 139–151, London & New York, NY: Routledge.

Sen, A. (1992). Conduct, ethics and economics, in his *On Ethics and Economics*, pp. 88–89, Oxford, UK: Basil Blackwell.

Sraffa, P. (1960). *Production of Commodities by Means of Commodities*, Cambridge: Cambridge University Press.

Shackle, G.L.S. (1972). *Epistemics and Economics*, Cambridge: Cambridge University Press.

Smith, A. (1976). *The Wealth of Nations*, Create Space Independent Publishing Platform.

Zarkah, M.A. (1992). Methodology of Islamic economics, in *Lectures on Islamic Economics*, eds. Ahmad, A. & Awan, K.R., Jeddah: IRTI-IDB.

5

THE FORMULATION OF THE ISLAMIC ECONOMIC MODEL

LEARNING OBJECTIVES

This chapter intends to provide an overview of the important modelling of both the microeconomics and macroeconomics context incorporated with Islamic standards so that students may:

- realize that a complete model formulation of Islamic economics with consensus from all economists does not exist (as in the case of mainstream conventional economic theory), hence a detailed account of a single-system Islamic epistemological model for unity of knowledge with an extension of Islamic economic formulation to multi-systems of sustainability and well-being functions are emphasized
- provide a fair base on the nature of microeconomics and macroeconomics which reflects the method of circular causation that responds to the Islamic methodology
- understand a comparison between the mainstream study of political economy and Islamic political economy in the multi-system extension of the Islamic String Relations as it applies to the learning dynamics of multi-group cooperation, intra-country political and institutional cohesion, globalization with a human face, and institutional global governance for common well-being.

This chapter begins with the application of the theory contrasting Islamic unity of knowledge and the rationalist world-systems that we substantiated in Chapters 3 and 4. In this regard we will first translate the premises of Chapter 3 in a formal model and explain the details. This chapter will also explain several important concepts that emanate from the formal model, and treats the essence of the Islamic instruments within this formal model that carries with it the contrasting concepts, differentiating Islamic methodological worldview and the rejection of rationalism depicted in mainstream economics.[1] The same kinds of arguments and formalism apply to the generality of the world-system study and its details.

From Chapters 3 and 4 we bring forward the definitions and explanations of the critical terms that will be used throughout. The following terms ought to be well-understood and are premised in the epistemology of Islamic unity of knowledge.·

1. We will refer to this epistemic premise of socio-scientific study in general as *consilience* (Wilson 1998), and *Tawhid* as the cardinal basis of belief and the core of Islamic methodological worldview along with its methodical functional applications in analytical depth (Choudhury 2014).

2. Rationalism is the opposite of *Tawhid* though necessarily of the nature of consilience. That is because other than unity of knowledge and its induction of the good things of life and the essence of the pairing universe, *Tawhid* does not accept any other way of defining unity of 'being' and 'becoming' on the generality and details of 'everything' (Barrow 1991). Rationalism is the human idea that bases its explanation of universal phenomena on scarcity, conflict, competition, differentiation, and marginalism. These conditions are treated as humanly designed and postulated in mainstream economic science. They are untenable in the understanding of the Islamic methodological worldview that is conceptualized and applied to Islamic economics, finance, science, and society, and their various intellectual diversities.

3. Complementarities and participation refer to the organic unity between things, which in the Islamic sense must comprise the good things of life. Hence these emanate from the domain of the purpose and objective of the Islamic law that is derived from the divine law and then discussed among the learned ones (*ulul amr*).[2] In the general sense of the world-system, complementarities are between all things approved by God Almighty and reflected in decisions in the discursive medium of the *maqasid as-shari'ah*. This is the *Qur'anic* idea of consilience that invokes unity of 'being' and the dynamics of 'becoming' as representing the organic dynamics by way of pairing[3] or unification. While complementarity applies to things symbolized by their variables, participation is an attribute of the same nature that may be appropriately applied through the meaning of complementarity between agents and agencies. The Islamic worldview of unity of knowledge and the process of unification between all good things of life (*halal at-tayyabah*) – i.e. in 'being' and 'becoming' – form the monotheistic organic unity of knowledge and of unification. The dynamic process of 'becoming' comprises the dynamics of interaction, integration, and evolutionary learning over knowledge, space, and time. Of the coordinates of the non-Cartesian universe so spanned, knowledge is the most substantive. Both space and time depend for their configuration on knowledge, derived from the Islamic epistemology of unity of knowledge. Time cannot create or originate anything. It simply records events that happen. Events happen, appear, disappear, and unravel inter-temporally by the causation of knowledge-flows

derived from Islamic ontological origin. This point was explained in Chapters 2 and 3 in terms of the supercardinality concept.[4]

4. Well-being is the objective criterion function that measures the degree to which complementarities or participation exists between the variables, agents, and agencies representing the good choices of life and rejecting the false and unwanted ones. The Well-being Function is therefore a criterion of pairing, equivalent to unity of knowledge premised in monotheistic consilience. This quantification of the well-being function is first taken up in the 'as is' state of complementarities between the choices. The 'as is' state is then improved to the normative 'as it ought to be' state by appropriately changing the estimated coefficients into simulated coefficients of a system of circular causation structural relations. See below for a definition of circular causation as the modelled quantification of the degree of unity of organic relations between representative variables.

    A similar kind of estimation and simulation also exists for the opposite kinds of choices. These reflect extensive differentiation between the choices made. An example is conveyed by the conflict and differentiated model based on the dialectical property of rationalism. In this case, the coefficient of relationships between the good and the bad choices will be indicated by a negative coefficient. This will require a normative approach to improve the choice of the good thing by reducing and replacing the unwanted one. Likewise, the relationship between the bad choices will be indicated by a positive sign of the coefficient in their negative sense of organic relations. The simulation focus would then be to reconstruct the choices such that the coefficient moves towards zero.

5. The circular causation equations appear in their structural form so as not to generate the problem of multi-co-linearity in the econometric estimation. These equations explain interdependencies between the variables of the relations as they exist (*estimation*) and as they ought to be related (*simulation*). Such a system of circular interrelations explains the pairing and complementary (*participatory*) properties of the Islamic postulate of unity of knowledge and unification between the particular choices.

6. The multiverse extension of a single systemic circular causation relationship denotes the particular methodological superiority of the monotheistic postulation contrary to rationalism, which is embedded in mainstream economic theory. The multiverse system of interactive, integrative, and evolutionary learning relations points out the multidimensional pairing (complementary, participatory) relationship between diversely distributed systems.

An example here is the sub-system of the grand world-system as markets and economies related to the physical systems of energy, cosmology, and inter-disciplinary fields. An example of such multiverse circular causality is depicted in the *Qur'anic* chapter, *R'ad*[5]. Here the multiverse systems are exemplified by, but not limited to, the following: the earth, cosmology, environment, geography, and diversity in relational unity of 'being' and 'becoming'.

The multiverse concept is also a multidimensional one that spans knowledge, space, and time. Consequently, the multi-systems of the unifying multiverse and the formal method of circular causation and well-being remain valid for the measurement of intensity of unity of knowledge in knowledge-embedded pairing. This phenomenon is spread over all dimensions, each and all being spanned by knowledge, space, and time.[6] Thus the unique and universal methodology of Islamic unity of knowledge conceptualizes the Islamic worldview, and is applied over all details of the multiverse.

It can be inferred from the above summary of certain key points in Islamic economics and general socio-scientific work that the evidence of degrees of unity of knowledge and simulated unification between critical variables is given by measured complementarities (participation). This is signified by the various coefficients of the circular causation system of equations.

The other inference drawn from the above discussion on unity of knowledge, complementarities (participation), and estimated (simulated) well-being functions, subject to circular causation system of equations, is the following: the degree of complementarity or participation is the most significant social indicator as concept and empirical measure regarding unity of knowledge. Islamic economics differs significantly from mainstream economics in terms of its permanent axiom of participative resource mobilization on the good choices as opposed to the permanence of the postulate of scarcity in mainstream economics. Chapter 4 has explained this critical difference in the basics of the two systems. The policy, institutional, social, and scientific implications are vast as well. We will return to this important point later in this book.

EXAMPLE 5.1

Consider capital formation in two opposite ways: first, by trade, and contrariwise, by interest rate. We denote the corresponding relative price by (r/i), where 'r' denotes the rate of return on trade (market exchange) and 'i' denotes the real rate of interest. The wealth equation is given as:

$W = X_1.r + X_2.i$.

X_1 and X_2 are trade versus interest-bearing outlays, respectively. The indifference curve between X_1 and X_2 in mainstream economic theory implies that both trade and interest are acceptable and good activities. This choice is reprehensible to Islam. It is also an illogical one, as interest impedes investment and favours bank-savings. On the other hand, investment is spending on trade-related activities. Savings is withdrawal (Ventelou 2005). Investment is spending today for future rewards of '$r.X_1$'. Savings is present withdrawal for future spending of '$i.X_2$'.

In the state of optimal allocation of wealth we would have:

$dW = r_1.dX_1 + i.dX_2 = 0$

The result then is this: As 'r' increases relative to 'i', then X_1 increases relative to X_2. Consequently, $dr/di = -dX_2/dX_1 > 0$. But such a result remains similar when X_2 increases relative to X_1. Consequently, the Islamic significance to the avoidance of interest is not explained by the neoclassical economic postulate of marginal rate of substitution.

Furthermore, in the optimal state of allocation of wealth between the two sources of wealth we would have the result

$-d(r.X_1)/d(i.X_2) = -(rdX_1 + X_1.dr) / (idX_2 + X_2.di) > 0$

in either case of r and i increasing in opposite forms of allocation of wealth between X_1 and X_2. The Islamic case of avoidance of interest in favour of trade is thus not addressed in mainstream economics.

In the Islamic economics and ethical case, the principal factors underlying the avoidance of interest are an integrated combination of economic and ethical factors. These two factors are endogenously interrelated in the sense of unity of knowledge and positive complementarities between two possible ways of generating wealth. These ways ought to remain complementary to each other. This means that the financial instrument to use must be a participatory one between two instruments of trade, so as to produce positive socioeconomic returns of spending in such good choices.

Examples in such a case would be of the following kinds and many more:

1. Complementing the instruments of profit-sharing and equity-participation; trade financing and return on trade as market exchange; cost-plus pricing and yield on real assets. These are economic and financial complementarities.
2. The ethical factor realized together with the economic activities would be poverty alleviation by complementing this goal in respect of the resources of the participants (X_1, X_2); increasing worker empowerment by means of cooperative production and decision-making between workers and management, the rich and the poor.
3. Participation between the largest possible nexus of participants would be implemented as stakeholders' group activity. The resulting risk-diversification and production diversification would further enhance appropriate technology, innovation, and all that these yield.

The complementarities between X_1 and X_2 by various ethico-economic factors are encapsulated in the knowledge parameter, say 'θ'. The **X**-vector of variables is now changed into $\{W, X_1, X_2, r_1, r_2\}[\theta]$, all variables being commonly induced by 'θ' to establish a fully circularly causal participatory system of choices and allocations. 'r_1' and 'r_2' are the rates of return in two complementary financing and ethical choices. (Note: the word *ethics* here stands for the degree of complementarity gained from the participatory financing instruments of allocating wealth.)

Figure 5.1 shows the two opposite cases of allocation of wealth in mainstream and Islamic cases, respectively. As pointed out in Chapter 4 there cannot logically be any optimum and steady-state equilibrium point for the Islamic case of resource allocation in its continuous evolutionary learning property of unity of knowledge. The Islamic case, based on its perturbation effects (Choudhury 2013) caused by ethical factors that remain embedded as knowledge induction in the economic variables and all other kinds of socio-scientific variables, causes probabilistic fields around the points of occurrence of events. Such perturbations cannot be removed by methods like data envelopment analysis, or the stochastic surfaces method. The reason is the persistence of a continuous field of simulacra of perturbations and the unattainability of the specific optimum point. The optimum and steady-state point remains in the core of economic processes (Debreu 1959). The core is not accessible, and therefore, is not real in treating the conjoint learning interrelations between unity of knowledge and the knowledge-induced variables at hand that are scattered over knowledge, space and time. Consequently, as pointed out earlier, the mainstream postulates of scarcity, marginal rate of substitution or opportunity cost, competition, conflict and methodological individualism in mainstream dialectics, and thereby, the results

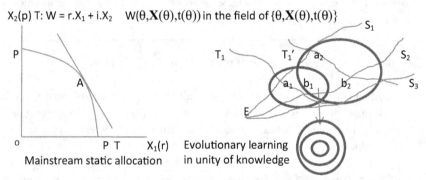

$X_2(p)$ T: $W = r.X_1 + i.X_2$ $W(\theta,\mathbf{X}(\theta),t(\theta))$ in the field of $\{\theta,\mathbf{X}(\theta),t(\theta)\}$

Mainstream static allocation

Evolutionary learning in unity of knowledge

T_i's are now the corrugated surfaces. E is an instantaneous equilibrium that becomes like A. All other points like a's and b's are Evolutionary learning points as perturbations along the allocation paths like S's. Islamic allocation of resources take place in the topological surfaces in knowledge, space, and time. Hence these do not take place in Cartesian spaces like in mainstream economics.

FIGURE 5.1 Contrasting resource allocation between Islamic and mainstream economic formulations

that we are accustomed of assigning to formulas of pricing, marginal productivity, rates of return, and general equilibrium models, cannot be copied over into Islamic economic formulations by its methodology of unity of knowledge. Now none of the postulates of rationalism that influence the axiom of economic rationality can abide in the Islamic evolutionary learning formulation invoking knowledge, space, and time dimensions in the vector of variables $\{\theta, \mathbf{X}(\theta), t(\theta)\}$ and in the functions of such vectors, such as the well-being function, $W(\theta, \mathbf{X}(\theta), t(\theta))$, and the system of circular causation relations that explain organic interrelationship in respect of the states of complementarities between the variables or otherwise.

Detailed formal model of Islamic consilience: single system (Islamic economics)

How does each of the evolutionary paths in Figure 5.1 (ES$_i$) correspond with the single-system depiction of Islamic ethico-economic learning universe? We will now formalize this one-system explanation under the precept of Islamic unity of knowledge. Following this the multi-system case will be taken up. We exemplify the one-system case with the example of sustainability in socioeconomic development. The sustainability concept is different from sustainable development. Very briefly we note the differences here in order to then formulate the sustainability index as an example of the well-being function defined above.

Sustainability is the organic unity between the knowledge-induced choices of development showing the interaction, integration, and evolutionary learning (IIE) experience in an ever-widening domain of life-sustaining systems. This is also the meaning of the multiverse unity that is set by complementarities between the good things as life-sustaining choices. These are the *maqasid*-choices. Sustainability is based on the concepts of social and spiritual capital (Halpern 2005; Zohar & Marshall 2004). These concepts – of capital and wealth, growth, development, and social choice – depend upon the interactive, integrative, and evolutionary (IIE) learning processes of ethico-economic choices to sustain well-being at large. In this sense of being an organic relationship between ethics and diversity of capital with the idea of consilience within it, the meaning of sustainability comes near to the idea of organic unity of morality in choices of capital, and thereby of the artefacts wherein capital is used for moral construction (Stehr 2002). In such respects of the nature of continuously replenished capital within the life-sustaining concept, the nature of capital is an output of relational unity of knowledge. The property of evolutionary learning under sound consciousness, which is the function of knowledge derived from Islamic epistemology, automatically (endogenously) sustains capital by its wider field of organic interrelationship with wealth, technology, innovation, and the life-fulfilment development outlook. Capital may depreciate but is continuously replenished by these vastly complementary relationships between diverse possibilities according to the episteme of unity of knowledge.

Sustainable development (World Commission for Environment and Development 1987) treats capital as a depreciable good. Although the role of ethics and consciousness is invoked, this is not of the self-motivational type. Endogeneity of evolutionary learning and the induction of unity of knowledge are not embedded in choices. Policies and regulations become externally induced ways of directing the recovery of capital depreciation. Consequently, the ethical imposition being externally applied, the policy and regulatory instruments are exogenous in nature. This is contrary to the case of organic relationship of capital in the concept of sustainability.

EXAMPLE 5.2

The case of sustainable development is a mainstream concept and its welfare concept is a utilitarian one. In Figure 4.1 we can think of two substitutes (X_1,X_2), which can be X_1 = environment and X_2 = employment. In the mainstream economic parlance of opportunity cost, as environment conservation (X_1) increases, forest employment (X_2) drops as clear-cutting drops. The reverse is also true. These manifest the opportunity cost and marginal rate of substitution underlie resource allocation between X_1,X_2 as competing alternatives.

Contrarily, in the case of Islamic economic formulation, X_1 and X_2 are endogenously embedded with the ethical and appropriate technological and innovation effects. This means that, environment conservation or clear-cutting can increase, but the use of seeding and replantation via discursive learning between foresters and management will continuously diversify plantation and replant trees, as the case may be. The three factors, namely $\{\theta_{discourse},X_1(\theta),X_2(\theta),t(\theta)\}$ are thus interactive, integrative, and continuously evolutionary through the discursive medium of innovation creating θ-flows by induction. Figure 5.1 explains the Islamic case for sustainability. Many other cases of environment conservation studied intertemporally can be formulated. The student can try the following exercise.

EXERCISE 5.1

Formulate the contrasting cases of sustainability issue in mainstream economics and Islamic economics for the following problem:

Allow for forest clear-cutting, but diversify the forest into fruit-bearing trees that can generate a secondary linked industry. Consequently, show how the revenue flow takes place among the fruit industry, the forestry industry in diversifying products, and the producers and managers as shareholders. Use a system diagram for explanation.

Formulation of the single-system Islamic epistemological model for unity of knowledge

The starting point of the knowledge-induced world-system, of which economics is a part, is the absolute and perfect law of unity of knowledge – the divine law. Thus, through *Tawhid*, in the socio-scientific field we do not associate the theology of God and the metaphysical implications of God's Oneness, the '*dhat*' or essence ('*a'sas*'). Such quiddity is beyond human understanding and is sheer speculation without benefit to the lived experience. We avoid all such metaphysical queries. Instead, we associate *Tawhid* with the unity of the law of God and its induction in the process of unification of the generality and details of the world-system. In the case of economics for instance, the precept of unity of knowledge is explained by the organic complementarities between the chosen artefacts in the light of the nature of the Signs of God (*ayat Allah*)[7] that unravel the unity of 'being' and 'becoming' and its negation of falsehood to establish the truth.

God is not a metaphysical being in Islam, removed from the world-system and its details. Rather, He makes Himself known through His Signs in the order of reality, which comprises the Signs of God in its completeness. The Law of God is incrementally prepared and explained by the Signs of God (*ayat Allah*) for human comprehension. Therefore, we take the domain of law of God as the complete and absolute knowledge that creates everything. Yet by itself it remains uncreated.

The Law of God as the law of complete and absolute unity of knowledge assumes a non-dimensional mathematical precept. This is referred to as the topology of the supercardinal order (Chapter 2);[8] as a mathematical concept, it has no dimension and encompasses all of knowledge (Maddox 1970). We denote this supercardinal topology by the symbol Ω. The unravelling of the Law of God through the message of the *Qur'an* is done by the *Sunnah* (teaching) of the Prophet Muhammad. Let the *Sunnah* as mapping of the *Qur'an* to the details of the world-system be denoted by 's'. Then the further discourse among the learned in Islam (*ulul umri*) is denoted by {f}. The compounding between {s}*unnah* and {f}*urther* discourse is denoted by, s•{f} = S, say.

We have avoided identifying Ω with the *Qur'an*, because as a functional artefact of the world-system it is part of the *Qur'an*. It presents the Law of God that is functional as a conceptual and an observational category in its operation. Also note that, the *Qur'an* includes certain verses of '*muqatt'at*', divinely secret meanings. These meanings are in the realm of the hidden (*ghayb*), about which the *Qur'an* forbids effort to extract meaning. Those who indulge in this kind of futile speculation are among the weak in belief. Yet the *Qur'an*, *Tawhid*, and the *Hereafter* (*Akhira*) are relationally identically precepts of belief as the *Qur'an* declares in the chapter, *Naba*. Thus the unravelling of unity of knowledge as the meaning of the *Tawhidi* epistemology (theory of knowledge) is denoted by[9]

$$[\Omega \to_{(s \cdot f) = S} \to \{\theta\}]$$
(5.1)

The function of the flow of knowledge, $\{\theta\}$ derived as shown in expression (4.1) is to unravel the Signs of God in its generality and details as between the heavens and the earth.[10] Yet because $\{\theta\}$ is incrementally derived, and so also the 'de-knowledge' $\{\theta'\}$ is incrementally rejected with the growth of certainty of knowledge, therefore the Signs of God manifest themselves surely but incrementally to our human limitations in acquiring full knowledge. We thereby write:

$$\{\theta\}\to\mathbf{X}(\theta) : \{\theta,\mathbf{X}(\theta)\}$$

where $\mathbf{X}(\theta)$ denotes the observational entities as multivariants of Signs of God (being positively induced by knowledge $\{\theta\}$ or by 'de-knowledge' $\{\theta'\}$ in order to unravel the truth of knowledge).

We write in combined form:

$$[\Omega\to_{(s\cdot f)=S}\to\{\theta\}]\to(\mathbf{X}(\theta),t(\theta)) : \{\theta,\mathbf{X}(\theta),t(\theta)\} \tag{5.2}$$

The well-being conveyed by the blessings derived from the Signs of God is a functional criterion explaining and unravelling the degree to which complementarities exist or fail to exist so as to be corrected into moral reconstruction. We write the well-being function as:

$$W(\theta) = W(\theta,\mathbf{X}(\theta),t(\theta)) \tag{5.3}$$

By combining the above expressions we can write:

$$[\Omega\to_{(s\cdot f)=S}\to\{\theta\}]\to(\mathbf{X}(\theta),t(\theta)) : \{\theta,\mathbf{X}(\theta),t(\theta)\}\to W(\theta,\mathbf{X}(\theta),t(\theta)) \tag{5.4}$$

We denote expression (5.4) as the start and end of one process of evolutionary learning under the precept of unity of knowledge shown in the bracketed [.].

The commencement of the second process of evolutionary learning follows evaluation of the well-being function under the condition of circular causation that represents degrees of complementarities between the variables as expressed by the coefficients of the interrelating variables $\{\mathbf{X}(\theta)\}$. The resulting equations bringing out the inter-causal dependencies between the variables are the circular causation relations (Toner 1999a, 1999b). We write these as:

$$\mathbf{X}(\theta) = \{X_1,X_2,\ldots,X_n\}[\theta]$$

The circular causation equations for this vector are:

$$X_1(\theta) = f_1\{X_2,\ldots X_n\}[\theta]$$
$$X_2(\theta) = f_2\{X_1,\ldots X_n\}[\theta]$$
$$\ldots\ldots\ldots\ldots\ldots\ldots\ldots\ldots\ldots\ldots\ldots$$
$$X_n(\theta) = f_n\{X_1,\ldots X_{n-1}\}[\theta] \tag{5.5}$$

These equations are used as structural ones (not reduced forms) to estimate the well-being function by statistically observing the coefficients of the various equations of (5.5). The 'as is' functional form of the well-being function is thus generated by the following estimation exercise:

Estimate $W(\theta) = \theta$ (say by linear approximation; but this can be non-linear) (5.6)

Subject to equations (5.5)

There are now (n+1) equations in (n+1) variables. While the observations of $\mathbf{X}(\theta)$-variables can be obtained from the actual data base, the values of $\{\theta\}$ for each of the $\mathbf{X}(\theta)$-variables must be assigned in accordance with the ranking and averaging across the data set. We show this kind of ranking and averaging in the appendix to this chapter.

When estimation does not show an appropriate degree of complementarities between relevant variables in accordance with the precept of unity of knowledge, then simulation for a better moral reconstruction can be carried out. This is done by discursively changing the estimated coefficients into better complementary values. The theoretical meaning underlying this transformation is that, coefficients are dynamic under repeated simulation (simulacra) while leaving the data set at the observed level. The economy and economic problems in microeconomics are thus affected by the ethico-economic embedding by way of the perturbations caused by $\{\theta\}$ inducing the $\mathbf{X}(\theta)$-variables. The resource allocation consequences are of the nature shown in Figure 5.1.

With the above explanation of estimation and simulation of well-being function subject to circular causation equations (5.5), the complete one-process P_1 of the Islamic epistemic explanation of the Islamic economic formulation can be written down as:

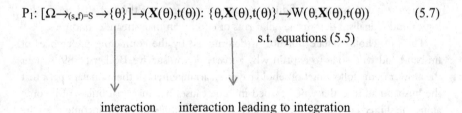

$$P_1: [\Omega\rightarrow_{(s,f)=S}\rightarrow\{\theta\}]\rightarrow(\mathbf{X}(\theta),t(\theta)): \{\theta,\mathbf{X}(\theta),t(\theta)\}\rightarrow W(\theta,\mathbf{X}(\theta),t(\theta)) \qquad (5.7)$$

s.t. equations (5.5)

interaction   interaction leading to integration

At the end of every process, thus P_1, evolutionary learning commences to engender P_2, and then likewise P_3 following P_2, etc. At the start of every process, the primal ontology denoted by [.] must repeat to refer everything to *Tawhid* once again and so on continuously along the evolutionary learning paths.

Expression (5.7) is now completed along interactive, integrative, and evolutionary learning paths as:

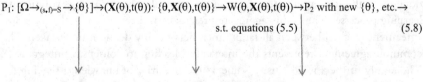

$$P_1: [\Omega\rightarrow_{(s,f)=S}\rightarrow\{\theta\}]\rightarrow(\mathbf{X}(\theta),t(\theta)): \{\theta,\mathbf{X}(\theta),t(\theta)\}\rightarrow W(\theta,\mathbf{X}(\theta),t(\theta))\rightarrow P_2 \text{ with new } \{\theta\}, \text{ etc.}\rightarrow$$

s.t. equations (5.5)   (5.8)

Interaction   interaction leading to integration $\rightarrow$ evolutionary learning

Note that the process meaning of including [.] in every evolutionary learning process indicates simulated levels of comprehending the Islamic unity of knowledge, and thus the moral reconstruction of the economic system (world-system).

Expression (5.8) is the final single-system formulation of Islamic economics in its microeconomic and macroeconomic states under the theory of Islamic unity of knowledge. Yet the same string relation also holds for the 'de-knowledge' case. Take the example of dialectical models of rationalist genre as in Marxism/Hegelianism (Resnick & Wolff 1987). According to Marxist theory of economic planning the price relatives are set by central planning. Hence the resource allocation trajectory follows a given path over the planning period. The production possibility curve PP in Figure 5.1 becomes kinked in shape. The variables become perfect complements but not endogenously, rather by the command of central planning.

The nature of microeconomics and macroeconomics in Islamic methodology

It is worth noting how microeconomics and macroeconomics are treated by the Islamic String Relational formulation of expression (5.8). In this formulation, most importantly, the method of aggregation by interaction, integration, and evolutionary learning determines the level of economic analysis. An example here is of preference formation from the individual to the level of social preference. In mainstream economic theory, social preferences and thereby the social welfare function are established by linearly independent individual preferences by virtue of the fact that methodological individualism determines all forms of choices in mainstream economics.

The household welfare function is determined by the competing preferences of husband and wife, so as to explain why a marriage can survive, Becker (1989) sought the answer in the following household payment arrangement: If the monetary perk that the husband adds to the wife's earned income causes her marginal utility of income along the shifted curve to be higher than the marginal utility of earned income, then the marriage survives. Otherwise it breaks down. On the other hand, if the 'real' marginal household utility before and after the income transfer remains equal for the husband and the wife, then the marriage remains in balance (social equilibrium). Otherwise the family breaks down. Such a result remains independent of children in the family. In the sense of social welfare, this welfare function becomes a linearly additive function of the totality of society's husbands and wives. Now there are two competing groups of welfare functions. The above utilitarian criterion for the national family welfare applies.

In the Islamic formulation of social choices with Islamic values, aggregation is done through interaction, integration, and sustainability conferred by evolutionary learning processes. The family aggregate preference is determined by the common agreement reached between all family members on any decision undertaken. The common agreement represents the interaction leading to consensus (integration). The family furthers its discursive value, as the maturity of knowledge seeking for the common good continues by evolutionary learning in continuums.

When such household interactive, integrative and evolutionary learning values are promoted at the societal level, a greater nexus of behavioural patterns takes place along the same line. Now the well-being function represents the tree of nexus of interrelationships for the common good. The *Qur'an* declares that divorce is the worst of the permissible acts in the eyes of God. On the other hand, ceremonious prayer at its appointed time is the most liked by God. The implications of such declarations are that, knowledge-gaining activity by prayer cements participation and pairing in and across families in the social order (Choudhury 2011).

The microeconomic nature of the family in the case of mainstream economics now disappears through the presence of the knowledge-induced interrelations that extends from the family to society at large. Likewise, the macroeconomic nature of an estranged nation in familial agreements is replaced by the interactive, integrative and evolutionary learning preferences that are induced by ethical behaviour denoted by knowledge-flows $\{\theta\}$ within families and across the families of the nation as a whole. An aggregate social ideal thus arises out of such evolutionary learning behaviour.

EXERCISE 5.2

In the case of economic planning by keeping capital/labour ratio fixed how would you use Figure 4.1 to explain these three cases:

1. the mainstream neoclassical case with X_1, X_2;
2. the Marxist fixed endowment case with X_1, X_2; and
3. the Islamic case using the complementary case of evolutionary learning.

EXAMPLE 5.2

Let us now take parts of the Human Development Index (HDI) and fit it into the Islamic formulation by expression (5.8) while undertaking a critical view of it. HDI (developed by the UNDP) is a geometric mean of three critical indicators – real GDP, life expectancy, and years of schooling by levels of education. These indicators can be further disaggregated as by age, gender, and sources of incomes (earned, wealth and transfer by poor brackets). However, such disaggregation is not done; rather, different indexes are developed, such as the Poverty Index, and the Gender Empowerment Index. HDI as it is used to rank countries (not only according to income levels but also by social causes) is a mono-causal indicator. Contrarily, if we were to treat the HDI as a well-being index, then this would be estimated and simulated first in one process and then in more complex undertakings by subsequent evolutionary processes. In each such case, circular causation equations will be used as the relations signifying degrees of existing complementary relations and the expected complementarities that can be induced via the coefficients of the variables.

Now, using the Islamic String Relation of expression (5.8) we denote the following indicators:

1. X_1: real GDP per capita; thus $X_1(\theta)$ would denote a degree of complementarity with the other variables
2. X_2: life expectancy; thus $X_2(\theta)$ would denote a degree of complementarity with the rest of the variables
3. X_3: enrolment ratio; thus $X_3(\theta)$ would denote a degree of complementarity with the rest of the variables
4. The well-being function replacing HDI would be $W(\theta) \approx \theta = W(X_1,X_2,X_3)[\theta]$
5. The estimation and simulation of the well-being function subject to circular causation equations are given by:

Estimate $\theta = W(X_1,X_2,X_3)[\theta]$

Subject to:

$$X_1 = f_1(X_2,X_3)$$
$$X_2 = f_2(X_1,X_3) \quad \}$$
$$X_3 = f_3(X_1,X_2)$$

(5.9)

Each of these equations and the well-being function can be taken in linear, log-linear, and other complex forms. For reasons of interpreting the coefficients as elasticity of well-being in respect of each of the variables it is preferred to estimate in the log-linear form. In the light of the Islamic epistemology the HDI estimation in respect of the inter-variable causality means that a balance ought to be established between the list of critical variables to impart well-being as a common good to all. This too is the idea of sustainability that was explained earlier. The variables can be disaggregated further. Without the Islamic epistemic foundation the need for circular causation, complementarity, and the meaning of well-being (*maslaha*) would not arise. The entire problem would then devolve into the HDI as the mainstream mono-causal problem.

Next we fit in all the different parts of the multi-causal meaning of HDI as well-being as follows:

Unity of knowledge $\{\theta,X_1(\theta),X_2(\theta),X_3(\theta);(t(\theta)\}$ $W(\theta) \approx \theta = W(\{\theta,X_1(\theta),X_2(\theta),X_3(\theta);(t(\theta)\}$ etc

Subject to equations (5.9)

$P_1: [\Omega \to_{(s,f)=S} \to \{\theta\}] \to (X(\theta),t(\theta)): \{\theta,X(\theta),t(\theta)\} \to W(\theta,X(\theta),t(\theta)) \to P_2$ with new $\{\theta\}$, etc. $\to$

s.t. equations (5.5)

(5.10)

interaction   interaction leading to integration $\to$ evolutionary learning

Extension of the Islamic economic formulation to multi-systems

Consider two systems construction of the Islamic String Relations formulation of Islamic economics (world-system) – heavens and earth, as the *Qur'an* declares that God is the Lord of the heavens and the earth and all in between. In mainstream economic theory, the nexus of relations between different variables belongs to a single-system process relations divided into sectors. Thus in the generalized system of organic interrelations between the product market, the labour market, the fiscal sector, and the monetary sector, all these sectors and their variables form interacting sub-systems within the same economic system. This can be further expanded to the open economy with trade and international factors and services as interrelations. Nonetheless, in the widest form of the generalized system model there are exogenous variables, such as fiscal and monetary policies, and all other policies that are exogenously applied in mainstream economics. Consequently, unlike this case, in the Islamic self-regulatory case the circular causation relations generate pervasively endogenous variables including the endogenous type policy variables. Preferences of all kinds we have shown are not datum, being θ-induced. Technology and innovation are all θ-induced. Only a free choice stands out under conditions of conscious decision-making with righteous guidance. The *Qur'an* says in this regard that only truth stands out. Truth is the principle of unity of knowledge and its induction of the good things of life – the *maqasid*-choices.[11] Policies must therefore interrelate with all other endogenous variables and thus become endogenous themselves by the force of the underlying principle of organic 'pairing' that reflects the Truth of the Islamic episteme of unity of knowledge and its induction of the unified economic sub-system.

Besides, the multi-system Islamic String Relations (ISR) in the formulation of the Islamic economic system points out that the economy and its variables and functions are only a part of the nexus of systemic interrelations. Indeed, as we will explain towards the end of this book, science and economics span the entire universe with meaning and consciousness. Thereby, the universal design of the monotheistic law is indeed that of science and economics. These mind-spaces form the grand design of the science of the Signs of God and of the comprehensive order and scheme of the embedding of Islamic economic science with every other discipline and conduct of life. This life experience embraces the moral and ethical order. It is the order of *maqasid al-shari'ah* derived in, from, and towards the deepening knowledge of the monotheistic law and its induction of the world-system in its generality and details. Because of the multi-systemic depiction of the consciously evolutionary learning, the world-system becomes the true depiction of reality (Choudhury *et al.* 2003). Therefore, Islamic economics does not stand alone as an isolated system. It cannot be studied as such. The meaning of knowledge-flows, 'θ' derived from the divine source $(\Omega;S)$, as we have explained, now implies the unity of all interacting, integrating, and evolutionary systems, both intra-systems and inter-systems, in the entire nexus of experience.

Multi-system model formulation: Islamic political economy *contra* mainstream political economy

A depiction of such an inter-nexus of unifying relationships is conveyed by the discipline of Islamic political economy and world-system study (Choudhury 2014).

Here too there is a substantive difference between the mainstream study of political economy and Islamic political economy. In either case though, the study of political economy encompasses a broad field of interactive study across a nexus of factors that impinge on economic activities. Among such extraneous forces impressed exogenously on economic variables, mainstream economic thought adds on political, social, cultural, and recently religious forces (Witham 2010). Such is the impossibility of the problem of heteronomy that has moved away from consciousness as intrinsic value.

Political economy in its mainstream context (Staniland 1985) is a study of the dynamics of conflict and strategies underlying the nature, formation, and distribution of wealth among its contending claimants. These can be groups within countries, regions, and among countries in the global economy, which is the study of the world-system in its capitalistic and socialistic meanings of conflict and competition, acquisition and deprivation. Thus there is the classical political economy and the global political economy that grew on the heels of capitalist globalization (Nitzan & Bichler 2000). Political economy taken in the context of global conflicts also addresses the deeply theoretical issues of epistemology (Ruggie 2003a, 2003b). It reflects the alternative views of social reality across nations, culture, and historical developments.

Nitzan and Bichler (2000, p. 67) contrast the picture of global political economy with neoclassical political economy (Srinivasan 1985), and the neoliberal political economy as follows:

> And so from Smith onward, it became increasingly customary to separate human actions into two distinct spheres, 'vertical' and 'horizontal'. The vertical dimension revolves around power, authority, command, manipulation and dissonance. Academically, it belongs to the realm of politics. The horizontal axis centres around well-being, free choice, exchange and equilibrium – the academic preoccupation of economists. The consequence of this duality was to make modern political economy an impossible patchwork: its practitioners try to re-marry power and well-being, but having accepted them as distinct spheres of activity to begin with, the marriage is inherently shaky.

Islamic political economy of the Islamic epistemological genre is substantively different from the mainstream study, but its methodology subsumes the mainstream one by changing the knowledge model into a 'de-knowledge' model that is based on methodological individualism, conflict, competition, and a belief in the scarcity of resources that otherwise can be shared. Islamic political economy as an epistemological study is premised on unity of knowledge across diversity of partners who can complement the claims on resources, wealth, and markets. Such a foundation of Islamic political economy rests on the Islamic epistemology of unity of knowledge. This methodology was explained earlier. In the multi-system extension of the Islamic String Relations (ISR) the interactive, integrative, and evolutionary learning properties of this formulation applies to the learning dynamics of multi-group cooperation, intra-country political and institutional cohesion, glo-balization with a human face, and institutional global governance for common well-being.

Examples of Islamic political economy studies are: economic integration of the *ummah* (whole community), the world nation of Islam via trade, development, resource sharing, and common institutional policies and strategies, such as monetary and development policies, and shared spirit and practice of discourse (*shura*). Islamic political economy can contribute significantly to global well-being by suggesting such cooperative (participatory) models to the United Nations Organization, UNCTAD, World Bank, and the IMF (Commission on Global Governance 1995). The Islamic worldview can also contribute to the goal of development of the South. The South Commission (1990, p. 13) writes: "To sum up: development is a process of self-reliant growth, achieved through participation of the people acting in their own interests as they see them, and under their own control." In the light of such a broad perspective of political economy as cooperation, participation, and complementarities in the common heritage of man and global society the Islamic multi-systems model has much to offer.

Yet in the multi-system framework of Islamic political economy there are a number of critical details that need to be studied. First, there is the theory of the *shura* evolutionary learning process and institution. The *shura* means the Qur'anic medium of consultation:[12] broadly, a discursive process of multi-system enlightened discussions and decision-making at all levels. There is an even broader meaning associated with the *shura*, regarding what the *shura* consults about. At this stage of the Islamic existence, the *shura* becomes a discursive process that studies and consults mutually within and across it on the substantive issues of diverse depth and meaning of enlightened arguments. Such *shuras* belong to diverse ranks of scholarly discourse and also of policy-makers. In this way the *shura* model extends to all levels of the social order – the family, community, society at large, institutions, the marketplace and all the smaller and larger bodies that are involved in these. This encompasses the totality of Islamic economics and science. The *shura* thus discourses on the details of interrelated issues of mind and matter. These are equivalent to investigating the nature of the worshipping world-system in its generality and details. The recognition of the conscious world-system in perpetual abeyance to God is termed *tasbih* (glorification of God). The Qur'an (42:53) says in this regard: "The Way of God, to Whom belongs whatever is in the heavens and whatever is on earth. Behold (how) all affairs tend towards God!" The central role of *tasbih*, consciousness of the worshipping world of matter and mind in the *shura* process, is brought out elsewhere in the Qur'an (21:79);[13] see also Qur'an (59:24).[14]

Multi-system formulation of Islamic political economy

Let S_1 denote the system comprising heavens; S_2 denote the system comprising the earth. The multi-system Islamic String Relation (ISR) is shown by:

$$\to \{\theta_1\}] \to (\mathbf{X}_1(\theta_1), t(\theta_1)): \quad \{\theta_1, \mathbf{X}_1(\theta_1), t(\theta_1)\} \to W(\theta_1, \mathbf{X}_1(\theta_1), t(\theta_1)) \to P_2 \quad \text{with new}$$

$\{\theta_1\}$, etc.

$$[\Omega \to_{(s,f)=S} \to \{\theta_1, \theta_2\}] \qquad\qquad\qquad\qquad\qquad\qquad\qquad\qquad (5.11)$$

$$\to \{\theta_2\}] \to (\mathbf{X}_2(\theta_2), t(\theta_2)): \quad \{\theta_2, \mathbf{X}_2(\theta_2), t(\theta_2)\} \to W(\theta_2, \mathbf{X}_2(\theta_2), t(\theta_2)) \to P_2 \text{ with new } \{\theta\},$$

etc.

According to the *Qur'an*, the heavens and the earth are paired realities in the worship of God. They therefore share a common law, which is derived from the divine law that governs the domains of the heavens and the earth. Examples of these domains are solar energy, rain, and taming and tapping the wind and the cosmic environment. These elements are associated with the cosmic domain. The earth as the other domain has its vegetation, produce, markets, and yields as rewards. These belong to the economic and social domains. While these domains have their distinct dynamics of learning (*tasbih*), yet they collectively unite to define the common well-being of the multi-system universe through their common worship of God in terms of divine law.[15]

Thus the expressions in (5.11) are combined according to the dynamics of interaction, integration, and evolutionary learning. The resulting system of circular causation comprises the computational general equilibrium model of the multi-system universe.

The multivariates are denoted by the vector $\mathbf{X}(\theta) = \{\mathbf{X}_1, \mathbf{X}_2\}[\theta]$, where $\theta = (\theta_1 \cap \theta_2)$. This implies the well-being function assumes the form $W(\theta) = W(\mathbf{X}(\theta))$. The circular causation model is given by $\mathbf{X}_1(\theta) = f_i(\mathbf{X}_2(\theta))$, where the vector-variables are expanded over as many elements as they can possibly have, say n_1-number for $\mathbf{X}_1$, n_2-number for $\mathbf{X}_2$. Thus the various functional relations are structural equations for $i = 1, 2, \dots n_1, \dots n_2$ (say). There are $(n_1 + n_2)$ number of circular causation equations. The final $(n_1 + n_2 + 1)^{th}$ equation gives the *quantitative* empirical form of the well-being function as defined earlier: $\theta = W(\mathbf{X}(\theta))$, say by a linear approximation obtainable by the implicit function theorem of differential calculus. We will explain the assignment of θ-values later in this chapter.

One form of these various equations can be log-linear. This form helps in a ready interpretation of the estimated and simulated coefficients as elasticity coefficients of the dependent variable in respect of the independent variables. The quantitative form of the well-being function can be taken in the product for $\theta = \prod_{i=1}^{(n1+n2)} \mathbf{X}_1{}^{a} \mathbf{X}_2{}^{b}$; $\mathbf{a}, \mathbf{b}$ are vector coefficients of the various variables of the vectors as shown. They explain the degrees of complementarities between θ-values and the variables; and between the variables as shown in the circular causation estimates and simulated values. Thereby the coefficients '**a**' and '**b**', because of their simulacra of variations according to the policy-theoretic changes in θ-values, are themselves also θ-induced. The result now is that the entire system of simulation of well-being, subject to the system of inter-variable circular causation relations, becomes a non-linear and dynamic functional.

EXERCISE 5.3

Adapt the multi-system formulation of the Islamic String Relation (5.11) to verses 1–5 of the chapter *R'ad* of the *Qur'an* and explain all details. In reference particularly to verse 5, set up and explain the 'de-knowledge' model of rationalism of mainstream multi-systems in terms of its characteristics of differentiation, methodological independence and individualism, competition, and both denial or exogeneity of moral and ethical values in socioeconomic methodology.

Assignment of θ-values for circular causation estimation/simulation

The following tabulation shows how θ-values corresponding to the socioeconomic values are assigned to represent the ranking of knowledge both within given columns and across rows of variables by averaging. Within given columns of the socioeconomic variables that are considered admissible according to the *Shari'ah*, the best selected θ-value may be assigned to say θ =10. The remainder of the θ-values are prorated by the formula: $\theta_s = (10/x_c{}^*){\star}x_s$, where $x_c{}^*$ denotes the socioeconomic value corresponding to that selected for θ =10. 'x_s' denotes the other socioeconomic values; s =1,2,... θ_s denotes the pro-rated θ-values for the socioeconomic variables s=1,2,... Note that the attributes of *asma al-husna* are used to qualify the kind of moral and ethical values and their levels of significance in this respect that are reflected by the given socioeconomic variables.

For instance, variables are shown in columns representing peace (*salam*) for stability; Bestower of Forms (*bariul musawwir*) representing diversification; strength (*matin*) representing growth; safety (*muhaimin*) representing sustainability, etc. Such attributes associated with the characterization of socioeconomic variables may also be surveyed. An example of such a case is the survey of managers on their managerial qualities responding to selected attributes of *asma al-husna*. The responses can be ranked.[16]

In multi-system estimation and simulation using the circular causation method responding to the Islamic methodology of unity of knowledge, the tabulation is done in Table 5.1. Table 5.2 shows this with θ-values. This is an example that is applicable to both the single-system and multi-system cases. It is also an example applicable for cross-sectional and time-series values of socioeconomic variables, and for cross-sectional questionnaire survey responses on socioeconomic variables as these are tallied with given qualities reflected by *asma al-husna*. Among the cross-sectional cases there can be regions and countries as in trading blocs. There can be firms, corporations, and small and medium-size enterprises and their managers.

Data can also be generated by panel. In this case, cross-sectional variables can be first averaged by time series and θ-averages developed as discussed above. The time series of θ-averages can be next used for running the time-series circular causation equations. The final results in every case now involve the estimation and simulation of the following circular causation model:

$$\text{Estimate/simulate } \theta = W(\mathbf{X}(\theta_{avg})) \tag{5.12}$$

Subject to circular causation equations in the elements of the vector variables $\mathbf{X}(\theta_{avg})$ corresponding to the $\mathbf{X}(\theta_{avg})$-variables for every θ_{avg}-values.

Note that in estimating/simulating the circular causation equations it is not absolutely necessary to use the θ_{avg}-values. These equations may be estimated/simulated as structural relations between the socioeconomic variables solely, without θ-variable. But in the estimation/simulation of the well-being function θ_{avg}-values are required to be one column of observations corresponding to the socioeconomic variables. Without this column of values the coefficients of the variables in (5.12) cannot be estimated/simulated.

Furthermore, the phases of simulated θ-values over stages of evolutionary learning are depicted in Table 5.3. Likewise, the simulacra of simulated socioeconomic variables corresponding to series of θ_{avg}-values are shown in Table 5.4.

TABLE 5.1 Primary/secondary data tabulation

Socioeconomics Variables: activities	Attributes from asma al-husna (a_i)	Responses by numbered responses	Averaged to denote θ-values
x_1^k	i–1	θ_{11}^k	
	2	θ_{12}^k	
	,	.	$\theta_1^k = Avg(\theta_{11}^k,..,\theta_{2n1}^k)$
	n_1	θ_{1n1}^k	
x_2^k	i–1	θ_{21}^k	
	2	θ_{22}^k	
	.	.	$\theta_2^k = Avg(\theta_{21}^k,..,\theta_{2n1}^k)$
	n_1	θ_{2n1}^k	
x_n^k	i–1	$\theta_{n,1}^k$	
	2	$\theta_{n,2}^k$	
.		.	$\theta_n^k = Avg(\theta_{n,1}^k,..,\theta_{n,n1}^k)$
.	n_1	$\theta_{n,n1}^k$	

TABLE 5.2 Tabulations with socioeconomic values and θ-values

t	x_1^t	x_2^t	....	x_n^t	θ_1^t	θ_2^t	...	θ_n^t	$\theta^t - Avg(\theta_1^t, \theta_2^t,.., \theta_n^t)$
1	x_1^1	x_2^1	...	x_n^1	θ_1^1	θ_2^1	...	θ_n^1	θ^1
2	x_1^2	x_2^2	...	x_n^2	θ_1^2	θ_2^2	...	θ_n^2	θ^2
.									
T	x_1^T	x_2^T	...	x_n^T	θ_1^T	θ_2^T	...	θ_n^T	θ^T

TABLE 5.3 Simulated θ_{avg}-values over phases of evolutionary learning

$$\theta_1 \rightarrow \theta_2 \rightarrow \theta_3 \rightarrow \ldots\ldots \rightarrow \theta_n$$
$$\downarrow \quad\quad \downarrow \quad\quad \downarrow \quad\quad\quad\quad\quad \downarrow$$
$$\theta_1^* \rightarrow \theta_2^* \rightarrow \theta_3^* \rightarrow \ldots\ldots \rightarrow \theta_n^*$$
$$\downarrow \quad\quad \downarrow \quad\quad \downarrow \quad\quad\quad\quad\quad \downarrow$$
$$\theta_1^{**} \rightarrow \theta_2^{**} \rightarrow \theta_3^{**} \rightarrow \ldots\ldots \rightarrow \theta_n^{**}$$

TABLE 5.4 Simulated socioeconomic variables in respect of simulated θ_{avg}-values over phases of evolutionary learning

$$x_1(\theta_1) \rightarrow x_2(\theta_2) \rightarrow x_3(\theta_3) \rightarrow \ldots\ldots \rightarrow x_n(\theta_n)$$
$$\downarrow \quad\quad\quad \downarrow \quad\quad\quad \downarrow \quad\quad\quad\quad\quad \downarrow$$
$$x_1^*(\theta_1^*) \rightarrow x_2^*(\theta_2^*) \rightarrow x_3^*(\theta_3^*) \rightarrow \ldots\ldots \rightarrow x_n^*(\theta_n^*)$$

$$x_1^*(\theta_1^*) \rightarrow x_2^*(\theta_2^*) \rightarrow x_3^*(\theta_3^*) \rightarrow \ldots\ldots \rightarrow x_n^*(\theta_n^*)$$
$$\downarrow \quad\quad\quad \downarrow \quad\quad\quad \downarrow \quad\quad\quad \downarrow$$
$$x_1^{**}(\theta_1^{**}) \quad\quad \rightarrow x_2^{**}(\theta_2^{**}) \quad\quad \rightarrow x_3^{**}(\theta_3^{**}) \quad\quad\quad \rightarrow \ldots\ldots \rightarrow x_n^{**}(\theta_n^{**})$$

EXERCISE 5.4

1. Fit the variables shown in Tables 5.1–5.4 into the multi-system model explained in expression (5.11).
2. Explain the steps in the multi-system construction of the Islamic String Relations. Use one of these: (i) time series data; (ii) cross-sectional data; (iii) panel data approach.
3. In each case write down and explain the corresponding circular causation model.

Conclusion

Throughout the earlier chapters; and it will be the same throughout this book, that the central methodology of Islamic economics in particular and the Islamic world-system in general is the Islamic methodology. It has its deep analytical premise that takes its shape and form in describing the multi-causal world-system with economics as a particular but most profound study of inter-variable circular causal relations with the nexus of multi-systems. Nothing escapes this methodology. The results borne out by the circular causation based on the epistemology of unity of knowledge arising from the Islamic methodological worldview are profound.

The Islamic methodology of unity of knowledge explained and quantitatively reflected through the model of circular causation is found also in the books of the sociological thinkers. On the circular causation issue Fitzpatrick (2003, p. 128) writes "everything is a reproduction of other reproductions. Society explodes in on itself and we cannot liberate ourselves from the *simulacra*…" In science likewise, Hawking (2010, p. 80) writes regarding the scientific method with the property of simulacra:

> Feynman showed that, for a general system, the probability of any observation is constructed from all the possible histories that could have led to that observation. Because of that his method is called the 'sum over histories' or 'alternative histories' formulation of quantum physics.

This and earlier chapters have derived Islamic methodology from the *Qur'an* and the *Sunnah*. They have provided several examples and have set several exercises for general readers to work out in detail. It is necessary for serious readers and students to understand the nature of and scientific discovery by Islamic methodology that is universally and uniquely reflected by the method of circular causation. This method describes and analytically calculates the degrees of complementarities (partnership, participation) between the variables representing the good things of life.

By the same methodology, the circular causation method can also explain the behaviour of the 'de-knowledge' model. This is the model that arises from the epistemology of rationalism as defined in this and earlier chapters. Consequently, the Islamic methodology of unity of knowledge is in most cases contrary to the axiom of mainstream economics. The results and consequences of this contrariness remain unique yet universal to the case of Islamic economics in particular and the Islamic world-system in general.

Notes

1 This oft-recited verse of the *Qur'an* (2:3) carries a deeper meaning: "Who believe in the unseen, establish prayer, and spend out of what We have provided for them." The 'unseen' here would encompass the abstraction that enables to fathom the recesses of meanings of praises of God (*Tawhid*) and the ways of conscious worshipping of the God in the functioning of the world-systems (*tasbih*). The instruments to delve into such deep recesses of abstraction could be abstract mathematical concepts, cybernetic systems, and onto-logical inquiries. The part 'establish prayer' is to extend intellection across the domain of consciousness to know the true reality (*Tawhid* and its illogical opposition by polytheism,

see Chapter *Al-Haqqa*, 69). Thus the conscious worshipper is perpetually and continuously in the presence of *Tawhid* (God and *Qur'an*). The part 'spend out of what We have provided for them' means the divulging and dissemination of the experience of conscious worshipping by all the means and awakening of righteous acts. These would involve both the dissemination of Islamic worldview and the material spending in the way of God by exerting the efforts of mind and matter. This is the pursuit of *Tawhid* as divine *law* of monotheism in action in the generality and details of the world-system. The *Qur'an* (29:69) says, "And those who strive for Us, We will surely guide them (to) Our ways. And indeed, God surely (is) with the good-doers."

2 *Qur'an* (4:59): "O ye who believe! Obey God, and obey the apostle, and those charged with authority among you. If ye differ in anything among yourselves, refer it to God and His Apostle, if ye do believe in God and the Last Day: That is best and most suitable for final determination."

3 *Qur'an* (36:36): "Glory to God, Who created in pairs all things that the earth produces, as well as their own (human) kind and (other) things of which they have no knowledge."

4 Because time is premised on the primacy of knowledge-flows that arise and continue on the basis of $\{ \theta \} \in (\Omega, S)$, we therefore write time as $t(\theta)$. A saying (*hadith*) of the Prophet as the inspired one called *hadith al-qudsi*, goes as follows: "Sons of Adam inveigh against (the vicissitudes of) Time, and I am Time; in My hand is the night and the day" (narrated by Al-Bukhari and Al-Muslim cited in Ibrahim and Johnson-Davies n.d.). The exegesis of this hadith is that time belongs to *Allah* who is the absolute in knowledge. Thus time belongs to knowledge that is *Allah's*. It can therefore be written $t(\theta \in (\Omega,S)) = t(\theta)$. Thus the dimensions of knowledge, space, time are written in the non-Cartesian coordinate as $\{\theta, \mathbf{x}(\theta), t(\theta)\}$, with $\{\mathbf{x}(\theta)\}$ as the continuum spanned by *Tawhidi* knowledge. $\{\mathbf{x}(\theta)\}$ spans the entire continuum of space induced by the primacy of knowledge. But the events in the universe unravel a little at a time as knowledge evolves and proceeds on.

   The non-Cartesian nature of the Islamic universe of the Signs of God is defined by the non-commensurate nature of the topology denoted by $\{(\Omega,S) \rightarrow \theta\}$. From this is defined the equally non-Cartesian nature of space and time premised on knowledge-flows. Thus any good is measured by the service it provides to be of relational importance. Mere size does not matter in the valuation of goods (e.g. land). '$\{\mathbf{x}(\theta)\}$' can thus be interpreted as the total valuation of the goods by the unity between essence and materiality. This integration yields the consciousness of total evaluation of things.

5 *Qur'an* (13:1–5): "Alif, Lam, Meem, Ra. These are the verses of the Book; and what has been revealed to you from your Lord is the truth, but most of the people do not believe. It is Allah who erected the heavens without pillars that you [can] see; then He established Himself above the Throne and made subject the sun and the moon, each running [its course] for a specified term. He arranges [each] matter; He details the signs that you may, of the meeting with your Lord, be certain. And it is He who spread the earth and placed therein firmly set mountains and rivers; and from all of the fruits He made therein two mates; He causes the night to cover the day. Indeed in that are signs for a people who give thought. And within the land are neighbouring plots and gardens of grapevines and crops and palm trees, [growing] several from a root or otherwise, watered with one water; but We make some of them exceed others in [quality of] fruit. Indeed in that are signs for a people who reason. And if you are astonished, [O Muhammad] – then astonishing is their saying, 'When we are dust, will we indeed be [brought] into a new creation?' Those are the ones who have disbelieved in their Lord, and those will have shackles upon their necks, and those are the companions of the Fire; they will abide therein eternally."

6 *Qur'an* (65:12): "It is God who has created seven heavens and of the earth, the like of them. [His] command descends among them so you may know that Allah is over all things competent and that God has encompassed all things in knowledge."

7 The signs of God (*ayat al-Allah*) are all-pervasive over the dimensions of knowledge, space, and time. Nothing is left out either in generality or details. The world-system (*a'lameen*) comprises the signs of God. They encompass the universe of mind and matter in their details of conceptions, formalism, empirical nature and inferences for the construction of the generality and details of the world-system. The *Qur'an* (55:13) declares in this regard: "Which then of the bounties of your Lord will you deny?" Furthermore the *Qur'an* (41:53) declares: "Soon will We show them our Signs in the (furthest) regions (of the earth), and in their own souls, until it becomes manifest to them that this is the Truth. Is it not enough that thy Lord doth witness all things?"

8 The *Qur'an* repeatedly declares: "Verily with God is full knowledge and He is acquainted (with all things)." Man has been given a small part of this knowledge as Mercy, and the totality of which is with God.

9 *Qur'an* (78:1–5): "About what are they asking one another? About the great news – that over which they are in disagreement. No! They are going to know. Then, no! They are going to know." Yusuf Ali explains the Great Event as the equivalence, The Hereafter ≈ *Qur'an* ≈ The Prophetic Message of *Tawhid*.

10 *Qur'an* (42:52–53): "…We have made the (*Qur'an*) a Light, wherewith We guide such of Our servants as We will; and verily thou dost guide (men) to the Straight Way, – The way of God to Whom belongs whatever is in the heavens and whatever is on earth. Behold (how) all affairs tend towards God!"

11 *Qur'an* (10:32): "Such is God, your real Cherisher and Sustainer: Apart from Truth, what (remains) but error? How then are ye turned away?"

12 *Qur'an* (42:38): "Those who hearken to their Lord, and establish regular prayer; who (conduct) their affairs by mutual consultation …"

13 *Qur'an* (21:79): "To Solomon We inspired the (right) understanding of the matter: to each (of them) We gave judgment and Knowledge; it was Our power that made the hills and the birds celebrate Our praises, with David: It was We Who did (all these things)."

14 *Qur'an* (59:24): "He is God, the Creator, the Evolver, the Bestower of Forms (of Colours). To Him belong the Most Beautiful Names: Whatever is in the heavens and on earth, do declare His Praises and Glory: And He is the Exalted in Might, the Wise."

15 *Qur'an* (22:18): "Seest thou not that to God bow down in worship all things that are in the heavens and on earth, – the sun, the moon, the stars; the hills, the trees, the animals; and a great number among mankind…"

16 Let $i = 1, 2, \ldots m$ denote number of managers surveyed cross-sectionally in respect to specified socioeconomic variables, $j = 1, 2, .., n$ to respond to a given attribute of *asma al-husna* corresponding to the socioeconomic variable by the quality of managers' responses. Let such responses be ranked as $\theta_{ij} = 1, 2, \ldots 10$ along with fractions between these numbers. The averages across the columns represent row-averages: $[\Sigma_{j=1}^{n} \theta_{ij}.j]/n = \theta_i \text{avg}, i = 1, 2, .. m$.

References

Barrow, J.D. (1991). *Theories of Everything: The Quest for Ultimate Explanation*, Oxford: Oxford University Press.

Becker, G.S. (1989). Family, in *The New Palgrave: Social Economics*, eds. Eatwell, J., Milgate, M., & Newman, P., pp. 64–76, New York: W.W. Norton.

Choudhury, M.A., Umar, Y., & Al-Ghamdi, M. (2003). *Ummatic* globalization versus neoclassical capitalist globalization, *Review of Islamic Economics*, 12(1): 5–45.

Choudhury, M.A. (2013). Perturbation theory in cognitive socio-scientific research: Towards sociological economic analysis, *Mind and Society*, 12(2): 203–217.

Choudhury, M.A. (2011). The family as a socioeconomic management system, *International Journal of Management Systems*, 18(1): 99–115.

Choudhury, M.A. (2014a). *Tawhidi Epistemology and Its Applications: Economics, Finance, Science, and Society*, Cambridge: Cambridge Scholarly Publishing.

Choudhury, M.A. (2014b). Islamic political economy: A methodological inquiry, *Social Epistemology:* Review and Reply Collective (SERRC). Available at: http://social-epistemology.com.

Commission on Global Governance. (1995). Global civic ethic, in *Our Global Neighbourhood: A Report of the Commission on Global Governance*, New York: Oxford University Press.

Debreu, G. (1959). *Theory of Value: An Axiomatic Analysis of Economic Equilibrium*, New York: John Wiley.

Fitzpatrick, T. (2003). Postmodernism and new directions, in *Social Policy*, eds. Alcock, P., Erskine, A., & May, M., pp. 125–133, Oxford: Blackwell.

Halpern, D. (2005). *Social Capital*, Cambridge: Polity Press.

Hawking, S.W. & Mlodinow, L. (2010). Alternative histories, in *The Grand Design*, London: Transworld Publishers.

Ibrahim, E. & Johnson-Davies, D. (n.d.). *Forty Hadith Qudsi*, translated. (personal publication)

Nitzan, J. & Bichler, S. (2000). Capital accumulation: Breaking the dualism of 'economics' and 'politics', in *Global Political Economy, Contemporary Issues*, ed. Palan, R., pp. 67–88, London: Routledge.

Resnick, S.A. & Wolff, R.D. (1987). *Knowledge and Class: A Marxian Critique of Political Economy*, Chicago, IL: The University of Chicago Press.

Ruggie, J.G. (2003a). Introduction: What makes the world hang together? Neo-utilitarianism and the social constructivist challenge, in his *Constructing the World Polity*, pp. 1–40, London: Routledge.

Ruggie, J.G. (2003b). The new institutionalism in international relations, in his *Constructing the World Polity*, pp. 45–61, London: Routledge.

South Commission. (1990). *The Challenge to the South*, Oxford: Oxford University Press.

Srinivasan, T.N. (1985). Neoclassical political economy, the state and economic development, *Asian Development Review*, 3(2): 38–58.

Staniland, M. (1985). The fall and rise of political economy, in *What is Political Economy? A Study of Social Theory and Underdevelopment*, pp. 10–35, New Haven, CT: Yale University Press.

Stehr, N. (2002). Knowledge societies, in his *Knowledge and Economic Conduct: The Social Foundations of the Modern Economy*, pp. 63–73, Toronto: University of Toronto Press.

Toner, P. (1999a). Gunnar Myrdal (1898–1987): Circular and cumulative causation as the methodology of the social sciences, in his *Main Currents in Cumulative Causation: The Dynamics of Growth and Development*, Chapter 5, Houndmills, Hampshire: Macmillan.

Toner, P. (1999b). Conclusion, in his *Main Currents in Cumulative Causation: The Dynamics of Growth and Development*, Chapter 7, Houndmills, Hampshire: Macmillan.

United Nations Development Program (UNDP) several annual reports. *Human Development Index (HDI) Report*, New York: Oxford University Press.

Ventelou, B. (2005). Economic thought on the eve of the General Theory, in *Millennial Keynes*, Chapter 2, Armonk, NY: M.E. Sharpe.

Wilson, E.O. (1998). *Consilience: Unity of Knowledge*, New York: Vantage Press.

Witham, L. (2010). *Marketplace of the Gods: How Economics Explains Religion*, Oxford: Oxford University Press.

World Commission for Environment and Development (Brundtland, G.H. Report), (1987). *Our Common Future*, Oxford: Oxford University Press.

Zohar, D. & Marshall, I.N. (2004). *Spiritual Capital: Wealth we can live by*, San Francisco, CA: Brett-Koehler.

6

ISLAMIC PARTICIPATORY INSTRUMENTS AND THE ETHICAL DIMENSIONS

LEARNING OBJECTIVES

This chapter aims:

- To provide students with the scope of the *maqasid al-shari'ah*, broadened into the widest socio-scientific inquiry to help in developing *muamalat* (socio-economic affairs).
- To show the institutionalizing possibility of an integrative financing instrument in trade and development in the *ummah* (community) according to the theory of unity of knowledge (*Tawhid*) and unity of the knowledge-induced specific case of the participatory instruments.

Introduction

An intellectual critique is launched on the prevalent nature of knowledge and scope of thinking in Islamic economics and finance. Such thought and the practices that emanate from them have resulted in a meagre showing in the development of the present state of Islamic knowledge and financial institutions worldwide. No revolutionary worldview has arisen. The missing paradigm in intellection, application, and practice is the distinctive Islamic worldview concerning the functional nature of the epistemology of unity of knowledge that emanates from the mono-theistic law in the *Qur'an* and is guided into action by the *Sunnah*, and thereby, by Islamic discourse. This chapter recommends that the worldview of unity of knowledge (*Tawhid*) have its epistemology and functionalism be formalized and applied at the highest educational and institutional levels. On the path of such intellectual and applied reconstruction, this chapter upholds the importance of *fiqh* in Islamic jurisprudence, and thus recommends returning every inquiry to the *Qur'an*, the *Sunnah*, and Islamic discourse for a fresh search and discovery in all socio-scientific matters each time an issue is raised. The scope of the *maqasid al-shari'ah* is thus broadened into the widest socio-scientific inquiry to help in developing *muamalat* (socioeconomic affairs).

The chapter then gives an example to show the institutionalizing possibility of an integrative financing instrument in trade and development in the *ummah* according to the theory of unity of knowledge and unity (*Tawhid*) of the (Islamic) knowledge-induced specific case of the participatory instrument. This Foreign Trade Financing Certificate (FTFC) can be commercially viable and academically rewarding according to the underlying theory of unity of knowledge and the unitary world-system.

Background

There is a debate that has been waged for a considerable time now by Islamic economists and finance experts calling for resorting to mainstream methods and models of these fields with some *fiqhi* colouring to them. *Fiqh* means canonical Islamic jurisprudence or rules of the *Shar'iah*, the Islamic law, based on religious interpretation. *Fiqhi* inferences colour that these experts would like to qualify as 'Islamic'. The result has been that Islamic financial institutions have embraced this retrogressive and mechanistic approach to what they call Islamic economic and financial instruments and *Shari'ah* compliance.

There are multiple methodological errors in such an approach to what has come to be referred to as 'Islamic Economic' and 'Islamic Finance' activities and the many themes they comprise. In the end, the result of this intellectual enterprise leaves the observer in a predicament of intellectual poverty and loss of self-reliance toward establishing a *Qur'anic* worldview transcending both mainstream imitation (*taqlid*) and also sheer *fiqhi* (interpretive) origin of Islamic thinking.

In regards to the latter case, Asad (1987) writes:

> In consequence, our current theology (*kalam*) and canonical jurisprudence (*fiqh*) now resemble nothing so much as a vast old-clothes shop where ancient thought-garments, almost unrecognizable as to their original purport, are mechanically bought and sold, patched up and re-sold, and where the buyer's own delight consists in praising the old tailors' skill.

Such problems multiply during the new millennium even with the rise of post-modernist questioning in intelligentsia and with a deepening Islamic crisis with the Western world. We want to address this Muslim predicament as it is presently premised in the mainstream mould against the backdrop of what otherwise can be truly an Islamic approach to and worldview of problems of economics, finance, institutions, social ordering and the whole world-system of Islam (Choudhury 2004).

Objective

This chapter argues that the submissive attitude and advice on equating the Islamic and mainstream *methodologies* and even empiricism, thereby calling for adopting mainstream *methods* of analysis, constitutes a flawed reasoning; a defeated apologia.

To revert to Islamic economics and finance as an embedded study in the ethico-epistemology of divine oneness as the foundation of Islamic Law, is the principal objective of this chapter. This critical examination is built up by an examination of the idea and practice of Islamic economics and finance during present times. Epistemological issues are examined in the socio-scientific reconstruction of what this chapter surmises should be the true methodology in Islamic economics and finance.

Critical methodological issues of Islamic economics and finance

This chapter draws a major difference between the concepts of *Method* and *Methodology*. Choudhury (1999) explains that these two concepts are interrelated scientific primitives. They are together used for understanding the praxis and applying this to inferential consequences arising from the methodological premise by the corresponding analytical methods that apply.

The original praxis is invariably epistemological in nature. Epistemology is subsequently integrated by a scientific discursive approach with applied models, and thereafter deriving the evidences from the models and analysis of applications. Methods belong to the engineering (functional) ontological domain (Gruber 1993); the evidence forms Heidegger's consequences of 'being' (Heidegger 1988), when the analysis and application of the original methodological premise is to be formulated and applied for understanding real world facts.

Yet, in the absence of the epistemological methodology it is possible for methods to be used independently of the methodological understanding. When this is the case, methods fail to have substantive relevance in the light of methodology. They exist merely as procedural artefacts for conducting an analysis, but not necessarily the true and relevant one. Choudhury (1999, p. 348) writes,

> Methods can exist without methodology as was explained in the earlier chapters for the case of the reductionist design of rationalism. Yet methodology cannot exist without the corresponding determined methods. Such methods must be derived from the essence of the methodology itself. They must be such instruments that mobilize the entire methodological nature of divinely unified systems into explanatory relations.

We referred to this premise as the Islamic epistemology of unity of knowledge. In this chapter we will explain the difficulties encountered in such academic ventures from the Islamic side.

Contrary to this assertion is the felt distancing of the prevailing Islamic socio-scientists from a substantive reference to the *Qur'anic* worldview, its epistemology of oneness of the divine law (*Tawhid*), and the inter-causal understanding of unification of knowledge in issues of world-systems by the epistemological methodology that remains embedded in the generality and details of such world-systems. The field of economics and finance are subsets of the grand domain of the Islamic world-system. Consequently, a vacuum has remained in the construction of the Islamic phenomena *vis-à-vis* its epistemology, the reality in the world-system, and the moral reconstruction of a socio-scientific normative module. Such normative questions are empirically studied by what we have explained to be the circular causation model of estimation and simulation of well-being. Such an approach can result in simulacra of possibilities in converting the normative picture into a positive picture (Choudhury 1998).

Within the broad arena of human inquiry are massive questions that span methodology, methods, and both normative and positive constructions, in the light of the *Qur'an* and the *Sunnah*. Without this fundamental epistemological reference there cannot be an authentic foundation stone for the Islamic revolutionary paradigm of the socio-scientific worldview. We have explained this in detail in Chapter 4. Within the Islamic methodological worldview, the embedded field of Islamic economics and finance is a subset of the generalized study of the generality and particulars of the world-system. In an otherwise rationalist development of Islamic economics and Islamic finance, during the last seventy years of their existence and the last thirty years of Islamic banking and Islamic development finance organizations, no positive challenge and transformation has come about in the Muslim world, as it slips into intellectual decadence. No revolutionary reconstruction of the socio-scientific methodological worldview could be rendered. Thus, the Islamic epistemological foundation along with its methodological applications in the generality and details of 'everything' remains the decisive criterion of Islamic reality.

An example: Ambivalence of Islamic methodological goals in Islamic financing institutions

The ambivalence of the goal of the Islamic intellectual world-system in the light of the *Qur'an*, *Sunnah* and the Islamic methodology is proved by the case of a cursory and unplanned use of Islamic charity for human uplift. A haphazard approach presently exists despite much talk on the issues of human development by Islamic intellectuals and practitioners. The same state of Islamic thought and practice has prevailed for quite some time now. There is hardly any will to change despite the flaws of Islamic economics and finance in the absence of the Islamic methodological worldview.

High announced rates of return on earnings, rates of return on assets, and the profitability and stability of Islamic banks still do not point towards social well-being. Islamic banks make large profits to safeguard shareholders' wealth but remain distanced from the Islamic philosophy of financing assets in the real economy within market integration and commonly spread-out capital that can be shared by stakeholders. The complementary and participatory nature of Islamic financing, capital formation, and banking and non-banking activities without sound stakeholding activity causes the ultimate result of maximizing shareholders' wealth. These approaches remain unchanged from the conventional corporations and banking practices.

On the other hand, only by the participatory spread of capital and investment in society at large, and by deepening financing in the real economy, can the rate of interest be decreased. Such a possibility comes about by replacing loan capital with share capital among stakeholders at large; and expanding the nexus of inter-sectoral and inter-firm participation with a broad diversified investment portfolio. The result in the end would then be a market-driven injection of capital and financing into the money–real-economy linkage for the general participatory framework.

Such a broadened perspective on stakeholding across a wide nexus of participation is equivalent to adopting the proven meaning of the Islamic unity of knowledge and knowledge-induced activities in terms of well-being (*maslaha*). Without such an approach Islamic banks are in a permanent misunderstanding regarding the objective and goal of Islamic financial transformation, which ought to realize social transformation by adopting the Islamic principle of unity of knowledge and the knowledge-induction of the social economy. The pronounced cases of the social economy would be caused by the organic linkages between money and the real economy, engaging society at large, and the nexus of enterprises big and small sharing in diversified production and risk. The particular instruments that can bring about such participatory socioeconomic change ought also to be of the participatory type between the nexus of producing firms and financing enterprises. The participatory realization of Islamic economic and financial change would require the correct portfolio of all such single instruments that can be organically unified together in the form of development-financing instruments.

Yet the Islamic development-financing portfolio today is very weakly diversified. Much of the portfolio remains concentrated in cost-plus financing instrument, equity-financing, and foreign trade financing. The role of the profit-sharing financing instrument (*mudarabah*) has declined. The accumulation of funds in equities (*musharakah*) and mark-up financing (*murabaha*), and securities in the secondary financial market that revolve around the above-mentioned secondary ones, has caused lack of risk-diversification and production diversification in the face of a concentration of foreign trade financing of short-term funds. In the end, the efficiency ratios quoted by Islamic banks fail to bring out the true status of the social effects of Islamic bank financing. The social effects in fact remain very weak. The complementary relations are required between the economic and financial variables on the one side, and the social variables together with the economic ones. Most important of these are self-reliant human development, and sustainability of development and growth in human resources. In the absence of these important social factors for the common stakeholders, the financial results of many of the high ratios only project the benefits in terms of private depositors' returns with the high equity/liability ratios. Consequently, the goal of social well-being (*maslaha*) that we highlighted in Chapter 5 cannot be realized.

These empirical facts – see also Table 6.1 – point out that Islamic banks have to date failed to attain the participative complementarities between their economic and social goals. The complementary kind of organic embedding of unity between all good things of life arises from the episteme of unity of knowledge and of its knowledge-induced understanding of the world-system. This is the essential principle underlying the Islamic worldview, and thereby Islamic economics, finance, and the social order. Such kinds of complementary interrelations between the *Shari'ah*-driven possibilities mark the *functional* ontology of unity of knowledge. This functional ontology forms the Islamic epistemological applications of the Islamic methodological worldview that we explain in the previous chapters. The Islamic epistemological premise is the be-all and end-all of the Islamic worldview. It grounds Islamic economics and finance as well as society and science in it.

Figure 6.1 depicts the knowledge-induced embedding of systems according to the ever-expanding discursive impact of learning in the Islamic unity of knowledge on issues of the world-system. This though is not the nature of Islamic financing as it prevails today.

From published data from Islamic Bank Bangladesh (IBBL Annual Report 2008), considered among the best internationally according to the Global Finance Forum, *murabaha* (mark-up) financing comprised almost 51 per cent of total financing in 2007. PLS financing (*mudarabah* and *musharakah*) held a distant 0.13 per cent financing ratio. No data on social spending (Islamic *zakah* and *sadaqah* for the needy) are available in the bank balance sheets or otherwise. This is one of the persistent problems of disclosure and transparency of Islamic banks in declaring their social spending and social assets. If we approximate microenterprise development

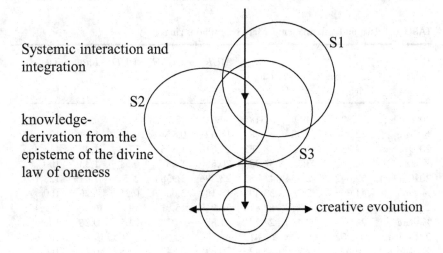

FIGURE 6.1 Systemic expression of knowledge-induced unity of knowledge as episteme

financing as a rough representation of a kind of social spending, the ratios held by the Islamic Bank Bangladesh were as follows: 0.02 per cent of total investment in 2007, and 0.005 per cent in 2006. These are despicable figures for social spending. In spite of these low social standings and in the absence of transparency and disclosure and the inadequacy of the balance sheets of Islamic Bank Bangladesh, its ROE-ratio (return on equity) stood at a high 13.42 per cent in 2006 and 13.00 per cent in 2007. The conclusion is reinforced: Such efficiency ratios, while they favour shareholders' returns and wealth, are not representative of the social and ethical meaning of Islamic economics and finance.

In the case of Islamic banks in Indonesia, published data (Bank Indonesia 2009) indicates a slightly better but yet questionable financing trends for microenterprises. Medium- and small-scale microenterprise (MSMEs) financing ranked at approximately 15 per cent of total financing in 2008, up from approximately 9 per cent in 2007. Yet Islamic financing of rural sector projects ranked between 4.00 and 4.50 per cent between 2006 and 2008. The return on equity (ROE) was wide-ranging: 37 per cent to 68.85 per cent between 2006 and 2008. Thus, once again, the inadmissibility of Islamic bank financial reporting in respect of the ethical social context remains unchanged.

In the case of Malaysian Islamic banks, published data shows that the Islamic bank social financing ('community, social and personal services') stood at 0.69 per cent in January 2005 and 0.91 per cent in December 2005. This ratio decreased to 0.88 per cent in March 2006. Given the high watermark of Malaysian Islamic banks in Islamic banking and finance in the secondary financing markets, the social financing figures shown in their consolidated balance sheets augurs poorly for the Islamic ethical and social objective.

The trend towards secondary financing in Malaysia is significantly away from the main basis of Islamic participatory financing, which is the Profit–Loss instruments comprising M1 = *mudarabah* and *musharakah* = M2. The overwhelming

TABLE 6.1 Islamic Bank financing, Malaysia, millions ringgit

End of period	Bai Bithaman Agil	Ijara	Ijara Bai	MUR	MUSH	MUD	Istisna	Total
2006 (Dec)	15,822	499	9,518	3,501	157	148	494	30,139
% share	52.50	1.65	31.58	11.62	0.52	0.49	1.64	100
2009 (Dec)	42,732	4017	38,353	23,016	1,875	376	1,487	111,856
% share	38.20	3.59	34.28	20.58	1.68	0.34	1.33	100
2010 (Dec)	52,642	2,834	43,487	23,296	3,958	275	1,615	128,107
% share	41.09	2.21	33.49	18.18	3.06	0.21	1.26	100
2011 (Dec)	83,148	6,332	62,878	56,940	15,817	146	696	260,476
% share	26.07	2.43	24.14	21.85	6.07	0.05	0.26	100
2014 (Jan)	83,452	6,526	63,812	58,746	16,636	148	900	284,616
% share	29.32	2.29	22.42	20.64	5.84	0.05	0.31	100

Source: Bank Negara Malaysia (2014)

concentration is in *bai bithaman agil*, *ijara thumma bai*, and *murabaha*, all of which are secondary financing instruments. Besides, there is now debate around the over-concentration of *murabaha* at the expense of PLS-portfolio diversification. We note this trend as the usual feature of Islamic financing structure over the time period 2006–2014. Such a trend throughout this time period proves that the Islamic portfolio has remained non-diversified.

The inference derived from Islamic bank financing on the ethical front

From 2001 to present times, the Islamic bank financing facts point out a clear pattern. This is that Islamic financial institutions are evolving along a line of activities based on a mechanistic understanding of the *Shar'iah*. In fact, the *Shar'iah* conception based on learning dynamics did not evolve in Islamic banks through a participatory discourse of the learned with diverse agencies of the Muslim community. There is no effective process in place in the Islamic institutions to understand the foundational methodology of the Islamic worldview. This is the unity of knowledge emerging from the divine law (*Tawhid*) in action in the world-system in all details of problems and issues. The *shura*, the Islamic consultative medium, which generates an extensive learning process spanning all of human order including science and complexity, is not a mechanistic institutional consultation. Rather, the *shura* learning process is premised on knowledge reproduction by developing insight into the intellection process of unity of knowledge integrated with intellectual discourse. These together evolve directions and rules on how the Islamic episteme of unity of knowledge can be actualized in the problems and issues at hand (*Qur'an* 42:38, 49–53).

A purely literal interpretation of a particular injunction of the *Shar'iah* to safeguard shareholders' wealth, and thus the preservation of the net worth of the Islamic institution, despite being a necessary condition of justice, fairness, and accountability, remains devoid of the purpose and objective of the *Shar'iah* (*maqasid al-shari'ah*). This happens when the understanding of complementary and causal relations between different parts of the economic, financial and social order for attaining well-being is not understood as belonging distinctively to the episteme of unity of the divine law in action with issues concerning the world-system.

EXERCISE 6.1

Search the internet for financing data on various primary, secondary, and ethical instruments to demonstrate the current state of relative financing being carried out by Islamic banks to attain the endogenous mix between economics, financial, and ethical goals.

The principle of pervasive complementarities applied to Islamic financial instruments

The resulting state of trade-off in resource allocation and decision-making *vis-à-vis* mainstream economic roots of the prevailing thinking in Islamic economics and finance is contrary to the principle of the paired universe presented by the *Qur'an* (36:36). The *Qur'anic* pairing of entities in world-systems is the defining basis of what we refer to here as the *Principle of Pervasive Complementarities* across diversity. This is the principle that arises from the episteme of Islamic unity of knowledge and explains that all the good things of life are complemented in pairs, being unitary.

Also by the same principle, the ensuing model of circular causation explaining Islamic consilience of unity of knowledge also explains the 'de-knowledge' model in terms of its characteristics of association between the rejected things according to the Islamic methodological worldview. The difference between the knowledge worldview and the 'de-knowledge' worldview is that, in the former case the central perspective is of unity between the good things of life (*hallal at-tayyabah*) creating consilience. In the latter case, the association is between the rejected things from the domain of goodness. The dynamics are now characterized by the increasing conflict, competition, methodological individualism and independence between the groups of rejected things. In the absence of understanding and applying the principle of pervasive complementarities for Islamic transformation, Islamic economics and finance and the Islamic organizations have lost their way by still holding on to the principle of marginal rate of substitution and trade-off as in mainstream economics.

In earlier chapters we explained the rejection of this latter postulate in Islamic economics by virtue of the interactive, integrative, and evolutionary learning dynamics according to the Islamic methodological worldview. When these properties cease to exist, the entire economic system relents on the postulate of marginal rate of substitution. This postulate is linked with the axioms of scarcity of resources, competition, optimization, and steady-state equilibrium conditions. On the other hand, even in the dialectical nature of the rationalist world-system there are no dynamics left to extend such a dialectical process of evolutionary learning to the *a priori* domain of God and thereby the derivation of knowledge therefrom. The result is the problem of heteronomy. It partitions the moral domain of the *a priori* from the material domain of the *a posteriori*. Without realizing these foundational *problematique* of mainstream economics and finance and of the entire generality and details of the world-system, the carriage of Islamic economics within such axioms has severed itself from the true Islamic epistemic roots, which is the Islamic methodological worldview.

The *Qur'an* clearly differentiates the dialectical befriending nature of Truth from Falsehood. The *Qur'an* (21:92) declares regarding the brotherhood of Truth: "Verily, this Brotherhood of yours is a single Brotherhood, and I am your Lord and Cherisher: therefore serve Me (and no other)." Regarding the brotherhood of Satan with its false attitude of human conflict, the *Qur'an* (4:119–120) declares:

I will mislead them, and I will create in them false desires; I will order them to slit the ears of cattle, and to deface the 'fair' nature created by God! Whoever, forsaking God, takes Satan for a friend, hath of a surety suffered a loss that is manifest. Satan makes them promises and creates in them false desires; but Satan's promises are nothing but deception.

The true nature of Islamic economic and financial studies

The above arguments give an illustrative example, though not meant to be exhaustively detailed, that can be objectively launched against the present state of Islamic economics and finance. Yet the field of Islamic economics and finance bears a revolutionary mastery in the world of learning. This intellection must be pursued as the final ideal of moral reconstruction in this field.

This leads to a critical review. We reiterate here the nature of Islamic economic and financial studies in a different light in reference to the *Qur'an* and the *Sunnah* as the basis of its epistemology. By Islamic epistemology we mean the epistemology of organic unity of divine knowledge in relation to the schemes of issues of the world-system, particularized here to economics and finance. The same analytical design holds true for the most general nature of the world-system by virtue of the methodological worldview of Islamic universality and uniqueness.

We therefore need to examine the nature of Islamic economics as an interdisciplinary paradigm that explains interaction over the domains of moral guidance, divine law, and their impulses in the issues of world-systems. These elements are evolved according to discursive impulses and learning processes. Such interactive and integrative learning systems governed by evolutionary learning *processes* have remained outside mainstream economic analysis and mainstream economic doctrine, yet not the epistemological worldview of unity of knowledge.

The *fiqh* (juridical interpretation) tradition has succumbed to this catching-up fervour in the midst of capitalist globalization and the resulting inadequate human resource development. These problems today influence Islamic institutions and their mainstream intellection. Yet this is not the true nature of Islamic intellection and its methodological implementation according to the Islamic worldview of consilience in the revolutionary world of learning.

The substantive question of interaction, integration, and creative evolution by learning between diverse issues of embedded social, economic, and scientific systems in accordance with the epistemology of oneness of God, equivalently the unity of divine knowledge, which is particular to the Islamic worldview, is fundamental in understanding the nature and logic of economic behaviour and Islamic transformation in embedded systems with endogenous variables of circular causation relations. Such a knowledge-centred process model transcends the level of the individual, family and shareholders into society, markets, stakeholders, institutions and the global order (Choudhury, Umar, & Al-Ghamdi 2003). Such a discursive society was exalted by Foucault (1992).

Without the Islamic episteme spearheading Islamic economic, financial and social investigations, and thereby the delineation and analysis of the emergent problems, Islamic reasoning cannot emerge regarding the abolition of interest rate, money, finance, and real economy; and institutional, social and Islamic global orders. Consequently, the mainstream model of money and macroeconomic dynamics will continue to prevail. Yet the Islamic and mainstream approaches of economics and finance are fundamentally different. On this issue see Oslington (1995) for a criticism of Ghazzanfar and Islahi's (1990) mainstream historical orientation of the Islamic scholastic scholars, notably Imam Ghazali. In none of these studies has there been any attempt to critically study the history of economic thought and of Islamic economic thought from the *Qur'anic* point of view vis-à-vis *Tawhid*, its methodology, and impact on the moral construction of the economic and financial world-system.

Instead, the Islamic world-system is truly established and its analytics constructed on the basis of the Islamic worldview as unity of divine knowledge spanning inter- and intra-systems that continuously interact, integrate, and evolve. They thus learn in concert with the existential phenomenon of discourse, participation, and paired organic linkages. These properties of the learning processes realize the worldview of unity of the divine law in relation to the unified nature of variables and issues in the economic and financial multi-causal world-systems. The model of such multi-causal Islamic induced world-system in unity of knowledge was explained in detail in Chapter 5.

The principle of pervasive complementarities as the explanatory form of inter-causal participation and organic unity of knowledge initiates the discursive *tasbih–shura* process of evolutionary learning through the dynamics of the *shuratic* process. Such elements and their characteristics are discovered by the application of the circular causation model. The underlying inter-causal relations between the selected variables explain the formulation and application of the functional or engineering ontology (Maxwell 1962). Functional ontologies are explanatory functions derived from the Islamic *methodology* of consilience in unity of knowledge. This is the way to extract the implications of the paired universe of pervasive interaction, integration, and evolutionary learning in unity of knowledge, as explained in previous chapters.

How to get to the Islamic methodological formulation from the mainstream economic approach

First, education along the lines of the Islamic epistemology of global change, with particular emphasis placed on the dynamics of economics and finance, must instil such awareness and education at the intellectual and practitioning levels. Specifically, we will deal with the theme of money, finance, and real economy later on in this book, as a major example of the concept and application of the Islamic methodological worldview applied by using the circular causation model derived from the Islamic methodological worldview. The Research and Development sections of Islamic banks around the world, in concert with seats of higher education in the

Muslim world ought to spearhead such discourses under the right kind of Islamic intellectual and scientific leadership with the correct form of human resource development along the lines of the Islamic methodological, analytical, and applied worldview with critical examination of the comparative studies both in mainstream and in existing Islamic economic and finance studies. Such original and revolutionary approaches do not exist yet. Yet they are of the utmost importance for the world of learning.[1]

Second, a conglomerate of pilot projects can be established, such as diversity of processes interrelating primary goods with agrarian and petroleum production. Such interfaced goods would be developed and traded internationally. In international trade, the gold standard will become the basis of inter-communal trade agreement in the Muslim World. The Islamic Development Bank (IDB) should establish this pilot mechanism on the basis of maintaining the principle of 100 per cent reserve requirement monetary system between the central bank and the Islamic banks in the trading countries (Choudhury 1997). The pilot project can be subsequently expanded to include many traded items of similar kinds of diversified goods. We will have occasion to explain the nature of the 100 per cent reserve requirement monetary system in the macroeconomic part of this book.

There may be a special need to protect such expanding segmented markets of goods, services, and financial instruments. This can be done by targeting specific markets for trade promotion in goods and services that can be generated in the pilot project and traded by the 100 per cent reserve requirement monetary system with the gold standard (Choudhury & Hoque 2004).

A value-contract will be established between the central bank and the commercial bank on holding a residual (small) amount of gold, which IDB will guarantee. This gold stock will support the 'residual' amount of unmobilized currency (say the IDB Dinar in the gold standard) that may remain unused after a maximum quantity of money is mobilized into the real sector (i.e. trade and development) by means of Islamic financial instruments. This 'residual' amount of the IDB Dinar needs to be backed up by a quantity of gold that will be sufficient to assign value to the unit of currency in circulation in the real economy (i.e. resources mobilized in market exchange, trade and development).

Consequently, the quantity of gold required for shoring up the value of currency in circulation will be small as resource mobilization remains inversely proportional to the quantity of gold required to shore up the residual un-mobilized resource. The amount of gold held in the central bank for shoring up the value of residual unmobilized monetary resource would thus be inversely related to the speed and quantity of finances mobilized into the real economy. On the structure of 100 per cent reserve requirement monetary system see Choudhury (2004b). On the gold standard respecting 'residual' quantity of gold required to lubricate trade and development see Mydin (2004) and Mydin and Larbani (2004). While these explanations may be too advanced for the student reader, the dynamics underlying them in respect of the Islamic methodological worldview will be explained in details in the macroeconomics part of this book.

EXAMPLE 6.1

A small amount of gold is required to maintain the value of monetary circulation in the real economy

Here is a formal explanation of the gold-backing or real asset-backing of currency as an essential choice of prescribed medium in Islamic economics and finance kept in active in circulation in relation to the real economy.

Let total of monetary resources $R = Rc + Re$;
 Rc: unmobilized and thus with central bank;
 Re: mobilized into the real economy.
Let G: quantity of Gold required for shoring the total monetary resource (stock Rc and flow Re).

Let the Central Bank set $R/G = a$, a money/gold ratio. If all money is measured in terms of gold standard, then $a = 1$.

Now, $d(R/G) = 0 = d(Rc/G) + d(Re/G)$, implying that change in the gold-value of money in reserve is cancelled by the change in the gold-value of money in circulation. In other words, the higher the need for the gold-value of money in circulation, the less the need to hold an equivalent gold-value of money with the central bank, and vice-versa.

Furthermore, $[d(Rc/G)]/(Rc/G) = [d(a\text{-}Re/G)]/(a\text{-}Re/G)$. Therefore the monetary elasticity coefficients $(\varepsilon(.))$ between the central bank holding and circulation yield, $\varepsilon(Rc/G) = \varepsilon(a\text{-}Re/G)$, an inverse relationship in terms of the gold-standard of monetary valuation. Thus decreasing amounts of gold are required for shoring the money in circulation. Figure 6.2 explains this case on the two sides of G affecting Rc and Re.

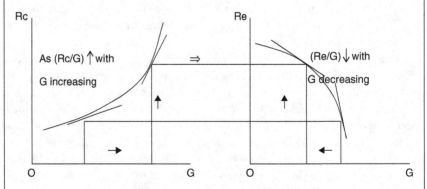

FIGURE 6.2 Central Bank relations on shoring currency in circulation

The opposite signs of elasticity coefficients further establish the fact on the smaller scale of gold to shore up Rc in terms of the gold standard as Re increases and vice-versa. Thus the response to an increase in gold to shore up the value of Re mobilized in the real economy is negligible when full mobilization of R is realized into the real economy, with a $= 1$ in this case.

Obviously, the above result is true also in the case of partial mobilization of monetary resources into the real economy with a >1. The amount of G remains between zero and a small amount with the central bank under condition of full to partial mobilization of monetary resources in the real economy. With a further impact of knowledge, technology and innovation in financial resource mobilization the curves as shown will shift rightwards for (Rc,G) and upwards for (Re,G). One such case is the joint mobilization of financial resources by the pooled fund idea. This is formalized below. The converse is also true.

An Islamic epistemological application to a unified Islamic financing portfolio: Pooled Fund Model

The Islamic epistemology of unity of knowledge can be applied to the construction of a complementary portfolio of Islamic financing instruments. We call it the Pooled Fund (PF) *vis-à-vis* the amounts floating in Islamic financing instruments (M_i); i $=$ *mudarabah, musharakah, murabaha, ijara, sukuk,* foreign trade financing, *bay-muajjal,* and various other secondary participatory financing instruments mobilizing funds across the real economy, with both secondary portfolio diversification and production diversification in the real economy in respect of serving the international trade and development goal for the benefit of the *ummah* and otherwise. The PF negates the treatment of Islamic financing instruments as isolated and differentiated ones. We formalize the PF as follows:

$$PF = \{M_i\}_i, \text{ with } M_i \leftrightarrow M_j; M_i \geq M_i\star \tag{6.1}$$

$M_i\star$ are critical minimum values for retention in its instrument; $i,j = 1,2,..,n$ number of participatory instruments that can be complemented in the PF.

M_i funds are required to be complemented together in order to diversify PF. This would serve a number of financing benefits. The risk and production in relation to the real economy financing will be effectively diversified. The medium to attain such diversifications can be realized by means of Foreign Trade Financing (FTF) in relation to economic development for product diversification in the real sector in agreement with the *Shari'ah*.

In this way, each M_i and the PF ensemble is maintained by inter-flow of returns between FTF and PF through the medium of production (Q) and unit-risk diversification (Risk/Q). Production and unit-risk diversifications are further spread across various sectors (s $= 1,2,..,S$) and projects, k $= 1,2,...K_s$. Hence, $Q = \{Q_s\}$; $Risk/Q = \{(Risk/Q)_s\}$. The diversification bundle (D) is the tuple of production (return) and unit-risk diversification, that is, $D = \{Q_s, (Risk/Q)_s\}$. In the more diversified form of sectors by projects the diversification bundle would be $D = \{Q_{ks}, (Risk/Q)_{ks}\}$; $k=1,2,..,K; s=1,2,..,S$.

The characteristic interrelations between the participatory variables are shown by

$$PF = \{M_i \leftrightarrow M_j\} \leftrightarrow D = \{Q_s, (Risk/Q)_s\} \tag{6.2}$$

EXERCISE 6.2

Put the expression (6.2) in its matrix form with projects by sectors in the real economy conformable to the *Shari'ah*.

$$PF = \{M_i \leftrightarrow M_j\}_{ks} \leftrightarrow D = \{Q, (Risk/Q)\}_{ks} \tag{6.3}$$

Now use the Islamic functional ontology (function based methodologically on a given epistemology) to explain the (k,s)-matrix construction in the Islamic methodological context.

Stakeholding and shareholding in the PF for purposes of risk and production diversifications

Shares in unit amount (S_{PF}) are sold revolving around PF for the purpose of achieving expression (6.2). S_{PF} is spread over PF without it being necessary to identify which particular S_{PF} is locked into specific instruments. S_{PF} as financial resources are allowed to flow freely across the instruments that are complemented in PF for the purpose of realizing the diversification bundle denoted by D so as to sustain the relationship shown in expression (6.2).

The interactive, integrative, and evolutionary interrelations of the Islamic methodological genre acting by circular causation between all the variables are denoted by:

$$S_{PF} \leftrightarrow PF \leftrightarrow D; \text{ that is}$$

$$S_{PF} \leftrightarrow \{M_i \leftrightarrow M_j\} \leftrightarrow \{Q_s, (Risk/Q)_s\} \tag{6.4}$$

Production, development and innovation effects in expression (6.2) are shown by the value imputation of a qualitative θ-variable, which is shown to acquire ordinal values in respect of the other variables of the system of interrelations. Expression (6.4) is now written in its θ-induced form as follows:

$$\theta \leftrightarrow [S_{PF} \leftrightarrow \{M_i \leftrightarrow M_j\} \leftrightarrow \{Q_s, (Risk/Q)_s\}][\theta]. \tag{6.5}$$

That is, 'θ', which is derived from Islamic epistemological roots, influences all the variables uniquely as the enabling and responding variable to put the FTF system in its interactive, integrative, and creative dynamics. Because of this primal influence of the θ-variable on all the variables by virtue of the principle of pervasive complementarities and choices in the context of *maqasid al-shari'ah*, the induced consequences acquire an ethical dimension. This ethical dimension comprises the actualization of sustainable development and growth with equitable distribution of resources across diverse interlinked economic sectors. The social consequence is also poverty alleviation by developing microenterprises and activating medium and small enterprises (MSMEs); realizing productivity and production and risk diversifications as gains to diversify the economy; and increased participation in the economy induced by ethical value. See below for further explanation regarding sectoral linkages. In this way, the resulting well-being criterion becomes a conceptual and empirical measure of degrees of complementarities between the variables. This is the empirical manifestation of the Islamic methodological application at work in the midst of ethical construction of the Islamic financing instruments to realize economic and social complementarities by virtue of linkages as organic unity of knowledge and knowledge-induced artefacts.

Thus the episteme underlying θ-value is in the learning processes generated by it and its induction of the variables of the entire system of relation defined by expression (6.4). Such a systemic interrelationship conveys the meaning of organic unity between the different parts of the total system of variables-specific interrelations. The interrelations are implied by $\leftrightarrow$.

Consequently, the origin of such a system of organic unity as a learning system of interrelations must epistemologically arise in reference to a certain methodological foundation that fundamentally defines the knowledge-induced function of organic unity. The underlying epistemological foundation of the complementary relations of the selected *maqasid al-shari'ah* choices is the divine law of unity of knowledge. *Tawhid* as the unitary law maps on to the world-system of 'everything' in the framework of unity of knowledge and knowledge-induced unified systems. We denote the epistemological foundation of *Tawhid* in terms of its fundamental knowledge base, namely the *Qur'an*, the *Sunnah*, and the discourse of the learned ones through the medium of the *shura* and *ijtihad* (practice of deducing knowledge from the epistemological sources).

We denote this foundational basis of θ-value by $\Omega = (Q,S)$: Q as the knowledge universe of the *Qur'an*; S as the ontological mapping of the *Sunnah* on to the world-system. That is, $\theta \in [\Omega = (Q,S)]$, as this formulation was explained in the earlier chapters. Expression (6.5) is now extended to its comprehensive primal form:

$$[\Omega = (Q,S)] \rightarrow \theta \leftrightarrow [S_{PF} \leftrightarrow \{M_i \leftrightarrow M_j\} \leftrightarrow \{Q_s, (Risk/Q)_s\}][\theta]. \tag{6.6}$$

In the circular causation system (6.6) of learning interrelations between the variables, every variable including θ-variable is endogenously interrelated. The exception is $[\Omega = (Q,S)]$, which remains primal, and hence exogenous in defining the rest of the relations. This is the picture of the small-scale universe, as of a project such as FTF. But if the objective of any project is extended with its ultimate objective and purpose of the *Shari'ah* (*maqasid al-shari'ah*) to comprehend the beginning until the end of worldly experiences, then the Closure (see earlier chapters) is created by the very large system of learning interrelations extending up to the Great Event of the Hereafter (*Akhira*). We denote this kind of completion of expression (6.6) by the Closure as:

$$[\Omega = (Q,S)] \rightarrow [\theta \leftrightarrow [S_{PF} \leftrightarrow \{M_i \leftrightarrow M_j\} \leftrightarrow \{Q_s, (Risk/Q)_s\}][\theta]] \leftrightarrow$$
$$\text{repeat the sequence } [..] \text{ in continuum until} \leftrightarrow [\Omega = (Q,S)]. \qquad (6.7)$$

In this form of the complete learning system in unity of knowledge and its induced world-system generated by $[\Omega = (Q,S)]$ through θ, the *maqasid al-shari'ah* becomes (θ) – derived from $[\Omega = (Q,S)]$. The *maqasid al-shari'ah* thereby actualizes the world-system. We note that with Mq denoting *maqasid al-shari'ah*, $Mq \subset (Q,S)$ and $\theta \in (Q,S) \Rightarrow \theta \in Mq$.

$$[\theta \in [\Omega = (Q,S)] \leftrightarrow [S_{PF} \leftrightarrow \{M_i \leftrightarrow M_j\} \leftrightarrow \{Q_s, (Risk/Q)_s\}][\theta]] \qquad (6.8)$$

Conversely, the pursuit of the PF and D with all forms of complementarities in them, as the Islamic economic and financial sub-system of the grand world-system is attainable through the learning experience, regenerates new means and learning through fresh evolutionary θ-values. Hence, unity of knowledge embodied in the *maqasid al-shari'ah*, $\{\theta\}$, is regenerated through the evolutionary learning processes in unity of knowledge. This process of unity of knowledge and its social reconstruction of the world-system never ends until the end of worldly time; that is at the Great Event of the Hereafter (*Akhira*). The learning process in unity of knowledge arising from $[\Omega = (Q,S)]$ and closing on itself through the learning processes of the finite world-system is referred to in the *Qur'an* as the learning mediums of *shura* and *ijtihad*.

Underlying the system of interrelations given by (6.4) are the roles played by the institutions. These comprise the private sector further divided between the urban and rural sectors in order to actualize the developmental effects and social consequences on poverty alleviation. Other categories of sectoral diversification would be the development of non-banking institutions like finance houses, corporations interrelated with microenterprises, small and medium enterprises (MSMEs), and industrial sectors and various other projects according to the context of *maqasid al-shari'ah*. The public sector comprises the government, central bank, Islamic banks, development banks, and organizations. The stakeholders will be both national and international, as in terms of integration within the *ummah* and otherwise. These categories will all be sources of participatory holdings and projects for embedding economics, financial, and social results. The Islamic banks ought to act as the brains of such an idea and generate the synergistic relations as pointed out in (6.4).

The circular causation system of the complete system of interrelations given by expression (6.8) is shown in Figure 6.3.

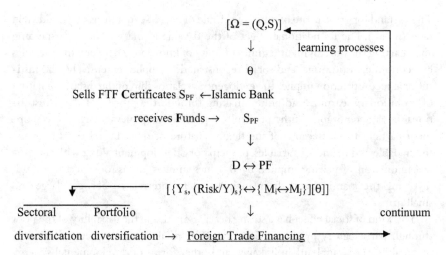

FIGURE 6.3 Circular flow of resources for sustaining FTF in the economic development process

---

EXERCISE 6.3

1. Reformulate expression (6.8) in terms of projects by sectors in matrix form as in Exercise 6.1.
2. Explain the Islamic ontology underlying the interaction, integration, and evolutionary learning characteristics of unified systems in terms of PF and D as explained.

Foreign Trade Financing Certificate (FTFC) in the PF-formalism

Why is the above formalism particularly attractive for FTFC? Although the mechanism and arguments in favour of Islamic financing is true of any particular tradable instrument replacing interest rates, it has a particular appeal for FTFC. Tradability under FTF is of the nature of merchandise, capital, and contracts supported by real-assets. Consequently, the rates of return on FTF are short-term, fairly risk-free yield rates (r_f). This prospect of the yield rates causes short-term risk-free effects on the other variables. When further induced by θ-values the real economy advances with production and risk diversifications. Circular causation is generated between r_f and the returns on the other variables according to the same principle of pervasive complementarities between Islamic financing instruments. Thus for example:

$$r_f \leftrightarrow [\{Y_s\uparrow, (Risk/Y)_s\downarrow\} \leftrightarrow \{M_i\uparrow \leftrightarrow M_j\uparrow\}][\theta]] \equiv [\{r_{Ys}\uparrow, r_R\downarrow\} \leftrightarrow \{r_{Mi}\uparrow \leftrightarrow r_{Mj}\uparrow\}][\theta]$$

$$(6.9)$$

The r's stand for growth rate of output (r_{Y_s}), rate of decrease in unit risk (r_R), and yield rates (r_{Mi}, r_{Mj}). The foundational effect of the θ-value as the way of understanding and enacting the development regimes of unity of knowledge between the variables by economic, institutional and social reconstruction, applies extensively. The institutional reconstruction implies the endogenous relationship of the discursive nature of evolutionary learning and policy-making through the process of *shura* (institutionalism) in cognizance of the principle of pervasive complementarities (development participation). Because of the flexible nature of the FTF-relations between the tradable and financing variables, participatory development along with the ethical injunction of pairing implied by θ-values implies a grassroots access towards involving the marginal and the principal traders, interrelated between large and small firms.

This kind of social effect has a strong bearing on raising the capability of the poor through participatory productive activities. The result then is poverty alleviation. Sectoral linkages, rural–urban linkages, and other forms of developmental synergy are enhanced for realizing micro–macro unified complementarities in participatory development planning. Microenterprises and small and medium businesses prosper alongside large corporations that complement each other. A dynamic grassroots interactive and integrative development regime is promoted with endogenous technological induction through the organic evolutionary learning processes of systemic pairing. Pairing as cause and effect that are circularly established in the learning processes of participatory development implies strong endogeneity of unity of knowledge (θ) and unity of the system comprising FTF in relation to the real economy along with the proper direction of institutional strategic and policy variables.

Conclusion

After seventy years of Islamic economics and finance and thirty years since the inception of Islamic banks, there remains a great gap in true Islamic intellection in the scholarly field that Islamic economics and finance can potentially give to the world. Thus far, it is only the goals of capital formation, organizational survival by competition in the capitalist globalization scene, profit-making in an intensifying global financial competition, and the protection and maximization of shareholders' wealth by Islamic banks that have activated the Islamic financing institutions and development organizations. The study of Islamic economics and finance has thus remained a 'normal' science replicating mainstream economics and finance. Contrary to this, what Islamic economics and finance truly ought to be is a 'scientific revolution' (Kuhn 1970). Such a contribution would bestow something new and challenging to the world of learning as a whole by concept, methodology, and applications. This emergent field would also bestow well-being on all.

Likewise, on the academic side, the absence of the epistemological worldview in Islamic economics and finance has failed to treat the study of endogenous ethics and economics as a substantive scientific theme (Edel 1970) of Islamic economics and finance. Such a failure has been due to the subservience of vision and intellect to mainstream rationalist thought that is already subject to questioning on the theme of ethics and unity of knowledge and consilience *contra* heteronomy. Consequently, the true intellection of Islamic economics and finance is lost to mainstream rationalist and rationality postulates. The Islamic methodological worldview of unity of knowledge and the knowledge-induced world-system has been increasingly taken away from the Islamic methodological worldview by its mainstream mould of thinking, analytics and applications. The vision, mission, understanding, and use of Islamic economics and financial instruments and Islamic institutions have thus been misplaced. New and fresh directions are required. This is the cardinal foundation of Islam and its uniqueness and universality in the world of intellection and applications.

One can still ask the question: Why is it necessary to invoke the Islamic unity of knowledge and God and the study of the world-system in the plane of socio-scientific inquiry? The answer to this query will be unravelled throughout this book. For the present it may simply be noted that, without God and *Tawhid* in the highest echelons of socio-scientific thought, human inquiry will be forever trapped in the belief of methodological independence and differentiation between the economic and financial interests on the one side and the moral and social well-being on the other. Consequently, neither the conceptual background nor its dissemination in intellection and its practical results would be realized. Such is the moral heteronomous picture regarding the conflict and competition over scarcity over resources between marginalist substitutes. These kinds of postulates of economic rationality make up the core axioms of mainstream economics. Contrarily, the reality of evolutionary learning in the Islamic context of organic pairing, distributive sharing, and complementarities offers the possibility of abundance, and thus the emergence of embedded economic and moral possibilities.[2]

In this chapter the important areas to focus upon (as mentioned in Chapter 1) are:

1. The formulation of the Islamic economic model
2. Islamic participatory instruments and their ethical dimensions

The teacher will be required to extract the essential elements of these topics, though the chapter discusses many issues of Islamic economics and finance.

Notes

1 Thomas Kuhn (1970), the historiographer of science, writes regarding the nature of scientific revolution, on which the Islamic methodological worldview shares: "… scientific revolutions are here taken to be those non-cumulative developmental episodes in which an older paradigm is replaced in whole or in part by an incompatible new one." In our present times, the birth of a new, more inclusive and extant, meaningful and beneficial way of looking at science and the world-system in terms of an organic and holistic model

rests on the emergence of a new epistemology. Albert Einstein (1954), writing to his friend Niels Bohr, remarked that there cannot be science without epistemology. Likewise, there cannot be a new science without a new epistemology. Indeed it appears that the intellectual vision of the new millennium is essentially a search for and discovery of this new epistemology. But when any particular discipline is awakened by the touch of a new epistemology, all other disciplines are too. This was the way that economics was touched by the mathematical novelty of the eighteenth-century Enlightenment.

2 *Qur'an* (17:20): "Of the bounties of thy Lord We bestow freely on all – these as well as those: The bounties of Thy Lord are not closed (to anyone)."

References

Asad, M. (1987). *This Law of Ours*, Gibraltar: Dar Al-Andalus.

Bank Indonesia. (2010). *Indonesian Islamic Bank Outlook 2009*, Jakarta, Indonesia: Islamic Banking Directorate.

Bank Negara Malaysia. (2014). Annual report. Available at: www.bnm.gov.my/index.php?ch=en_publication_catalogue&pg=en_publication_msb&eId=box1&mth=1&yr=2011&lang=en

Choudhury, M.A. (1997). *Money in Islam*, London: Routledge.

Choudhury, M.A. (1998). *Studies in Islamic Social Sciences*, London: Macmillan.

Choudhury, M.A. (1999). Methodological conclusion, *Comparative Economic Theory: Occidental and Islamic Perspectives*, Chapter 21, Norwell, MA: Kluwer Academic Publishers.

Choudhury, M.A. (2004a). *The Islamic World-System: A Study in Polity-Market Interaction*, London: Routledge.

Choudhury, M.A. (2004b). Islamic political economy, *Review of Islamic Economics*, 13(1).

Choudhury, M.A. & Hoque, M.Z. (2004). *An Advanced Exposition in Islamic Economics and Finance*, Lewiston, NY: Edwin Mellen Press.

Choudhury, M.A., Umar, Y., & Al-Ghamdi, M. (2003). *Ummatic* globalization versus neoclassical capitalist globalization, *Review of Islamic Economics*, 12(1): 5–45.

Edel, A. (1970 reprint). Science and the structure of ethics, in *Foundations of the Unity of Science*, eds. Neurath, O., Carnap. R., & Morris, C., 2(1–9), pp. 273–378, Chicago, IL: The University of Chicago Press.

Einstein, A. (1954). Considerations on the universe as a whole, in *Relativity: The Special and the General Theory*, trans. R.W. Lawson, London: Methuen.

Foucault, M. (1972). *The Archeology of Knowledge and the Discourse on Language*, trans. Sheridan, A.M., New York: Harper Torchbooks.

Ghazzanfar, S.M. & Islahi, A.Z. (1990). Economic thought of an Arab Scholastic: Abu Hamid al-Ghazali, *History of Political Economy*, 22(2): 381–403. Reprinted in S.M. Ghazzanfar, ed. (2003). Medieval Islamic economic thought: Filling the "Great Gap", *European Economics*, pp. 23–44, London: Routledge.

Gruber, T.R. (1993). A translation approach to portable ontologies, *Knowledge Acquisition*, 5(2): 199–200.

Heidegger, M. (1988). *The Basic Problems of Phenomenology*, trans. Hofstadter, A., Bloomington, IN: Indiana University Press.

Islamic Bank Bangladesh. (2017). *Annual Report 2007*, Dhaka, Bangladesh: Islamic Bank Bangladesh (IBBL).

Kuhn, T.S. (1970). *The Structure of Scientific Revolution*, Chicago, IL: University of Chicago Press.

Maxwell, G. (1962). The ontological status of theoretical entities, in *Minnesota Studies in the Philosophy of Science, Vol. II: Scientific Explanation, Space and Time*, eds. Feigl, H. & Maxwell, G., pp. 3–27, Minneapolis, MN: University of Minnesota Press.

Mydin, A.K. (2004). *The Theft of Nations*, Kuala Lumpur, Malaysia: Pelanduk.

Mydin, A.K. & Larbani, M. (2004). The gold dinar: The next component in Islamic economics, banking and finance, *Review of Islamic Economics*, 8(1): 5–34.

Oslington, P. (1995). Economic thought and religious thought: A comment on Ghazzanfar and Islahi. *History of Political Economy*, 27(4): 781–5. Reprinted in S.M. Ghazzanfar ed. (2003).

7

THE DUAL THEORIES OF CONSUMER BEHAVIOUR AND MARKETS

LEARNING OBJECTIVES

This chapter intends to provide the students with:

- a clear portrait of the consumer behaviour that Islam expects from its followers
- an evaluation of the assumptions made in the conventional theory of consumer behaviour, like consumer sovereignty, rationality, selfish attitude and utility maximization, etc.
- a critical review of supply and demand, market equilibrium and the concepts of scarcity of resources and multiplicity of wants.

In the previous chapters the foundational topics of Islamic methodology and some of the methods and formulations arising from it were laid down in terms of the Islamic theory of knowledge. This theory was laid down in terms of first, ontology: the theory of existence where the primal origin of knowledge is the *Qur'an* and its implementation through the *Sunnah*. Second, there is epistemology: the theory of knowledge. In Islamic intellection, epistemology is derived from the *Qur'an* and the *Sunnah* in terms of the cardinal law of *Tawhid*. It is logical for the purpose and establishment of an abiding theory of Islamic economics, and, broadly, of Islamic socio-scientific intellection utilizing the foundational topics. The analytical results arising from these methodological foundations will then be carried over into quantitative perspectives. This last part of the comprehensive theory of Islamic economics is referred to as the unravelling element of consciousness. In scientific language it is referred to as phenomenology.

The all-encompassing robust theory of any scientific endeavour, and thereby of Islamic economics, should establish the continuity of inter-variable relations by circular cause and effect across a variety of specific problems. In Islamic economics, therefore, we invoke the study of analytical economics from the perspective of the Islamic theory of moral, ethical, and material valuation for the common good of all. The *Qur'an* is clear on such an analytical formulation, but which the *Qur'anic* exegesis must extract and develop. There is, first, the Belief in *Tawhid* as the Purity of God (*Allah*) as the One. Second, there is the derivation of *Tawhid* as Law. This explains the world-system (*a'lameen*) in terms of the nexus of unity of things caused and continued by extension of the unity of knowledge affecting the organic connectivity, continuity, and extendibility of the attributes of organic relational unity in and across systems.

The *Qur'an* (36:36) deepens human intellection in the principle of organic pairing. The multi-systemic connectivity by means of the organic complementarities, also meaning participative systems represented by their multi-entities and variables, can be derived by the exegesis of the following *Qur'anic* verses. The *Qur'an* (13:1–5) points out the embedded moral and material reality of the divine law in terms of multi-systems of interrelations with their inter-causal multivariates signifying the Islamic unity of knowledge by organic causality. On dimensions of reflection that ignite extended human intellection and that enter the study of economics and socio-scientific systems, there is the *Qur'anic* verse (45:36): "All praise belongs to God, the Lord of the heavens and the Lord of the earth, Lord of all the worlds." For the multi-system and multi-stage denoted by their variables as observations embedded in moral actualization, there is a verse of the *Qur'an* (81:15–21) raising the consciousness of the morally embedded material reality. Then there is a further deepening realization of the worshipping world that consciously recognizes the oneness of God as conscious worship (*tasbih*) in the scheme and order of all things (*Qur'an* 59:24): "Whatever is in the heavens and the earth, do declare His Praises and Glory: and He is the Exalted in Might, the Wise." Over all these attributes of the nature of existence is the intrinsic learning property of all things, animate or inanimate, caused by the process of organic pairing as well as by human endeavours to learn and discover the truth.

The *Qur'an* says in this regard in many verses, including the following:

> … see in the creation of the Most Merciful any inconsistency. So return [your] vision [to the sky]; do you see any breaks?
>
> *67:2–3*

> Have they not considered how God originates creation and then repeats it? Indeed that, for God, is easy.
>
> *29:19*

> Indeed, in the creation of the heavens and earth, and the alternation of the night and the day, and the [great] ships which sail through the sea with that which benefits people, and what God has sent down from the heavens of rain, giving life thereby to the earth after its lifelessness and dispersing therein every [kind of] moving creature, and [His] directing of the winds and the

clouds controlled between the heaven and the earth are signs for a people who use reason.

(2:164)

And how many a sign within the heavens and earth do they pass over while they, therefrom, are turning away.

(12:105)

Do they not contemplate within themselves? God has not created the heavens and the earth and what is between them except in truth and for a specified term. And indeed, many of the people, in [the matter of] the meeting with their Lord, are disbelievers.

(30:8)

Or were they created by nothing, or were they the creators [of themselves]? Or did they create the heavens and the earth? Rather, they are not certain.

(52:35–36)

Indeed, We created man from a sperm-drop mixture that We may try him; and We made him hearing and seeing.

(76:2)

These verses and many more of their kind point out the properties of the essential building blocks of the Islamic theory of unity of knowledge that governs over all morally embedded constructs of mind-matter reality. The unity of the world-system in its generality and particulars is then pointed out as the unique truth by the properties of:

1. Organic pairing in unity of knowledge. This is explained by the discursive process of discovering and reconstructing the mind–matter reality along the precept of pervasive complementarities, as also participation between all the good things of life – the *maqasid*-choices. The process in diversity as the principle of *interaction* leads to convergence as the principle of *integration*.
2. The principles of *interaction* leading to *integration* are followed by continuity and extendibility across systems represented by their multivariates. This marks the principle of evolutionary learning.
3. Thus the *interaction, integration, and evolutionary learning process* (IIE) marks out the continuous and extended inter-causal properties of the Islamic methodology of incessant organic learning in unity of being and becoming of the phenomenological essence of mind and matter occurring in 'pairs'.
4. The phenomenological attribute, that is, scientific consciousness combines conception with application, quantitative or discursive, to lead into an evaluative stage of completion followed by regeneration of the whole evolutionary process inter-temporally across processes, and within processes cross-sectionally or over a given period of time.

It was proved in the previous chapters that the above derived properties of the Islamic methodological worldview (as the only possible foundation of all Islamic disciplines including economics and finance, science and society) leads into the formulation of a unique and universal formalism arising from the inner properties of *Tawhid* as law applied to systemic study. We recapitulate it, a good deal of detail having been given earlier.

First, we note the following description of the multivariate construct in the embedded field of the divine law of unity and its induction of materiality. We also note, in the following summary representation (Figure 7.1), the recursive interrelations between ontology, epistemology, and phenomenology as the scientific properties of the nature of the divine law of unity of knowledge acting in material cognates. Also inherent in this representation is the process-oriented nature of Islamized disciplines of knowledge, including Islamic economics.

Step 4 of Figure 7.1 is formalized as *evaluation* of the social well-being function, $W(\mathbf{x}(\theta))$, which measures the degree of complementarities between the selected variables $\mathbf{x}(\theta)$ that are embedded in the moral consciousness denoted by 'θ' derived from the primal ontology of Islamic unity of knowledge. This law was denoted by (Ω,S). These symbols were explained in the previous chapters.

The recursive or continuous re-emergence of the evolutionary learning process in unity of knowledge is shown by the circular causal paths moving to its terminal, equilibrium, and optimal point only in the Hereafter and at the very Beginning,[1] and nowhere else along the IIE-learning processes spanning knowledge, space, and time. The Hereafter as the Great Event in the *Qur'an* (*surah* 78) equates this End as the only other point of perfect completion besides the Islamic Beginning. There is no other such point in any issue and problem of the entire world-system. Thereby, the theory of Islamic economics, and likewise all such specific studies, have no optimality and steady-state equilibrium; only 'expectational' evolutionary learning equilibriums remain. Yet the attainment of any event within the universal

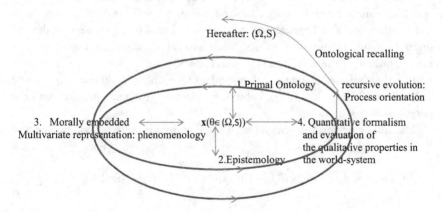

FIGURE 7.1 Circular interconnectivity (complementarities) through recursive evolutionary evaluation

history of $[(\Omega,S) \rightarrow \text{World-system} \rightarrow (\Omega,S)]$ must have a *closure* for completion of a learning process across IIE-processes. On the other hand there is the final *Closure*, which is the ultimate point of the learning world-system in the Hereafter. All other closures within the world-system are evolutionary ones of the punctuated kinds (Grandmont 1989). In the physical and social sciences such non-convergent, continuously evolutionary biological equilibriums are of recent discovery (Hull 1988; Thurow 1983; Burstein 1991).

The inter-causality between the representative variables of the systems experiencing interaction, integration, and evolutionary learning processes (IIE) is explained by the recursive gyration of Figure 7.1. Such inter-causality is evaluated by what we have referred to before, as the evaluation of the social well-being function, subject to circular causation relations. Evaluation includes estimation followed by simulations. This complete quantitative formalism is included in step 4 of Figure 7.1 and its evolutionary continuity across the dimensions of knowledge, space, and time marking the evolutionary learning processes.

We write the above phenomenological nature of socio-scientific thought according to the *Qur'an* in the following formalism. It is written down here once again as in the previous chapters:

Evaluate $W(x(\theta))$ (7.1)

Subject to $x_i(\theta) = f_i(\mathbf{x}_j(\theta));$ $\{\theta\} \in (\Omega,S);$ $\theta = \lim_{\text{interaction,integration}}\{\theta\}$ (7.2)

$i,j; i \neq j = 1,2,3,\ldots$

$\mathbf{x}_j(\theta)$ denotes the vector of variables excluding the interrelated variable $x_i(\theta)$ by way of testing the degree of complementarities between all the variables. The degrees of inter-variable complementarities are denoted by the signs of the estimated coefficients in the system of circular causal relations denoted by expression (7.2).

We have noted earlier that the social well-being function given by the expression (7.2) cannot be empirically evaluated. This is because we do not have observation values for $W(.)$. For such values of the social well-being we need to depend on ordinal assignment of θ-values. Such ordinal θ-values are computed pro rata according to the $\mathbf{x}(\theta)$ observations. A specific $\mathbf{x}(\theta)$ observation is fixed, say $\mathbf{x}^\star(\theta = 10)$ is selected along the column values for each of the different columns of $\mathbf{x}(\theta)$-values. Then the rest of the column θ-values are generated pro rata with the corresponding $\mathbf{x}(\theta)$-values.

The following formula can be used for computing the final computation of θ-values:

θ_{ic} corresponding to $\{x_i(\theta_i)_c = [\theta^\star \text{ (say} = 10)].(x_i(\theta_i)/x^\star(\theta=10))\}_{\text{given columns, } c}$ (7.3)

$\theta_i = [\Sigma_c \theta_{ic}]/\#c, i=1,2,3,\ldots$ (7.4)

by observations over all columns to generate the final average column of θ_i-values.

The table of complete vector values (bold notations) would now appear as follows:

$$\boxed{\mathbf{x_i}(\theta_1) \quad \theta_i \quad \theta} \tag{7.5}$$

In the process of evaluation by regression relations with the learning coefficients expression (7.5) can be written down as:

$$\theta = F(\mathbf{x}(\theta)) \tag{7.6}$$

Expression (7.6) is a 'similar' function, with expression (7.1) being functions of the same variables and explaining the phenomenon of unity of knowledge. This derivation also means that, because of the continuity and non-zero property of the well-being function in terms of θ-values, the implicit function theorem of differential calculus will apply to the result in expression (7.6). The estimation and simulation by policy-theoretic changes in the estimated coefficients to generate desired complementarities between the variables and thus improving the estimated values, and which together perform the evaluation of the well-being function, can now be completed by the system comprising expressions (7.2)–(7.6).

The attributes of the Islamic unity of knowledge and its applications now conclusively state that the mainstream economic axioms of optimization and steady-state equilibrium, along with its postulates of scarcity, rational choice, full information, competition, and optimal allocation of resources between competing ends, cannot hold up for the case of Islamic economics, which by its Islamic axiom and attributes of unity of knowledge we refer to as Islamic economics.

The mainstream economic assumptions are all replaced by the postulates of continuously evolutionary learning with interaction and integration in circular causation between the selected variables. The analytical explanation underlying all these inferences arising from the Islamic epistemology, contrary to mainstream rationalist assumptions, was given in the earlier chapters. The present chapter will investigate the imminent differences between the Islamic epistemological approach and the mainstream rationalist approach. Regretfully, the latter has been blindly followed by the existing study of Islamic economics and thus has no socio-scientific novelty to offer to the world of learning as can be discovered in the Islamic methodological worldview of unity of knowledge and its application to the unity of organic relations between systems and their representative variables.

In the case of differentiated systems, especially those characterized by methodological individualism and rational choice axioms of mainstream economics, the same system of evaluation comprising expressions (7.2)–(7.6) would apply. However, the ontologically determined choices would be differentiated from the good choices as recommended by the divine law. Besides, the estimated coefficients will show to be negative or weakly positive showing marginal substitution between the variables and their corresponding entities. Finally, many of the variables, such as technology and innovation, will be exogenous in character. Consequently, the organic evolutionary behaviour will be annulled in the system of inter-variable circular causation.

EXERCISE 7.1

1. Explain in your own words the evaluation method of the social well-being function, subject to circular causation relations given by expressions (7.1)–(7.6).
2. Take the case of continuous reproduction of household income with human capital and innovation as forms of resources in formulating a model of the type (7.1)–(7.6).
3. What is the exogenous and endogenous nature of technological change in equating the seller's revenue with household income in mainstream economics and in Islamic economics?

We will now use the contrasting approaches of Islamic methodology against the mainstream methodology of rational choice on the topic of the theory of consumer choice. We will use the method and models laid out above and in the previous chapters. At the outset we lay down definitions of some terms and concepts that will be used to develop the theory of ethically oriented idea of consumer choice and individual and collective behaviour in Islamic perspectives.

Definitions

Economic choice among complementary 'possibilities' rather than among marginalist 'alternatives'

The ethically/morally embedded vector of variables in the Islamic sense explained in Figure 7.1 forms possibilities rather than alternatives in their state of extensive complementarities rather than marginal substitutes. Even local complements between goods are replaced by extensive complements between the good things of life intra-system followed by extension to inter-systems. The good and bad things cannot form substitutes, nor complements. Allowing for imperfect learning about the nature of goods between good and bad, that is the hybrid, which the *Qur'an* refers to as *mutashabihat* (unclear of *ayat* of *Qur'an*), the role of knowledge-flows derived from the Islamic ontological law through the enabling medium of the *Sunnah* and social discourse, i.e. $\theta \in (\Omega, S)$, soon separates the good and the bad into different baskets. Thereby, with the progress of knowledge of unity of being through the process of discourse the bad is completely removed from the consumption basket. National and *ummah* policies and regulations must then be made to eradicate such 'bads' from the consumption basket.

Examples of the process of removing the bad through a discursive separation in reference to the divine law, as in the case of the *maqasid al-shari'ah*, are avoidance of smoking, eliminating environment degradation, and the gradual avoidance of acts such as temporary marriages (*mutah*), alcohol consumption, and slavery according to the *Qur'anic* law. In the end, when a clear distinction is ascertained between truth and falsehood, good and bad, permissible and forbidden through social discourse, the *Qur'an* then bans the bad. Individuals, communities, nations, and the *ummah* are collectively asked to ban the bad by the force of legislation, regulation, and public policy. These are discursively set by gaining moral consciousness of learning from lesser to higher levels of certainty. The *Qur'an* (2:42) says in this regard: "And cover not Truth with falsehood, nor conceal the Truth when ye know (what it is)." There are many other similar commands and evidences in the *Qur'an*.

Choice in terms of the cost–benefit mechanism in mainstream economics and otherwise

The term 'choice' in Islamic consumer behaviour is therefore not based on the sheer material assessment of cost and benefit (pain and pleasure). For example, this notion is explained by the pleasure of social smoking and drinking, and the pain of losing social friends caused by not indulging in these when the group meets.

Economic wealth is massively increased by smoking, drinking, and pornography. Governments raise heavy tax revenues from the profits of these industries. They claim that these taxes can be recycled for spending in social welfare, and are assumed, from an economic perspective, to be the benefits raised from social oddities. Yet the pain caused by them is the sustained culture of environmental decadence, health problems, and a sexually devastated society that cannot be reformed over time after the ravages of social destruction have run their course. The cost–benefit formula of rational consumer and social choice must therefore be rejected as an acceptable approach for social evaluation, within which are embedded individual choices. The idea of 'alternatives' between 'responsible' drinking, 'responsible' smoking, 'consensual' sex, and 'adult' pornography as benefits which allow resource allocation at the level of consumption and production, form untenable social practices. They fall short of reasoned behaviours.

The oppositeness of the concepts of possibilities and alternatives is inherent in the nature of moral/ethical embedding versus marginalism, respectively. In the Islamic framework, the consumer choices of possibilities annul the regime of marginal substitution found in consumer rational choices. Thereby, the axioms of rational choice behaviour become untenable in the morally embedded case of pervasive complementarities between the good things of life and avoidance of the bad choices. Sustainability and ethico-economic possibility can only be possible in this kind of regime of social and individual choices. These attributes of a good society are degraded to oblivion in the differentiated economic and social orders of marginalism determining the cost–benefit mechanism of alternatives poised between economic transactions and social well-being.

In this contrast of meaning between truth and falsehood, the same model and method of Islamic methodology of unity of knowledge apply. But the limiting trend of 'de-knowledge' (falsehood by differentiation and methodological individualism; Holton 1992) is towards differentiation arising from marginal substitution. Consequently, the moral, ethical, and social effects of choices of 'alternatives' lead into methodological individualism that becomes a logical effect of the rational choice axiom universally in respect of mainstream economic doctrines (Buchanan 1999).

The system model given by the expressions (7.1)–(7.6) will apply as well in the perverse sense of negative coefficients signifying marginalist substitution as the mark of differentiation and the parting knell of complementarities. The epistemological praxis of unity of knowledge is denied in this system in the limiting case of 'de-knowledge' increasingly deepening the marginalism of resource allocation.

Even local forms of complementarities that are considered in mainstream economic theory of consumer behaviour cannot be acceptable in the case of Islamic episteme of unity of knowledge. The Islamic economic resource distribution results in pervasive complementarities between the good things. The same method of circular causation explains the limiting case of complements departing in the limiting case into marginalist disjoint states, conflict, competition, and cost–benefit notions of rational choice of allocation of resources between scarce alternatives.

In the above examples, Islamic methodology premised in unity of knowledge resolves the cost–benefit problem of 'alternatives' of mainstream economics by inducing evolutionary process learning that continuously and endogenously learns with the knowledge-induced variables. This attribute of Islamic economics is explained in Figure 7.1 which shows continuous reproduction of resources under θ-induction. Consequently, the core axiom of scarcity in mainstream economics is replaced by abundance of the good things of life in Islamic economics. Consequently, a continuous reproduction of this kind can flow into increased payments and usage of inputs of production and enjoyment of different consumption goods of life-sustaining type. Marginal substitution and limited complementarities between the good and the productive inputs are together annulled along the expansion path of resources, outputs, and payments. Even though this kind of distribution and ownership of goods and resources may have *differential* increments pertaining to the consumer goods, inputs and production outputs, these are positively acquired as the good things of life. It was explained in the earlier chapters that evolutionary learning processes in unity of knowledge by pervasive complementarities between the knowledge-induced resources, goods, inputs, and outputs leave the decision-making points to be perturbation points due to evolutionary learning in complementarities.

Marginalism, priorities, and complementary possibilities

Consider Figure 7.2 in regard to the above topics to prove that the idea of 'priorities' in choices by marginal substitution is untenable in Islamic methodology.

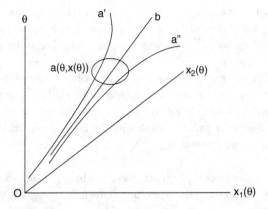

FIGURE 7.2 Complementarity versus marginalism and priorities

Priority of resource allocation among possibilities carries a different meaning in the case of continuously reproduced resources.

Here is how the concept of allocation among priorities is explained contrary to the marginal substitution idea of neoclassical economics.

Let $(x_1(\theta), x_2(\theta)) = (10, 20)$ at the point 'a' for a given θ-value within a system of relations under the expressions (7.1)–(7.6).

Let $(x_1(\theta), x_2(\theta)) = (5, 25)$ at the point 'a"' for a given θ-value within a system of relations under the expressions (7.1)–(7.6).

Let $(x_1(\theta), x_2(\theta)) = (15, 25)$ at the point 'a"'' for a given θ-value within a system of relations under the expressions (7.1)–(7.6).

Le, $(x_1(\theta), x_2(\theta)) = (15, 30)$ at the point 'b"' for a given θ-value within a system of relations under the expressions (7.1)–(7.6).

1. Now $[dx_1(\theta)/d\theta]_{a-a'} = -5; [dx_2(\theta)/d\theta]_{a-a'} = 5; [dx_1(\theta)/dx_2(\theta)]_{a-a'} = -1$. This is the case of substitution in the mainstream frame, but only if a steady-state point is maintained at 'a' and 'a"'. But this is impossible within the perturbation set 'a' and along the non-linear expansion path Oa'.

   Hence the meaning of 'evaluation' of the well-being function as conveyed, subject to simulation of the coefficients of the circular causation relations, becomes an effective way of policy and strategy changes affecting Oa' towards a social reconstruction of consumption towards attaining greater degrees of complementarities between the good things of consumption while avoiding the bad consumptions.

2. By calculation from the above data on diverse points:
   $[dx_1(\theta)/d\theta]_{a-a'} = 5; [dx_2(\theta)/d\theta]_{a-a'} = 5; [dx_1(\theta)/dx_2(\theta)]_{a-a'} = 1$.
   This is the case of complementarity between $x_1(\theta)$ and $x_2(\theta)$ with the possibility of resource reproduction from a to a". But this is impossible within the perturbation set 'a' and along the non-linear expansion path Oa'. Hence the meaning of evaluation of the well-being function is conveyed, subject to

simulation of the coefficients of the circular causation relations. In the idea of 'evaluation', simulation of the well-being function becomes an effective way of policy and strategy changes affecting Oa" towards gaining greater degrees of complementarity.

3. The same implications as above remain true of complementarity and evolutionary learning across non-linear regimes of possibilities along the Ob path. This path cannot remain linear, as shown within evolutionary learning regions that engulf the linear path shown despite the complementarity between $x_1(\theta)$ and $x_2(\theta)$ for increasing θ-values.

The above conditions of complementarities and changes made to the marginalist path by policy induction endogenously affecting the $\mathbf{x}(\theta)$-variables holds strictly in the topological space. A topological space is non-Cartesian in geometric coordinates. Therefore, the inferences drawn above hold true everywhere in the positive quadrant of Figure 6.2, now configured as a non-Cartesian topological space.

Case 2 negates the idea of priorities according to Islamic methodology as long it is equivalent to invoking the marginalist condition as shown. But the idea of priority can be interpreted along the policy-induced reconstructed path of Case 1 causing the marginalist condition to change into complementarity by θ-induction. In this case the following results are found: $[dx_1(\theta)/d\theta] > 0$; $[dx_2(\theta)/d\theta]$; but it is possible that $[dx_1(\theta)/d\theta] > 0$; and $[dx_1(\theta)/d\theta] > 0$; yet $d^2x_1(\theta)/d\theta^2 > $ or < 0; and oppositely, $d^2x_2(\theta)/d\theta^2 < $ or > 0.

Here take an example in respect of Case 2 above: $[dx_1(\theta)/d\theta]_{a-a'} = 5$; $[dx_2(\theta)/d\theta]_{a-a'} = 5$; furthermore, $[dx_1(\theta)/d\theta] = 2$; $[dx_2(\theta)/d\theta] = 7$. Then, $(d/d\theta)[dx_1(\theta)/d\theta] = d^2x_1(\theta)/d\theta^2 = -3$; $(d/d\theta)[dx_2(\theta)/d\theta] = d^2x_2(\theta)/d\theta^2 = 2$.

Since the above possibilities occur everywhere in the non-Cartesian space spanning the positive 'quadrant', by taking away the axes, therefore, both marginalist allocation of resources by competing choices of mainstream economics and its correction to complementary choices can be explained. Islamic methodology and the imminent method encased in expressions (7.1)–(7.6), can therefore explain both the mainstream case of optimality and steady-state equilibrium; and oppositely the case of evolutionary learning by processes in unity of knowledge.

The idea of priority in scarce allocation of resources as marginal substitution between 'possibilities', has been erroneously upheld in some existing neo-classically orientated Islamic economics. Even in the Islamic literature, this idea has been upheld but it is flawed, unless explained in the technical way. Examples of such flawed ideas of 'priority' is that of 'consequentialist rationality' that was upheld by Imam Shatibi (Attia 2008) as an inductive thinker of *maqasid al-shari'ah*. He viewed the legitimacy of choices in terms of cost–benefit conception. The mistaken concept of priority has sometimes been used by Islamic economists without explaining a technical basis of how priority can be explained not in the neoclassical economic sense.

EXERCISE 7.2

Take the case of allocation of household budget between tea and coffee. Since both of these goods are considered as acceptable under the *Shari'ah*, therefore they can be abundantly marketed for consumption.

1. Name some of the complementary variables that would keep the prices of these goods stable and affordable as basic commodities. Give especial consideration to advertisement of the benefits from the complementary goods under the *Shari'ah*.
2. Resources for consumption can then be socially used in these kinds of consumptions. Would then the case of marginal rate of consumption be true? Would the axiom of scarcity of resources and thereby its allocation in competing alternatives be true in reality?
3. Explain the consumer choice problem of tea and coffee in respect of Islamic methodology underlying the equations (7.1)–(7.6) in the case of these goods.

Consumer preference and social preference formation according to Islamic circular causation theory

With the rejection of the axioms of rational choice in consumer socio-economic behaviour embedding moral and ethical values through the processes of interaction, integration, and evolutionary learning in unity of knowledge and its applications to real-world phenomena, the idea of consumer preferences assumes a vastly different meaning. In forming the *maqasid-* choices of Islamic economics all of the following mainstream economic assumptions are untenable:

1. Scarcity of resource; and thereby of goods in consumption and production.
2. Consequently, optimization and steady-state equilibriums, and diminishing returns cannot be upheld as objective goals of the consumer.
3. The concept of utility function that gives rise to marginal utility, marginal rate of commodity substitution, and indifference curves at the point of optimal utility and steady-state equilibrium with scarcity of household resources are unacceptable in forming pervasively complementary goods. This is the representation of Islamic unity of knowledge functioning in Islamic economics.
4. Price relatives of substitutes cannot be determined by marginal rates of commodity substitution in the case of *continuous* evolutionary learning and consequential reproduction of resources.
5. Static preferences as datum are abandoned. Instead, dynamic preferences result as the cause and effect of the above negations concerning the axiom of rational choice theory of consumer behaviour in economics.

Unfortunately, the assumptions of neoclassical and mainstream economics are passionately replicated by some contemporary Islamic economists.

The neoclassical assumptions form contradictions to consumption decisions concerning any kind of goods and choices in the real world. Consider the case of selecting any two basic needs (name them as your example) that are recommended by the *Shari'ah*. Such basic needs are continuously augmented by the basic-needs production technology, and thus, the continuous and abundant information generation to the consumer on the basis of *dynamically graduated basic needs* being the good things of life according to the *Shari'ah*. Consumer information such as, 'An apple a day keeps the doctor away!'; 'recycle and reuse!' form the central design of Islamic economics.

The topic of the life-fulfilment regime of consumption and production was formalized in previous chapters in terms of the derived nature of Islamic methodology. This methodology was applied to complementary discursive preferences formed at various levels of the resulting interactive, integrative, and evolutionary learning processes resulting in terms of dynamic preferences. We now extend the earlier formalism by adding in the consequential effects on the type of negations mentioned above respecting assumptions 1 to 5.

Formation of dynamic household preferences in Islamic economics

This is how dynamic preferences are formed in the Islamic economic process-oriented social system. The head of the family does not coerce a household decision on any matter as the '*amir*' or self-righteous teacher of knowledge, good manners and attitudes. Instead, he wins his respect by love, affection, and the approval of all. This is the idea of the respectable leader, '*murabbi*'. On matters of consumer behaviour, interactive (discursive), integrative (consensual), and evolutionary learning forms a dynamic and coordinated decision on qualities, quantities, and choice of goods. The influence of the head of the family remains in galvanizing the members' preferences towards determining basic-needs consumptions. The circular causation relations then imply that organic reinforcing relations of inter-variable causality of complementarities are expected to emerge or to be simulated by policy, strategy, technology, and knowledge (*tarbiah*) implications between the variables.

Now evolutionary learning, generating flows of knowledge in terms of unity of knowledge between the good (*maqasid*) choices, is denoted by: $\theta \in (\Omega,S)$.

The specified vector of choice-variables are denoted by:

$\mathbf{x}_1(\theta) = \{$wages and income $\mathbf{y}(\theta)$, wealth $\mathbf{w}(\theta)$, quantities $\mathbf{q}(\theta)$, prices $\mathbf{p}(\theta)\}$

$\mathbf{x}_2(\theta) = \{$quality $\mathbf{\alpha}(\theta)$, technologies $\mathbf{T}(\theta)\}$

Household preference vector of 'i' members are denoted by $\{\wp_i(\theta)\}$ including that of head of the household, '$\wp\star(\theta)$'. The vector of participatory preferences is denoted by $\wp(\theta) = \{\wp_i(\theta), \wp\star(\theta)\}, i = 1,2,3,\dots$

Now all through the variables in the vectors as shown, the same properties of inter-action, integration, and evolutionary learning built in the formalism of expressions (7.1)–(7.6) will operate. This circular causation relationship with the induction of the θ-values must be explained. Yet the explanation need not be through mainstream and neoclassical economic theory; we question rational choice theory of consumer behaviour throughout the theory and application of Islamic economics. Rather, the rhetoric of socioeconomic interrelations can be an alternative to explain (McCloskey 1985). Observant and conscious understanding of real-world inter-variable causality can unravel the explanation of the circular causation results.

These results can now be explained in respect of these vectors of sequences of variables in a realist common understanding. The inferences drawn by automaticity of analysis would be contrary to those derived from mainstream economic theory. First, we formulate the full model of evaluation of well-being, subject to the circular causation relations in Islamic economics. Then in contrast, we develop the critique and prove the unacceptability of consumer theory based on the theory of rational choice.

Formulation and explanation of a problem of consumer economic theory in Islamic economics

We re-state the problem mentioned above as follows:

$$\mathbf{x}_1(\theta) = \{\text{wages and income } \mathbf{y}(\theta), \text{ wealth } \mathbf{w}(\theta), \text{ quantities } \mathbf{q}(\theta), \text{ prices } \mathbf{p}(\theta)\}$$

$$\mathbf{x}_2(\theta) = \{\text{quality } \mathbf{\alpha}(\theta), \text{ technologies } \mathbf{T}(\theta)\}$$

Household preference vector of 'i' members, $\{\wp_i(\theta)\}$ including that of head of the household, '$\wp^\star(\theta)$' is denoted by $\wp(\theta) = \{\wp_i(\theta), \wp^\star(\theta)\}$, i = 1,2,3,…

According to the Islamic methodology of unity of knowledge and its underlying analytics, we invoke the simulation problem of evaluating well-being subject to circular causation relations. Thus,

1. Circular causation relations in unity of knowledge, endogenous interrelations, and organic inter-variable pairing yields:

$$y(\theta) = f_y(w, q, p, T, \alpha, \wp)[\theta] \tag{7.1}$$

A positive relationship expressed by the estimated coefficients of $w(\theta)$ would mean that as wealth increases the prospect of generating income also increases. An example is of shareholders in a participatory Islamic firm. A negative estimated coefficient could also be possible if, for example, high levels of wealth could be saved for old age in active young life. Yet because of retirement, old age will reduce these earnings. In such a case, continued productive life would require activity in indus-tries that are amenable to old age. A simulation of the coefficient is then required in the light of policies and strategies. An example is to implement the policy of non-mandatory retirement. Now the organic unity of knowledge is expressed by the endogenous circularity between $y(\theta), w(\theta), T(\theta)$. These together would embody the specific policy and strategy consideration.

Likewise, the estimated coefficient of $q(\theta)$ would imply that, as consumption levels increase the increased derived demand for the consumption basket of basic needs comprising necessaries (*dururiyath*), comforts (*hajiyath*), and refinements (*tahsaniyath*) would sustain the levels of earnings from productive activities and spending in the basic needs of life. We note also that, if the resulting dynamics of interrelations are sustained between $(y, q, p, T, \alpha, \wp)[\theta]$ by estimated results, then a complementary set of organic relations is thereby generated between all the variables. A special explanation is required now for the interrelations concerning $(\alpha, \wp)[\theta]$ with the other variables. Because it is difficult to obtain data for these variables over time-series, therefore, cross-sectional data can be used by regions and other characteristics. The estimation followed by simulation of all the variables in the series of equations is done by cross-sectional data that can be generated by attending to ordinal values from sample surveys using questionnaires. Increasing quality of consumed commodities measured by ordinal responses in the questionnaires in respect of the requirements of *maqasid al-shari'ah*, as for example by the upgrading of the *dhururiyath, hajiyath, tahsaniyath* basket, relates positively with spending, quantity, prices and technology in a sustainable way across diversified levels of development.

EXERCISE 7.3

As in the case of explaining the circular causation relations for expression (7.1) and (7.2), the reader can complete a similar explanation for the expressions (7.3)–(7.7) keeping in view the social well-being objective function given by expression (7.11).

$$w(\theta) = f_w(y, q, p, T, \alpha, \wp)[\theta] \tag{7.2}$$

On a circular causality

$$q(\theta) = f_q(y, w, p, T, \alpha, \wp)[\theta] \tag{7.3}$$

$$p(\theta) = f_p(y, w, q, T, \alpha, \wp)[\theta] \tag{7.4}$$

$$T(\theta) = f_w(y, w, q, p, \alpha, \wp)[\theta] \tag{7.5}$$

$$\alpha(\theta) = f_w(y, w, q, p, T, \wp)[\theta] \tag{7.6}$$

$$\wp(\theta) = f_w(y, w, q, p, \alpha, T)[\theta] \tag{7.7}$$

with

$$\wp_i(\theta) = g_i(\theta, \wp^*(\theta), y, w, q, p, T, \alpha)[\theta] \tag{7.8}$$

$$\wp^*(\theta) = g^*(\theta, \cup_{interaction} \cap_{integration} \{\wp_i(\theta)\}, y, w, q, p, T, \alpha,)[\theta]) \tag{7.9}$$

i = 1,2,3,....
The discursive nature of the formation of $\wp^*(\theta)$ is given by its topological form,

$$\wp^*(\theta) = A(\theta).[\theta_{interaction} \cap_{integration} \{\wp_i(\theta)\}] \tag{7.10}$$

Expression (7.10) is an explained formula regarding the properties of interaction, integration, and evolutionary (IIE) learning in unity of knowledge concerning household preferences in decision-making and choices of possibilities. It does not have numerical and empirical values. Such IIE-preferences are influenced by the consciousness of knowledge and the state of the *Shari'ah*-determined variables through their property of pervasive complementarities. These attributes together signify the functioning of unity of knowledge and its induction of the organic inter-variables by circular causation. A(θ) explains the multiplier learning effect on the IIE-process produced by household decision-making. Therefore, we can proxy $\wp(\theta)$ by 'θ', the knowledge parameter.

Now any of the expressions (7.7)–(7.9) can be interpreted as the well-being function. This can be expressed as before in the case of the empirical version of the conceptual well-being function, W(.), as:

$$\theta = f_\theta(y, w, q, p, \alpha, T)[\theta], \tag{7.11}$$

$$df_\theta(.)/d\theta = (\partial f_\theta(.)/\partial y).(dy/d\theta) + (\partial f_\theta(.)/\partial w).(dw/d\theta) + (\partial f_\theta(.)/\partial q).(dq/d\theta)$$
$$+ (\partial f_\theta(.)/\partial p).(dp/d\theta) + (\partial f_\theta(.)/\partial \alpha).(d\alpha/d\theta) + (\partial f_\theta(.)/\partial T).(dT/d\theta) > 0 \tag{7.12}$$

identically, over basic-needs stages of participatory development.

After using the implicit function theorem applied to expressions (7.7)–(7.9), given the properties of continuity and differentiability of the θ-variable, and thereby of its induced variables, expression (7.11) would then yield the empirical meaning of the positive relationship signifying degrees of complementarities between the circular causal variables. The meaning here is also regarding the endogenous nature of circular causation relations that form inter-variable relations according to the epistemology of unity of knowledge.

Contrasting the model of circular causation in Islamic economics to utility-maximization in mainstream consumer theory

1. According to the Islamic methodology of unity of knowledge the well-being function is the criterion signifying degrees of complementarities existing and

gained, estimated and simulated, between the selected variables of *maqasid al-shari'ah*. The well-being function negates the assumptions underlying the axiom of rational consumer choice. Likewise, the numerical approximate derivation of the well-being function by the θ-variable according to unity of knowledge replaces the epistemology of rationalism by the primacy of *Tawhid* as law and its induction of unity of knowledge in the circular causation variables. Now all the variables being θ-induced, they become endogenously interrelated along the IIE-learning processes over knowledge, space, and time.

2. In the case of rational consumer choice theory, the well-being function devolves into the utility function, the axiom of economic rationality. Then the assumptions hold of scarcity of resources, self-interest by methodological individualism, and full-information in allocating resources such as income across competing alternatives. The consequences of these assumptions are found to set-up the so-called mainstream and present-day Islamic economic 'objective' criteria as utility maximization under income and resource constraints.

    Preferences are pre-determined and static in nature. This enables rational choices to be pre-ordered, as an alternative: $A \wp B; B \wp C \Rightarrow A \wp C$; $\wp$ symbolizes preference ordering. This postulate of transitivity of rationality preferences is proved to be a rational fallacy, which Amartya Sen (1977) refers to as the behaviour of "rational fools". Condorcet (1785) noted the emptiness of such preference pre-ordering. Besides, if evolutionary learning is induced via induction by θ-variable then preferences cannot remain static; and pre-ordering is rejected. Thereby, variables like technological change and innovation, resource augmentation, and taste and moral/ethical values, are exogenous in the utility function and in its optimizing constraints.

3. Thus we consider the above-mentioned differences between Islamic economic approach and the mainstream one within which also is Islamic economics at the present juncture.

We form the Lagrangian $L(\theta) = f(\mathbf{x}(\theta)) - f^\star(\mathbf{x}^\star(\theta^\star)) + \Sigma_{i=1}^{n} \lambda(\theta)[x_i - f_i(x_j(\theta))]$

$$(6.13)$$

$dL(\theta)/d\theta = df(x(\theta))/d\theta + \Sigma_{i=1}^{n}(x_i - f_i(x_j(\theta))).(d\lambda(\theta)) + \Sigma_{i=1}^{n}\lambda(\theta)[dx_i/d\theta - df_i(x_j)/d\theta] \neq 0$.

This result is contrary to the constrained maximization problem of the Lagrangian function in neoclassical consumer theory of constrained utility maximization.

EXERCISE 7.4

Set up the classical problem of maximization of the household utility function, subject to the budget constraint, and show how the circular causation approach in such a household well-being simulation problem is contrary to the Lagrangian approach in the case of the mainstream consumer theory of rational economic behaviour.

Formation of social preferences and implications

The concept of being 'social' implies a complex and interactive aggregation of micro-organic preferences, objectives, and goals that are represented by their specific variables. Therefore, in the moral/ethical sense of social preferences, there is a progressive aggregation of these indicators rising from the microeconomic to the macroeconomic levels. This implies that, in the case of the moral and ethical foundations of economics, the true component of the embedded social and economic perspective corresponding to any economic problem is at the microeconomic level. From the micro-level, appropriate complex aggregations are enacted to form social behaviour and choices. In the Islamic worldview, individual preference and consumer choices are necessarily embedded in a social order via circular causation. This gives rise to circular causality as recursive feedback between the various preferences, well-being, and their inherent variables, all of which together experience organic interrelations governed by the epistemology of unity of knowledge according to the Islamic methodological worldview. In reference to such a complex and interactive aggregation arising from the microeconomic level to the social level, the Islamic methodological orientation becomes a study in microeconomic foundations of the total social order, while being governed by organic evolutionary learning characterized by the IIE-dynamics, as explained earlier.

Formalism

The micro-foundations of social preferences and social choice in the Islamic methodological context pose a complex accumulative formalism. We take the following steps towards the construction of such social complexity and non-linear aggregation. The inference to be drawn is that the foundational grassroots representation plays the most important formative basis in Islamic decision making; and the cumulative role of morality/ethicality determines the formation of individual, household, and social consumer behaviour throughout.

1. *Individual and household preferences:* This was formalized in earlier chapters and in this chapter as:

$$\wp(\theta) = \{\wp_i(\theta), \wp^\star(\theta)\}, i = 1,2,3,\dots \tag{7.14}$$

The discursive nature of the formation of $\wp^\star(\theta)$ is given by its topological form:

$$\wp\star(\theta) = A(\theta).[\cup_{\text{interaction}} \cap_{\text{integration}} \{\wp_i(\theta)\}]$$ (7.15)

$$\wp(\theta) = f_w(y, w, q, p, \alpha, T)[\theta]$$ (7.16)

with:

$$\wp_i(\theta) = g_i(\theta, \wp\star(\theta), y, w, q, p, T, \alpha)[\theta]$$ (7.17)

$$\wp\star(\theta) = g\star(\theta, \cup_{\text{interaction}} \cap_{\text{integration}} \{\wp_i(\theta)\}, y, w, q, p, T, \alpha,)[\theta])$$ (7.18)

$i = 1,2,3,\ldots.$

EXERCISE 7.5

Consider the following way of organizing cross-sectional data or data raised from a questionnaire survey. Each of the vectors of variables is θ-induced, although this is not symbolized.

y	W	q	p	T	α	$\wp_i$=1,2.3...	$\wp\star$	$\wp$	θ

How would household consumer behaviour be evaluated in the two cases?

1. Rational choice theory of mainstream economics.
2. Islamic methodology of unity of knowledge explained by the evaluation of the well-being function (*maslaha*) as a microeconomic aggregation of preferences and variables.
3. How is the moral and ethical context explained in case 2?
4. How is ethics exogenous in case 1?

Finally, in respect of social choices, well-being, and aggregation of ethically induced preferences, and consequently its effect on the ethically induced variables, a robust theory of the well-being function (*maslaha*) can be formalized. *Maslaha* arises from the study of the purpose and objective of the *Shari'ah* called *maqasid al-shari'ah*. This formalism reflects the microeconomic complex aggregation of the variables and preferences involved in forming the corresponding social verities. The inference here is that, ethical induction and moral context of all decision-making and their induction by the *maqasid al-shari'ah* choices represented by the corresponding variables as symbols can exist as micro-level realities.

Contrarily, it is impossible to identify an ethical behaviour and ethical agent as an institution at the macroeconomic level. It is also impossible to disaggregate from the macroeconomic level to the microeconomic level of economic and social behaviour. That is because aggregation in mainstream macroeconomics does not mean the lateral aggregation of variables. In macroeconomics there is no behavioural study, consumer choice issues, and household decision-making to reflect any kind of ethical behaviour. Even when governments are studied in respect of decision-making it becomes a study of microeconomics or microeconomic foundations of macroeconomics as in public choice theory.

In Islamic economics as it presently exists, the *maslaha* function turns out to be of the utilitarian type. This means a lateral addition of additively linear utility functions distributed over individuals and households in the nation as a whole. Even if there are ethical decisions, the utilitarian version of additive utilities implies ethical exogeneity in decision-making.

The following models arise from the above-mentioned Islamic economic method of formalization as it presently exists: The much-misconstrued idea of welfare ($W(U(x))$ in mainstream economics, which is now copied zealously by the present cadre of Islamic economists is formalized as follows. Bold symbols denote vectors:

$$W(\mathbf{U}(\mathbf{x})) = \Sigma_{i=1}^{n} U_i(\mathbf{x}) \qquad (7.19)$$

This is a utilitarian expression with independently distributed utility functions over society in terms of the basket of goods denoted by quantities: $\mathbf{x} = \{x_1, x_2, x_3, \ldots x_m\}$. The property of independent distribution of utilities and quantities is reflected in the linear aggregation of utilities. This does not allow for interaction between the utilities and all that interaction, integration, and evolutionary learning otherwise employs.

Furthermore, in the case of interdependent utility function we write:

$$U_i = f_i(U_j(\mathbf{x})), i \neq j = 1,2,3,\ldots,n \text{ (say)} \qquad (7.20)$$

If expression (7.20) holds for the entire domain of utility functions and commodity space then the postulate of marginal utility and marginal rate of commodity substitution would either hold, or else complementarities would exist between all possibilities. In the former of these cases, all the neoclassical economic postulates abide in contrast to the postulates of unity of knowledge under Islamic methodology. In the latter case, neoclassical economic theory is rejected. Islamic economics as science now reverts to the well-being analytics of circular causation in the light of the Islamic methodological worldview of unity of knowledge. But in the latter case, the systemic view of IIE-processes would be much more extensive and complex than the linear and *ceteris paribus* nature of neoclassical economics. We turn to this imminent complex functional picture of circular causation involving the objective criterion of evaluation of the well-being function, technically defined as the *maslaha* function of *maqasid al-shari'ah*.

We note now that none of the variables comprising $\mathbf{U}$-functions and $\mathbf{x}(\theta)$ vector of variables remains independent of each other. Thus, the $\mathbf{U}$-functions and $\mathbf{x}(\theta)$-variables establish themselves in corresponding relations as follows:

quantities:	1	2	3.........	n	Final Market Demand, $x_j(\theta)=$ $X_j(\theta) -\Sigma_j x_{ji}(\theta)$ $i = 1,2,..m$ goods $j= 1,2,..n$ consumers
$\mathbf{x}(\theta)$: Total Quantity					
$X_1(\theta)$	$X_{11}(\theta)$	$X_{12}(\theta)$	$X_{13}(\theta)$	$X_{1m}(\theta)$	X_1
$X_2(\theta)$	$X_{21}(\theta)$	$X_{22}(\theta)$	$X_{23}(\theta)$	$X_{2m}(\theta)$	X_2
$X_3(\theta)$	$X_{31}(\theta)$	$X_{32}(\theta)$	$X_{33}(\theta)$	$X_{3m}(\theta)$	X_3
.	.	.	.	.	.
$X_m(\theta)$	$X_{m1}(\theta)$	$X_{m2}(\theta)$	$X_{m3}(\theta)$	$X_{mm}(\theta)$	X_m

$$(7.21)$$

Total consumption for each good, say for good 1 of m can be expressed as:

$$X_1 = [(\Sigma_{j=2}^{m}.a_{1j}X_j) + x_1(\theta)]/(1-a_{11})$$

The equations of material exchange for other consumptions can similarly notated. The coefficients a_{1j}, a_{11}, and likewise for other equations of material exchange can be simulated. The simulated coefficients convey the meaning of the dynamic coefficients model of exchange in the input–output expression (7.21) (Miller *et al.* 1989). We therefore have a non-linear dynamic coefficients model of economy-wide consumer goods and preferences all included in the θ-values, that make the model the dynamic coefficients type.

Expression (7.21) in goods consumed by individuals (aggregate households, community, society) corresponds to the following disaggregate well-being functions of consumers:

$U_i(\mathbf{x}(\theta))/i$:	1	2	3............	n	Final Market Demand, $x_j(\theta)=$ $X_j(\theta) -\Sigma_j x_{ji}(\theta)$ $i = 1,2,..n$ consumers $j = 1,2,..m$ goods

Interactive consumer-specific well-being from specific goods

$U_1(x_1(\theta))$	$U_{11}(x_{11}(\theta))$	$U_{12}(x_{12}(\theta))$	$U_{13}(x_{13}(\theta))$	$U_{1m}(x_{1m}(\theta))$	$U_1(x_1(\theta))$
$U_2(x_2(\theta))$	$U_{21}(x_{21}(\theta))$	$U_{22}(x_{22}(\theta))$	$U_{23}(x_{23}(\theta))$	$U_{2m}(x_{2m}(\theta))$	$U_2(x_2(\theta))$
$U_3(x_3(\theta))$	$U_{31}(x_{31}(\theta))$	$U_{32}(x_{32}(\theta))$	$U_{33}(x_{33}(\theta))$	$U_{3m}(x_{3m}(\theta))$	$U_3(x_3(\theta))$
.	.	.	.	.	.
$U_m(x_m(\theta))$	$U_{m1}(x_{m1}(\theta))$	$U_{m2}(x_{m2}(\theta))$	$U_{m3}(x_{m3}(\theta))$	$U_{mm}(x_{mm}(\theta))$	$U_m(x_m(\theta))$

$$(7.22)$$

An equivalent set of equations like the derived dynamic coefficients equation of consumption of expression (7.21) can be derived. From the dynamic model we deduce the equations:

$$U_1(X_1(\theta)) = [(\Sigma_{j=2}{}^m.b_{1j}U_j(X_j(\theta)) + U(x_1(\theta))]/(1-b_{11}) \qquad (7.23)$$

$$\text{Likewise, } U_l(X_l(\theta)) = [(\Sigma_{k=1}{}^m.b_{kl}U_l(X_l(\theta)) + U(x_l(\theta))]/(1-b_{ll}) \qquad (7.24)$$

$$k,l = 1,2,3,\ldots,m; k{\neq}l.$$

One can readily see that the well-being function in both its non-linear and linear forms with the utility functions given in terms of the *maqasid*-choices represented by the variables would be a complex system. This property of IIE-systems, governed by circular causation, best fits into the definition of complex non-linear systems formalized by Bertuglia and Vaio (2005, p. 269):

> The fundamental characteristic of complexity is the fact that, in the study of the evolution of dynamical systems that complexity deals with, the nature of the system in question is usually irrelevant. In the vision proposed by complexity, we can identify forms and evolutive characteristics common to all, or almost all, systems that are made up of numerous elements, between which there are reciprocals, non-linear interactions and positive feedback mechanisms. These systems, precisely for this reason, are generally called complex systems.

On a simple scale we can write the well-being function as follows:

$$W(\theta) = W(U(x(\theta))) = W(x_{ij}(\theta), x(\theta); \wp(\theta))$$

This expression means that evaluation of the well-being function in terms of the dynamic coefficients input-output analysis is premised on the formation of choices by preferences under the effect of θ-values. We have explained above that the measurement of the preference function can be subsumed in the evaluation of the θ-values.

Demand functions

Two forms of demand function need to be examined. In usual economic theory consumer demand is that of Robinson Crusoe and of Man Friday. These are independent of each other. Thus no inter-causality is shown between the variables to specify how the two consumer demand functions interactively. Interaction though is not denied, except that it is not analytical, studied in economic terms.

Next, market demand is defined in economic theory as the locus of the sum-total of quantities demanded at given prices along the consumer demand curve.

Once again it is noted that inter-causality between quantities and prices is not considered analytically. Simply, *ceteris paribus* situation of demand is assumed. The same assumption is made for any other variable in the demand function. The example is of the income variable, which is treated as an exogenous variable to cause shifts in the demand curves of the consumer and the aggregate market demand. In the same way, taste, technology, and ethics as charitable behaviour are exogenous variables affecting shifts in the demand curve.

None of these assumptions hold up for the case of evaluating well-being, subject to circular causation between the variables. In this case, the price and quantity variables are interrelated endogenously by their interrelationship. We now derive the price vector $(\mathbf{p}(\theta))$ and quantity vector $(\mathbf{q}(\theta))$ relations in multi-markets by the following equations of the entire set of other circular causation equations.

$$p_1(\theta) = f_1(q_1,\ldots,q_n, p_2, p_3,\ldots p_n, Y, \alpha)[\theta] \qquad (7.25)$$

$$p_n(\theta) = f_n(q_1,\ldots,q_n, p_1,\ldots,p_{n-1}, Y,\alpha)[\theta] \qquad (7.26)$$

$$q_1(\theta) = f_1(q_2,\ldots,q_n, p_1,p_2, p_3,\ldots p_n, Y, \alpha)[\theta] \qquad (7.27)$$

$$q_n(\theta) = f_n(q_1,q_2,\ldots,q_{n-1}, p_1,p_2, p_3,\ldots p_n, Y, \alpha)[\theta] \qquad (7.28)$$

The above kinds of multivariate specification of the demand function in its two forms are essential in the case of circular causation relations of endogenous inter-variable relationships caused by the Islamic methodology of unity of knowledge.

Now preferences can be different among consumers in respect of prices and quantities and the other variables. This is caused by the different effects of the θ-variable on the variables. Besides, the random variations in the θ-variable will cause no unique positioning of the demand curves. The consumer demand curve is therefore undetermined. Demand remains only a notion of hurt and pain between relative prices for the relative quantities of goods in demand. Since the consumer demand curve remains a notion rather than reality, therefore, the market demand curve is not determinate. It is notional.

Market demand, market supply, and market equilibrium

The market demand curve in the case of the circular causation method of deriving price and quantity equations given a basic-needs regime of consumption and production – as exemplified by the Shatibi basket of *dururiyath*, *hajiyath*, and *tahsaniyath* – is an *almost* perfectly elastic curve DD as shown in Figure 7.3. The endogenous effect of θ on $\mathbf{p}$ and $\mathbf{q}$ in multimarkets gravitates the demand functions, DD_1, and many more of these towards the *approximately* perfectly elastic demand curve shown by DD as the θ-induced market demand curve of basic-needs. These induced goods are also the *maqasid*-choices. They enter the *maslaha* function, which we evaluate in the light of complementarities between the choices

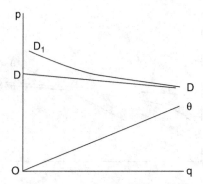

FIGURE 7.3 Market demand specification by endogenous relationship between $(p(\theta), q(\theta), \theta)$ in the dynamic basic-needs regime of consumption

as 'possibilities', rather than by substitutes ('alternatives'). Simulation by means of strategies, policies, and knowledge induction are some of the instruments that induce the convergence of D_1D to DD. This kind of specification of the temporary consumer and market demand function implies a change from the marginalist regime of scarcity of resources caused by the absence of endogeneity of knowledge and learning in a complementary regime of approximation to life-fulfilment (basic-needs) regime of consumption. The approximation rather than perfection into a fully realized basic-needs regime of consumption is shown by a slightly negatively sloped shape of DD.

The supply function

Construction of the supply function is similarly specified by the method of circular causation model as with the demand specification. In reference to the problem that we formalized above in respect of the market demand function, we will repeat the use of the same variables for the supply function and explain the construction.

Specification of the supply function

$$p_1(\theta) = f_1(q_1,\ldots,q_n, p_2, p_3,\ldots p_n, Y, \alpha)[\theta] \tag{7.29}$$

$$p_n(\theta) = f_n(q_1,\ldots,q_n, p_1,\ldots,p_{n-1}, Y, \alpha)[\theta] \tag{7.30}$$

From the perspective of complementarities signalled by the epistemology of unity of knowledge, which is projected by the circular causation between the variables, the above equations describe the supply functions in multimarket. The degree of complementarities gained between the price, quantity, income and taste (or technology) variables is a matter of the function of knowledge induction in the supply

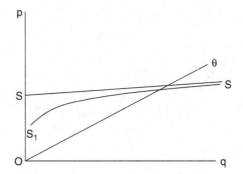

FIGURE 7.4 Supply function according to the precept of Islamic unity of knowledge projected in circular causation method of extensive complementarities

specification between the variables and by the strategies and policies used to simulate the desired levels of complementarities.

Extensive complementarities between the variables would suggest that the simulated coefficients of the expressions (7.29) and (7.30) would mean: As quantities of any good increase, its own price increases but remains stable along an *approximately perfectly elastic* supply curve. The price of any good increases as the supply prices and quantities of the other goods increase. These results happen because of the *continuous* increase in resources, such as in inputs, technology ($\alpha(\theta)$), revenues ($Y(\theta)$), and stable cost of production in the basic-needs regime of supply specification, i.e. production of goods and services. This in turn meets the demand side of the basic-needs regime of consumption.

Similar relations are confirmed from the side of supply specification of complementarities between any specific supply quantity of a good in relationship with other supply of goods and all with all the prices. The same implication of complementarities and increased resource effect applies as explained above. The *Qur'an* (7:156) declares the blessings and mercy of God lies on all that is good for this world and the Hereafter: "And decree for us in this world [that which is] good and [also] in the Hereafter; indeed, we have turned back to You." [God] said, "My punishment – I afflict with it whom I will, but My mercy encompasses all things. So I will decree it [especially] for those who fear Me and give *zakah* and those who believe in Our verses."

Specifying supply function in multimarket

$$q_1(\theta) = f_1(q_2,\ldots,q_n, p_1,p_2, p_3,\ldots p_n, Y, \alpha)[\theta] \tag{7.31}$$

$$q_n(\theta) = f_n(q_1,q_2,\ldots,q_{n-1}, p_1,p_2, p_3,\ldots p_n, Y, \alpha)[\theta] \tag{7.32}$$

The above kind of specification details hold.

Market equilibrium

The important controlling basis of the complementary interrelationships between the *maqasid al-shari'ah* choices specifying the demand and supply functions is the continuously augmenting resource variable induced by the property of θ-variable. Resources include physical and financial inputs, technology and suchlike inputs that enhance the values for demand and supply. The resource effect on the formation of complementarities changes the nature of market equilibrium into a plethora of non-steady-state evolutionary equilibriums. The evolutionary processes in the IIE-learning field of equilibriums occur around the 'final' equilibrium point, which cannot be attained. In Islamic terminology the final yet unattainable equilibrium point is hidden as '*ghayb*' (unseen). The *Qur'an* (6:59) declares in this regard:

> With Him are the keys of the unseen (*ghayb*). No one knows them other than Him. He knows what is in land and sea. No leaf falls but He knows it; nor there is not a grain in the darkness (or depths) of the earth nor anything fresh or dry (green or withered), but is (inscribed) in a Record Clear (to those who can read).

Now we bring together Figures 7.3 and 7.4 in Figure 7.5 to explain the nature of evolutionary market equilibrium in reference to the Islamic unity of knowledge reflected through circular causation.

The results of the Islamic methodological worldview of unity of knowledge reflected in the method of circular causation and simulation for complementarities contrast with the mainstream economic theory of market equilibrium (Choudhury 2011). The resulting evolutionary learning world-system of inter-variable complementarities caused by unity of knowledge between the *maqasid*-choices in the well-being (*maslaha*) function contradicts the steady-state market equilibrium concept of mainstream economics. That is because of the assumptions underlying the axiom

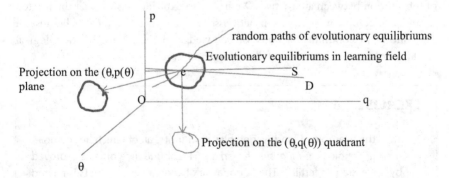

FIGURE 7.5 Evolutionary market equilibriums as the consequence of circular causation and simulacra of demand and supply with respect to Islamic precept of unity of knowledge

of rational economic choice. Its core assumption in mainstream economics is that of scarcity of resources.

Abundance versus scarcity in Islamic and mainstream economics

What does scarcity of resources mean in an economic theory where the *Qur'anic* meaning of abundance is distinctly against scarcity? According to the *Qur'an*, abundance as mercy is caused by God's blessings in all good things. Across the domain of such good things flow his blessings and mercy? The *Qur'an* (31:20) declares:

> Do ye not see that God has subjected/made of benefit to you all things in the heavens and on earth, and has made his bounties flow to you in exceeding measure, (both) seen and unseen? Yet there are among men those who dispute about God, without knowledge and without guidance, and without a Book to enlighten them!

The meanings of scarcity and abundance arise from the nature of resources. If resources remain scarce, the logical yet unethical consequence is reflected in the marginal rate of substitution, opportunity cost, competition, and thereby self-interest and methodological individualism. On the other hand, the existence of abundance of resource regeneration is caused by search and discovery of interactive, integrative and evolutionary knowledge that arise from interaction across diversity of organisms. As we have explained earlier, under the condition of abundance of resources caused by organic unity of knowledge, marginal substitution and opportunity cost do not exist in the resource distribution theory over complementary possibilities of the life-fulfilling regimes of consumption and production – that is of demand and supply. Thus in the Islamic methodological worldview there is neither the notion of absolute scarcity nor the relative scarcity conveyed by marginal rate of substitution between alternatives. We have also explained earlier that the limited meaning of complementarity as in neoclassical economics is untenable, because of the concept of continuity of unity of knowledge in the Islamic methodological worldview prevailing over knowledge, space, and time.

EXERCISE 7.6

1. Take the example of land, vegetables, and fruits, all of which are complementary choices of *maqasid al-shari'ah*. The abundance of land is proved by increasing its fertility. The abundance of vegetables and fruits is related to the acceptance of the basic-needs regime of development. But in this regime of three resources, the enhancement to fertility and production of land will end.

How then can complementarities be extended to sustain organic relationship between land, vegetables, fruits, and the other complementary
factors? Answer by using an example.

2. In the life-fulfilling regime of consumption and production, the demand
and supply curves tend to converge to establish continuously evolutionary
equilibriums.

Re-draw Figure 7.5 to explain this phenomenon. Can the demand and
supply curves coincide *perfectly* under the induction of θ-values on the
demand and supply sides? Explain.

3. In the case of complements and substitutes, for example between tea
and milk, the following implications would hold with tea and coffee as
substitutes:

(%change in the quantity of tea consumed)/(%change in the price of
coffee) > 0, implying tea and coffee are substitutes.

(%change in the quantity of tea consumed)/(%change in the price of
coffee) < 0, implying coffee and tea are complements.

How can this happen in the case of extensive complementarities
between tea and coffee with θ-effect? Can the assumption of *ceteris paribus*
be true in this case?

4. Without the relevance of *ceteris paribus*, how could the degree of complementarity be evaluated in the presence of resource augmentation by
θ-values? (Use the objective *maslaha* criterion of evaluation of well-being
subject to circular causation between *maqasid*-choices.)

5. Explain the extended idea of inter-variable complementarities using
expressions (6.25) and (6.28).

Conclusion

Throughout this book there appears an increasing quantity of critical and formal
analyses to prove that the Islamic *epistemological* basis of Islamic economics is distinctive and rich in explaining, evaluating, and measuring complex fields of social
and economic study. On the other hand, the assumptions of the axiom of economic
rationality and rational choice theory cannot achieve such an extended methodological worldview.

Islamic economic methodology is indeed the most generalized nature of economics and socio-scientific intellection. It dispels the postulates of rational choice,
ceteris paribus, and partial equilibrium. Islamic economics replaces these with the
axiom of abundance arising from the IIE-learning processes by the presence of
continuously endogenous inter-variable complementarities. Mainstream economic
theory does not have the capability to undertake such a knowledge-induced evolutionary learning domain of interdependent study. Contrarily, the emergent field
of Islamic epistemology in the building stages of a new socio-scientific theory with

economics as a particularity can universally and uniquely answer the deficiency of mainstream economics and its Islamic economics offshoots. Thereby, in the present age of heterodox economics with new epistemological ways, as of unity of knowledge premised in *Tawhid*, the emergence of the heterodox Islamic economics with its Islamic epistemology can offer a revolutionary platform of socio-scientific thought, theory, formalism, and applications for all intellection.

In this chapter the focus of study has been on the following, combining with earlier chapters:

1.   Islamic economics *contra* mainstream consumer theory
2.   Islamic economics *contra* mainstream theory of the firm.

Note

1   *Qur'an* (57:3): "He is the First and the Last, the Evident and the Imminent: and He has full knowledge of all things."

References

Attia, G.E. (2008). *Towards Realization of the Higher Intents of Islamic Law: A Functional Approach of Maqasid as-Shari'ah*, Herndon, VA: International Institute of Islamic Thought.

Bertuglia, C.S. & Vaio, F. (2005). Dynamical systems and the phase space, in *Non-linearity, Chaos and Complexity: The Dynamics of Natural and Social Systems*, pp. 49–70, Oxford: Oxford University Press.

Buchanan, J.M. (1999). The domain of constitutional economics, in *The Collected Works of James M. Buchanan: The Logical Foundations of Constitutional Liberty*, pp. 377–395, Indianapolis, IN: Liberty Press.

Burstein, M. (1991). History versus equilibrium: Joan Robinson and time in economics, in *The Joan Robinson Legacy*, ed. Rima, I.H., pp. 49–61, Armonk, NY: M.E. Sharpe, Inc.

Choudhury, M.A. (2011). The family as a socioeconomic management system, *International Journal of Management Studies*, 18(1): 99–115.

Condorcet, M.J.A.N. (1785). *Essai sur l'application de l'analyse a la probabilite des decisions rendues a la pluralite des voix*, Paris, France: Imprimerie Royale.

Grandmont, J.-M. (1989). Temporary equilibrium, in *New Palgrave: General Equilibrium*, eds. Eatwell, J., Milgate, M, & Newman, P., pp. 164–185, New York: W.W. Norton.

Holton, R.L. (1992). *Economy and Society*, London: Routledge.

Hull, D.L. (1988). *Science as a Process: An Evolutionary Account of the Social and Conceptual Development of Science*, Chicago, IL: University of Chicago Press.

McCloskey, D.N. (1985). *The Rhetoric of Economics*, Wisconsin, MN: The University of Wisconsin Press.

Miller, R.E., Polenske, K.R., & Rose, A.Z. (1989). *Frontiers of Input–Output Analysis*, New York: Oxford University Press.

Sen, A. (1977). Rational fools: A critique of the behavioural foundations of economic theory, *Philosophy and Public Affairs*, 6(4): 317–344.

Thurow, L. (1983). *Dangerous Currents: The State of Economics*, New York: Random House.

8

DUAL THEORIES OF THE FIRM

LEARNING OBJECTIVES

This chapter is oriented towards:

- a comparative discussion of the contrasting nature of the firm in Islamic economics and mainstream perspectives
- an understanding of the complexity of the Islamic concept of the firm with its institutional, organizational, and factual role in the Islamic social economy
- a brief discussion on marginal productivity theory of wages in Islamic economics and economic efficiency, marginal cost, marginal productivity, and returns to scale concepts in Islamic economics
- a critically comparative discussion on social values, perfect and imperfect competition in partial and general equilibriums, and monopolistic and oligopolistic competition of mainstream conventional and Islamic economics.

The general theory of *evaluation* of the objective function of well-being (*maslaha*) in the light of the epistemology of unity of knowledge with *maqasid*-choices and using the method of circular causation has been laid down in previous chapters. The same method and the underlying idea meeting Islamic analytical methodology have also been particularized for special problems of economics. The building blocks of this theory will not therefore be revised here. What will be accomplished is the *application* of the Islamic theory of unity of knowledge with the method of evaluation of the well-being function subject to circular causation relations.

In the theory of the firm, the contrasting nature of the firm in the Islamic Economic and mainstream perspectives needs to be understood. The firm uses factors of production, subject to cost of production to produce goods out of the efficient use of resources and the productive use of inputs of production. This is the usual viewpoint of all approaches to the theory of the firm. The difference between the Islamic methodological approach and its *maqasid al-shari'ah* viewpoint is established by the embedding of θ-values in the organic participatory relationships between all the variables comprising the well-being function and the circular causation relations pertinent to the objective of the firm.

Islamic analytical methodology and the *maqasid*-viewpoint make the objective criterion not simply that of production. Rather, this activity is a subset of the total social picture. The firm then is an institutional entity of this social nexus. An example of such kinds of firms could be the Islamic firm promoting consumption and production, and thereby the complementary nature of these activities, in a life-fulfilling regime of development in the good things of life (*hallal at-tayyabah*). Take another example, of an Islamic bank as an Islamic firm. The principal function of the Islamic bank, differently from any other bank, is to mobilize savings according to the *maqasid al-shari'ah* directions. This comprises a portfolio of morally and ethically embedded objectives. The principle of resource mobilization in the *maqasid*-choices involves a participatory financial portfolio that must thereby necessarily avoid financial interest (*riba*). *Riba* causes holding back of bank-savings against allowing resource mobilization. The complementarities between the good things of life in the evaluation of the *maslaha* function, subject to circular causation between the representative choice variables as the sign of organic evolutionary learning forming inter-variable complementarities stand for the sign of unity of knowledge and its induction of reality in all details. The evaluation of the well-being function, subject to the system of circular causation relations constitutes the actual objective criterion of the Islamic firm. This approach endows the Islamic firm with its institutional, organizational, and factual role in the entire Islamic social economy (Choudhury 2017a).

Now taking stock of all the details of the method of evaluation of the well-being function (*maslaha*), subject to circular causation relations, the formal model of the Islamic firm is written as follows:

The following variables are defined:

Q denotes output; K denotes stock of capital; L denotes employment; H denotes human capital; E denotes enterprise; T denotes technology and innovation; R denotes resources such as cost of production, and in the Islamic case participatory joint financing instruments are used. (The last case is one of joint venture in a 'pooled fund' of various Islamic financing instruments. This case of pooled financing was explained earlier.)

Evaluate $\{\theta\}$ $W(Q, K, L, H, E, T, R)[\theta]$ $\qquad$ (8.1)

Subject to $Q = f_1(K, L, H, E, T, R)[\theta]$ $\qquad$ (8.2)

$K = f_2(Q, L, H, E, T, R)[\theta]$ $\qquad$ (8.3)

$L = f_3(Q, K, H, E, T, R)[\theta]$ $\qquad$ (8.4)

$$H = f_4(Q, K, L, E, T, R)[\theta] \tag{8.5}$$

$$E = f_5(Q, K, L, H, T, R)[\theta] \tag{8.6}$$

$$T = f_6(Q, K, L, H, E, R)[\theta] \tag{8.7}$$

$$R = f_7(Q, K, L, H, E, T)[\theta] \tag{8.8}$$

$$\theta = F(Q, K, L, H, E, T, R)[\theta] \tag{8.9}$$

Expression (8.9) is the empirical form of the well-being function, with θ being assigned ordinal values in terms of the socioeconomic variables, as was explained earlier.

In reference to the mainstream economics of production, which is also copied by Islamic economics of the mainstream genre, the resource variable includes more than the cost of production, for the factors of production earn dividends besides factor payments.

In mainstream economics the cost of production is given by either of the following equations shown by their internal specifications:

$$C = C(Q) = wL + rK \tag{8.10}$$

Contrarily, the resource equation in Islamic analytical concept is given by the full gamut of inputs of production as shown by expression (8.8). Besides, the payments equation to such inputs of production is given by:

$$R(\theta) = (wL + r.K + p_1.H + p_2.E + p_3.T + d.Q)[\theta] \tag{8.11}$$

with 'w' being wage rate; 'r' being rents; 'p_i' being prices of the ith inputs as shown; 'd' being the dividend rate on the production of units of Q. dQ therefore denotes the total dividends on the financing of the production levels.

Expression (8.11) is 'similar' to expression (8.8). Each one of the variables, including the price coefficients and 'd', is induced by the θ-variable. The meaning of this is that, in a life-fulfillment regime of production, consumption and distribution of resources, prices and the variables remain sustainably stable. This state of the variables requires organic pairing between the variables along intra-systems and inter-systems of the Islamic economics processes. If otherwise, any two of the comparative variables and prices are represented, as an example, by the price relative (w/r), for matters of incremental choice of the corresponding inputs, then this would mean marginal rate of substitution between those variables. This would be contrary to the principle of abundance of resources and complementarities between the pairing variables, which is the principal consequence of Islamic methodological implications.

The production function of the firm is represented by expression (8.2). All the expressions (8.2)–(8.9) are derived functions of the computational general equilibrium functions of the interactive, integrative, and evolutionary type. The meaning of the well-being function (*maslaha*) implies that each of the functional variables is complementary to all other variables. In this regard one can put an important institutional explanation in the production milieu.

Consider the simple case of expression (8.2) in the form, $Q = f(L,K)[\theta]$. The embedding of both L and K in the θ-value implies that there must be an institutional arrangement of cooperation between capital (owners) and workers in determining the *maqasid*-choices. The result then is, as shown earlier, the demand function and the supply function are together near-perfect elastic curves, subject to evolutionary equilibrium all along the continuous organic complementarity between capital and labour demand curves. This would likewise be of the same nature of complementarity and continuity as between variables of the demand and supply functions. Such is the case of participatory financial and organizational instruments in Islam contrary to the effect of the instrument of *riba*.

EXERCISE 8.1

1. Formulate and explain the empirical version of the objective criterion comprising the circular causation relations (8.1)–(8.9) with the following complementary variables: $(Q, K, L, F)[\theta]$.
2. Explain the difference and the necessity of having H and θ in any and all of the expressions (8.2)–(8.9).
3. Explain the following result derived from expression (8.5) taken in the following form:

   $\log H = A(\theta) + a_1.\log Q + a_2.\log K + a_3.\log L + a_4.\log E + a_5.\log T + a_6.\log R$

   Each and every variable and the learning coefficients are θ-induced.
   How do you explain $d\log H/d\theta$ with the distinctive meanings for $H(\theta)$ and 'θ' ?
4. What is the difference between the result of Question 3 and the marginal productivity idea of the mainstream economic theory of the firm? Does this difference in these results change in the intertemporal case along the output expansion path?
5. How is the idea of increasing returns to well-being different from the case of increasing returns to scale of production in the case of mainstream economics? You can work with the case of expressions (8.2) and (8.9).

Non-viability of the marginal productivity theory of wages in Islamic economics

The principle of pervasive complementarity that spans all functions in Islamic economics rejects the relevance of every marginalist formula. In this sense the marginal productivity theory of wages, rents, and other input payments are not tenable in Islamic economics.

Formally, let us consider the following mainstream formula that is untenable:

$$w = p.\text{Marginal Productivity of } L = p.(\partial Q/\partial L) \text{ in perfect competition} \quad (8.12)$$

and

$$w = p.\text{Marginal Revenue Product of } L = MR \times p.MP_L =$$
$$p.(\Delta\text{Total Revenue}/\Delta Q) \times (\Delta Q/\Delta L) = \Delta TR/\Delta L \quad (8.13)$$

in imperfect competition.

'w' is set by the labour market. No institutional and policy implication is invoked to affect wage setting other than the market. In the basic-needs economic regime the supply curve of goods and services causes abundance of demand for inputs of production including labour, leaving aside those who cannot work and are therefore not in the active labour force. Temporarily, they may be in exit and re-entry flux in the potential labour force in the periphery. Consequently, the role of θ-induction in the demand and supply functions of the basic-needs economic regime will cause the supply of production of Q to remain fluctuating around the evolutionary labour market equilibriums. Consequently, the MP_L curve remains random and the wage rate undetermined in both the perfect and imperfect markets for goods, services, and factors of production.

Formulas (8.12) and 8.13) being untenable in the case of the sensitive effect of θ-values, the Islamic economics method suggests the multivariate empirical determination of Q, K, L and all prices. This of course does not mean that statistical variations can be avoided. Rather, the random behaviour of factor and product markets is accepted as a fact. Thereby, only simulation in the complementary field of multivariates is upheld to be the way to regulate prices by policies and strategies, along with market realities. This proves that Islamic economics is always a domain of IIE-processes playing out its course in a market-institutional conjoint discursive interrelationship. Such is the case also with the implication of circular causation inter-relations between the variables of the good things of life. In the case of contrary variables, as of *riba* (i) against trade (rate of gains from trade, π), the well-being function given in (8.1) [and thereby, expression (8.9)], the variable representation for *riba* would be either $(1/i)$ or (π/i).

In expression $(7.11), R(\theta) / d\theta = (d / d\theta)(wL + r.K + p_1.H + p_2.E + p_3.T + d.Q)[\theta]$

$$> 0 \qquad\qquad > 0 \qquad\qquad > 0 \qquad > 0$$

yields, $w(dL / d\theta) + L(dw / d\theta) = R(\theta) / d\theta - (d / d\theta)(r.K + p_1.H + p_2.E + p_3.T + d.Q)[\theta] \quad (8.14)$

Let $\lambda(\theta) = (d/d\theta)(r.K + p_1.H + p_2.E + p_3.T + d.Q)[\theta] > 0 \quad (8.15)$

Expression (8.14) explains that payments for increases in employment plus increments in wages as bonus paid to the employed labour force are possible as long

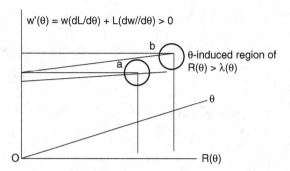

FIGURE 8.1 The capability of paying wages and wage increments as incentive payment under the impact of knowledge induction to generate increasing returns in resources in the basic-needs economic regime

as the resources increase under the θ-impact of θ-values above the θ-induced positive increases in the payments to all remaining inputs of production.

These consequences can be shown in Figure 8.1.

The region 'b' is above the region 'a' indicating the possibility of paying wages and bonuses to labour by size and increments as long as the resources of production increases. This is possible under the condition of θ-induced resources being in excess of the positive changes in the rest of the factor payments as shown (Mansfield 1985).

Islamic economics of resources in production

We have pointed out that the theory of pervasive complementarities in light of the Islamic unity of knowledge in the domain of the most extended meaning of *maqasid al-shari'ah* (Choudhury 2017b) depends on the positive augmenting effect of θ-induction of resources. Without this critical case, no possibility of complementarities can be attained. The neoclassical economic theory of marginalism via scarcity of resources as the core property would return lock, stock, and barrel. The possibility of Islam in the face of its methodology of unity of knowledge would drown.

As defined by expression (8.11), resources of production comprise payments to all factors of payments including the dividend payments. That is because in the cooperative firm as institution in the Islamic economy with its participatory financing, a factor of production by its entities is a shareholder. The rest of the community in which the firm exists is the stakeholders' social order. This feature of resource formation is signified by the nature of market-institution of the Islamic firm and its growing degree of consciousness implied by increasing θ-values.

The nature of θ-induced resources as the total cost of production is now examined in the contrasting cases of mainstream economics and Islamic economics. In the mainstream theory of cost and production of the firm, the total cost of production remains as the direct cost. Other important cost components such as implicit costs and social costs are not included. For example, in the control of violence two kinds of cost escalation may be used. First, in the mainstream economics of the firm, the production of lethal armaments and punishment as control are used. In Islamic economics, a lesser use of lethal armaments is replaced by rehabilitation methods to regenerate human resources. Such is presently the case with the Scandinavian approach to its welfare state and rehabilitation policies – an institutional effect (James 2013).

In expression (8.10), the θ-induction of cost makes the cost function sensitive to direct cost, indirect implicit cost, and social cost. The sum total of these cost components for the production of Q as social good causes a learning effect on the cost function by way of the IIE-learning processes. The randomness in the total cost component while being caused by statistical observations is also caused in respect of the IIE-learning processes experienced via evolutionary equilibrium changes along the total cost curve. The statistical randomness can be smoothened by certain statistical methods, such as by the smoothening of value estimators, and Data Enveloping Analysis (DEA). But there is no method to smoothen the effects of the simulacra of IIE-effects that arise from continuous simulations after simulations that arise along the IIE-learning processes, and so on. The nature of evolutionary equilibriums being a consequence of market-institution interaction and discourse around moral/ethical values, such discursive interventions form in the neighbourhood of evolutionary equilibrium points consequential to the intensifying learning processes; yet not reaching the core of the finality because of the inextricable presence of the hidden, the unseen (*ghayb*).

From the above-mentioned nature of intrinsic variations of the total cost function along the IIE-processes, it is obvious that the shape of the average variable cost and average fixed cost of production cannot be smooth, as shown in mainstream theory of the firm. This is because the fixed cost is θ-induced around the continuous plethora of points around its evolutionary learning equilibriums. Consequentially, the shape of the θ-induced fixed cost curve, FC(θ), is not perfectly elastic. Therefore, the average fixed cost curve, AFC(θ) = FC(θ)/Q(θ), cannot be expected to remain asymptotically smooth along the increasing θ-induced outputs. The simple case of expression (8.10) now takes the form:

$$TC(\theta) = w(\theta).L(\theta) + r(\theta).K(\theta) + FC(\theta) \qquad (8.16)$$

That is:

$$TC(\theta) = AVC(\theta) + AFC(\theta) \qquad (8.17)$$

From these expressions the formula of the average total cost curve is:

$$ATC = TC(\theta)/Q(\theta) = (ALC + AKC + AFC)[\theta] \qquad (8.18)$$

Where ALC denotes the average cost in labour use:

$$\{w(\theta).L(\theta)\}/Q(\theta) \qquad (8.19)$$

Average capital cost is denoted by:

$$\text{AKC} = \{r(\theta).K(\theta)\}/Q(\theta) \tag{8.20}$$

Between expressions (8.19) and (8.20) we can write:

$$[w(\theta).L(\theta)]/[r(\theta).K(\theta)] = \text{wage bill relative to capital cost} \tag{8.21}$$

Since labour and capital are complementary to each other in Islamic economics, therefore the wage bill and capital cost will be proportionate to each other. This result is opposite to the wage–rental relationship of neoclassical economics. The proportionate relationship is caused by the continuous change in θ-values, thus causing pervasive complementarities between all 'possibilities'. Such is the case with labour and capital, which otherwise in mainstream economics are substitutes along the production isoquants even though they are proportionately increasing along the expansion path of output. Yet every point on the expansion path denotes marginal rate of substitution between factor inputs.

The shape of the average cost curves in Islamic economics

Figure 8.2 shows the shape of the average cost curves on the basis of the above explanations. The important point to note now is how the prices of goods are determined, given the price determination method of factor inputs, most importantly labour and capital, as explained above. It is quite clear, from the type of learning curve of average cost with continuously increasing θ-values, technological change, and resource augmentation, that no minimum point of the average cost curve can be found. The average cost curve loses its smooth shape in the case of the IIE-learning processes along it. Consequently, the price of goods in an perfectly competitive goods market in equilibrium cannot be determined by the marginal cost curve. Such a curve does not exist either by construction or by nature in the perfectly competitive markets of goods and services.

The idea of perfectly competitive markets turns out to be a fictive concept. There are none such. Islamic economics proves this by its realist arguments based on organic complementarity phenomena based on Islamic methodology. In heterodox mainstream economics too, the idea of perfectly competitive markets is rejected by its replacement with the theory of evolutionary economics (Burstein 1991; Rima 1986).

Figure 8.2 depicts the case of non-existence of marginalism in the cost and production context of mainstream economics by the IIE-properties of evolutionary learning in Islamic economics context. The following symbols are explained: Let SAR denotes the financial value of average total cost. TT denotes the long-run average cost curve. The long-run adjustment is caused by adaptation to θ-induction. Points a, b, c, and d denote short-run average curves during the adaptive period of θ-induction. Note that the long-run average curve as a learning curve is shown by uneven curves that are caused by perturbations caused by θ-induction.

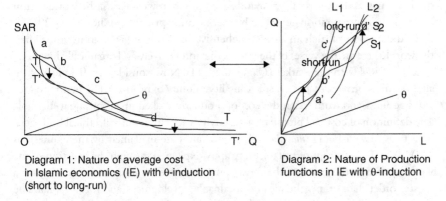

Diagram 1: Nature of average cost in Islamic economics (IE) with θ-induction (short to long-run)

Diagram 2: Nature of Production functions in IE with θ-induction

FIGURE 8.2 Corresponding inter-relations between average cost and production function in $(\theta, Q, L, TC)[\theta]$

On the production side of output corresponding to the average cost of production we have the cause and effect circularity shown in Figure 8.2. The circular causation is explained by the double-arrows. The corresponding short-run output curve and the long-run output curve are shown. The variable factor shown is only labour (L); whereas a mathematical formulation will analyse the multivariate case. The short-run production points a',b',c',d''' correspond recursively with the short-run average cost points a, b, c, d, respectively. The domains comprising such points are the IIE-learning points that evolve intra-system with θ-induction (short-run) of the inter-processes in the long-run. The important point to note in the shifts shown by the one-directional arrows is that endogenously caused changes by the circular causation effects of all the interrelating variables in both diminishing average cost of production and the corresponding ascending production levels, reinforce the complementarities between the circular causation relations in these two production and cost regions.

EXAMPLE 8.1

A distinctive example of the above explanations that bring out the unbridgeable contrasts between Islamic economics and mainstream economics is the architecture of the *masjid* (mosque) in the context of the meaning of sustainability. How does the concept of *masjid* play its distinctive role in the architecture of sustainability?

The world is a comprehensive *masjid* with all its values and artefacts of felicity, balance, and extensions of the observations conveying the Signs of God (*ayat Allah*; Lings 1991). These comprise Islamic unity of knowledge and its induction in the generality and particularities of consilience in the world-system. The world-system then assumes its stature as the great and all-comprehensive *ummah*, the world nation of balance and moderation governed by Islamic unity principle (Choudhury 2017b).

In the context of such an all-comprehensive meaning of *masjid* in its embedding the world, there are the verses of the *Qur'an* that interactively and organically interconnect the *masjid* with the market (*Qur'an* 62:9–11). Now consider the θ-induction in all these transformations and organic causality of unity of relations. The bestowed felicity, goodness, and truth lessen the cost of production taken up according to the holistic definition of cost and production as activities within the moral, ethical, and social objectives of well-being (*maslaha*). These attributes are explained by the expressions (8.1)–(8.9). The concept of sustainability aptly explained through the function of the world-system in the midst of the most comprehensive meaning of *masjid* involves a greater order than simply the idea of sustainable development and social capital. The greater rewarding moral, ethical, and social values of the *masjid*-world-sustainability interrelationship are the grand example of the consciousness in circular causation and organic complementarities represented by θ-induction of 'everything' (Barrow 1991).

The reader can think of moderation, social cohesion, consciousness in control of crime and punishment costs, rehabilitation as the control of illness, and abundance in the production regime of life-sustaining goods, services, and artefacts for well-being. Altogether these attributes decrease the total costs asymptotically, as shown in Diagram 1 of Figure 8.3. The average cost curve learns along the ever-expanding IIE-processes of learning in organic unity of knowledge and all such variables as would be in the sustainability vector. An example of such a vector is what was given below, namely: $\{Q, K, L, H, E, T, R\}[\theta]$.

EXERCISE 8.1

1. Interpret the idea of fairness as social justice ($J(\theta)$) in regards to complementarity (θ-induction) between labour and capital in the theory of the firm (Choudhury 1998) using the vector $\{Q,L,K,J\}[\theta]$.
2. If perfect competition is untenable in Islamic economics, how is cost and benefit equalized according to $C(\theta)$ as cost and revenue as benefit, $Rev(\theta)$? Answer by using the idea of resources in TIE as against cost of production in mainstream economics.
3. Use the additional variable of financial dividends received by shareholders, $D(\theta) = d(\theta).Q(\theta)$ to explain how this is at the same time a financial return and a resource requirement in the theory of cost and production of the firm in Islamic economics.

Irrelevance of the marginal cost, marginal productivity, and returns to scale concepts in Islamic economics

The ideas of all marginals – marginal cost, marginal revenue, and marginal productivity – are logically untenable in Islamic economics methodology. That is because the continuous learning points along the average cost curve, in Figure 8.3 caused by evolutionary learning processes and not simply by statistical variations in the data for average cost, do not allow for the marginal cost to exist. Besides, the corresponding total cost curves do not allow for smooth curve structure for the same reason. On the corresponding plane for production curves too, there cannot exist smooth points, as shown by the rough curves. These are noticeable cases for both the short-run and the long-run. More formally, the simple mathematics of marginal formulas would not yield smooth curves to be meaningful in product and input pricing.

For instance, $MC = \partial C / \partial Q = [\partial C / \partial \theta] / [\partial Q / \partial \theta]$ (8.22)

is not measurable around any evolutionary equilibrium point along the θ-induced total cost curve. Thereby, the *ceteris paribus* nature of the resulting cost curve in mainstream economics of the firm does not allow for complementarities between all the variables of the total cost curve, as in the case of expression (8.11), to uphold. Thereby also, the circular causation relations are untenable in such a case of a marginalist formula.

The case of the marginal revenue results of mainstream economics of the firm as untenable was proved before. It is now equally untenable for the marginal productivity curve to be possible. The nature of random fluctuations around the evolutionary learning points, apart from the statistical variations, establishes circular causation results as implied and explained by the recursive interrelations between Diagram 1 and Diagram 2 in Figure 8.3.

The impossibility of having the marginal cost and marginal productivity curves implies also that the average cost and average productivity curves cannot be used for empirical and strategic inferences. This is because of the random variations of evolutionary learning processes. It is further noted that the idea of marginals is a nicety rather than reality in the midst of multivariate endogenous interrelations. The latter is the case that results from the evaluation of the well-being function. This is the *maslaha* function of *maqasid al-shari'ah* as the firm's objective function in a targeted regime of *dynamic* basic-needs regime of development with the effect of consciousness generated in and by the θ-variable. The circular causation relations then must abide along with the *evaluation* of the well-being function.

Consequently now, with the irrelevance of the marginal, it is impossible for the optimum scale of output and the short-run and long-run curves of marginal cost and productivity curve to be tenable. The only way though that the increasing returns to scale and economies of scope in production can exist in Islamic economics is by the evolutionary learning processes. We can summarize this case by the following formalism:

$$Q = f_1(K, L, H, E, T, R)[\theta] \qquad\qquad (8.23)$$

yielding, $dQ / d\theta = (\partial f_1 / \partial K).(dK / d\theta) + (\partial f_1 / \partial L).(dL / d\theta) + (\partial f_1 / \partial H).(dH / d\theta)$

$$+ (\partial f_1 / \partial E).(dE / d\theta) + (\partial f_1 / \partial T).(dT / d\theta) + (\partial f_1 / \partial R).(dR / d\theta)$$

$$(8.24)$$

Each of the terms on the right-hand side is positive under the *maslaha* effect of 'θ' on the variables. Consequently, $dQ/d\theta > 0$ for all positive learning effects of θ-values intra-system (short-run) and inter-system (long-run). Both of these are continuous phenomena over knowledge, space, and time. Now no first-order optimal conditions can exist for the mainstream case of maximization of output, and thereby of the attainment of maximum returns to scale, as in the case of perfect competition. Paradoxically too, the firms in imperfect competition also aim at the objective of maximization of profit and output, although it is a fallacy. This fallacy was pointed out in the theory of satisficing behaviour of firms formalized by Simon (1987).

The first-order necessary and sufficient conditions of optimal production function of the variables in expression (8.23) of the mainstream genre, like:

$$MP_L/w = MP_K/r = MP_H/p1 = MP_E/p2 = MP_T/p3 = MP_R/p4 = 1/MC$$
$$(8.25)$$

are replaced by the following conditions of IIE-process learning for evaluation (estimation followed by simulation) of the well-being function with circular causation relations, of which is the expression (8.23) as one.

(Elasticity coefficient

Of Q in respect of L)$\varepsilon_{QL} / \varepsilon_{QK}$ $\qquad\qquad\qquad$ (8.26)

= either positive (complementary) or negative signifying marginalist substitution in the partial sense between K and L in respect of Q. In the latter case, policy, strategy, and consciousness by θ-induction are needed to correct for complementarity or lesser marginalist substitution reducing to complementarities as resources increase continuously under θ-induction.

EXERCISE 8.2

1. Write down and explain the formulas for complementarities contrary to marginal rate of substitution between all the variables of expression (8.23) according to their various circular causation equations.
2. Draw relevant diagrams for the complementary cases along the IIE-learning processes originating from the answer to the previous question.

The fallacy of the economic efficiency concept in mainstream economics, in light of Islamic economics

Economic Efficiency is a concept that corresponds with the minimization of total average cost of production, and the corresponding maximization of output and profits. Erroneously, the same concept of economic efficiency of a firm is applied to perfect and imperfect competition in terms of their self-same objective criterion of maximization of output and profits. In this case, the long-run marginal cost curve and the short-run marginal cost curve intersect at a level that determines the minimum price level and the level of output at which production can continue. At prices below this level, efficient production ceases. The fallacy arising from this phenomenon is that no explanation and process of policy, strategy, and techno-logical change that become important to evade the point of the firm's operational closure can be endogenously explained, except by means of exogenous impact of such forces. Learning by discourse, manifest in the field of evolutionary equilib-rium points of the short-run and the long-run, remain absent in the firm's closure or restarting points of decision-making. Such alternative possibilities were indeed studied by Schumpeter (Cantner, Gaffard, & Nesta 2009) to explain his theory of creative destruction and rejuvenation.

In the end therefore, the mainstream neoclassical theory of the firm yields a static theory of economic efficiency and its corresponding theories of maximiza-tion, steady-state equilibrium, and exogenous effects. The dynamic concept of effi-ciency remains impossible in such a neoclassical theory of economic efficiency. It is impossible to carry a sequence of economic efficiency points along the time trend to represent the dynamic efficiency concept (Choudhury & Hoque 2004). Finally, it is equally impossible to use an optimal control model to explain economic effi-ciency in the case of the endogenously learning field of knowledge-induced par-ticipatory economic behaviour (Choudhury & Korvin 2002). The TIE model yields its genre of evaluation of well-being function with desired and evaluated variables for complementarities, subject to the circular causation relations. The variables and coefficients of such a model of inter-variable relations are all θ-induced.

Figure 8.3 explains the impossibility of endogenously determining the price and quantity adjustment between the short-run and long-run in the neoclassical

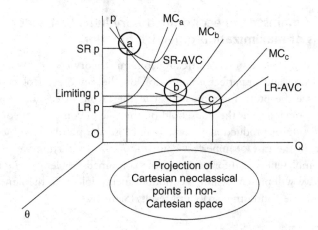

FIGURE 8.3 Rejecting the postulates of imperfect competition of mainstream economics by Islamic economics

economic theory of the firm. Note that the presence of the θ-axis to define the coordinates of $(\theta,p,Q)[\theta]$ causes non-Cartesian transformation all over the economic space. This space encompasses the diffusion of perturbation points of evolutionary learning, such as around points a, b, c and the like. Each such point would then be formed and regenerated by coordinates of $\{\theta,p,Q\}[\theta]$.

In neoclassical analysis the gap between the short-run and the longer-run in the case of imperfect competition is marked by the change from point 'a' to point 'b'. Then compared to the firm in perfect competition as the most efficient firm, the gap in price, output, and profit is shown between the points 'b' and 'c'. The adjustment between these gaps 'b' to 'c' would change the nature of the firm in imperfect competition to perfect competition. This is an undesired case for a firm in imperfect competition to rise above normal profits.

Contrarily, an evolutionary learning firm in Islamic economics would interrelate the points $(\theta,p,Q)[\theta]_a$, $(\theta,p,Q)[\theta]_b$, $(\theta,p,Q)[\theta]_c$ and many more of these kinds all over the non-Cartesian generalization so as to revert to the objective of evaluation of well-being (*maslaha*), subject to inter-variable circular causation relations. The formulation is as before but now introducing time $(t(\theta))$ to mark evolutionary processes of intra-system and inter-systemic adjustments as follows:

$$\text{Evaluate } \{\theta\}\, W(\theta,p,Q,t)[\theta] \tag{8.27}$$

$$\text{Subject to } p(\theta) = f_1(\theta,Q(\theta),t(\theta)) \tag{8.28}$$

$$Q(\theta) = f_2(\theta,p(\theta),t(\theta)) \tag{8.29}$$

Empirical θ-function as measured well-being (*maslaha*):

$$\theta = F(\theta,p,Q,t)[\theta]$$

Fallacies of mainstream economic theory in its first order conditions of maximization objective functions

One of the many fallacies of mainstream economic theory is to premise both perfect competition and imperfect competition on the same set of objectives. That is to maximize the profit function subject to the axiom of economic rationality, although it is obvious that the household on the side of consumer theory and the firm on the side of production theory would lose the possibility to acquire full information in the case of imperfect competition. In this section we provide the case of incompleteness of information in the combined problem of the following type. Next, we will present Islamic economics methodology to the same problem and bring out the contrasting analytical results (Samuelson 1970):

$$\text{Max. } Q = F(x_1, x_2, x_3, \ldots, x_n) \tag{8.30}$$

Subject to the derived demand function for inputs of the following type:

$$x_i = f_i(\mathbf{x}_j), i = 1,2,3,\ldots,n \tag{8.31}$$

Here some of the variables would be necessarily exogenous according to neoclassical economic theory. Examples of such variables are technological choice and innovation, population, and resource augmentation. These factors are injected from outside the production system to cause shifts. But there does not exist a system of endogenous variables like (Q,K,L) to cause changes. For instance, the choice of the (K/L)-ratio is internal to the firm as institution. In empirical work a representative value is selected by observing the statistical trend in the (K/L)-ratios to come up with a target value. This ratio is not an input of production. Hence technological change, T = (K/L), must be used along with endogenous variables in the production function. But T cannot be determined conversely by the market determined output of production. All this means that the following functions would be untenable: T = f(Q); Q = g(T). There must be additional endogenous variables to form meaningful functions as: Q = h(K,L,T).

Furthermore, we can use the constraints on the demand side of output by consumers in a general equilibrium theory of production in mainstream economics. We formalize as follows:

$$U_k = U_k(\mathbf{Q,x,l,T}) \tag{8.32}$$

Bold letters denote vectors. 'l' denotes leisure off work or usage of input $(\mathbf{x})$.

The combined production and consumption problem is stated as follows:

$$\text{Max.} \quad Q_s = F_s(\mathbf{x,l,T}), s \text{ as system of produced outputs;}$$
$$s = 1,2,\ldots,s \tag{8.33}$$

$$\text{Subject to, } x_i = f_i(\mathbf{x}_j,\mathbf{l,T}), i = 1,2,3,\ldots,n \tag{8.34}$$

$$U_k = U_k(\mathbf{Q,x,l,T}); k=1,2,\ldots m \tag{8.35}$$

A detailed classical maximization of the above system of functions is by the Lagrangian (L):

$$L = \text{Max}[F_s(\mathbf{x,l,T}) + \lambda_1(x_i - f_i(\mathbf{x}_j,\mathbf{l,T}) + \lambda_2(U_k - U_k(\mathbf{Q,x,l,T})] \tag{8.36}$$

$$\partial L/\partial x_i = \partial Q/\partial x_i + \lambda_1(1 - \partial f_i/\partial x_i) - \lambda_2(\partial U_k/\partial x_i) = 0 \tag{8.37}$$

$$\partial L/\partial x_k = \partial Q/\partial x_k + \lambda_1(1 - \partial f_i/\partial x_k) - \lambda_2(\partial U_k/\partial x_k) = 0 \tag{8.38}$$

$$\partial L/\partial \lambda_1 = x_i - f_i(\mathbf{x}_j,\mathbf{l,T}) = 0 \tag{8.39}$$

$$\partial L/\partial \lambda_2 = U_k - U_k(\mathbf{Q,x,l,T}) = 0 \tag{8.40}$$

$s = 1,2,\ldots,S; i = 1,2,3,\ldots n; k=1,2,\ldots m.$

Consider for example equation (7.41) as

$$\partial Q/\partial x_i = \lambda_2\left(\partial U_k/\partial x_i\right) - \lambda_1\left(1 - \partial f_i/\partial x_i\right)$$

$$\left.\begin{array}{c}\end{array}\right\}$$

$$\partial Q/\partial x_k = \lambda_2\left(\partial U_k/\partial x_k\right) - \lambda_1\left(1 - \partial f_i/\partial x_k\right) \qquad (8.41)$$

When solved for λ_1 and λ_2 we obtain an expression that depends critically on the marginal rate of substitution between x_i and x_k, for all values of $i = 1,2,\ldots n$ number of production; and k number of consumers. Besides, the values of **T** cannot be solved for as an independent vector of variables. The l-variables are substitutes with **x**-variables according to the income and substitution effects on final choices of consumers (Pindyck & Rubinfeld 2001).

The meaning of these results is that a solution to the Lagrangian depends on the postulate of marginal rate of substitution. That is, in the case of work and leisure, the meaning of leisure is unproductive activity in things like self-help, community involvement; informal teaching and learning that do not carry direct pecuniary benefits. The results also convey that some variables must necessarily remain exogenous (like **T**) in determining the solutions for λ_1 and λ_2. Only recently, Paul Romer (1986) published on the theory of new growth, which is also known as endogenous growth theory. But there is no such contribution presently in microeconomics of the firm's production function.

Perfect and imperfect competition in partial and general equilibriums of mainstream economics, critiqued by Islamic economics

The equations (8.30)–(8.40) explain the general equilibrium analysis. While we can treat this case only mathematically, the diagrammatic explanation needs to devolve into a partial equilibrium case. The assumption of *ceteris paribus* of endogenous variables and the exogenous effects of other variables can now be explained by Figure 8.4 (Diagram 1) in the case of perfect competition and by Figure 8.4 (Diagram 2) in the case of imperfect competition.

In perfect competition scarce resource allocation takes place between goods (x_1,x_2) along the expansion path that is driven by the exogenous effect of technology. The point 'a', as the meeting point of the smooth production possibility curve PP and the smooth consumer indifference curve II on the resource line curve (income line) TT, denotes the general equilibrium case of perfect competition. All these cases are shown in Diagram 1 of Figure 8.5.

In imperfect competition the market is independently segmented between private goods (x_1) and public goods (x_2) along their expansion paths EP_b and EP_a, respectively. The allocations are still described by the same kinds of production possibility frontiers and the indifference curves. This is the fallacy of mainstream

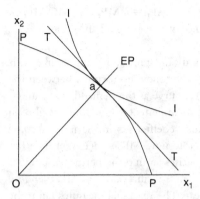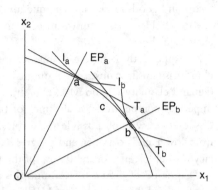

FIGURE 8.4 Resource allocations in partial equilibrium under perfect and imperfect competition

economics in describing the objective function of the two kinds of goods in production and consumption, respectively. In both cases the objective function is based on output maximization, profit maximization, and utility maximization. The substitution between 'a' and 'b' in terms simultaneously of consumer goods and producer goods is the case of the market resource allocations being divided independently between private goods and public goods. This is the case of imperfect competition.

The fallacy here is that, in such marginalist substitution there are transaction costs both ways, and policies that are not implicated. If these were put into effect then either of the points 'a' and 'b' would be perturbation points. The effect would be widespread all over the production possibility surface and the consumer indifference curve. The mainstream economic theory of marginal rate of substitution is annulled. Relative prices of the goods do not have a determinate role in setting market price relatives or putting policy directions and resource allocations in a specific way by means of marginalist study. Finally, the point 'c' is supposed to be the linear combination of the points 'a' and 'b'. This point shares in the problems of perturbations and non-smooth production possibility surface and the consumer indifference curve under the impact of policies, strategies, and technological change. The smooth surfaces cannot hold.

Fallacy in the pricing theory of the firm in imperfect competition

In Figure 8.5 the meeting points like 'a' in the case of Diagram 1 is where the first order conditions of profit and output maximization hold: $p = MC$ along the long-run MC curve, Average Revenue curve, and MR curve, all coincide at the minimum of the U-shaped average cost curve. At this point as well, $MP_L/w = MP_K/r = 1/MC$, on a limited case of productive inputs in perfectly competitive factor and goods markets. Consequently, $w = MC.MP_L = p.MP_L; r = MC.MP_K = p.MP_K$. Problems of mainstream economic theory regarding all these issues were examined above.

In imperfectly competitive market for goods and productive inputs like 'a, b, c' in Diagram 2, mainstream economics gives the following formula between the demand elasticity (ε) and MR. Thereby, the AR curve as the demand curve under imperfect competition for all kinds of firms in imperfect competition is also an elastic curve with all possible values of elasticity coefficients in the interval $(0,\infty)$ from lower end to upper end progressively. Note now, $MR = p(1-1/\varepsilon)$. The fallacy of such niceties of the theory of the firm arises around the perturbed point 'a' in Diagram 2 of Figure 8.5. Around this point no specific values of AR, therefore ε-values, and thereby values of MR can be read. The marginal measures fail to be determinate. The pricing and output (MR=MC) relations of imperfect competition are annulled. No market values of profit-maximization, policy effects, technological change and similar exogenous effects can be read by using the formulas of the theory of imperfect competition.

EXERCISE 8.3

1. Consider the allocation of land as a resource to grow life-sustenance. In mainstream economics land is seen as in scarce supply, whereas demand for land is perfectly elastic if land is seen as a right of all to own (Sattar 2015). The market equilibrium for mainstream economic idea of land rights is limited to a scarce quantity at a certain fixed price for a quantity of land. Under these conditions can any global governance allocate an increased quantity of land to Palestinians to relieve them of their present refugee status under Israeli rule? How does mainstream theory of the firm explain land allocation in this case?

2. What can be the role of discourse as an endogenous force to attain fairness in the Israeli occupation of Palestinian lands?

3. Extend the above land-problem to the case of allocation of space. Can you write on the global governance of the air-space problem of East–West détente caused by the mainstream kind of pricing of space use between competing countries?

Irrelevant concept of value in mainstream economics of consumer and production theory

In mainstream economics the concept of value arising from the side of consumer theory is marginal utility ($MU(x)$) of consumption of a certain *ceteris paribus* quantity of good (x). This is a market-oriented concept. By the fact that there is no endogenous relationship between ethics and x, therefore, there cannot be any continuously differentiable utility gained from such ethical induction. Consequently, every MU(x) is in respect of market goods. Thereby, the price of the good, which represents the MU(x), is assumed to be a market price. This is the case of perfectly competitive market exchange.

In the case of imperfect competition, as for the case of public goods, the fallacy of mainstream economics is that the same deductive formulas of marginal utility and marginal productivity are used. Now $MR = MC = p.(1-1/\varepsilon)$, as explained in respect of Diagram 2 of Figure 7.5, also conveys the meaning of ethical independence in the determination of price as value in imperfect competition. Now the demand curve of the firm's output is given by $AR = (1/2).MR$. Along this demand curve the values of price elasticity of demand $\varepsilon(p,Q)$ are computed.

Mainstream economic theory is thereby totally independent of any ethical context. Only a *ceteris paribus* concept of inter-variable relations of the market-determined types holds. The consequences of such a narrow concept of the theory of value, output, and price are far reaching in limiting the study of policy-making, behavioural and technological endogenous effects and the like.

Welfare consequences of the market theory of consumption and production

The independence of the utility function and the firm's production function in a combined general equilibrium case formalized by the system of equations (8.33)–(8.40) implies that the welfare function so studied remains simply a market-centred criterion. There is no ethical embedding in the *welfare* function in neoclassical economics as there is in the well-being function (*maslaha*) in Islamic economics.

The extended form of the general equilibrium model of welfare including consumer utilities and production functions takes the form,

$$\text{Max } W(\mathbf{x}) = W(U_1(\mathbf{x}), U_2(\mathbf{x}),\dots U_n(\mathbf{x})) \tag{8.42}$$

for n-number of consumers competing for a vector $\mathbf{x}$ of m-number of goods, subject to the system of equations (8.33)–(8.35). Figure 8.5 explains the nature of ethically independent correspondence of relations between the welfare function, its component utility functions, and the commodity space, all taken up in pure market venue.

Consider the utilities of the poor $(U_p(\mathbf{x}))$ and the rich $(U_R(\mathbf{x}))$. Both P and R consume the same produced quantities of goods of the $\mathbf{x}$-vector. In a market venue they compete for these goods by their scarce resources T_p of the poor; T_R of the rich. Similar labels explain the goods quadrant. While the points a and thereby a', b and thereby b', are efficient and optimal points of perfect competition; the point c is a suboptimal and inefficient point. 'c' is driven from its inefficient allocation point to the surfaces of Diagrams 1 and 2 by exogenously imposed policies, strategies, technological change and the like. Yet the second-order conditions of such reconstructed optimal points cannot reach the desired optimal and efficient surfaces.

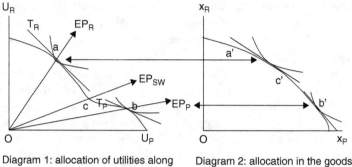

Diagram 1: allocation of utilities along the welfare surface WW showing suboptimal point 'c' having a social indifference curve (not shown) below the ones at 'a' and 'b'

Diagram 2: allocation in the goods market at the corresponding points a', b', c' on the production possibility curve with specific indifference curves

FIGURE 8.5 Fallacy in the allocation of scarce resources in welfare concept between the poor and the rich

The theorem in this regard is that, if the first-order conditions of profit maximization are not attained, then there is no need to utilize second-order conditions to improve the market failure to restore efficiency (Henderson & Quandt 1958).

The case of monopoly, monopolistic competition, and oligopoly with mainstream fallacies

Disintegrating monopoly in Islamic economics

The case of any kind of monopoly is untenable if social discourse and inter-variable complementary relations are promoted. In the case of natural monopoly the non-substitutable nature of the good can be completely altered by allowing for participation via technology, and product and risk diversifications, and transformation of the economic behavioural patterns of consumption and production into dynamic life-sustaining goods and services (basic-needs).

In the case of regulated monopoly, the fair return to the monopolist could be used to generate sharing of cost, risk and production, and technology to bring about stable prices and increased production through the employment of resources in constructive reformation of the production structure. Dominant firm case and industry concentration could then be made to share diversified production, as would be the case of supply outlets in MSEs and microenterprises. These are all signs of transformation into a life-fulfilling dynamic basic-needs regime of development in Islamic economics. On the other hand, sustainability of the dynamic basic-needs regimes of development would necessarily be characterized by the rise of SMEs and microenterprises. Thereby the regime of large monopoly firms will be automatically restricted by endogenous effects in industrial development. The inter-causality between consumption and production activities in a dynamic basic-needs regime of constructive transformation for inter-causal functioning in ethicality is actualized by the complementary relations between increases in information flow that comes about by the discursive medium of partners, stakeholders, and policy-makers.

Diminishing monopolistic competition in Islamic economics

Discursive experience that embeds policies, strategies, technology and growing ethical consciousness in consumers and producer behaviours through interaction would cause monopoly to be transformed into the state of monopolistic competition as a mid-way transformation. But if such a transformation is considered to be continuous under the flow of information and consciousness then all the variables would have to be taken as endogenously related. Thereby, the various critiques of marginalism and *ceteris paribus* nature of exogeneity of variables would be upheld to re-establish the fallacies of the monopolistic transformation by the underlying analytical problems encountered, as mentioned above.

The neoclassical explanation of price adjustment as information increases out of chiselling behaviour of representative firms in monopolistic competition conveys the overall static pictures of AR, MR, MC, price and output determination over the long-run. This is a fallacy in explaining the transformation from the short-run to the long-sun, and much more so when continuity and endogeneity are invoked. Monopolistic competition theory has no analytical grounds in such cases to explain the real case of continuously endogenous θ-induced change.

Oligopolistic competition in Islamic economics

Oligopoly as a production and differentiated price-output decision-making industrial arrangement with number of member firms in it beings less than that in monopolistic competition survives because of its closed membership. Such a structure needs to be sustained by abidance of institutionally decided collusive rules of setting prices and output levels. Yet as an example, in the case of Petroleum Development Oman, openness to oil production and pricing has helped industrial development in the country through enhanced production, technological change, and economic diversification launched by the Petroleum Development Oman (PDO) activities.

Over-reliance on oligopoly production, pricing, and internal decision-making has been found to artificially protect the monopoly character of oil in the world market in the absence of substitutes for oil. The implication is that oil-dependence in such a scenario of development continues on. On the other hand, oil to non-oil diversification is urgently needed to relieve dependence on oil in every aspect of economic and social development. But such a transformation ought not to come out of the neoclassical economic idea of marginal substitution of oil and non-oil productions. Rather, the transformation is to be brought about by a continuous change in pricing, production and technological change, as information increases via open-ended institutional and inter-country discussions.

The kinked point on the demand curve of oligopolistic pricing and production would then dissolve into a continuously changing decision-making point. The end point of such transformation is again towards the *dynamic* life-sustaining regime of development. It has its objective criterion of well-being as defined earlier, quite different from the concept of welfare in mainstream economics, which was critically examined above.

Addressing dynamic market shares and industrial structure: return to Islamic economics methodology

What then is the realist picture of consumption and production in economic terms? The central points are to restore continuity in the pervasively inter-variable endogenous relations. This comprises establishing inter-variable relations by means of their organic causality arising from pervasive complementarities. This signifies unity of knowledge as the abiding characteristic of Islamic economics in terms of its methodology. It was amply explained in this and other chapters that the central episteme of unity of knowledge dispels the mainstream economic axiom of economic rationality totally. Within the resulting reformulation, the derived postulate of marginalism, optimization, and steady-state equilibrium are *logically* rejected.

With the above summary critique of mainstream economics and keeping the methodological nature of Islamic economics in view, the mainstream economic idea of imperfect competition is replaced by the continuous process of IIE-learning to simulate socially a marginalist or dialectical system of competition into a pervasively partnered complementarity (pairing). These attributes and the imminent circular causation for evaluating social well-being in its equivalent conceptual and empirical forms comprise the computational general equilibrium model of consumption and production with moral/ethical social embedding. Equations (8.1)–(8.9) form an exemplary system. The system can be enlarged as the variables and their numbers of observations increase. The price, output, resource, cost, and technological results are empirically determinable now.

The implications of intra-systemic and inter-systemic evaluation are brought into play to obtain empirical and policy, strategic, and technological implications of the θ-induced effects. The entire system, with their 'estimated' results followed by 'simulated' coefficients is thus made up of dynamic conditions of *maslaha* (well-being). This implicates a progressively evolutionary transformation of the truly Islamic economic and social order into a life-sustaining, basic-needs regime of consciousness towards development by the attributes of IIE-process-oriented preference functions and production menus.

The example of such aggregate preferences is:

$$\wp(\theta) = U_{\text{interaction}} \cap_{\text{integration}} \{\wp_C, \wp_P\}[\theta] \tag{8.43}$$

C denotes consumer choices. P denotes production choices.

$$d\wp/d\theta > 0 \tag{8.44}$$

Expressions (8.43) and (8.44) mean that *maqasid al-shari'ah* choices intensify as consciousness of the Islamic unity of knowledge deepens. This too is a fully inclusive discursive undertaking, shown by $\cup_{\text{interaction}} \cap_{\text{integration}}$ in expression (8.43) by way of market-institution organic interrelations in the context of IIE-process-oriented learning.

Special case of oligopolistic generalization in determining prices and outputs with discursive effects, endogenous technology, and resources

In respect to the kinked demand curve for the oligopoly good and at which point the collusive price and output are determined by market-institutional interactive realities in the case of Islamic economics in reference to the variables as example $\{\theta, Q_i, p_i, T_i, R_i\}[\theta]$, the price and output equations for each of the participatory members (i) are as follows:

$$p_i = f_{1i}(\theta_i, Q_i, T_i, R_i)[\theta] \tag{8.45}$$

$$Q_i = f_{2i}(\theta_i, p_i, T_i, R_i)[\theta] \tag{8.46}$$

The well-being function beyond the pricing and output mechanisms are evaluated by:

$$\theta_i = F(Q_i, p_i, T_i, R_i)[\theta_i] \tag{8.47}$$

In these equations we assign the following sets of meanings to the variables: $\{\theta_i\}$-values denote the individual participatory member's (i) perception of his assessment of depth of unity of knowledge, represented by personalized ordinal value in respect of socio-economic variables. From the interaction and integration between the partners there arises a convergence of θ-values for all the participants. That is:

$$\theta = \cup_{\text{interaction}} \cap_{\text{integration}} \{\theta_i\} \tag{8.48}$$

In the same way, any of the variables $x_i \in \{Q_i, p_i, T_i, R_i)[\theta_i]\}$ aggregate to:

$$x = \cup_{\text{interaction}} \cap_{\text{integration}} \{x_i\} \tag{8.49}$$

The personalized variable of technological change denotes that which is used by the specific partners, such as between Saudi Arabia, Indonesia, and Nigeria at different levels of oil production as members of OPEC.

Now the forms of evaluative equations emergent from (8.40)–(8.42) are:

$$p = f_1(\theta, Q, T, R)[\theta] \tag{8.50}$$

$$Q = f_2(\theta, p, T, R)[\theta] \tag{8.51}$$

$$\theta = F(Q,p,T,R)[\theta] \tag{8.52}$$

The expressions (8.48)–(8.49) as the aggregative preference formulas are not quantifiable, being simply conceptual for explanation. Their equivalents in the forms of (8.50)–(8.52) can be empirically evaluated. The price and output variables for the oligopoly resulting from collusion are determined in Islamic economics by an extensive vector of variables that enter the market-institutional interactive determinants of choices. All such variables are critically influenced by the evolutionary learning θ-variable as consciousness based on the attainment of complementarities between the *maqasid*-choices in the light of Islamic unity of knowledge.

The kinked colluded form of demand function in mainstream microeconomics is now a function of a plethora of similar possibilities in the region of IIE-processes in continuity of expanding vector of possibilities. While the above formalism is specified for the oligopoly, the same approach is valid for the monopolistic competition based on the attributes that were mentioned earlier in this section. Even so, the various price and output adjustment from economic surplus to normal profit condition would not be the case in Islamic economics. That is because the surplus, little or more, must always exist to be distributed as participatory Islamic dividends. The chiselling behaviour of monopolistic competition does not exist because of its logical non-existence in the face of *maqasid al-shari'ah*, the Islamic economic methodology of unity of knowledge that is embedded in the IIE-processes and that characterizes the dynamics of expressions (8.48) and (8.49). These dynamics play their critical transformative role in the IIE-processes towards the life-fulfilling regime of development.

As it was mentioned before, Islamic economic methodology can revert to the disintegrated situation when the episteme of unity of knowledge weakens and its induction of the variables becomes weak and results in variables and entities of the differentiated type. In such a case, the evaluation of the well-being function subject to circular causation will show deepening degrees of marginalism by the negative values of the coefficients of the inter-variable causality in the circular causation system. Besides, the focus on *maqasid al-shari'ah* for making consumption, production, and social choices will dissipate into oblivion. Marginalism will thereby arise. Reversion to mainstream economics will occur. Thus Islamic economics methodology with its method of circular causation can answer both the case of learning dynamics in unity of knowledge and the differentiated system of marginalism where considerations of morality, ethicality, and endogenous inter-variable relations do not exist and are taken exogenously.

TIE cannot arise from marginalist mainstream economics. That is, the Islamic methodological worldview of Islamic economics cannot arise from the neoclassical or any mainstream approach, because the absence of the endogenous nature of morality/ethics and sociality, as in the case of the Islamic economics precept of unity of knowledge, would not allow for the rise of consciousness that characterizes the analytical dynamics in Islamic economics. In this kind of dichotomy between materiality and morality/ethics and sociality, mainstream economics invokes the nature of dichotomy between *a priori* reasoning and *a posteriori* reasoning; between deductive and inductive reasoning; and between *noumena* and phenomena. These topics were studied earlier in this book. Such is the perennial nature of all of Western science. It was pointed out by Husserl (1965).

No such dichotomy can logically exist under the axiom of Islamic unity of knowledge and its induction of the generality and particulars of diverse world-systems. A specific case of such particulars is economics, finance, science, and society. Thus the divine law (ontology) is inter-causally embedded with the mind–matter world-system and the evolutionary small 'closures' of IIE-learning processes and the eventual 'Closure' of the Hereafter. The world-system embodies the possibility of knowledge that is the epistemology. The small closures via IIE-processes and the eventual large Closure of the Hereafter establish socio-scientific meaning of Islamic methodological worldview.

On such a unity of knowledge between ontology and epistemology, Neville Spencer (2000) writes:

> However, for any theory that we have about what knowledge is, we must have a presupposition about what the world is like. That is, we must assume that the world exists in such a way that it makes our theory of knowledge possible. There is no escaping having a theory of ontology, it is only a question of whether or not it is consciously acknowledged and studied or whether it is left as an implicit presupposition of one's theory of epistemology.

EXERCISE 8.4

1. The nickel production project has decided to form an oligopoly of ten firms to collude on price and output setting. What kind of market and institutional interaction would establish the nickel oligopoly as a social oligopoly meeting its objective of collusion and social well-being? Select appropriate variables, and set up the system of relations for explaining the market-institutional causality for the oligopoly to realize its integrated objectives.
2. In the process of its dissolution under the impact of competition policy what would be the final status of the social oligopoly? Explain the process of such reorganization of the oligopoly to address the life-fulfillment regime of development in Islamic economics.
3. Construct a participatory relational model between a dominant firm and small and medium enterprises (SMEs) in regards to product sharing and joint pricing decision. How can such a social transformation of production be realized by market and institutional functions?
4. Illustrate by suitable diagrams the price and output relations in an ethically induced Islamic economics environment for a dominant firm that starts off with the following schedule: monopoly pricing; monopoly output; monopoly profit; regulated monopoly condition; predatory pricing mechanism.

The concept of value in Islamic economics

From our study of the concept of value in regards to the mainstream and the ethical perspectives it is clear that such markets come to have transactions in private goods and public goods that function independently of each other in their own separate markets. In the case of Islamic economics, there is no such good as a purely private good or a purely public good, for these are not independent of each other. An example is of oil drilling in offshore Newfoundland in Canada. The government would like to have participation by private firms. It will not risk public tax dollars by doing the venture alone for the sake of national enrichment.

In this book throughout we have represented the morally/ethically embedded knowledge-induced material variables by increasing degrees of consciousness. Such knowledge-induced variables in the light of unity of knowledge denoted by $\mathbf{x}(\theta)$ are uniformly social goods, irrespectively of being privately or publicly consumed, produced, and owned. There is no independence of relationship between private goods, so as to turn them into social goods – or more strongly still as ethical goods. The social good is thereby a common good with consciousness of unity of participation by complementarities defining the organic inter-causal relationships between the consumers and producers at all levels of these activities. In this sense, Islamic economics becomes an ethico-economic particularity in the study of generalized computational equilibrium as an evolutionary system within the expanded domain of the world-system.

Now consider the concept of value of social good in the following example: A group of companies and researchers (e.g. producers and consumers) together make a discovery that is not substitutable (but not complementary) or scarcely substitutable. Mainstream economic theory would characterize such a production group as monopoly and oligopoly, respectively. Any possible dissolution from such production types to more social types will make them representative of monopolistic competition. Thus the social cleavages of imperfect competition remain. The conditions of a differentiated economic system located apart in the social milieu establish the attributes of self-interest, absolute private property rights, bounded economic rationality, and the like.

The question then is this: Differently from the pricing theory of the firm in imperfect competition for goods without or with scarce limits of commodity substitution or factor substitution as in the labour market, how would *maqasid al-shari'ah* recommend such pricing and output generation? What otherwise would be the resulting price and output levels endogenously determined in Islamic economics?

The central characteristic to note in this case is the role of consciousness and the market-institution interface that promotes such consciousness through active realization of Islamic unity of knowledge in relation to *maqasid*-choices. The momentum in this direction of moral reconstruction of market-institution inter-relationship and the goal of sustainability within the life-fulfillment regime of participatory development will incite such policies, strategies, and education. The implementation of such endogenously relational forces will generate the way to attain social choices (Vanek 1971; Streeten 1981; Korten 1995). Examples of such policies, strategies, and development regimes centre on participatory development and its production and consumption designs. This is the nature of consumption and production that characterizes the Shatibi-menu of necessaries (*dururiyath*), comforts (*hajiyath*), and refinements (*tahsaniyath*), altogether belonging to the life-fulfilling regime of participatory development.

The rare metal discovery we have referred to above must enter its social goods portfolio in Islamic economics market-institutional interfaced arrangement. Its price and output setting is determined in the following way: We recall expressions (8.48) and (8.49) for the particular case of interactively integrating private and public goods in the context of forming social preference embedding these attributes in social goods. Thereafter, the equations (8.50)–(8.52) show the partial equilibrium case of the more generalized system that can be formulated to yield price, output, and social well-being in terms of the consumption and production of social goods.

The social value formed in Islamic economics in respect to this problem is given by the evaluated (estimated and simulated) value of the well-being function, conceptually explained by $W(\theta)$ and log linearized to θ-function in terms of the variables $\mathbf{x}(\theta)$ for quantitative viability. The value added by the vector of variables is given by: $d\theta = \Sigma_s (\partial W(\mathbf{x}(\theta))/\partial x_s).dx_s$.

EXERCISE 8.5

1. Set up a theory of social value in Islamic economics by taking all variables in their logarithmic form. Thereby, explain the meanings of the coefficients as elasticity in the circular causation equations and the total well-being function that can be first estimated and then simulated to attain better levels of complementarities between the variables. Why would there be increasing returns to scale in value added if $\Sigma_s \text{coeff}_s > 1$?

2. The *Qur'anic* model of life-fulfilling participatory development is of the ecological type centred on agricultural abundance, gardens, and fauna and foliage. Such a regime of development is contrasted with the marginalist model where some alternatives survive at the expense of others, such as the contest between labour and capital along any given production possibility surface. See *Qur'an* (14:24–27). How does this verse invoke the permanence of increasing returns to value added between complementary variables in their organic interrelations between consumption, production, and knowledge induction?

3. Explain the meaning of sustainability of value added in the IIE-process model over the dimensions of knowledge, space, and time; that is intra-system and inter-systems with material and moral valuation.

Conclusion

Like earlier chapters, this chapter, along the generalized way of integrating the consumption and production activities of consumer theory and the pricing theory of the firm, has proved that epistemic methodology and its applications through methodical formalism are completely opposite in Islamic economics and mainstream economics. Critical realism does not see the practicality of mainstream postulates in real life. On the other hand, the methodology and immanent formal methods of Islamic economics are complex and extensive in nature. For this reason there are two approaches to solving economic and social problems in Islamic economics. First, there is the discursive approach. According to this approach the market-institutional relational perspectives of generality in Islamic economics are settled discursively in the venue of market realities, policy, strategy, technology and consultation. According to the empirical approach, Islamic economics methodology and its imminent formalism call for the generalized model of *evaluating* well-being (*maslaha*), subject to the system of circular causation equations based on diversely selected *maqasid*-choices represented by their specific variables for investigating different problems at hand. Thus out of the generalized formulation of the objective problem in Islamic economics there arises the specific problems of consumption and production in their ethical embedding according to the Islamic principle of unity of knowledge. This is made functional through the analytical method involving *maqasid*-choices (Choudhury 2016).

Mainstream epistemology and its cultural background of material acquisition, economic rationality, and self-interest born out of competition for scarce resources over competing alternatives paint a picture of an acquisitive society. Thereby, the contorted reality is either of optimization and steady-state equilibrium, which is not of the real world (Shackle 1971), or is dialectics based on perpetual conflict. The consequential *ceteris paribus* nature of the socio-scientific problems generates an unrealistic approach to solving the economic problems.

Islamic economics is perpetually premised on the episteme of Islamic unity of knowledge. This is explained by *continuous* and *extensive* complementarities through organic inter-variable relations. The consequential analytical absence of endogenous nature of the variables negates marginalism everywhere in Islamic economics. Thus, all the formulas of marginalist pricing and production are rejected in Islamic economics and are upheld in mainstream economics. Thus the contrast between Islamic economics and mainstream economic theory continues everywhere and in everything of economic analytics and beyond.

In Islamic economics as well, the emergence of the essentially Islamic methodological way of formalizing ethico-economic theory in particular and the generalized socio-scientific worldview, shows how this field has moved deeper into the clutches of mainstream economics. Thus existing Islamic economics is found to be deeply embroiled in mainstream economic theory. Thereby, no revolutionary contribution to socio-scientific thought in general and Islamic economics and finance in particular has evolved out of the existing methodological orientation that is contrary to the essential one of Islamic economics. It is now necessary to leave this enslaved situation of Islamic economics and examine the *Qur'an* and the *Sunnah* for the revolutionary epistemological light that the intellectual world and its practitioners so badly need.

In this chapter the following areas of Islamic economics should be focused upon by the teacher for the students:

Islamic economics *contra* mainstream consumer theory
Islamic economics *contra* mainstream theory of the firm
Islamic economics *contra* mainstream imperfect competition
Islamic economics *contra* mainstream general equilibrium theory.

References

Barrow, J.D. (1991). Laws, in his *Theories of Everything: The Quest for Ultimate Explanation*, pp. 12–30, Oxford: Oxford University Press.

Burstein, M. (1991). History versus equilibrium: Joan Robinson and time in economics, in *The Joan Robinson Legacy*, ed. Rima, I.H., pp. 49–61, Armonk, NY: M.E. Sharpe.

Cantner, U., Luc Gaffard, J., & Nesta, L. (eds.) (2009). *Schumpeterian Perspectives on Innovation, Competition, and Growth*. New York: Springer Verlag.

Choudhury, M.A. (1998). *Reforming the Muslim World*, London: Kegan Paul.

Choudhury, M.A. & Hoque, M.Z. (2004). *An Advanced Exposition of Islamic Economics and Finance*, New York: Edwin Mellen Press.

Choudhury, M.A. (2016). Res extensa et res cogitans de *maqasid as-shari'ah*, *International Journal of Law and Management*, 58(3).

Choudhury, M.A. (2017a). *The Islamic Epistemological Worldview and Empirical Study of Socioeconomic Integration in the Ummah*, Kuala Lumpur: International Islamic University of Malaysia Press.

Choudhury, M.A. (2017b). *God Conscious Organization and the Islamic Social Economy*, Gower: Ashgate Group.

Choudhury, M.A. & Korvin, G. (2002). Simulation versus optimization in knowledge-induced fields, *Kybernetes: International Journal of Systems and Cybernetics*, 31(1).

Henderson, J.M. & Quandt, R.E. (1958). *Microeconomic Theory: A Mathematical Approach*, New York: McGraw-Hill Book Co.

Husserl, E. (1965). *Phenomenology and the Crisis of Philosophy*, trans. Lauer, Q., New York: Harper & Row Publishers.

James, E. (2013). The Norwegian prison where inmates are treated like people, *The Guardian*, Monday 25 Feb.

Korten, D.C. (1995). *When Corporations Rule the World*, London: Earthscan.

Lings, M. (1991). *Symbol and Archetype: A Study of the Meaning of Existence*, Cambridge, UK: Quinta Essentia.

Mansfield, E. (1985). *Microeconomics*, New York: W.W. Norton.

Pindyck, R.S. & Rubinfeld, D.L. (2001). The degree of economies of scope, in *Microeconomics*, fifth edition, p. 231, Upper Saddle River, NJ: Prentice-Hall.

Rima, I.H. (ed.) (1986). *The Joan Robinson Legacy*, Armonk, NY: M.E. Sharpe.

Romer, P.M. (1986). Increasing returns and long-run growth, *Journal of Political Economy*, 94: 1002–1037.

Samuelson, P.A. (1970). *Foundations of Economic Analysis*, New York: Atheneum.

Sattar, N. (2015). Land rights in Islam, *Dawn Daily Newspaper*, 2 January.

Shackle, G.L.S. (1971). *Epistemics and Economics*, Cambridge: Cambridge University Press.

Simon, H. (1987). Decision making and organizational design, in *Organizational Theory*, ed. Pugh, D.S., pp. 202–223, Harmondsworth, UK: Penguin Books.

Spencer, N. (2000). On the significance of distinguishing ontology and epistemology, available at: www.ethicalpolitics.org/seminars/neville.htm.

Streeten, P. (1981). From growth to basic needs, in his *Development Perspectives*, New York: St. Martin's Press.

Vanek, J. (1971). The participatory economy in a theory of social evolution, in his *The Participatory Economics: An Evolutionary Hypothesis and a Strategy for Development*, pp. 51–89, Ithaca, NY: Cornell University Press.

9

MACROECONOMIC THEORY IN MAINSTREAM AND ISLAMIC ECONOMIC PERSPECTIVES

LEARNING OBJECTIVES

This chapter intends to give a comparative overview of macroeconomics in the mainstream context and then shows how Islamic ethical norms can be incorporated in Islamic macroeconomic models, so that students may:

- learn something about the implications of the norms of Islamic injunctions if introduced in letter and spirit on the aggregate behaviour of economic agents. For example the introduction of Islamic profit-sharing arrangement in the banking and financial system instead of interest (*riba*) based transitions will positively affect investment demand
- realize the Keynesian macroeconomic approach into the harmonization of human behaviour within the representation of the emergent models, such as marginal propensity to consume and marginal propensity to save
- understand about the general flows of goods and services according to macroeconomics with ethical valuation
- learn something about government spending as fiscal policy, monetary policy, all other policies, technology and innovation effects while looking at the implication of Islamic ethics in the economy
- appreciate that both the style of income determination and the nature of its distribution are likely to change in an Islamic economy.

Nature of macroeconomic analysis

At first sight, the field of macroeconomics is seen as the study of the increasing stabilization in the coterminous relationship between price, output, money and employment for the economic system that is seen to remain in perpetual disequilibrium, more or less. Consequently, the functioning of an economy – in other words, the inquiry as to how the economy works – is rendered to the empirical visage of interactive functioning of the critical variables at the economy-wide level. In such a case aggregation is necessary. Yet it is the intricacies faced in the problem of aggregation that poses one of the outstanding questions on how the economy works.

But the nature of macroeconomics as an interactive system study of aggregate economic variables taken in terms of mathematical modelling invokes a deeply epistemological issue (Lawson & Pesaran 1989). Keynesian concepts in this project were centred on the issue of harmonizing certain human behaviours within the representation of the emergent models, such as marginal propensity to consume and marginal propensity to save. That is how the epistemological outlook of economic rationality was induced by the Keynesian macroeconomic approach to the harmonization of human behaviour. This was a nicety of reasoning, not the critical realist nature of reasoning; for Keynes' *Treatise on Probability* (see O'Donnell 1989) was unable to fathom a way out of the legion of subjective probabilities in which economic problems and human behaviour remain immersed. Consequently, to resolve this problem Keynes had to take recourse to the simplifying assumptions of economic rationality. That is, he reduced human behaviour into one unique and uniform standard based on economic rationality.

Thus in the core of his reasoning Keynes was a thoroughbred neoclassical economic thinker. The difference between the neoclassical economic school and the Keynesian school was essentially in the nature and at the level of aggregate analysis in the latter. Yet, by the formalism of independence of the macroeconomic aggregation from any trace of its microeconomic premises, Keynesian aggregation, and thereby macroeconomics, remained a field of study totally different and independent of microeconomic theory. In recent times, despite the emergent theory of microeconomic foundations of macroeconomics (Phelps 1970), such efforts have remained explorations in rational expectations and social choice theory and public choice theory (Lucas 1975; Arrow 1951), all of which are aspects of neoclassical economic theory. Hence the entire field of economics comprising microeconomics, macroeconomics, and microeconomic foundations of macroeconomics is found to be premised on the epistemology of the economic behavioural axiom of rationality.

Besides, the cultural root of the axioms of macroeconomics, as of other aspects of economic reasoning, was inherent in its building blocks. For instance, Keynes' theory of the low-level liquidity trap is an example in this regard. Keynes abhorred interest rates for a prosperous economy. Yet he held on to a low-level interest rate that allows for high mobilization of financial resources to establish the fullest expansion of the real output of the economy; and thereby establish full-employment of productive resources. Thus although Keynes would have liked to see an economy function at a zero rate of interest, his economic analysis could not uphold this possibility. Such approval of interest rates has been in the cultural heritage of all Western culture. Thomas Aquinas abhorred the existence of interest rate but accepted a 'market rate of interest' in economic dealings (Schumpeter 1968). This idea came to overshadow later Austrian economic thinking, despite its leaning on Thomism.

The place of ethics in economic activities was strong in Keynes' thought. Yet ethics as a social force lost its functional relevance because of several factors of a decisively analytical nature. First, ethics is part of human behaviour. It is therefore capable of inclusion in the microeconomics of preference formation. As pointed out in the previous chapters, the resulting knowledge-induced conscious preferences also carry on their endogenous effects on the selection of goods and services, such that ethical effects are inter-causally related with socio-economic variables. The symbolization of such inter-causal relations between knowledge and choices was shown to be $\mathbf{x}(\theta)$, and its functional transforms. A macroeconomic theory of aggregate variables disjoint from microeconomics cannot unravel ethical preferences and choices.

Also ethical choices if possible at the macroeconomic level are thought of as being *exogenously* included in government austerity measures, direction of spending into social functions, such as of generating full-employment level of real output; and as combining fiscal policy and monetary policy to create real economic expansion towards full-employment level of output, and attaining price stabilization out of the attenuating balancing role of spending, increase in productivity, and employment of productive factors. Yet when it comes to enacting fiscal and monetary policies to realize social goals and economic stabilization, such underlying policies are exogenously implemented by public actions. Policies, technological change, and ethics are introduced discontinuously as exogenous factors. Thereby, the continuity and endogenous sustainability of consciousness are annulled. This is a case similar to that of neoclassical economics wherein ethics is exogenously transmitted to shift the production possibility curve along the expansion path of output and employment of factors. When the endogenous nature of policies, strategies, technology and ethics withers away in sustained economic expansion, then the effect of the resulting exogenous factors distort price level. The consequent distortionary effects are felt in the principal macroeconomic goals, such as price stabilization, economic growth, employment, international competitiveness, and attainment of equitable distribution of resources.

Keynes wanted to make economics to be a handmaiden of ethics. His encounter with G.E. Moore was the basis of this academic trend. Yet Keynes, being a rationalist, could not agree with Moore's metaphysical approach to ethics (1903). What resulted from such a partitioned view of ethical reality is similar to the divided view between *a priori* and *a posteriori* reasoning in the model of heteronomy presented by Kant. Consequently, a dichotomy remains between deductive reasoning of mainstream microeconomics and macroeconomics; and also between the *noumenon* and the *phenomenon* aspects of reasoning. Scientific reasoning under heteronomy as the central perspective of rationalism became the way of thinking on economic matters and social functions between the fields of microeconomics and macroeconomics. These problems of Western thinking on socio-scientific matters were discussed earlier as methodological problems.

Macroeconomics has thus a wide scope. Yet its methodological orientation turns out to be inept in addressing the pressing expectations of economic epistemology today. That is regarding bringing together ethics and economic theory as a comprehensive study of socio-scientific consciousness. The dichotomy between microeconomics and macroeconomics is the continuing representation of the Western way of thinking regarding all scientific fields. This is seen in quantum mechanics for the smaller scale of physical phenomena and relativity physics for the larger scale of physical phenomena. The same characteristic is also found in the divide between economics and politics that barred the rise of political economy (Staniland 1985). Likewise it is true of the small-scale psyche projected by the field of psychology and the large-scale characterization of social phenomena in sociology, and so on. The demand for a new epistemological orientation to a methodology that integrates ethics and economics by the endogenous dynamics of socio-scientific consciousness is the march of the future (Heisenberg 1958; Nicolau 1995).

Despite the shortcomings of Keynes in developing a pure theory of ethical dynamics embedded in his aggregate analysis, thus leaving the Keynesian econometric system with exogenous policy, technological, and other external variables, he may be considered as an epistemological thinker in the field of economics, ethics, and society. He wrote wonderfully as follows:

> The strenuous purposeful money-makers may carry all of us along with them into the lap of economic abundance. But it will be those peoples, who can keep alive, and cultivate into a fuller perfection, the art of life itself and do not sell themselves for the means of life, who will be able to enjoy the abundance when it comes.
>
> *Keynes 1963, p. 368*

The project of endogenously embedding economic variables at the microeconomic level and its aggregation to the economy-wide level (macroeconomics) remains in an analytical void. It calls for fresh epistemological inquiry in socio-scientific discipline in general, and in economic theory in particular.

General flows of goods and services according to macroeconomics with ethical valuation

The general flow of goods and services (GFGS) is a logically accepted accounting measure of the value of spending and Gross Domestic Product economy-wide. The GFGS is not a valuation measure for either the firm or industry-specific level of the flows of goods and services. GFGS does not represent the valuation of the so-called non-economic effects, as of morality, ethics, and consumer and producer consciousness. This book has contended in analytical ways that there cannot be a separate home for economics fortified in itself alone. Keynes, and later Myrdal (social causation), and today the ontological heterodox school of new economic theory all intellectualize economics as deeply embedded in moral, ethical and social phenomenology. Such is also the analytical approach of this book in order to correctly reflect the Islamic valuation of well-being (*maslaha*) as part and parcel of Islamic economics as science.

Exogenous effects in the GFGS

Figure 9.1 points out the effect of variations in policies and consumption and spending behaviour caused on and by the income multiplier effect (Schiller, Hill, & Wall 2012). This shift is not caused by endogenous effects that convey learning and consciousness in behavioural patterns, yet Keynes wanted to see such patterns to be built into economic theory. But as pointed out above, he devolved into rational economic behaviour to resolve the endless problem that he faced in respect of subjective probability and expectations in his macroeconomic reasoning. Consequently, there is no reason to construct continuously evolutionary linked loops of GFGS, as shown in Figure 9.1 as separated loops.

Consequently, none of the economic activities in any of the economic sectors can be truly continuous in nature in respect of the endogenous nature of socially embedded effects. Take an example here. An increase in income via the income multiplier effect takes place first through government expenditure, along with other spending. Yet government expenditure represents fiscal policy that exogenously affects the increase in income. Second, the increase in income multiplier is also positively affected by the increasing marginal propensity to spend and the decrease in the marginal propensity to save within a given GFGS. Such household propensities are affected by the assumption of resource scarcity. The assumption poses the continued problem of scarcity of resources. Now all the postulates of economic rationality reappear in rational economic analysis. Economic analysis thus fails to acquire the realist basis of formalism and analysis on the wider. The possibility of dynamic effects caused by the property of diversification by continuity of complementarities is negated. Consequently, dynamic effects influencing household behaviour does not exist in the traditional form of the GFGS as shown in Figure 9.1. Consequently, the example here proves that the dynamic effects on the increase

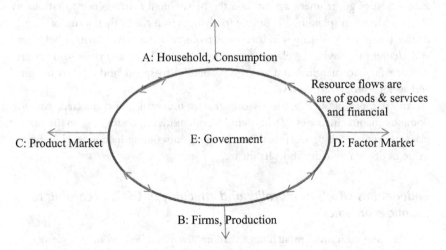

FIGURE 9.1 Economic independence of relations caused by exogenous policy shifts

in income multiplier enter an exogenous cycle of relations denying interrelations between endogenous variables.

The circular causation problem of exogenous property of macroeconomic variables in the GFGS is explained by means of Figure 9.2. Its formal ramification is the following:

$$Y = C + I + G \tag{9.1}$$

G is an exogenous economic variable and thereby not continuous, unless the government has an endogenous function, such as 'a government by discussion', participatory democracy, and discursive institution-market interaction. (For more on this, we can refer to Amartya Sen's keynote lecture to Institute for New Economic Thinking (2012).)

Therefore in the mainstream case:

$$d\Delta Y = k.d\Delta G + \Delta G.dk = \Delta G.dk \tag{9.2}$$

in the sense of discontinuity by the property of exogeneity of G representing fiscal policy. Furthermore, if k was to be endogenous this would result in the following expression:

$$dk = ds_p/(1 - s_p)^2 \tag{9.3}$$

is true only if the marginal propensity to spend is to be continuous with either time or behaviour. According to the rational economic assumptions there is no variation in the presumed behavioural propensities. Besides, if the marginal propensity to spend (thereby marginal propensity to save) was continuous with respect to time, then this would imply that government policies and household behaviour is continuously changing. Neither of these cases is true in respect of applying exogeneity assumption of government actions and the behavioural convergence to rationality. When changes in spending occur due to changes in income, then a smoothly predictive behaviour to changes in income is required. Interactive learning behaviour and changes in predictive elements continuously will not ascertain smooth predictive values to marginal and average propensity to spend, and thus to marginal and average propensity to save.

An example of such a case is one that is universally encountered. As gross domestic income increases (Y), households and business spending (S_p) in the market place are replaced by government spending in outstanding liabilities. Thereby, the shape of dS_p/dY remains indeterminate.

Endogenous effects of morality and ethicality in GFGS according to Islamic economics

Morality and ethicality are attributes that are always embedded in complementary (participatory) forms of inter-causal relations between variables and their social representations. Hence every such relationship is endogenous between the social representations and the variables that symbolize them. In such a case the implications of Figure 9.1 fail to explain economic and social reality. Now the GFGS conveys not simply an accounting way of valuation of the economy-wide flows of goods and services. Rather each of the goods and services in real, monetary, and financial terms that flow are ethically endogenized. That is the **x**-variables of mainstream economics are replaced by $\mathbf{x}(\theta)$. These are defined in the extended field of events that happen in on the knowledge, space, and time horizon. Yet time is simply a result of recording the state of the event after the event is caused to occur by the will of God in knowledge in space and time. Such ontology of the law of God – *Tawhid* – causes all things to happen in the causality, that is: $(\Omega,S) \ni \theta \rightarrow (\mathbf{x}(\theta), t(\theta)) \rightarrow (\theta, \mathbf{x}(\theta), t(\theta))$.[1] Such an endogenous transformation invokes consciousness in the choice of the good things of life. The meaning of this is to explain the social and economic universe in the inter-causal way of complementarities between all 'possibilities' replacing competing 'alternatives' (substitutes) of all of mainstream economics and social system.

The formal explanation of the above kind of difference in valuation of the GFGS in the social economy is as follows:

All variables are embedded in consciousness as we represent them by the vector of extended domains as knowledge increases, spreads, and endogenizes across diversely complementary systems. Thus we denote any such variable by $\mathbf{x}(\theta)$. Included in this vector are variables like government spending as fiscal policy, monetary policy, all other policies, technology and innovation effects and the ethicality of consciousness, and thus continuity by way of inter-causal relations. All such variables are endogenous. Thus:

$$(d/d\theta)(dY(\theta)/d\theta) = d^2Y/d\theta^2 = (d/d\theta)[(d/d\theta)(k(\theta).S_p(\theta)]$$
$$= (d/d\theta)[k(\theta).dS_p(\theta)/d\theta + S_p(\theta).dk(\theta)/d\theta]$$
$$\quad >0 \qquad >0 \qquad\qquad >0 \qquad\qquad >0$$
$$= (dS_p/d\theta).(dk(\theta)/d\theta) + k(\theta).(d^2S_p(\theta)/d\theta^2) + S_p(\theta).d^2k(\theta)/d\theta^2 + \quad (9.4)^2$$
$$>0$$
$$(dk(\theta)/d\theta).(S_p(\theta)) > 0$$

Regarding the explosive nature of the income multiplier on spending in the good things of life see Choudhury (1999). Keynes, despite his problem of exogenous effect of discontinuous policy, technology, and similar variables, promoted the activity of spending on productive things. He did also write regarding the good things of life as well.

Figure 9.2 can be explained by means of the interconnectivity of various parts of Figure 9.1. The schematic diagram would be like the following one. The symbols are defined as in Figure 9.1. The double arrows explain the pervasively endogenous effects in all parts of the GFGS including the nature of its evolution.

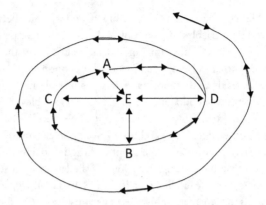

FIGURE 9.2 Continuously endogenous GFGS in respect to the complementary effect between all variables by the θ-induction

The income multiplier in the ethico-economic valuation process of GFGS according to Islamic economics

From the above explanation of the difference between, yet need for, an ethically induced valuation process in the GFGS it is clear that a great deal of such valuation is missed out from a purely accounting approach to valuation in the GFGS. By upholding the importance of the extended scope of valuation we now define the spending function as:

$$S_p = S_p(Y,k)[\theta] \tag{9.5}$$

The symbols have been defined throughout this work.

In the system of endogenous relations between the variables $\{Sp,Y,k\}[\theta]$ we derive the relation:

$$Y = Y(S_p,k); \text{ with } k = k(S_p,Y)[\theta] \tag{9.6}$$

From expression (9.6) we obtain:

$$dY/d\theta = (\partial Y/\partial S_p).(dS_p/d\theta) + (\partial Y/\partial k).(dk/d\theta) \tag{9.7}$$

Expression (9.7) yields, $(\partial Y/\partial S_p) = [dY/d\theta - (\partial Y/\partial k).(dk/d\theta)]/(dS_p/d\theta)$

$$= dY/dS_p - (\partial Y/\partial k).(dk/dS_p)$$

yielding, $\qquad\qquad dY/dS_p = (\partial Y/\partial S_p) + (\partial Y/\partial k).(dk/dS_p)$

$$\tag{9.8}$$

Expression (9.8) implies that the total positive effect of S_p on Y is higher than the marginal propensity to spend, $(\partial Y/\partial S_p)$, by the positive amount, $(\partial Y/\partial k).(dk/dS_p)$.

This is the same as noting that marginal propensity to consume is less than the total contribution of the change in spending as a ratio to the change in gross domestic product of mainstream economics by the amount $(\partial Y/\partial k).(dk/dS_p)$. This amount can be interpreted as the change in gross domestic product per unit of change in the multiplier 'k', applied to the quantity, dk/dS_p. This quantity in turn denotes the change in the multiplier 'k' per unit of the change in spending 'S_p'.

The conclusion to be drawn from the above analysis is that the role of ethical and social values in the valuation of GFGS plays a significant role to increase the role of the income multiplier by the total effect of spending in the good things of life (*maqasid al-shari'ah*), not simply in the productive things (earlier criticism of cost–benefit mechanism). We will soon find out how such a result affects the general equilibrium system in ethico-economics with focus on the pervasively evolutionary nature of inter-variable organic complementarities in Islamic economics and its income-generating capability.

Critical issues of consumption, savings, and investment functions

The important point to understand is that between the activities of consumption, savings and investment there is not merely an accounting interrelationship. More critically, the ethical consciousness in the social order introduces a complex system of inter-causal organic effects that must be noted in the various model specifications that finally lead up to the evolutionary generalized system model of economy-wide thinking.

In Keynesian macroeconomic modelling, the interconnection between the above-mentioned aggregate variables is via gross domestic output and prices that make up for real output, which in turn affects other macroeconomic variables. Contrarily, in the ethically induced modelling of macroeconomic activities, the ultimate basis is the premise of the θ-variable that induces output, prices, and all other variables. The resulting circular causation between the different variables is shown by Figure 9.3. The double arrows again show the circular causation between learning, and the knowledge, space, and time dimensions of the affected variables, and evolutionary learning occurring in continuums. The focus being on the cause and effect of θ-induction, the ultimate objective of the morally/ethically induced ethico-economic system is the well-being function. It is studied both conceptually and empirically. All the tenets of analytical methods are used, though in contextual relevance to the nature of the morally/ethically induced ethico-economic system.

The question first to be addressed is whether {C,S,I,Y} can all be complementary to each other. The meaning of savings needs to be understood to prove the complementarity of savings with consumption and investment. Savings that are held in banks as bank-savings form withdrawals from, not injections into, the economy (Ventelou 2005). Thus bank-savings cannot form positive complementarity with spending in the nature of consumption, investment, and also with the

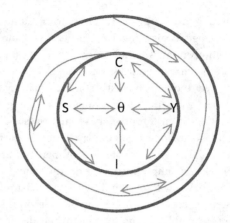

FIGURE 9.3 Inter-causal evolution by the foundational effect of moral/ethical values on ethico-economic variables

endogenous nature of government spending as would be the case with participatory governments – Amartya Sen's 'government by discussion' mentioned earlier.

For instance, the following equations would be untenable in Keynesian macroeconomics, but are meaningful in the endogenous nature of an ethically induced economic system in the inter-variable relational sense:

$$C(Y, \theta) = a_0 + a_1 . S(Y, \theta) + a_2 . I(\theta, Y) + a_3 . G(\theta, Y) \tag{9.9}$$

In mainstream economics, $C + S + G = C + I + G = Y$, with $S = I$ in all states of equilibrium of the macroeconomics systems, underemployment, and full employment states. But in the states of disequilibrium with $S < I$, savings are increased by the build-up of bondholding. The savings gap is closed up partly by market function and partly by policy effects. If $S > I$, the resulting lower rate of interest will increase investment, and thereby absorb the excess amount of savings. As the macro-economy is found to be always in certain states of disequilibrium, including underemployment equilibrium, therefore, it permanently alternates between $S > I$ (recessionary), $S < I$ (inflationary), $S = I$ denoting temporary equilibrium from the underemployment states to the full-employment state. All these economic states imply that resources remain scarce in full-mobilization to attain the desired, though not maximum, level of income multiplier effect. The presence of interest inherent in the macroeconomic system in mainstream economics does not allow sustainable full-employment levels of real output to be attained. Price stability is lost, as is also pointed out by the monetarists against the Keynesian defence of fiscal expansion for productive expansion, though with exogenous effect of $G(.)$ as an autonomous economic variable (Blaug 1993). Figure 8.4 displays the perpetual disequilibrium of the economy in the absence of continuous prevalence of sustainability.

Ironically, intertemporal bank-savings fails as a method to permanently stabilize a growing sustainable economy. We can prove this fact below. In the end, the inter-variable

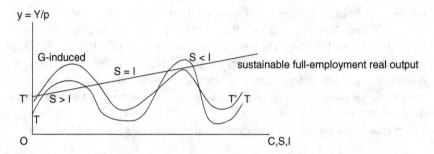

FIGURE 9.4 Perpetual disequilibrium of the macroeconomy in the absence inter-variable coterminous endogenous relations

relationship cannot be explained by equation (9.9) in the Keynesian consumption function. Yet this failure is because of the impossibility of the Keynesian general equilibrium system to get over the underlying assumption of resource scarcity; and to retain the interest rate as the key-player in economic adjustment. These two underlying conditions are foundational problems of the Keynesian argument and functioning. Therefore, for equation (9.9) to be meaningful, the structure and assumptions of the economy must be contrary to the above cases. This will reflect in the permanence of resource regeneration causing phasing out of interest rate continuously across all economic and social functions. The result would then be to cause increasing complementarities among the endogenous relations between {Y/p, C, S, I, G} and their positive transformation. An example of such positive effects is of the morally/ethically induced total valuation by the total valuation effect of the income multiplier.

EXERCISE 9.1

All over the world today, absolute poverty is a serious problem that must be reduced by means of social consciousness and economic activities and programs. Keynes' grand idea of economics as a handmaiden of ethics failed because of his economic model being incapable of being consciously inclusive of ethics as endogenous realization.

If each country was under the incidence of government fiscal policy, while resources remained scarce globally, what would be the effectiveness of global flow of resources on poverty alleviation? How can the underlying problem be changed with the endogenous consciousness of moral and ethical values in fiscal strategy?

Take the example of a two-country world, Rich and Poor (Singer & Ansari 1988). In Figure 9.5, scarcity will drive countries to think of a specific way of addressing the problem of the well-being competition between social justice (P) and economic growth (R). The mainstream optimal point of scarce allocation of resources in global governance and resource flows will be determined within the scatter of points shown by A, B, etc. (Rawls 1971). The complementarities between $\{y,C,S,I\}$ will evolve along the resource allocation path OT. If policy-induced points like a, b, etc. were selected then the paths OT_R, OT_P will explain complementarities between independently competing resource allocations between the competing 'alternatives'. The ethical endogeneity of consciousness for interrelating the Rich and the Poor is lost.

Yet true moral and ethical consciousness demands as the *Qur'an* (2:177) says:

> It is not righteousness that ye turn your faces Towards East or West; but it is righteousness – to believe in God and the Last Day, and the Angels, and the Book, and the Messengers; to spend of your substance, out of love for Him, for your kin, for orphans, for the needy, for the wayfarer, for those who ask, and for the ransom of slaves; to be steadfast in prayer, and practice regular charity; to fulfil the contracts which ye have made; and to be firm and patient, in pain (or suffering) and adversity, and throughout all periods of panic. Such are the people of truth, the God fearing.

Hence the extensive nature of complementary relations requires positive interdependence by inter-causality between $\mathbf{x}_P = \{y,C,S,I,G=S_p\}[\theta]$ and $\mathbf{x}_R = \{y,C,S,I,G= S_p\}[\theta]$.

In the endogenous ethical sense of interrelations between R and P, a combination of market and institutional interactions and integration with discursive learning will jointly generate the following two coterminous results simultaneously and correspondingly according to the IIE-learning process arising from the methodology of unity of knowledge and the world-system:

$$\theta = \cup_{\text{interactions}} \cap_{\text{integration}} \left\{ \wp_R, \wp_P \right\}, \text{yielding}$$
$$\mathbf{X} = \cup_{\text{interactions}} \cap_{\text{integration}} \left\{ X_R, X_P \right\} \tag{9.10}$$

Such a point of social choice is shown within the open domain encircled by $(R \cdot P)$ in Figure 9.5. Thus neither the Keynesian ethical concern nor Rawlsian control of the economy to allocate around the 45-degree line from the origin can gain the ethical endogeneity of a conscious ethico-economic transformation by extensive complementarities between the good things of life.

Further extensions of the problems of sustainability of the Keynesian general equilibrium

As before, we can prove that in a general equilibrium system of relations of the extensively complementary type, the nature of the interrelations between the critical variables changes into different ones. Thus the following equations can be explained in the pervasively complementary nature of an economic system. Yet they remain unexplained in mainstream economics:

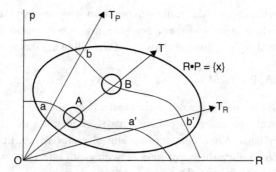

FIGURE 9.5 The impossibility of attaining complementarities between the possibilities of life in mainstream ethico-economic explanations – Keynes and Rawls

$$S(Y,\theta) = a_0 + a_1.C(Y,\theta) + a_2.I(\theta,Y) + a_3.G(\theta,Y) \tag{9.11}$$

$$I(Y,\theta) = a_0 + a_1.S(Y,\theta) + a_2.C(\theta,Y) + a_3.G(\theta,Y) \tag{9.12}$$

$$G(Y,\theta) = a_0 + a_1.S(Y,\theta) + a_2.I(\theta,Y) + a_3.C(\theta,Y) \tag{9.13}$$

The question of critical importance is this: How can we formulate and interpret the contrasting general equilibrium systems of relations in mainstream macroeconomics and the ethico-economics of pervasive complementarities? Let us address this question now. The mainstream general equilibrium is well-known to be as follows:

The general equilibrium treatment of mainstream macroeconomics

Expenditure sector equation

In reference to standard macroeconomic theory, so-called Islamic economists introduce the additional variable of price (profits) instead of the rate of interest 'i'. The *zakah* variable (Z) would also be introduced. The expenditure sector curve is then written in the form,

$$Y = a_0 + a_1.p + a_2.Z; a_0 > 0; a_1 > 0; a_2 > 0 \tag{9.14}$$

Monetary sector equation

$$Y = b_0 + b_1.p + b_2.Z + b_3 M_s{}^\circ; b_0 > 0; b_1 > 0; b_2 > 0; b_3 > 0 \tag{9.15}$$

For the present-day formulation of the Islamic version of mainstream general equilibrium the following relations would hold:

The same amount of *zakah* (Z) would hold from either the side of fiscal policy and monetary policy in the state of macroeconomic equilibrium in the present understanding of Islamic economy. Thus for all possible equilibrium points according to the various fiscal and monetary policy effects, the relationship between

Y and p will yield the general equilibrium points moving towards full-employment across all possible underemployment equilibriums. The equation for the Islamic version of general equilibrium we derive is of the following form:

$$Y = A_0 + A_1.P + A_2.M_s^0 \qquad (9.16)$$

The signs of the coefficients are not determinate. They would depend on the nature of effects of fiscal and monetary policies, that is, either on a substitution basis or complementary basis. When contractionary fiscal policy is substituted by expansionary monetary policy, there can be a crowding-out effect on income at lower prices. This can result in a stagflationary economic state.

When contractionary monetary policy is substituted by expansionary fiscal policy, inflationary forms of crowding-out effect on income can occur. When there is complementarity between fiscal policy and monetary policy, both expansionary, then non-inflationary economic growth can be realized. If both policies are contractionary, then non-inflationary economic deceleration can occur and cause the Dutch disease problem on a continued basis.

The lesson to learn from the above formulation of mainstream economics is that it contributes nothing original to economic reasoning. The economic expansionary effect of easy complementary monetary and fiscal policies is recognized. But the nature of learning type general equilibriums is non-existent, as needs to be explained by the continuously repeated simulation (simulacra) of the equations (9.9)–(9.13).

Generalized system model of evolutionary ethico-economic equilibrium in Islamic economics

We now bring back the essential elements of Islamic economics to characterize the nature of the generalized system model of evolutionary equilibrium. Keynes may have thought about a similar form of equilibrium system when he did not see the economy adjusting according to flexible price pressure affecting wage rates towards equilibrium in the labour market. The inflexible wage rate caused by the market-institutional interface causes a continuous system of underemployment conditions to prevail, although an economy in this state remains locked in stable (inflexible) prices and low level liquidity trap at a low level of interest. The problem with the Keynesian system arises at or around the full-employment level of real output at a given price level. The attainment of such an equilibrium state brings about scarcity of resources, competition, and resulting price escalation along the classical version of the supply curve of output. Contrarily, in the case of resource regeneration, technological change, entrepreneurship, and the like, the full-employment equilibrium can continuously shift along the elastic form of the short-run supply curve of real output. Complementarity between all variables including the policy variables cause the evolutionary equilibrium state of full-employment to occur. There remains no concept of the long-run full-employment rate at which the economy ceases to be reactive to further policies effects.

The objectives of mainstream macroeconomics are reformed in Islamic economics. In mainstream macroeconomics the objectives are: attaining non-inflationary economic growth; full-employment level of real output; price competitiveness in the open trading economy; and the goal of distributive equity. In the concept of economic welfare, these goals of macroeconomics combine together to translate into the objective of macroeconomic welfare maximization, given the relationship between the above-mentioned objectives. But in the process of attaining the maximization objective, the growth rate of the economy is assigned (Gordon 1967). The policy variables are exogenously applied; and thus inter-variable continuity of causality ends. Finally, under the assumption of scarcity of resources of the physical and financial kinds, the goal of attaining devolves into marginalist substitution between distributive equity and economic efficiency (growth). Thus we find that Keynes in his roots of thinking was a neoclassicist in a macroeconomic garb (Dasgupta 1987).

Islamic economics argues that any trace of marginalism and exogeneity of certain variables in macroeconomic models with their resulting mathematical discontinuity altogether must be replaced by pervasive continuity, endogeneity, and resource regeneration in the market-institutional discursive venue. The result of such relationships is extensive complementarities between all the good things of life (*maqasid*-choices) in the midst of interactive, integrative, and evolutionary (Islamic economics) learning processes intra-system and inter-systems. These consequences of the realist system of circular causation between the complementary variables or a transformation to such a system, introduces the perspective of unity of knowledge into the well-being function. The concept of well-being was substantially defined as the *maslaha*-function in terms of the *maqasid*-choices that continuously participate and complement.

The form of the generalized model of evolutionary system learning in aggregative Islamic economics

EXERCISE 9.2

Using the equations (9.9) – (9.13) and Figure 9.3 write down the problem of simulation of the objective function of *maslaha*, subject to the circular causation relations between the complementary variables. Explain the various circulation causation equations in this *maqasid-as shari'ah maslaha* function.

Keep in view that in Islamic economics, savings mean resource mobilization into *maqasid*-choices through the participatory forms of financial instruments. Savings in the form of financial flows form mobilized resources into consumption, investment, and government spending that merge with private resources in market-institution interface to share risk and enjoy returns.

See the section below on the contrariness of mainstream conclusion regarding savings and growth of economic output. If the savings function is discarded to be bank-savings then two questions are critical. First: What can be the role of interest, if at all, in the savings function? Second: What would the role of the central bank and commercial banks be in Islamic economics? The answers to these questions are interrelated and intertwined.

To investigate the first question, we note the simple reasoning that, if by savings we mean the transfer of liquid wealth into the real economy through the function of banks as an organized institution for this purpose, then a financial instrument must be used that heightens all kinds of resource mobilization. Contrarily, there must be the avoidance of instruments that hinder resource mobilization into the real economy, which is governed by ethico-economic possibilities as of *maqasid al-shari'ah*. In mainstream economics, the argument underlying a financial require-ment to nurture economic growth is capital accumulation via present abstinence to spend more in the future and with more to save. The financial instrument that renders this function is the rate of interest taken up in its various forms.[3]

On the second question we will treat it in the section on 100 per cent reserve requirement monetary system fully in Chapter 10 on this topic. We note though that the function of banks as bank-saving financial institutions ceases to exist. Islamic banks are defined as the financial intermediary to mobilize savings into productive spending in the light of *maqasid al-shari'ah* choices to increase the well-being objective criterion function and to avoid placing the non-permitted *maqasid*-'bads' in the recommended basket. Besides, we also include the objective of Islamic banks in this respect to be development financing institutions to actualize dynamic life-fulfillment regime of participatory development out of the encompassing prin-ciple of Islamic unity of knowledge as the governing episteme of belief, thought, and action.

The role of the central bank is to supervise the mobilization of money through financial intermediaries in sustaining the 100 per cent reserve requirement mon-etary system. In such a monetary and connected financial system, as the market-friendly institutional interface, the moral/ethical and material use of money is realized in full valuation of the good economy (Choudhury & Hoque 2004). The function of money and finance to mobilize resources towards sustaining the devel-opment of life-fulfillment regime of development the *maqasid*-way transfers the endogenous function of the circular causation relations exemplified by equations (9.9)–(9.13) and its further extensions to commercial banks and their associated financial institutions. This is an idea that comes closest to the theory of money found in the Austrian School of economics (Yeager 1997).

Resource mobilization through the above ways of circulating the quantity of good money and finance through the real economy of the *maqasid*-vintage and regenerating the quantity of money by doing so is the explanation that is necessary and sufficient in establishing the savings function as follows:

$$S = S(\theta,y,r,C,I,G,P)[\theta] \tag{9.17}$$

P denotes the endogenous policy vector, such as fiscal and monetary policies. Equation (9.17) is an extended form of the system of expressions (9.9)–(9.13) with the objective of simulating the well-being function, $W(\theta) \approx \theta$, in the linearized empirical and applied policy-theoretic form. Consequently, the fullest actualization of ethico-economic value is realized by mobilizing resources and regenerating it under the episteme, $\{\theta\} \in (\Omega, S)$, universally. Thus the domain of markets encompasses the ultimate playground of the divine law as the indicator of the Signs of God, unravelling the good and the bad choices of living experience end to end. Divine law includes *maqasid al-shari'ah* not as the complete law but as a subset of divine law at any moment of evolutionary learning explained by the Islamic worldview.

The following identity forms an accounting measure, not an ethico-economic *relational* one that can explain interrelations in the economy. In the relational order avoiding sheer accounting identity, the full scope of the moral/ethical valuation effect can be explained. For example, take the case of the caring, love, and affection that extends a total well-being relationship beyond simple physical love in marriage. Just so does the moral/ethical economy realize its heightened level of moral/ethical and material valuation, as explained earlier.

$$C = (Y - T) - S \tag{9.18}$$

Now include *zakah* (Z), and write:

$$C = (Y - T - Z) - S \tag{9.19}$$

Equation (9.19) is questionable in Islamic economics, as Z is not interpreted as deduction in disposable income when included in the *maqasid*-spending in Islamic economics.[4] The accounting nature of the identity cannot explain the moral/ethical valuation effect of Z in *maqasid* spending. Regarding explosive-type income multipliers under the effect of heightened Islamic transformation and endogenous consciousness, see Choudhury and Malik (1992).

Yet T is a withdrawal; it forms delayed spending in exigencies that the government faces in its expenditure in development. This may not have any ethical/moral valuation attached to it to be handed over to assuage social difficulties by productive and ethical means. Examples are the ineptness of T in reducing unemployment and poverty as is known to be the case with the welfare trap (Enke 1963). Thus the way to include the spending effect of Z in *maqasid*-spending is to use the circular causation relations of inter-variable causality, as shown before.

When T exists along with Z, this kind of relation causes resource scarcity and substitution between T and Z, thereby reducing the effectiveness of Z in the moral/ethical economic order. To increase ethico-economic effectiveness, the amount of T is to be reduced while the resource exposure of Z needs to be increased. The consequences of such a situation in the imperfect Islamic economics will be felt. This calls for a simulation procedure of well-being. Such simulations are represented by the continuous changes in the coefficients of the circular causation relations. This in turn calls for reorganization and endogenous (discursive) policy reconstruction. It is suggested as a matter of policy reorganization and increased valuation effectiveness in Islamic economics that the simulation form of the T,Z relationship should look thus This is a desirable goal, but not necessarily possible in real life.

$$Z(\theta) = f\overset{(-)\ +\ +\ +\ +}{(T,Y,C,S,I,P)}[\theta] \tag{9.20}$$

EXERCISE 9.3

Through an ethico-economic explanation, as shown above, and drawing on the *Qur'an*, describe the policy-theoretic and market-institutional relations underlying the following equation in an imperfect state of Islamic economics but aimed at moral/ethical reconstruction by way of simulation:

$$I(\theta) = f\overset{(-)\ +\ +\ +\ +\ +}{(T,Y,C,S,Z,P)}[\theta] \tag{9.21}$$

Figure 9.6 summarizes the kind of circular causation relations between institutions, their activities, and their representative variables as explained by expressions (9.17), (9.20) and (9.21). Figure 9.6 extends Figure 9.3. Figure 9.7 shows the inter-variable effects in respect of equations (9.20) and (9.21).

Adverse effect of bank-savings on potential real output

It is claimed in mainstream economics, which Islamic economics emulates, that savings are necessary for capital accumulation to finance future economic growth (Ramsey 1928). This is a fallacy; even as present savings are accumulated, it requires an incentive by banks, provided via the rate of interest or a similar instrument, say, bonds or capital market gambles between various risky instruments. The higher such rates on savings withheld in banks, the more the capital accumulation in the promise of future economic growth. However, one notes in such a regime of bank-savings *vis-à-vis* economic growth that all along the economic expansionary path there must be savings in banks to satisfy the needs of capital accumulation. Each withdrawal causes depressed output level lower than the potential level of real output or the full factor-employment level of potential output. This is the case in mainstream macroeconomic theory and its prototype usage in Islamic economics. This fact of a perpetual under-performing economy that can never reach the potential level of output to employ all its productive and moral/ethical factors fully is proved below in expression (9.22).

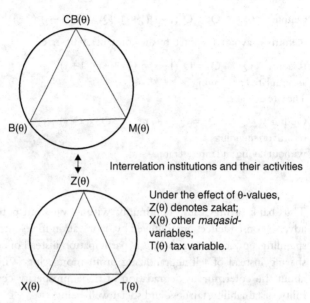

CB(θ) central bank with consciously induced policies such as 100% reserve requirement monetary policy and complementary spending policy with participating banks with similar conscious responses denoted by B(θ) and ethicizing markets denoted by M(θ). See Qur'an (62: 9.10).

CB(θ)

B(θ)   M(θ)

Z(θ)   Interrelation institutions and their activities

Under the effect of θ-values,
Z(θ) denotes zakat;
X(θ) other *maqasid*-variables;
T(θ) tax variable.

X(θ)   T(θ)

FIGURE 9.6 Institutions and their activities under the effect of evolutionary θ-values

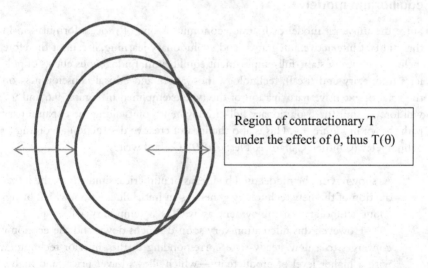

Region of contractionary T
under the effect of θ, thus T(θ)

FIGURE 9.7 Positive θ-effects on expansionary region of (Z(θ),X(θ)) and decreasing region of T under the simulation effect of θ, thus T(θ)

Time $\quad$ t = 0 $\quad$ t = 1 $\qquad\qquad\qquad$ t = 2 $\qquad\qquad\qquad\qquad$ t = n

Output $\quad Q_0 \quad Q_1 = Q_0(1-s)(1+i) \quad Q_2 = Q_0(1-s)^2(1+i)^2 \quad Q_n = Q_0(1-s)^n(1+i)^n$

Return on savings is denoted by the constant savings rate, s

Resources $Q_0 \qquad Q_1 = Q_0(1-s) = Q_0(1-s)^2(1+i) \qquad\qquad\qquad Q_n = Q_0(1-s)^n(1+i)^n$
accumulated post saving by
The rate of interest

Output $\quad Q_0 \quad Q_1 = Q_0(1+r) \qquad\quad Q_2 = Q_0(1+r)^2 \qquad\quad Q_n = Q_0(1+r)^n$
returns on spending
without saving and interest rate

$$(9.22)$$

Thus bank-savings cause continuous withdrawal from potential real output. The adverse consequences are followed by depravation in resource mobilization, goodly spending, employment generation, participation instead of competition, and profit-sharing instead of self-aggrandizing profit-mongering. Wherewithal, there comes about the coterminous degradation of trade, prosperity, economic and social stability, sustainability, fairness, and social well-being.

The nature of the generalized system of evolutionary equilibrium model

Since the universal model of Islamic economics is one of process formulation in the midst of interactive, integrative, and evolutionary learning, it cannot therefore include the idea of static full-employment equilibrium. Endogenous effects of policies (monetary and fiscal), technology, innovation, and ethical consciousness on the scale of extensive participation of the type exemplified in Figures 9.6 and 9.7 will forever shift the evolutionary full-employment points along the expansionary path shown in Figure 9.4. This is also the idea of creative destruction according to Schumpeter (Cantner, Gaffard, & Nesta 2009). Gaffard writes:

> As shown with the model used by means of numerical simulations, the introduction of the new technology generates an initial fluctuation, which brings about temporary unemployment as well as a temporary fall in productivity. However, this fluctuation very soon dampens down and the economy converges to a new steady-state corresponding to the superior technology, with a higher level of productivity—which allows lower prices and higher real wages—and full employment.
>
> *Cantner et al. 2009, p. 67*

Yet the Islamic economic phenomenon of dynamic supply curve of output is different from the Schumpeterian case. In the latter, temporary full-employment comes to a halt and needs to be re-started. Such temporary halting points are characterized by disequilibrium. Islamic economics solves this problem through its logical consequence of continuous evolutionary learning intra-system and inter-systems across knowledge, space, and time.

Thus, we can introduce more variables to any set of circular causation relations of the computational general evolutionary equilibrium model of Islamic economics as partially presented by the system of equations (8.9)–(8.13) and (8.17)–(8.21). In this respect we will study the system of interrelations between $(\theta, Z, T_r, y, r/i)[\theta]$. T_r denotes trade in its general meaning of market exchange; 'r' denotes the rate of return; 'i' denotes interest rate; (r/i) denotes the financial price, relative between real rate of return and the real rate of interest.

The example of generalized system of evolutionary equilibrium model in the vector of variables $(\theta, Z, T_r, y, r/i)[\theta]$

The *Qur'an* (2:275) declares:

> Those who devour usury will not stand except as stand one whom the Evil one by his touch hath driven to madness. That is because they say: "Trade is like usury," but God hath permitted trade and forbidden usury. Those who after receiving direction from their Lord, desist, shall be pardoned for the past; their case is for God (to judge); but those who repeat (the offence) are companions of the Fire: They will abide therein (for ever).

The important issue in the exegesis of this verse, in conjunction with the pervasive message of the organic pairing of the universe in all its details and particulars, is that trade as exchange of resources, and *riba* as withdrawal, create all the increase or obstruction of well-being (*maslaha*), respectively. Besides, via the extensive relationship that both trade and *riba* establishes with every opposite kind of thought, activities and artefacts, respectively, trade and *riba* become entangled through their continuously regenerative causality with every other such thing according to their categories.[5]

For instance, take the case of teaching generations of students in the field of trade and *riba*. Whichever way the morality and ethics-centred intellectual worldview tilts, there will be the results of the future generation comprising the minds, the belief, the action, and applications. That is what has happened with the morally and socially corrupting *riba* world at large.

Yet another subtle example is of *riba* and science as a human transaction of the purposeful mind. The actuarial mathematics of annuity calculation depends extensively on interest-rate-based accumulation, valuation, and discounting of assets. The closed life-table of mortality is used to standardize the risk premiums and returns. Yet the actuarial approach, despite its scientific approach, does not institutionally and socially consider the discursive medium of decision-making inherent in random variations of contingencies. It does not account for the epistemic of future versus present pricing of cash-flows (annuities).

Finally, we have already established that the inclusion of knowledge-induced variables in the general equilibrium system changes its nature radically by the episteme of the Islamic unity of knowledge and the ethico-economic world-system. Indeed, we note that in the case of the issue of trade and *riba*, reality and the world rely for meaning and purpose on the contrast between trade and *riba*. Reality commences through the law of Islamic unity of knowledge, whose instrument of continuous lubrication is knowledge and its relational interrelations with the world-system. Likewise, the reality of the *Akhira* is the end of the purposive nature of the Hereafter that is found through human activity of markets and institutions at large. Thereby, the reality of the world-system is enveloped by *Tawhid* in the Beginning and *Tawhid* in the End of the complete domain spanning knowledge, space, and time. This comprises the full moral and physical valuation of the socio-scientific universe of mind and matter. Thus everything in the universe is a representation of markets and institutions; that is, of exchange or *riba*. This is true for the social sciences and for the natural sciences: There is science and technology for the discovery of energy; and there is economic management of such discovery of new sources of energy. Thus there is the interplay between markets and institutions. This causes the intrinsic need for extension of resources (trade and exchange), and the diversion of resources into competing ends (*riba*). The *Qur'an* is a message of sustainability through market-institution relations. These are induced by the episteme of Islamic unity of knowledge as consciousness.[6]

Now returning to the intrinsic circular causation of organic forms of relationships of unity of knowledge between the good things of life while shunning the false things of life, we explore the relational meaning in the vector $(\theta, Z, T_r, y, r/i)[\theta]$ by their circular causation relations and the simulation objective of the well-being function (*maslaha*). It is essential to understand such a relational meaning by the exegesis of the verse mentioned above (*Qur'an*, 2:275).

EXERCISE 9.4

Write down and explain the objective of simulating well-being, subject to the circular causation relations between the variables of the vector, $(\theta, Z, T_r, y, r/i)$ $[\theta]$. The table of observations as explained earlier will be of the form:

$$(r/i)[\theta] = f\left(\overset{+}{g(Z)}, \overset{+}{g(T_r)}, \overset{+}{g(y)}\right)\theta]$$

(9.23)

$g(.)$'s denote rates of change of the bracketed variables.

with, $\theta = F(g(Z), g(T_r), g(y), r/i)[\theta]$

It is worth mentioning here that concepts, formalism, and empirical observations are recommended methods of the *Qur'an* and the *Sunnah*. The *Qur'an* invokes them in reference to the signs of God. The *Sunnah* invokes them by the authority of the Prophet. The Prophet Muhammad explained the worldly realities in reference to the *Tawhid* and thus *Akhira*.[7] That is why we write the embedding of all variables by the endogeneity of knowledge and consciousness as $\{\mathbf{x}(\theta)\}$.

Time	1 (r/i)	2 g(Z)	3 g(Tr)	4 g(y)	θ_1	θ_2	θ_3	θ_4	Avg.θ

Draw figures like Figures 8.6 and 8.7 to explain the circular causation relations among variables of the vector, $(\theta, Z, T_r, y, r/i)[\theta]$.

The law of *zakah* mandates all proceeds to be raised from the good things of life, the *maqasid*-choices. Some of these were noted earlier. In the form, shape, and objective of well-being (*maslaha*) in a life-fulfilling regime of sustainability, $Z(\theta)$ is mobilized in ethical and productive directions that raise the real economy and cause 'r' to increase as *riba* 'i' is decreased and vice-versa. Consequently, (r/i) increases. Likewise, trade 'T$_r$,' as market exchange in the life-fulfilling choices increases as the output (y = Y/p) of the real economy of the life-fulfilling kind increases.

None of the coefficients of the relation (9.23) is pre-assigned in signs. Firstly, the straightforward 'estimation' is carried out with actual data as would be collected in the box shown. In the case of non-complementary coefficient-signs the simulation of the well-being function subject to the 'estimated' circular causation equations will be taken. This would reflect the discursively endogenous effects of the market-institutional (IIE) learning processes on the circular causation relations between the variables. All such benefits of the reduction of *riba* by the organic causality of trade (exchange) in the *maqasid*-goods are summarized by the Qur'anic (2: 276) verse: "God destroys interest and gives increase for charities. And God does not like every sinning disbeliever."

EXERCISE 9.5

Even after keeping the usual goals of macroeconomic study the same as in mainstream economics, namely, non-inflationary economic growth and thus price stability, full-employment, international competitiveness, and distributive justice, how would you model the goal of price stabilization in relation to the other variables? Write down the objective function of the corresponding well-being (*maslaha*), subject to the circular causation relations. Thereby, attempt to answer the above question.

Conclusion

The principal characteristic of Islamic economics is the moral and ethical valuation of the economy-wide economic and social activities. In modelling such total valuation Islamic economics constructs a generalized system model of evolutionary equilibriums that endogenously unifies the moral/ethical values into the economic functions. This methodological approach arises from the Islamic episteme of unity of knowledge and its induction of the generality and particulars of the world-system, of which economics and society are specific cases. Such an endogenously embedded approach to economy-wide aggregation is necessary to realize the objective of attaining well-being (*maslaha*), the ethical *maqasid*-choices and dispelling the contrary goods and services from the choices. The resulting simulated choices that arise form the result and cause of unification between morality/ethics and economic variables which was unsuccessful in Keynes' approach to macroeconomics and his formulation of the general equilibrium model.

Thus Keynes' macroeconomic theory, and all of mainstream macroeconomics since, suffered from the dichotomy between ethics as an exogenous category, and partially endogenous economic variables. On the other hand, microeconomics does not treat the topic of endogeneity of preferences and ethical values. Besides, there is no mechanism known to fully formalize the microeconomic aggregation principle into macroeconomics. This is despite the attempts carried out by rational expectations theory and public choice theory.

The problem of ethical endogeneity and a fully endogenous system of circularly causation variables is the continuing problem of all Western scientific thought. Earlier we discussed the problem of heteronomy between the *a priori* and *a posteriori* ways of reasoning. That is the same as the demarcation between deductive and inductive ways of reasoning. As long as this problem remains in socio-scientific reasoning, the possibility of unifying morality/ethics with physical reality including economic variables remains distanced. The generalized system of evolutionary equilibrium model of simulating the well-being objective criterion, subject to the system of circular causation relations between all variables that are universally endogenous, is a formal consequence of the episteme of unity of knowledge in Islamic economics.

Mainstream macroeconomics, like microeconomics, can stand neither for the methodology nor for the formalism and explanations of Islamic economics. It is a pity that such deficient systems of formal reasoning continue to be ineptly used today in Islamic economics.

The results that arise are most misleading for Islamic economics. Take the example of interest rate setting as in the case of Exercise 9.4. In mainstream economics, interest rate is seen to be exogenously set by the central bank's prime rate that governs the commercial bank rates. In the process of transformation of an imperfect Islamic economics into the *riba*-free economy, the relationship between the central bank, commercial bank, and the market process as institutions, and the corresponding endogenous relationship with the other variables, are all endogenous in nature. This was explained with the help of Figures 9.6 and 9.7. The policy-theoretic inferences derived from these disparate approaches to the study of the role of interest in ethico-economic reconstruction are vastly opposite. The exogenous nature of interest rate determines the exogenous nature of fiscal and monetary policies. Interest rate is therefore seen as a financial policy instrument. On the other hand, in Islamic economics during its process of ethical reconstruction, interest rate exists as a diminishing financial instrument that disappears as the policy variable increasingly becomes endogenous and unified in nature. Interest rate in a transforming Islamic economics towards a deepening ethical state causes its reduction out of the inter-causal relationship with the rate of return. This is shown by the variations in (r/i) as is explained in Exercise 9.4.

Consequently, the Islamic economic theory and applications cannot be derived from or by the use of mainstream economics. This is true both on methodological grounds and by way of inferences and formal applications. One can conclude from all this on the premise of the *Qur'anic* verses (5:16–18):

> O People of the Book! There hath come to you our Apostle, revealing to you much that ye used to hide in the Book, and passing over much (that is now unnecessary):

> There hath come to you from God a (new) light and perspicuous Book, – Wherewith God guides all who seek His good pleasure to ways of peace and safety, and leads them out of darkness, by His Will, unto the light, – guides them to a Path that is Straight.

In this chapter the teacher should focus on the following topics for students: Islamic economics contra mainstream generation of outputs and macroeconomic variables; and *Maqasid al-shari'ah*, Islamization, and Islamic economic science.

Notes

1 *Qur'an* (14:32–34): "It is God who created the heavens and the earth and sent down rain from the sky and produced thereby some fruits as provision for you and subjected for you the ships to sail through the sea by His command and subjected for you the rivers" (14:32).
   "And He subjected for you the sun and the moon, continuous [in orbit], and subjected for you the night and the day" (14:33).
2 The *Qur'an* has many verses regarding the well-being effect of spending in the good things of life. One example is: "The parable of those who spend their substance in the way of God is that of a grain of corn: it groweth seven ears, and each ear Hath a hundred grains. God giveth manifold increase to whom He pleaseth: And God careth for all and He knoweth all things" (2:261).
3 Interest includes all kinds: simple and compound; real and expected; effective and term structure; small and large of any dimensions. In Islam the following two terms are used to define the complete idea of interest (*riba*). (This kind of definition though is unnecessary,

for there is always a one-to-one inter-relationship between financial transactions and the corresponding real transactions.) *Riba al-nasiya* is defined as excess in finance in real exchange. *Riba al-fadl* is defined as the corresponding excess in the commodities connected with the excess financial demand or supply by banks (including the central bank and commercial banks, and their financial derivatives, such as bond markets and financial companies, and individuals such as the *Kabliwala* who notoriously charges usury on loans). In fact there is no such thing as a simple rate of interest. Every so-called simple rate of interest is the compound result of a large number of term structures of interest rates over any length of time. Time is of the essence for interest rates to realize their full value. Therefore, there is no such concept as usury versus interest rate in the *Qur'anic* meaning of interest and usury taken synonymously. The *Qur'an* (2:278) declares: "O ye who believe! Fear God; and give up what remains of your demand for *riba*, if ye are indeed believers."

4 *Qur'an* (2:261): "The parable of those who spend their substance in the way of God is that of a grain of corn: it grows seven years, and each ear has a hundred grains. God gives manifold increase to whom He pleases and *Allah* cares for all and He knows all things."

5 The logical conclusion is this: Since exchange is the divine conferment over the entirety of creation from the beginning to the end in every detail and because *riba* obstructs the realization of trade as exchange in its widest sense of total valuation, *riba* is thus *the root cause* of all evil, misery, disorder and hardship. The *Qur'an* (2:278–279) declares regarding the universal evil of *riba*: "O ye who believe! Fear *Allah*, and give up what remains of your demand for usury, if ye are indeed believers. If ye do it not, take notice of war from God and His Messenger: But if ye turn back, ye shall have your capital sums: Deal not unjustly, and ye shall not be dealt with unjustly."

6 *Qur'an* (2:267): "O ye who believe! Give of the good things which ye have (honourably) earned, and of the fruits of the earth which We have produced for you, and do not even aim at getting anything which is bad, in order that out of it ye may give away something, when ye yourselves would not receive it except with closed eyes. And know that *Allah* is Free of all wants, and worthy of all praise."

7 *Al-Bukhari* (Vol. 8, Book. 76, Number 426): "Narrated Abdullah: The Prophet drew a square and then drew a line in the middle of it and let it extend outside the square and then drew several small lines attached to that central line, and said, 'This is the human being, and this, (the square) in his lease of life, encircles him from all sides (or has encircled him), and this (line), which is outside (the square), is his hope, and these small lines are the calamities and troubles (which may befall him), and if one misses him, another will snap (i.e. overtake) him, and if the other misses him, a third will snap (i.e. overtake) him.'"

References

Arrow, K.J. (1951). *Social Choice and Individual Values*, New York: John Wiley & Sons.

Blaug, M. (1993). *The Methodology of Economics*, Cambridge: Cambridge University Press.

Cantner, U., Gaffard, J.L., & Nesta, L. (eds) (2009). *Schumpeterian Perspectives on Innovation, Competition, and Growth*, New York: Springer.

Choudhury, M.A. (1999). *Comparative Economic Perspectives: Occidental and Islamic Perspectives*, Norwell, MA: Kluwer Academic.

Choudhury, M.A. & Hoque, M.Z. (2004). Micro-money and real economic relationship in the 100 per cent reserve requirement monetary system, *An Advanced Exposition of Islamic Economics and Finance*, Chapter 8, Lewiston, NY: The Edwin Mellen Press.

Choudhury, M.A. & Malik, U.A. (1992). The essence of the Islamic political economy, in their *The Foundations of Islamic Political Economy*, Chapter 1, London: Macmillan and New York: St. Martin's.

Dasgupta, A.K. (1987). Marginalist challenge, in his *Epochs of Economic Theory*, pp. 74–98, Oxford: Basil Blackwell.

Enke, S. (1963). Population and growth: a general theorem, *Quarterly Journal of Economics*, 77(1): 55–70.

Gordon, R.A. (1967). *Goals of Full Employment*, New York: John Wiley & Sons.

Heisenberg, W. (1958). *Physics and Philosophy*, ed. Anshen, R.N., New York: Harper & Brothers Publishers.

Keynes, J.M. ([1930] 1963). Economic possibilities for our grandchildren, in *John Maynard Keynes: Essays in Persuasion*, pp. 358–373, New York: W.W. Norton.

Lawson, T. & Pesaran, H. (1989). Methodological issues in Keynes' economics: An introduction, in their *Keynes' Economics, Methodological Issues*, p. 1, London: Routledge.

Lucas, R.E. Jr. (1975). An equilibrium model of the business cycle, *Journal of Political Economy*, 83: 1113–1144.

Moore, G.E. (1903). *Principia Ethica*, Cambridge: Cambridge University Press.

Nicolau, E. (1995). Cybernetics: The bridge between divided knowledge and interdisciplinarity, *Kybernetes: International Journal of Systems and Cybernetics*, 24(7): 21–25.

O'Donnell, R.M. (1989). Types of probabilities and their measurement, in his *Keynes: Philosophy, Economics and Politics*, pp. 50–66, London: Macmillan Press Ltd.

Phelps, E.S. (ed.) (1970). *Microeconomic Foundations of Employment and Inflation Theory*, New York: W.W. Norton.

Ramsey, F.P. (1928). A mathematical theory of savings, *Economic Journal*, 38(152): 543–550.

Rawls, J. (1971). *A Theory of Justice*, Cambridge, MA: Harvard University Press.

Schiller, B., Hill, C., & Wall, S. (2012). *The Macroeconomy Today*, 13th edition, New York: McGraw-Hill Education.

Schumpeter, J.S. (1968). The scholastic doctors and the philosophers of natural law, in his *History of Economic Analysis*, New York: Oxford University Press.

Sen, A. (2012). Keynote address, Paradigm Lost Conference in Berlin, April 14. Available at: www.youtube.com/watch?v=OBw5fJkjXiM.

Singer, H.W. & Ansari, J.A. (1988). *Rich Nations and Poor Nations*, London: Unwin Hyman.

Staniland, M. (1985). The fall and rise of political economy, in *What is Political Economy? A Study of Social Theory and Underdevelopment*, pp. 10–35, New Haven, CT: Yale University Press.

Ventelou, B. (2005). Economic thought on the eve of the General Theory, in *Millennial Keynes*, Chapter 2, Armonk, NY: M.E. Sharpe.

Yeager, L.B. (1997). *The Fluttering Veil: Essays on Monetary Disequilibrium*, Indianapolis, IN: The Liberty Press.

10

MONETARY, FINANCIAL, AND REAL ECONOMY ISSUES IN ISLAMIC ECONOMICS AND COMPARATIVE PERSPECTIVES

LEARNING OBJECTIVES

This chapter dilates further on the argument developed so far with the objective of introducing the students to:

- understanding Islamic financial instruments developed by the Islamic financial system to eliminate *riba* (interest) from financial operations despite certain conceptual problems and practical shortcomings
- understanding the basic issues in operating the prevailing system of financial transactions so that it can become comfortable with the capitalization of assets with interest-free instruments
- defining fundamental postulates of money, finance and real economy relationships in an interest-free regime of socioeconomic change
- modelling the alternative central banking practice adhering to Islamic norms.

This the starting premise of this chapter. In 1930, Keynes wrote:

> The strenuous purposeful money makers may carry all of us along with them into the lap of economic abundance. But it will be those people, who can keep alive, and cultivate into a fuller perfection, the art of life itself and do not sell themselves for the means of life, who will be able to enjoy the abundance when it comes.
>
> *Keynes, 1963, p. 368*

Such are the messages of moral worth and wisdom in this chapter. The fundamental point here is to establish the fact that, the only way of phasing out interest rates from Islamic transactions is to understand and implement the formalism of the inverse relationship that permanently exists between trade in the good things of life and the rate of interest as the impediment to the free flow of resources into such tradable activities. The central bank, the commercial banks, and financial intermediaries as practitioners must understand this organic relational concept of intellection in relation to money and the real economy. The monetary system and the real economy with the financial instruments in between would thus be shown to formalize the intellection paradigm – which indeed is a truly scientific revolution (Donzelli 2004). The result is the replacement of the fractional reserve requirement monetary system by the 100 per cent reserve requirement monetary system backed by the gold standard. Likewise, the organic relationships of such a monetary arrangement including its monetary policy and transmission mechanism would structurally change the nature of markets and its institutional relations and individual preferences. The end result will be a phased-out interest-rate regime changing into a trade-related one by the rise of the tradable relationships that are generated. The foundational methodology that enters this kind of organically relational worldview with the episteme of unity of knowledge (the divine law in Islam) provides the functional ontology of the socially and morally constructed money, production, and real economy circular causation relations. It models the legitimacy of trade as the resource mobilization instrument, while rejecting interest as the permanent impediment of resource mobilization.

Objective

Our objective in this chapter is to explain the necessary and sufficient conditions for economic and social bliss reached by the endogenous interaction between money, finance and the real economy.

The idea of endogenous relations is conveyed by the systemic interrelations between entities and variables of the socioeconomic problem under study. These internal dynamics generate causality and learning by interaction. The concept is similar to what Paul Krugman (1989) termed "self-governing equilibrium" resulting in self-organized behaviour. The social and economic change occurs simultaneously with the phasing down of interest rates. This kind of total change is also tantamount to the pursuit of endogenous interrelationships between the central bank, the commercial banks and the market economy exchanging in the good things of life (*hallal at-tayyabah* in the *Qur'an*) according to *maqasid al-shari'ah*.

The explanation of these kinds of changes is carried out in reference to the same fundamental Islamic model of unity of knowledge, upon which the Islamic methodological worldview governing 'everything' permanently and indispensably stands.

Zero rate of interest: a necessary but not sufficient instrument for Islamic economics

The experience with the now diminishing *mudarabah* (profit-sharing) and *musharaka* (equity participation) forms of financing proves that these instruments are replaced by secondary financial instruments, all of which are subject to *shariah* concerns (Choudhury 2008a). Likewise, despite earnest efforts to promote Islamic financing and profitability in the face of interest-free financing of projects and investments, Islamic banks in Malaysia could not herald even a distant prospect for the well-being of the *ummah* in the field of Islamic networked flow of resources and organization of institutions for resource sharing (trade). This assertion is borne out by the fact that Islamic banks and development planning in Malaysia never accounted for a clear direction of Islamic financing towards ameliorating either their own broader Islamic global picture or the momentum of trade, development and related policy instrumentation for the Muslim bloc.

The current lure of *sukuk* – bonds that revolve around the principal financing instruments of *mudarabah* and *musharakah* – and the market of sale of *musharakah*-linked bonds in real assets to the private sector to finance mega-projects have ended up in deep *Shari'ah* concerns (Usmani n.d.; Parker 2012). *Sukuk* financing problems arise from the sale of debt with interest to private outlets. The *sukuk* holders can then proportion this equity instrument between the government and private businesses through public shareholding. Consequently, the debt coverage in such projects passes on the debt as an intergenerational burden to debtor companies.

An alternative would be for such companies to engage in debt-equity swaps (Krugman 1989; Blackwell & Nocera 1989; Choudhury 1989). Debt-equity swaps involve large investors retiring the debt or a part of it for an indebted country by paying it out in these proportions, i.e. investing to buy the debt. In exchange, the debt-ameliorated country treats such an investment as an equity swap for the debt retired. Debt-equity swaps can be managed effectively in the case of equity-participation (*musharakah*). The debt overhang and the allowance for financing debt in the private sector is thus best extended over time, rather than being a comprehensive financing mode that can be instituted for phasing out the interest rate regime caused by debt overhang. The goal of financing interest-bearing, debt-ridden projects by interest-free financing instruments therefore does not cure the interest-rate enigma. Thereby, the true impact of financing by Islamic participatory instruments is not attained, even when the interest-free goal is targeted to reach a given level of acceptance. Yet in the name of interest-free financing as the focus of Islamic finance, Islamic banks and finance companies, Muslim governments, large businesses and projects are raising the flag of *sukuk* (Gassner 2008; *Business Islamica* 2008).

Capitalization of income flows and the rate of interest

The notion of a low interest rate or phased-down interest rate in economic and financial arrangements has prevailed in the literature. But the concept of how the rate of interest emerges in the economy, and how it can be phased out from this system, has not matured either in the mainstream literature and practice or within the theory and practice of Islamic economics and finance. The latter area remains inextricably submerged in mainstream academic thinking relating to money, finance, interest rate and the real economy relations.

The position of Islamic economics and finance in respect of capitalization of assets with interest-free instruments

Islamic economic and finance gurus have adopted a time-value of money discounting approach in asset valuation. They thus failed to understand the interest-rate implications of the discounting approach. The result in asset valuation is that a future market, which remains undetermined, would be capitalized at a rate either less or greater than the expected rate of return on the stream of future income flows. Especially, in such a case of discount-rate indeterminacy, microenterprises have difficulty in tying up commitment to a mark-up that determines the investors' and shareholders' dividends and profits. Microenterprises bear the burden of the excessive cost of capital. The problem arises when large shareholders aim at discounting their risk by taking a larger share of the profits in joint venture. This leaves smaller residual shares and dividends for the small borrowers and participants in Islamic funds. Microenterprises thus find it costly to refinance their assets by means of the lower share of total profits of joint ventures. The same result can swing in favour of microenterprises at the expense of shareholders when an under-valuation of the intergenerational flow of projected returns takes place. In such a case, the question is this: Can the investor be risk-averse and divert potential investments into risk-free alternatives, such as short-term trade using the *murabahah* (mark-up) financing instrument? None of these alternatives comes to the benefit of socioeconomic development of the community, and beyond of the *ummah*.

Indeed, a prevalent problem in Islamic banks is either a lack of investment or an over-subscription of shareholders' capital. These results are reflected in the variable 'financing/deposit ratio', which is found to move away on either side from the expected value of unity (Choudhury 2009) in Islamic banks. Islamic banks in Indonesia show such financing problems in their annual reports (Bank Muamalat Annual Report 2007; Bank Mandiri Annual Report 2006). Consequently, although interest-free financing has been promoted by Islamic banks, yet the method towards realizing this goal has not been well defined in terms of investment, liquidity problem, asset valuation, and socioeconomic development of the *ummah*. Besides, it was pointed out above that secondary financing instruments have been used in place of the principal Islamic financing instruments to legitimate operations in interest-free financing. Yet there are looming *Shari'ah* problems relating to interest rates in these secondary financing instruments. One of these problems is the absence of the idea of 'pooled funds' made by combining individual types of financing modes. The *Shari'ah* gurus have not looked into this possibility. We have referred to this kind of participatory portfolio earlier in this book. A second problem is the difference of the often-used jargon of '*Shari'ah*-compliance' from the great purpose and objective of the *Shari'ah*, known as the *maqasid al-shari'ah* (Choudhury 2009).

Both of these approaches in asset valuation and financing run into the same kinds of methodological problems. These problems in turn generate ineffective socioeconomic development effects.

The money, finance, and real economy relationships in an interest-free regime of socioeconomic change

Islamic economists argue on behalf of establishing an interest-free regime of socio-economic change by retaining the existing fractional monetary reserve system, despite introducing the compelling need for delivering social justice (Chapra 1985). The arguments, prescriptions, and implementation of such an approach through interest-free targeting are untenable. We explain this problem below in terms of a general system of comprehensive socioeconomic transformation.

It was explained in the previous chapter that, if interest-based financing is inverted by the rise of trade-based instruments in the Islamic case, then there is a decreasing need and incentive for holding savings in banks and capital markets. Consequently, Islamic banks become outlets of mobilizing savings *continuously* into spending in the good and productive things of life. This process, which is *continuous*, generates participatory dynamics between spending possibilities (relations) and between their entities. The entities are symbolized by their representative factors denoting socioeconomic variables and financing instrumental variables, as was formalized in Chapter 9. These variables define the relations and represent the agencies (e.g. agents, institutions, markets, etc., underlying the relations and their constituent variables). Indeed, the Islamic world-system, within which are studied the complementary relations between money, finance and the real economy, is fully participatory in nature (Choudhury, Zaman, & Harahap 2008). The result then is to interactively integrate the three domains – money, finance and the real economy in participatory ways, so that they learn continuously by circular causation between them.

How can an Islamic capital market arise from the circular causation relations of complementarities between money, finance and the real economy? The transformation into the complementary linkages remains hampered by the blockage in the flow of resources in the mere presence of the catchword '*Shari'ah*-compliance' idea. A better possibility for realizing the impact of interest-free financing in the real economy is to establish the wide range of linkages that money, finance and real economy interrelations generate and are sustained.

Therefore, to base all transactions on interest-free instruments in the Islamic economic and financial system is only *a necessary condition* of Islamizing the financing and banking system. By itself the abolition of interest financing is *not a sufficient condition* in establishing the alternative of trade and participatory development in the Islamic *ummah*. It is therefore necessary to combine the interest-free transformation as a process that is linked with a simultaneous change in monetary policies and money–finance–real economy relations. Such relations are generated between the central bank, the commercial bank, and the real economy by circular causation. The resulting new economic arrangement based on complementary circular causation between variables and their representative agents would cause the emergence of unified and synergetic interrelationships between the monetary system, financial instrumentation, and the real economy. We now turn to a formalism of the underlying dynamics in such a case.

The circular causation between the central bank, commercial banks, and the real economy in the midst of money, finance, and real economy relations

Consider the case of continuous regeneration and flow of all forms of resource that remain interconnected by causality. The emergent circular connections explain the circular-causation relations between the various entities. Most importantly, in this kind of circular-causation relations there occur the simultaneously complementary and participatory linkages between the central bank, the commercial banks (Islamic banks and other banks), and the resulting complementarities in the real economy between the good things of life, as ordained by the *maqasid al-shari'ah*. Such unifying relationships bring out the nature of monetary policy and the complementary money, finance and market relational transformation in Islamic economics. There is no equivalent explanation for such participatory relations in Islamic economics as we know it.

Islamic economics is essentially based on free-market orientation. But at the same time, it is guided by knowledge induction and appropriate *Shari'ah* instruments and policies to realize resource mobilization into the good things of life. In this respect, the central bank generates a supply of money as required by the market-oriented projects in which commercial banks become partners with the market-determined projects. Contrarily, the central bank avoids maintaining the supply of money to banks in excess reserve. This would otherwise cause multiple credit creation backed by promissory notes. Also, the intent of the underlying Islamic monetary policy is to attain a stable and productive macroeconomic state of the general (circular) flows of goods and services in physical and monetary terms and with total moral/ethical valuation, as explained in Chapter 8.

Thus in the Islamic case, the concept of money supply is replaced by the concept of 'quantity of *micro-money*' pursuing the needs of specific projects that are based on the tenets of *maqasid al-shari'ah*. The concepts of demand and supply of money are untenable. These concepts are now replaced by that of 'quantity of *micro-money that is specific to approved projects*'. In other words, such projects are financed by the full quantum of a given quantity of circulation of micro-money in specific projects, as needed. An example of such project-specific quantity of micro-money is given by the Real Bills (Green 1989). Real Bills can be endogenously generated by commercial banks under the authority of the central bank (Green 1989). Now there would be an automatic equilibrium circulation of currency through the commercial banks entering the real economy. This kind of an evolutionary equilibrium process of money, finance, and real resource linkage must however be governed by appropriate central bank regulations on sustaining a stable and growing economy in the absence of *riba* and in the presence of trade as exchange according to choices under *maqasid al-shari'ah*.

Case 1: Perfect 100 per cent reserve requirement monetary system

We note in the Islamic economics context of micro-money that there is no excess creation of money by the central bank when an automatic equilibrium process is maintained between the monetary flows generated by resource linkages between the commercial banks and the real economy. The commercial banks under the authority of central bank guidance can generate the real bills (micro-money) for the increased resource mobilization as needed. Alternatively, it is possible that central banks create the extra quantity of money needed to finance a growing real economy. The cost underlying this additional flow of a quantity of money will be recovered from bank seigniorage. This is revenue raised by the central bank to cover the cost of producing a quantity of money by gold-backing. The cost will be collected from the borrowing commercial banks that themselves earn participatory returns from the yields of the real economy funding of projects, also from market exchange in approved goods and services. The central bank and commercial bank interrelationship abides. The quantity of money required to finance additional projects in the real economy arises from the increased demand for goods and services that result in project development.

Now on the one side, there is the quantity of goods and services in demand. On the other side, this demand in the real economy is satisfied by monetary injection that is carried over by financial instruments including currency in circulation. This injection of money equals a quantity of currency in circulation. The carrier of this circularly regenerated monetary stock through the real economy in response to the demand for regenerated resources, comprise the bundle of trade-related instruments. Trade and commerce thereby replace interest-based businesses of all kinds. The principal meaning and objective of the quantity of money now becomes the need for currency to finance productive *maqasid* projects in response to the increased demand for the corresponding kinds of goods and services connected with such *Shari'ah*-aligned projects. An effective transmission of money through financial instruments would thus take place to finance the real economy of goods, services and projects in the light of *maqasid al-shari'ah*.

The result thus is contrary to bank-savings. We mean by bank-savings that part of the earned and national income that is withheld by banks to serve interest-bearing and speculative portfolio over time. Now, just as trade increases, the flow of resource into the real economy is enhanced. The quantity of micro-money increases in pursuit of such a real demand for goods and services connected with projects. The diversion of income into bank-savings to earn interest rate is diminished. This kind of internal adjustment in the financing medium brings out the logical and formal basis of trade, thus positively affecting resource mobilization through the market-oriented real economic transformation with linkage to monetary flows through financing instruments. The consequence of these kinds of circular flow dynamics is a continuous liquidation of savings at every moment of time in the life of the economy by its mobilization into approved spending outlets in a market economy that remains conscious of *maqasid al-shari'ah*. The emphasis on such an ethical market economy transformation is not the way of the current version of Islamic economics. The latter promotes excessive government and institutional governance that defies endogenous ethical market transformation.

Case 2: Imperfect 100 per cent reserve requirement monetary system with excess demand by commercial bank

However, when the total financing cannot be met by the available bank deposits by households, wherein savings = resource mobilization continuously generated, the banks call for additional financing from shareholders and depositors. The expansion of a quantity of money by the central bank can be loaned out to the commercial banks to finance projects. In such a case, the (financing/deposit)-ratio exceeds unity. The principal shareholder/stakeholder of the Islamic banks, in the sense of the lender of last resort, is the central bank. Besides, other principal shareholders' share-capital can be secured in the central bank for the benefit of lending to commercial banks in the situation of excess demand for funds to finance approved projects.

Case 3: Lower demand for financing the real sector

There is yet another type of monetary flow between the commercial banks and the central bank. When the demand for money to finance projects declines due to lower market demand, the 'excess reserve' in commercial banks is liquidated. The resulting amount of un-mobilized financial resources cannot remain in the commercial banks. The commercial banks are not allowed to hold this saving as excess reserve, for fear of causing multiple credit creation, and thereby all the ills this carries. Excess reserves held in commercial banks will otherwise negate the above-mentioned dynamics of trade over saving in regenerating resources and the quantity of micro-money to meet real demand for goods, services and projects. The unutilized savings must thus be deposited fully as 'reserve' with the central bank. Such transfer of central bank reserve forms inventory of un-mobilized monetary stock. Such reserve is now held with the central bank. They will form Islamic instruments once again when they are mobilized through the commercial banks upon demand. The fund remains with the central bank until it is called back by the commercial banks to finance subsequent rounds of enhanced demand in the real economy.

The central bank holds none of the statutory reserve. This though is the ideal case of 100 per cent utilization of commercial bank micro-money (real bills) in the real economy in pursuit of approved possibilities. Say, an initial amount from the central bank to the market via commercial banks is the case where the investment demand in the real economy is high and the commercial banks fall short of this amount to finance all projects. Consequently, the (financing/deposit)-ratio exceeds unity.

Case 4: Resource leakages from the banking system under fractional reserve requirement

We next examine the possibility of resource leakage from the banking system. The important issue here is to note that the quantity of money exists in circularity between the demand of the real sector, the availability of loanable funds by the banks, and the additional requirements from the central bank.

In the last case, certain amounts of funds could fail to meet the requirements of the real economy, thus causing leakages from the desired money, finance and the real economy interrelationship. Indeed, the usual case of resource mobilization must accept leakages through the commercial banks in the real economy linkages with financial instruments carrying money.

Consequently, the resulting contraction of yields in the real economy allows for say, $900 resource mobilization out of $1000 with the banks. This would then cause $100 to remain as savings in the commercial banks to yield interest income on idle financial resources when fractional reserves return is allowed. Thereby, the inter-bank flows of such savings in speculative assets will trigger multiple credit creation and an accumulating amount of interest cost on debt capital.

To avoid such a situation when the resources are not fully mobilized into the real economy, the commercial banks hand over the $100 unutilized financial resource to the central bank for safe-keeping. *This amount becomes the 100 per cent potential reserve of the commercial bank in a monetary arrangement with the central bank.* Note here that this definition of the 100 per cent Reserve Requirement Monetary System (100%RRMS) with the gold standard (explained below), is quite different from the 100 per cent reserve requirement monetary idea explained in the literature (Rist 1940; Friedman 1968).

The commercial bank would use this 'saved' resource at a later date on the basis of its legitimate claim based on credit-worthiness due to increased possibility in financing diversified projects. At the time of such a future release of funds from the central bank, the 100 per cent reserve converts to money in circulation in the form of a quantity of currency as money.

The central bank is entrusted with the protection of the value of the underutilized resources through the commercial banks. This exchange-value protection cannot be done by paper and promissory notes or by any such *numeraire* whose long-term stability is in question. The choice is gold as the required stable monetary *numeraire*. The long-term stability of gold has been proven historically (Choudhury & Hoque 2004). Thus a stock of gold (denoted by G) is stored by the central bank to stabilize the value of the central bank reserve, which subsequently becomes currency in circulation.

It can be proved that the value of gold, which protects the marginal amount of money by a corresponding marginal amount of gold stock simultaneously, protects the entire currency as money in circulation in the real economy. Thus only effective pricing in the real economy values the currency value per unit of gold-backing of temporarily un-mobilized commercial bank reserve held with the central bank as 100%RRMS.

Central bank functions in 100%RRMS

The conclusion now is astounding. A small amount of gold is needed to protect the entire stock of currency in circulation. The regulatory condition though is this: The central bank must regulate the stable price of gold over the long-run. Stability of the gold price can be maintained by regulating the stock of gold in the economy/ society. The Islamic country has the duty of moral suasion to attain this goal of moderation on holding gold as precious metal.

The same kind of regulation is extended to the mixed precious bi-metals, gold and silver. In the 100%RRMS, the role of the central bank in monetary management is reduced to policy-making and regulation for supervising a sustainable market economy in approved goods, services and projects. This situation would involve supervising the management of a stable and growing economy in concert with the participation of commercial banks as the principal medium for mobilizing money and finance between banks, the financial sector, and the real economy.

The power of creating money by the central bank is reduced to managing a stock of gold to maintain the value of money as currency in circulation (see *Money Matters* on 100%RRMS, n.d.). This function too is inversely related with the velocity and volume of the circularly mobilized money and finance through the real economy.

Gaining from the extensively participatory nature of the 100%RRMS and the real economy, the central bank also engages in a *continuous* activity of knowledge sharing with the central bank and the agents representing the real economy. This generates an overarching 'learning process' towards determining the general-system relations involving the central bank, the commercial banks, and the real economy. Thereby, technical analysis, the resulting information sharing, and development of such learnt policies and endogenous learning experience become the principal attributes in central bank function in the money, finance, and real economy interrelationships with 100% RRMS.

All functions conventionally endowed on the central bank cease to have effect. Undue governance as by government, central bank, and monetary policies is replaced by the participatory decision-making analytical forums of discourse and conscious invoking. The conventional functions including those promoted in contemporary Islamic economics, on the other hand, are money supply and monetary regulation, interest rate and exchange-rate setting by regulating the monetary reserve of the countries' balance of payments. All these targets are converted into endogenous causality in the 100%RRMS of TIE. Inflation targeting too is left to market adjustment in the midst of the features of 100%RRMS with the protection of exchange-value by the gold standard and the micro-monetary perspective of project financing.

The *laissez faire* concept of money and medium of exchange in the literature: micro-money

Our delineation of a predominantly commercial banking role in resource mobilization in the real economy with the central bank being a lender of last resort and an overseer of the currency value in market exchange in terms of a quantity of gold-backing, has strong precedence in the literature (Saving 1977; Klein 1975; Tullock 1976; Tobin 1963). Hayek thought about such a kind of private monetary system in which private banks will play the role of money in circulation (1976). In this case, private money would all be valued on the basis of a given standard, such as gold, but they would compete with each other. In other words, competing quantities of money would be held by private institutions, especially banks, and this would be like holding money in terms of financial and other assets.

Yeager (1997, pp. 412–413) writes in regards to privately supplied money: "Commercial banks would supply such funds. The central bank's authority in such a monetary system would be minimal." This is his prescription of monetary reform, expanding on the work of Black, Fama and Hall (Yeager 1983):

> Government would be banished from any role in the monetary system other than that of defining a unit of account or *numeraire*. We envisage a unit defined by a bundle of goods and services comprehensive enough for the general level of prices quoted in it to be practically steady. Merely by conducting its own accounting and transactions in the Unit – we tentatively so name it, with a capital U – the government would give private parties a strong incentive to adopt the same Unit.

Yeager continues (1983, p. 413):

> No longer would the size of the *numeraire*, one Unit, be determined by the supply and demand for any medium of exchange. The Unit would be defined by goods and services having supplies and demands of an almost entirely *non-monetary* character.

The praxis of the Islamic approach to trade and interest relationship

Our arguments establish the fact that interest-rate eradication in the Islamic economy cannot be enforced by exogenous imposition of policies and restrictive measures. If it is so, as is presently practised by Islamic venues, the replacement of the interest rate will not be sustained without simultaneously charting the constructive change that the trade and financing instruments must generate between money, finance, and the real economy. Presently, there is no such attempt by Islamic banks and Muslim countries in their Islamization experiment. Consequently, the programme of Islamization of the financial sector has not proceeded to the extent of contributing to the rise of the *ummah* endowed with its own capital markets, inter-communal international trade dynamics, coordinated markets, and socioeconomic development programmes along the direction of life-fulfillment regimes. This is the continued import of idea from our earlier mentioned ones. That is, merely a construal of interest-free financing modes does not form an adequate benchmark of the *Shari'ah*. Islamization is not an adequate approach in such a partial view of Islamic change. The *ummah* view, in which money, finance, and real economy interrelationships play the crucial role of structural change and monetary reform, must emanate from the general-system objective based on the epistemology of systemic unity of knowledge.

We have argued that the Islamic programme to phase out interest rate and replace it with trade instruments must be carried out within a generalized evolutionary equilibrium system of circular causal relations between money, finance, and the real economy. This would simultaneously involve pervasively complementary interrelations between the central bank, the commercial banks, and the functioning of the 100 per cent reserve requirements monetary system with the gold standard. Such pervasively complementary relations generate organic relations in reference to the epistemology of systemic unity of knowledge.

Thus the question arises: Can the central principle of pervasive complementarities be derived from any other epistemological premise other than the *Qur'anic* foundations? We note here the empirical and policy directional role played by the principle of pervasive complementarities in explaining the epistemology of unity of knowledge by using the constructed functional ontology of that unity in diverse problems of the world-system. In this chapter we have narrowed down such a treatment to the topic of money, finance, and real economy participatory unity of relations.

The answer to the above question is in the negative. The dividing line between Islam and all other comparative socio-scientific systems is the ultimate quintessence of epistemological reference to the oneness of God, *Tawhid* as belief and as law; or equivalently, the principle of unity as law in respect of organic relationals between the maqasid-goods. This worldview projects the episteme of unity of knowledge in relation to the world-system. In all other socio-scientific systems the origin of knowledge is premised on the epistemology of rationalism. Rationalism and its entire constructed system operate on the basis of methodological individualism, conflict, competition and notions of scarcity of resources, and thereby, of substitution between contested entities. The rationalist mind is inextricably rooted in such behaviour at the level of the individual, institution, society, and human relations. This characterizes behaviour around the globe in this rationalist world-system. Even socio-scientific theories and programmes of rationalist origin rely on this nature of the world-system and 'everything' in it (Barrow 1991; von Mises 1978; Choudhury 2008b).

Extending the arguments to the open economy case

Two cases need to be studied here. The first is when a regional group together adopts a common currency. Such arrangements are gaining ground. It is argued for strongly by Mundell (2000) in respect of his prescription for one world-currency. Likewise, there is the Euro, the American dollar, and there used to be a growing interest in a common Gulf Cooperation Council (GCC) currency following the inception of a future GCC common market and monetary union. In our case, the example is of an incomplete regional arrangement for the 100 per cent reserve requirements with the gold standard. Such an imperfect 100%RRMS can learn along evolutionary processes into higher echelons of its realization.

In the latter case, the fractional reserve monetary system is treated as dual with the Islamic banking system. Segmented markets would be necessary to establish the desired money, finance, and the real economy interrelations. This kind of an incomplete monetary transformation is presently practised by some Islamic financial outlets, notably the Islami Bank Bangladesh and the Islamic Society of North America Housing Co-operative. In general, the phasing out of interest rates in Islamic financial operations is embedded in a general system of simulated interrelations that must be realized with the simultaneous development of the emergent trade versus interest paradigm (Choudhury 1999). Following such a recent development, a return to the 100 per cent reserve requirement monetary system with the gold standard would be extended within the segmented region idea that would adopt this arrangement. The principle of resource mobilization is promoted in regional grouping to establish a complementary and participatory trade and development regime. A regulatory and combining market-institutional interactive learning medium is enhanced by means of active networking between partners and Islamic banks.

A given stock of gold is parcelled out through the medium of an Islamic bank for settlement of payments. This is a significant global project that can be considered by the Islamic Development Bank. Since the stock of gold required for stabilizing currencies would not be great, and would be inversely proportional to the extent and speed of effective resource mobilization, therefore a large stock of gold and its minting cost would be avoided. Besides, the cost of gold minting would be covered by the seigniorage that the central bank would collect from the commercial banks in terms of the cost of production of gold required to protect the currency value with a legitimate mark-up (Black 1989) of the reserve held. Seigniorage would also be collected by participatory arrangements that would exist in a cooperative agreement to share risk and returns between the central bank and commercial banks, and between the commercial banks and the clientele in the real economy. The latter case is well-known in the profit-loss (*mudarabah*) and equity participation (*musharakah*) arrangements of Islamic banks.

For the participatory sharing of risk and return between the central bank and the commercial banks the resulting seigniorage arises in the case of partial resource mobilization by the commercial banks. Now the commercial banks share the services that the central bank renders by paying for these services in terms of the cost of procuring gold stock by the central bank plus a service charge on the commercial banks. The commercial banks can roll over this cost to their clientele in the real economy by way of service charges. This shows that both service charges and interest rates are inversely related to productivity and product and risk diversifications. These positive changes are causally related to resource mobilization through commercial banks.

The principal cost that would exist is caused by leakages. This is where the full productivity of the use of money and finance in the real economy fails – always, partially, but increasingly so in the interest-bearing system. In order to reduce such leakages and share in the full realization of profitability and cost reduction, Islamic banks benefit from the joint consequences of risk and product diversifications.

These conditions always exist effectively in a joint pursuit of resource mobilization, which is exemplified by the Islamic economic and financial system in Islamic economics (Choudhury 1993).

The paradigm of the participatory, thus endogenous, relations between the central bank, commercial banks (Islamic banks) and the real economy remains unchanged for the open economy, as is the case with the closed domestic economy. In the open economy case, the national central bank, commercial and real economy relations are further extended by the bank of international settlements of payments in the Islamic networked monetary arrangement.

Productivity-determined exchange rate in 100%RRMS with the gold standard

The exchange rate (E) is defined on the grounds of productivity relations, avoiding the monetary intervention except in exigency of under-mobilization of financial resources. The following formula reflects this:

$$\text{Terms-of-trade, } t = p_X . X / p_M . M \tag{10.1}$$

X denotes volume of exports; p_X denotes price export.
M denotes volume of imports; p_M denotes price of imports.

Rewrite equation (9.1) as:

$$E = p_X / p_M = t.(M/X) \text{ is the nominal exchange rate.} \tag{10.2}$$

Because X and M are both determined by their similar dynamics within the country-specific or region-specific 100%RRMS with the gold standard, therefore, (M/X) assumes a stable value, say 'a'. Thereby,

$$E = a.t \tag{10.3}$$

E defines the exchange rate. It is shown to have a stable relationship with the terms-of-trade variable.

As free trade expands between partners in the region with full or partial 100%RRMS with the gold standard, as explained above, then M/X tends to 1. Hence trade liberalization along with a phase of transformation into a 100%RRMS arrangement within and across the integrating region, result in stability of the exchange rate and the terms–of–trade simultaneously.

It is implied from our continuing formalism below that with greater speed of economic integration, institutional networking of every kind, technological diffusion, factor mobility, and production and risk diversifications in the midst of the 100%RRMS arrangement, expression (9.3) will cause an upward trend in t, and thereby in E. The coefficient 'a' will be induced by the force of economic integration, which in our case of participatory trade and development is based on learning and endogenous interrelations in the spirit of systemic unity of knowledge.

The functions of money in the 100%RRMS

The issue of resource mobilization in trade versus financial interest implies that, increased complementarities in the system are required so as to simulate the well-being that is attained from such complementarities over learning processes. The function of money, finance, and Islamic banks is precisely to attain this well-being objective that yields the total valuation of the ethical economy.

So what are the functions of monetary aggregate in such a system?

Money is not a store of value in Islamic economics

Is money a *store of value*? The value of money arises from the real economy in terms of *maqasid*-approved exchange of goods, services and project financing. The absence of the property of a store of value in money means that there is no productive value in money as such. Rather, the stability of currency value in international exchange is attained by means of the gold standard in the way as we have explained for the 100%RRMS in money, finance, and real economy circular causation relations.

Money is indeed a unit of value in exchange in Islamic economics

Is money a *unit* of exchange? Yes, this is true; for money in 100%RRMS determines the true relationship between the unit value of money and the price of goods and services in exchange. Currency is equivalent to money in circulation in this system. This amount of money that remains in circulation is supported by the gold standard in order to be stable in international exchange value, forming this sound money as currency (von Mises 1981).

Indeed, the Prophet Muhammad informally denominated various values to monetary units called *danaq* and *mithqal* in terms of physical units of basic needs (Allouche 1994). The importance of denominations of weights and measures appears in the *Qur'an* (83:1): "Woe to the defaulters in weights and measures, those who take full measure when they take from men and who give less when they measure out to them or weigh to them."

Money is not necessarily a medium of exchange in Islamic economics

Is money a *medium* of exchange? This property of money is true only in the static case of exchange. In the intertemporal case of resource mobilization it is difficult to ascertain the state of demand and supply of goods and services at future time-periods. It is also difficult to ascertain the risk-contingencies that exist at future points of time. Also, consumer preferences, systemic risk, and costs of future flows of goods and services, and financial demand in projects are based on subjective factors, and are thus undeterminable. Consequently, it is impossible to ascertain the value of goods and services in exchange, and thereby the value of money that would back up such a real economic value. Therefore, money does not have any market of its own, which otherwise would result in interest rate as the price of money and financial instruments. Islamic money being micro-money and specific to projects that need to be financed, the quantity of money (currency) in circulation in the economy is determined by full quantum flows into projects. This requires such projects to exist to match up its market value with the quantity of micro-money that is mobilized by financial instruments. We write the equation of the quantity of micro-money as follows in this case between micro-money and project-specific financing as,

$$MxV = Pxy, \text{ or } M = (Pxy)/V \qquad (10.4)$$

When $V = 1$, or 100 per cent circulation (full micro-money mobilization through banks), then,

$$M = P^\star y \qquad (10.5)$$

Expression (10.4) means that the value of a stock of micro-money equals the total spending value in terms of the prices and quantities of approved goods and services in exchange pertaining to specific projects (activities).

Note that 'y' denotes real output. Thus an alternative definition of money is the value of GDP, which in turn represents the value of all spending (expenditures). But all these implications are specified in respect of projects, rather than by the economy as a whole. We therefore interpret that a quantity of money, M, is driven fully into financing a project(s). This is the meaning of full quantum financing of projects by micro-money.

Hence, $V \cong 1$. This is equivalent to the consequence of 100% RRMS, in which any saved (un-mobilized) money as currency is totally surrendered to the central bank. Otherwise, the micro-money as currency would be totally mobilized as resource to fit into projects in the real economy.

We can write equation (9.5) in the light of the project-specific condition of micro-money transmission (M*) through commercial banks as,

$$M^\star = \Sigma_i M_i = \Sigma P_i.y_i = P.y \text{ for economy-wide case} \qquad (10.6)$$

These kinds of project-specific circulation of micro-monetary 'units' were considered by Yeager (1983) in his *laissez-faire* approach to monetary reform. Yeager's *Unit* of money and Hayek's (1976) *competitive currency units* are weighted against a bundle of goods and services whose prices remain stable by the forces of supply and demand in market exchange against the value of the currencies used as monetary units for denoting exchange value of real goods and services. This kind of currency valuation against the real goods and services in market exchange can be used both in the regional and international sense. On top of this there is the multiplier affecting real goods and services, and thereby money in circulation that carry the total valuation of the transforming moral/ethical real economy.

For example, units of currency could be the Islamic Dinar. The common commodity base for valuation is gold and silver in the 100%RRMS with the gold standard. Yet the currencies in circulation may not be strictly in terms of these precious metals. Any government-certified way of holding money as a means of settling payments nationally, regionally, and internationally can be protected by the minting of the 'residual' stock of gold, G.

In the end: functions of money

We have debated against the notions of demand and supply of money and replaced the concept of quantity of micro-money mobilized into projects through the banking sector in complementary relations with the real economy and by appropriate participatory financing instruments. This chapter has also rejected the unquestioned acceptance of the notions of the mainstream functions of money in prevalent Islamic economic ideas. Of these, only the function of unit of exchange as it is actually realized or intertemporally established with market transactions is acceptable.

The function of store of value for money is untenable, for value is jointly claimed by money and market exchange of real *maqasid* related goods and services as they are temporally realized as payments get settled. The function of money as the medium of exchange is rejected in the absence of well-determined exchange values of goods and services over time.

Ludwig von Mises (1981, p. 84) wrote in regard to the notion of money as a medium of exchange (slightly edited):

> Its (state) task thus becomes that of determining, in accordance with the intent of the contracting parties, what is to be understood by money in commercial transactions. From the legal point of view, money is not the common medium of exchange, but the common medium of payment of debt settlement.

In Islamic economics, we go a step further by arguing that money is a convention to settle payment contracts at *every* determined moment of clearly realized market exchange in the real economy across the model of interaction, integration, and evolutionary learning. These are the logical properties of Islamic economics.

Conclusion: inferences on the Islamic alternative regarding global financial crisis

Islamic banks are claimed to have remained safe from the financial crisis that is sweeping the world today. Central banks in most countries have cut their prime lending rates to near zero to stimulate consumer and investment lending. Yet the deepening crisis continues. Islamic banks, although insulated from the global financial crisis due to their operations that do not involve the stock market and speculative financing, have not gained advantage of the situation to contribute to the future of the *ummah*, and thereby to show the path out of the crisis for the rest of the world, by demonstrating the zero interest agenda and the alternative trade financing instruments.

This chapter argued that reducing interest towards zero is not a new recommendation by any economic system during a financial crisis. Spending and innovation require venture capital to be freely mobilized by development-financing instruments through commercial banks. Yet such a central bank policy is not taking effect toward stabilizing the global financial system.

This chapter points out that simultaneously with the phasing out of the interest rate to zero, it is necessary to reconstruct the general-system design of the relations between the central bank, the commercial bank, and the real economy. Within such general-system reconstruction, all such circular causation synergies must be taken up that establish pervasive complementarities between the productive and socially good things of life. We have denied the label 'Shari'ah-compliant' to these goods. Instead, we have emphasized the currently neglected term, *maqasid al-shari'ah*. The *maqasid*-goods meet the demands of the greater purpose of well-being that is embedded in the wider field of valuation, including moral and ethical values with material ones (Choudhury 2008, 2009).

The result would be a panacea for the Muslim and non-Muslim alike – because unethical, unsocial, and thereby, immoral things are equally abhorred by all peoples and cultures. Most fundamentally, underlying this common heritage of mankind upon which to build, renew, or reconstruct old and fallen systems there is the epistemological shift away from rationalism. Rationalism breeds methodological individualism and the inextricable problem of heteronomy. This is the broken glass of reality breeding entropy. Contrarily, the epistemology of systemic unity of knowledge, as the core of unity of the divine law in relation to the unity of the world-system, establishes the world-system on the foothold of organic participation, and thereby cooperation in the good things of life while sorting out the unwanted ones.

Discourse with convergence towards consensus is the goal and the result universally. Discourse leads to a new pattern of monetary futures. The global financial crisis requires a change in monetary arrangements along with fiscal stimulus through reduced interest rates, to restore stability. Likewise, the reality of organic unity of relations between the good things of life that sustain a healthy society and economy, mind and material artefacts is the most natural order and scheme for everything. Any system that competes with itself and does not participate and complement in the attempt to interconnect amicably within the system is bound to fail by the futile objective of specialization and maximization of the acquisitive self. These social predicaments are not realities of systems. They are imposed by the rationality axioms of certain self-interested psyches. That is what we find in the artificial configuration of the mainstream and neoclassical economic science, which as a specialization left out moral, ethical, and social reality from its calculations. (See below for an exercise.)

Our above-mentioned recommendations can be extended for global institutional reform. In that case, the central banks of member states would be superseded by a regional bank of reconstruction and development. In the case of the Islamic *ummah* such a global monetary reform can be guided by Islamic Development Bank. On this issue the International Monetary Fund has an idea (2008):

> This is an important moment for the IMF and its future. The IMF has a critical role to play in the global resolution of the financial crisis. The proposed modernizing reforms will begin the process of making the IMF more representative of the global economy. It is strongly in the U.S. interest that the Fund fulfills these responsibilities in order to retain its relevance and preeminent place in the international monetary system. The need for a strong and effective IMF is all the more pressing in the challenging global economic environment we find ourselves in today.

The above quote signifies the urgency of the time to launch the blueprint of a future reform of the monetary system in conjunction with the outlook of the money, finance and real economy unity of organic relations to gain global economic and financial stability. This chapter has pointed out what structure of reasoning and institutional change will be required inside such an alternative form of money, finance and the real economy interlinked system in the Islamic economic and financial framework.

EXERCISE 10.1

1. Draw figures to explain the three kinds of monetary, financial, and real economy relations in 100% RRMS.
2. Now insert the following values in different loops in the figures to denote financial resource mobilization as in (9.1):
   (i) Full mobilization of SAR1000 into the real economy through the commercial banks; and recursive accumulation of savings as capital for re-mobilization at a rate of 5 per cent through each sequence of savings mobilized as financial resource.
   (ii) Mobilization of $900 of $1000 of financial resources into the real economy through the commercial banks at a yield on returning savings of 5 per cent per sequence.
   (iii) Mobilization of financial resource to meet excess demand of $1500 in the real economy in relation to the creation of additional money by the central bank for commercial banks to meet the excess demand.

3. Set up the objective criterion of well-being for simulating the money, finance, and real economy circular causation relations.
4. How is the total valuation measured by the well-being function (*maslaha*)?
5. Draw the figure of systemic interrelationships that we find in an interconnected enterprise with organic linkages to various sectoral parts of the social economy that aims at its total valuation with the good things of life (e.g. stakeholder model of social decision-making). As an example, define total valuation by the well-being function as usual as we have defined this concept of *maslaha* throughout this book.

EXAMPLE 10.1

Assume the following information:

1. Savings ($S(\theta)$) are formed in Islamic bank by continuous mobilization of funds and thus extensive *organic pairing, that is complementarities in the sense of total valuation* ($\{\theta\}$). Say $S(\theta) = S(\theta)$ to start with.
2. Let $r(\theta)$ denote rate of return from the total valuation ($\{\theta\}$).
3. R_i denotes resources in the real economy across total valuation $E(\theta) = \{\theta, \mathbf{X}(\theta), t(\theta)\}$.
4. Rounds of inter-causality around the system interconnecting money (central bank), finance (Islamic banks), and the real economy ($\mathbf{X}(\theta)$) depend upon knowledge regeneration over time ($t(\theta)$). Let $\mathbf{X}(\theta)$ include $S(\theta)$.
5. Thus money, finance, and real economy activities are regenerated over $E(\theta) = \{\theta, \mathbf{X}(\theta), t(\theta)\}$.

Consider the following cases of interrelations between Central Bank, Islamic Banks, Real Economy, that is between money, finance, and the real economy (MFRE) in the case of 100%RRMS:

1. **Full mobilization** of S_0 through financing (i.e. finance/deposit ratio = 1). This is the ideal case of 100%RRMS with the Islamic banks holding all the savings as reserve for continuous mobilization into the real economy. That is Excess Reserve = 100%. The central bank does not hold any reserve. That is Statutory Reserve = 0%.

$S_0(\theta_0, X_0, t_0)$

In the second round of resource mobilization,

$S_1 = S_0(1+r_1)$

All variables are θ-induced in rounds of total valuation. The assumption here is that all of savings when mobilized generates activities that increases at least by the rate 'r'.

The nth round of such regenerating of MFRE causes total resources allocation =

$$S_0\Pi_{i=1}^{n}(1+r_i)$$

The financial statements are as follows:

Central bank statutory reserve = 0; Islamic bank excess reserve = 100%; resource in the real economy = S_i, i = 1,2,…,n. and yield equals $S_0\Pi_{i=1}^{n}(1+r_i)$.

2. **Excess demand for mobilization**, resource $R_i > S_i$, i = 1,2,..,n. The same conditions hold relating to $E(\theta) = \{\theta, \mathbf{X}(\theta), t(\theta)\}$. This is the case of (i.e. finance/deposit ratio > 1)

    Now the central bank creates the excess demand of money worth of $(R_i - S_i)$ to Islamic banks to finance required projects in the real economy to year 'r'. The condition for 100%RRMS is once again completed with the central bank as the lender of last resort.

    The value of 'r' as profit-sharing rate is then shared between the central bank (r_c), Islamic banks (r_b), and the agents in the real economy (r_e). Note that the yield increases with the wider valuation meaning of 'θ' to include all forms of increasing returns to scale continuously over the events $E(\theta)$. The resources are regenerated in rounds of $E(\theta)$ and distributed by the respective shares. The central bank claim of $(R_i - S_i)$ is completed by the Islamic banks. The agents of the real economy participate in making up for this principle of excess demand for resources in the real economy.

    The financial statements are as follows:

    Central bank statutory reserve = 0; Islamic bank excess reserve = 100%, with $S_0 < R_0$; resource in the real economy = S_i, i = 1,2,…,n are generated as follows: $R_i*\Pi_{i=1}^{n}(1+r_{ei})$. '$r_{ei}$' denotes profit-sharing rate for the real economy in the ith round of real economic activity corresponding to circular causation by $\{\theta_i\}$-values explaining total valuation.

3. **Excess demand for mobilization**, resource $S_i > R_i$, i = 1,2,..,n. The same conditions hold relating to $E(\theta) = \{\theta, \mathbf{X}(\theta), t(\theta)\}$. This is the case of (finance/deposit ratio < 1).

In this case, the excess savings over resource used for *maqasid*-spending (emphasized by 'θ' values is $(S_i - R_i)$. i = 1,2,..,n. This quantity of financing is deposited by Islamic banks with the central bank in order to avoid multiple credit creation on excess reserves. The 100%RRMS is still satisfied at a lower level of *maqasid*-spending causing lower level of economic activity but still subjected to total valuation. For this reason the prospect of returning to improved economic levels remains to fill up the gap, $(S_i - R_i)$. i = 1,2,..,n over $E(\theta)$.

The central bank creates a small amount of gold (G) to shore up the quantity of financing $(S_i - R_i)$. i = 1,2,..,n over $E(\theta)$. We note that $[G/(S_i - R_i)]*R_i$ is the amount of gold that needs to be circulating in order to shore up the unit amount of money that is held with the central bank and the same unit gold for protecting R_i of resources in circulation. Now $[G/(S_i - R_i)] \star R_i = G/(S_i/R_i - 1)$ $i = 1,2,..,n$. This quantity decreases as S_i/R_i decreases until the states (1) and (2) are established. In this case the quantity of seigniorage decreases and r_b and r_e yield increased yields with the continuity of 'θ' effect across $E(\theta)$.

The financing conditions now are as follows: Central bank statutory reserve = $(S_i - R_i)$; Islamic bank excess reserve = 100%, with $S_0 > R_0$; resource in the real economy = R_i, $i = 1,2,...,n$ are generated as follows: $R_i' \star \prod_{i=1}^{n}(1+r_{ei}) -$ seigniorage for creating G of gold in the central bank. 'r_{ei}' denotes profit-sharing rate for the real economy in the ith round of real economic activity corresponding to circular causation by $\{\theta_i\}$-values explaining total valuation.

4. **The combination of these three cases** can happen, particularly in times of financial volatility. In that case, the sum-total of the yields from the money (central bank), finance (Islamic banks), and real economy – the MFRE-model – is the following:

$S_0\prod_{i=1}^{n}(1+r_i) + R_i \star \prod_{i=1}^{n}(1+r_{ei}) + R_i' \star \prod_{i=1}^{n}(1+r_{ei}') -$ seigniorage over all possible states of $E(\theta)$.

In the case of an average constant rate of return 'r_i', as may be approximated across $E(\theta)$, we obtain, $(S_0+R_i+R_i') \prod_{i=1}^{n}(1+r_i)$.

The above construction of the resource flow through the MFRE-model in 100%RRMS is shown in Figure 10.1.

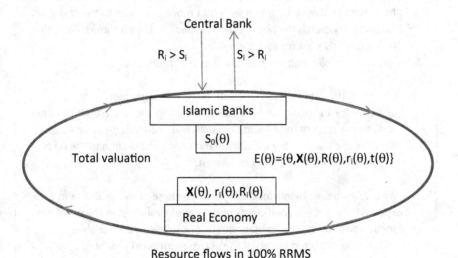

FIGURE 10.1 The MFRE inter-flow of resources signifying $E(\theta)$-activity in 100%RRMS in Islamic economics

EXERCISE 10.2

1. Discuss the money, finance, and real economy (MFRE) modelled system for the four cases mentioned in the example given above for a segmented market that is divided in assets between real rate of return and real interest rate. See also Choudhury (2015).

2. Neither the central bank nor the Islamic banks has any authority to create money at a price except to charge seigniorage for the minting of gold that the central bank uses to shore up the value of currency that stays with the central bank and also protect the residual financial resources that circulate in the real economy. Therefore, money in Islam is simply a resource. See also (Haines on Maritain, 1987). Its quantity and value depends directly on the amount of spending (Sp) that is in demand and supply in the real economy across the *maqasid* forms of $E(\theta)$. In such a case discuss the equation:

$$M(\theta) = Sp(\theta) = M(X,p,r,t)[\theta]$$

3. Because money circulates across events $E(\theta)$ in the real economy it causes well-being by organic linkages with the good things of life (*hallal at-tayyabah* of *maqasid as-shari'ah*). Explain this fact by writing down the model of simulating well-being in money and the variables shown in Question 2, subject to the system of circular causation relations.

4. Derive the meaning of your formulation and explanation in Question 3 in respect of the following verse from the *Qur'an* (18:19) relating money ($M(\theta)$) to resource (silver coins) and the good things of life (best food): "Now send ye then one of you with that money of yours to the town: Let him find out which is the best food (to be had) and bring some to you, that (ye may) satisfy your hunger therewith."

5. Consider the following illustrative values that represent:

   (i) Increasing rates of return indicating real economy performance;
   (ii) Relatively declining interest rates indicating the inverse relationship with the rates of return and thus with real economic performance;
   (iii) Rates of change in the quantity of money corresponding to the rates of return relative to the rates of interest.

   Write down a well-being function between these variables indicating the expected signs of the coefficients of the various variables in the well-being function and the circular causation relations between the variables.

   Draw the expected trends of the above-mentioned variables.

   Explain this expected system of relations with the selected signs of the coefficients.

Can you suggest an endogenous policy related with the total valuation concept of E(θ) that could be undertaken in the economy as a whole to attain the kind of reformation that you are suggesting?

t:	1	2	3	4	5	6	7	8	9	10
'r':	2	4	8	8	8	9	9	10	10	8
'i':	10	9	8	7	7	6	6	5	5	7
M:	------------------------- M=M(r/i,R,Sp,X)[θ]-------------------------

References

Allouche, A. (1994). *Mamluk Economics: A Study and Translation Of al-Maqrizi's Ighathah*, Salt Lake City, UT: University of Utah Press.

Bank Mandiri. (2006). *Bank Mandiri Annual Report 2006*, Jakarta, Indonesia.

Bank Muamalat. (2007). *Annual Report 2007*, Jakarta, Indonesia.

Barrow, J.D. (1991). *Theories of Everything: The Quest for Ultimate Explanation*, Oxford: Oxford University Press.

Black, S. (1989). Seigniorage, in *New Palgrave: Money*, eds. Eatwell, J., Milgate, M., & Newman, P., pp. 314–315, New York: W.W. Norton.

Blackwell, M. & Nocera, S. (1989). Debt-equity swaps. In *Analytical Issues in Debt*, eds. Frenkel, J.A., Dooley, M.P., & Wickhman, P., pp. 311–345, Washington, DC: International Monetary Fund.

Business Islamica. (2008). Gulf mega-*sukuk* issues: A rich man's club, March, pp. 18–19.

Chapra, M.U. (1985). *Towards a Just Monetary System*, Leicester, UK: The Islamic Foundation.

Choudhury, M.A. (1989). Privatisation of the Islamic dinar as an instrument for the development of an Islamic capital market, *Islamic Economic Co-operation*, pp. 272–294, London: Macmillan.

Choudhury, M.A. (1997). *Money in Islam*, London: Routledge.

Choudhury, M.A. (1999). A critique of econometric modeling for development studies: A political economy approach with special reference to Malaysia, in *Political Economy of Development in Malaysia*, eds. Ghosh, B.N. & Salleh, M.S., pp. 105–123, Kuala Lumpur, Malaysia: Utusan Publications.

Choudhury, M.A. (2006). The principle of complementarities in the *Shuratic* process and the implications for the socio-scientific order, *The Koranic Principle of Complementarities Applied to Social and Scientific Themes*, Chapter 1, Lewiston, NY: The Edwin Mellen Press.

Choudhury, M.A. (2008a). Islamic economics and finance: A fiasco, *The Middle East Business and Economic Review*, 20(1): 38–51.

Choudhury, M.A. (2008b). Islam versus liberalism: Contrasting epistemological inquiries, *International Journal of Social Economics*, 35(4): 239–268.

Choudhury, M.A. (2008–2009). Islamic asset valuation by using a terminal-value overlapping generation model, funded internal research project, College of Economics and Political Science, Sultan Qaboos University. A part appeared in M.A. Choudhury (2011). Overlapping generation model for Islamic asset valuation: A phenomenological application. Chapter 8 of his *Islamic Economics and Finance: An Epistemological Inquiry*. Bingley, UK: Emerald.

Choudhury, M.A. (2015). Monetary and fiscal (spending) complementarities to attain socio-economic sustainability, *ACRN Journal of Finance and Risk Perspectives: Special Issue of Social and Sustainable Finance*, 4(3): 63–80.

Choudhury, M.A. & Hoque, M.Z. (2004). Micro-money and real economic relationships in the 100 per cent reserve requirement and the gold standard, in their *An Advanced Exposition of Islamic Economics and Finance*, pp. 199–220, Lewiston, NY: The Edwin Mellen Press.

Choudhury, M.A., Zaman, S.I., & Harahap, S.S. (2008). An evolutionary topological theory of participatory socioeconomic development, *World Futures*, 63: 584–598.

Choudhury, M.A. (2009). *Money, finance and the real economy in Islamic banking and finance, perspectives from the maqasid as-shari'ah* (Unpublished doctoral dissertation). Department of Economics, Banking and Finance Program, University of Stirling, Scotland.

Donzelli, F. (2004). *Rise and decline of the notion of own rate of interest in Sraffa*. Working Paper No. 32. Universita degli Studi di Milano.

Friedman, M. (1968). Real and pseudo gold standards, in his *Dollars and deficits*, pp. 247–265. Englewood Cliffs, NJ: Prentice-Hall,

Gassner, M.S. (2008). Revisiting Islamic bonds: Are 85% of *sukuk haram*? *Business Islamica*, March: 22–23.

Green, R. (1989). Real bills doctrine, in *New Palgrave: Money*, eds. Eatwell, J., Milgate, M., & Newman, P., pp. 310–313, New York: W.W. Norton.

Hayek, F. (1976). Choice in currency. Occasional Paper 48. London: Institute of Economic Affairs.

Haines, W.W. (1987). A society without money: Reflections on Jacques Maritain, *International Journal of Social Economics*, 14(3/4/5): 97–104.

International Monetary Fund (IMF) (2008, Dec 2). Deputy Assistant Secretary Sobel Remarks on the Global Financial Crisis and the IMF's Response, Dec. 2, U.S. Department of the Treasury. Available at: www.treasury.gov/press-center/press-releases/Pages/hp1307.aspx.

Keynes, J.M. (1963). Economic possibilities for our grandchildren, *Essays in Persuasion*, New York: W.W. Norton.

Klein, B. (1975). The competing supply of money, *Journal of Money, Credit and Banking*, 4.

Krugman, P.R. (1989). Market-based debt-reduction schemes, in *Analytical Issues in Debt*, eds. Frenkel, J.A., Dooley, M. P., & Wickhman, P., pp. 258–278, Washington, DC: International Monetary Fund.

Mundell, R.A. (2000). Presentation, Economic forum: One world, one currency: destination or delusion?, Nov 8, Washington DC: International Monetary Fund.

Parker, M. (2012). Comments on al-Amine, M. al-Bashir's *Global Sukuk and Islamic Securitization Market*, *Arab News*, Jan 3.

Rist, C. (1940). *History of Monetary and Credit Theory from John Law to the Present Day*, London: Allen Unwin.

Saving, T R. (1977). A theory of the money supply with competitive banking, *Journal of Monetary Economics*, 3: 289–303.

Tobin, J. (1963). Commercial banks as creators of 'money', in *Banking and Monetary Studies*, ed. Carson, D., pp. 408–419, Homewood, IL: Irwin.

Tullock, G. (1976). Competing moneys, *Journal of Money, Credit and Banking*, 7.

Usmani, M.T. (n.d). Sukuk applications. Available at: www.failaka.com/downloads/.

von Mises, L. (1978). *The Ultimate Foundation of Economic Science*, Kansas City, KS: Sheed Andrews & McMeel.
von Mises, L. (1981). The return to sound money, *The Theory of Money and Credit*, Chapter 23, Indianapolis, IN: Liberty Fund.
Yeager, L.B. (1983). Stable money and free-market currencies, *CATO Journal*, 305–326.
Yeager, L.B. (1997). *The Fluttering Veil*, Indianapolis, IN: Liberty Fund.

11

FISCAL POLICY IN ISLAMIC ECONOMY

LEARNING OBJECTIVES

This chapter explains the concept of *zakah* within the physical policy in Islam. The objective is that students may:

- pinpoint the aims of physical policy in eradicating unemployment and just distribution of wealth, economic stability and faster economic growth in an Islamic economy
- understand the importance of *zakah* in poverty alleviation and fulfillment of basic needs, if implemented in letter and in spirit.

All actions and administrative measures of the government which are related to revenues and expenditures are called physical policy. The main purpose of this policy is to maintain a standard of full employment without inflation. On the other hand, the main objectives of fiscal policy in Islamic economy are: (1) eradicating unemployment, (2) just distribution of wealth, (3) economic stability, and (4) faster economic growth.

In an Islamic economy, physical policy holds greater importance because owing to the illegality of interest, prohibition of accumulation of wealth and property and the ban on speculation would probably be very effective. *Zakah* (alms giving) is one of the main instruments of fiscal policy in an Islamic economy; the next most important is tax revenue. We will discuss *zakah* and tax in this chapter in detail.

Zakah as an instrument of fiscal policy

Zakah is one of the five pillars of Islam. The *Qur'an* contains several verses which declare *zakah* obligatory for Muslims; detailed rules are given in the sayings of the

Prophet Muhammad (peace be upon him). The directives to pay *zakah* are almost as many as the directives to prayer five times a day in the *Qur'an:* "Establish Salat (prayer) and pay *zakah*" (2:431). It also occupies a central place in the Islamic fiscal policy. This section deals with the conceptual issues and shows the overall role of *zakah* in socio-economic development.

Issues of zakah

Meaning of zakah

Etymologically, the word '*zakah*' means 'that which purifies'. It purifies wealth. According to the *Qur'an*, it is an *ibadah* (an act of worship), just like obligatory prayers. From an economic point of view, it is a tax-like levy imposed on those rich persons who have a minimum level of wealth (called *nisab*), and hence represents transfer of payment from the haves to the have-nots. The *Qur'an* does not mention the rate of *zakah* and the amount on which *zakah* is to be levied. These details are to be found in the *Hadith* (sayings and practices of the Prophet Muhammad). Disbursement of *zakah* is mandatory on capital investment in merchandise, agricultural produce, business, hoarded gold and money, and silver holdings. Ordinarily, the rate of *zakah* is 2.5 per cent per annum.

Zakah-*able items*

Items subject to zakah

The principal items on which *zakah* is payable include: (1) cash in hand or in the banks, (2) gold, silver or ornaments made thereof, (3) trading goods, (4) produce of mines, and (5) herd of cattle.

Items which are not included in zakah

Zakah shall not be payable by an assessment in respect of the following wealth, not being stock-in-trade: (1) land, (2) all buildings that house such establishments as mills, factories, warehouses, stores, (3) shops, (4) houses, (5) cattle below one year of age, (6) all clothing and household linen, (7) paper, books and printed matters, (8) all household furniture, utensils and equipment, (9) all domestic fowls and birds, (10) machinery, tools and instruments, (11) conveniences, (12) arms and ammunition, (13) all perishable agricultural products, (14) seeds for sowing, (15) wealth acquired and spent within the assessment year, and (16) wealth devoted to charitable purposes owned by charitable organizations.

Rate of zakah and nisab

Although the rate of *zakah* is popularly known as fixed tax, it depends upon the nature of items concerned. The most popular items, *nisab* and the rates are given in Table 11.1.

TABLE 11.1 Items of *zakah*, *nisab*, and rates

Wealth	*Nisab*	*Rate of payment of zakah*
Agricultural production	1,568 kgs per harvest	5 per cent of the produce in case of irrigated land and 10 per cent in case of non-irrigated land
Gold, silver, or ornaments made thereof	(i) Gold: The *nisab* by the standard of gold is 3 ounces of gold (87.48 grams) or its equivalent in cash. It is almost $3,744 (19/05/2017) but may vary with the existing market price of gold	2.5 per cent of the value
	(ii) Silver: The *nisab* by the standard of silver is 21 ounces of silver (612.36 grams) or its equivalent in cash. It is roughly $331 (19/05/2017)	
Cash in hand or at bank	Worth of 21 ounces of silver (612.36 grams)	2.5 per cent of the amount
Trading goods	Worth of 21 ounces of silver (612.36 grams)	2.5 per cent of the value of the goods
Cows and buffaloes	30	For each 30, a 1-year old; for each 40, a 2-year old
Goats and sheep	40	One for first 40; two for 120; three for 300; and one more for each number
Produce of mines	Any quantity	20 per cent of the produce

Source: Islamic Relief Worldwide (n.d.)

Distinctions between zakah, tax, and sadaqa

At this stage it would useful to show the distinguishing features of *zakah* vis-à-vis tax and *sadaqa* (charity). This is shown in Table 11.2.

For the payment of *zakah*, certain conditions need to be fulfilled. Hameed (2009) specified some of the conditions:

1. **Muslim:** *Zakah* is a compulsory payment but only for Muslims, as it is one of the mandatory five pillars of Islam. God says, "Take from their wealth a *sadaqa* to sanctify them and purify them with it, and pray God for them. Verily! Your invocations are a basis of security for them" (*Qur'an* 9:103). This verse of the holy *Qur'an* is addressed to Muslims and not to disbelievers or non-Muslims.

TABLE 11.2 Distinction between *zakah, sadaqa,* and tax

Zakah	Tax	Sadaqa
Compulsory payment imposed by God	Compulsory levy imposed by the government	Compulsory payment imposed by God
A levy on accumulated wealth at a certain level, as mentioned in Table 11.1	A levy on income up to a certain level	Does not necessarily depend upon tangible income
Payment involves money	Payment also involves money	Payment does not necessarily involve money; can be simply a gesture
Religious duty applicable only to Muslims	A duty for all citizens of a country	Religious duty for Muslims
Must be spent as specified in the *Qu'ran*	Can be used for any purpose as decided by the government	Must be spent for God's pleasure
For the poor	It is for all	It is for all but mainly for poor
The payee cannot expect any *quid pro quo* in this world but can expect reward in the Hereafter (life after death)	The taxpayer individually cannot expect any direct *quid pro quo* from the receiver of tax	The payee cannot expect worldly benefit but can expect spiritual benefit
A defined minimum level of wealth below which it does not become due	For direct tax, there is a minimum level of income below which tax is exempted	There is no minimum level
Rate is taken as fixed and invariable	Direct tax rate is not fixed; may increase with level of income	No fixed rate
Paid every year	Paid every year	Not regularly paid

Spiritually by paying *zakah*, a Muslim purifies himself or herself. Therefore, *zakah* is not to be collected from non-Muslims.

2. *Al-Takleef* **(burden of duty):** This refers to legal aptitude for obligation. A few scholars have imposed the conditions of the age of sanity and puberty (emotional and intellectual stability) for the directive of *zakah*. They say that *zakah* is not compulsory on the wealth of those who are not capable of following the teachings of religion. After all, *zakah* is an act of worship.

3. **Intention:** The validity of *zakah* depends upon one's intent. Someone contributing the *zakah* should pay it to its receivers, trusting that this is an obligation to be settled. As one Hadith says, "The worth of one's actions is dogged by one's intents" (*Bukhari*). Since the *zakah* is an action of worship, it must be connected with intention.

4. **Comprehensive possession of wealth:** The meaning of complete possession of wealth is that the wealth must be in the hand of the person paying *zakah* and that the wealth should be free from any privileges by others. Somebody paying the *zakah* must have the right to use and dispose of the wealth as he or she wills.

5. **Ownerless wealth:** For ownerless wealth there will be no *zakah*. This money or wealth should, of course, belong to the state, and the poor can claim due share.

6. *Waqf* **(endowment):** According to Islamic jurists, money from sources of endowment such as mosques, schools and orphans are not subject to *zakah*.

7. **Illegal wealth:** This includes wealth from theft, forgery, extortion, bribery and cheating. Islamic code demands that this money should be returned to the legal holders or their successors. If the owner of this money is unknown, then the money would be distributed to the needy and the poor. If somebody insists upon keeping control of this kind of wealth, and that wealth is still in existence after a whole year, then it becomes accountable to *zakah*.

   Here questions may be raised: When a debt is engrossed, then who is accountable to pay *zakah* on it, the debtor or the lender? Is this type of debt subject to *zakah*? Mainstream Islamic scholars have categorized debts into two groups, namely bad debt and good debt. If a debt is recognized by the debtor with a readiness to pay back, this is called a good debt. According to the stated principles, the lender would pay *zakah* on it. On the hand, if there is no expectation of receiving back the debt, this is called a bad debt and there would not be *zakah* on it.

8. **Increased wealth:** Wealth ought to be such that its products should be profit or value to its owners. The Prophet (pbuh) clearly circumvented the *zakah* on wealth used to meet the sincere obligation for personal use or livelihood. Therefore, there will be no *zakah* on wealth kept for primary necessities such as clothes, food, housing and supplementary basic needs.

9. *Nisab: Zakah* is payable on any amount of increasing wealth that reaches *nisab*.

10. **One complete Islamic calendar year:** An important condition of *zakah* is that the wealth must be in the possession of the person for one lunar calendar year. This is true for money, commercial commodities and livestock.

Zakah *receivers*

As per the *Qur'an* and Hadith, there are eight types of recipients of *zakah*, which God Himself has specified. That is:

> The *zakah* (alms) are only for the needy and the poor, and those who gather them, and those whose hearts are to be submissive, and to free the prisoners and the debtors and for the cause of God, and (for) the travelers; an obligation enforced by God.
>
> *Qur'an 9:60*

The recipients as mentioned in this verse are described below.

1. **The poor (al-fukara)**
2. *Masakin* **or needy**: The poor and the deprived are defined as those who do not have their basic needs fulfilled. In other words, they do not possess the *nisab*, which is an amount in excess of their vital needs with regard to food, drink, clothing, drinking water, housing, tools of their trade, animals, and similar other requirements. They are qualified to receive *zakah*.

    It may be pointed out that in the Islamic literature, there are scholars who preach that *al-fukara* refers to those persons who are poor but 'do not beg' and *al-masakin* to those who are poor and 'beg'. There are others who hold the opposite view. That is, *al-fukara* refers to those persons who are poor and 'beg' and *al-masakin* to those who are poor but 'do not beg'. This difference of opinion has no impact on the method of selection of recipients. In this regard, the following Hadith may be taken into consideration:

    > *al-miskin* (needy person) is not one who goes around asking the people for a date or a mouthful, but someone who is too uncomfortable, or, who has not sufficient money to fulfill his or her needs and whose situation is not identified to others.
    >
    > *Bukhari and Muslim*

    What is important to remember is that both *fukara* and *miskins* are poor and they are the first recipients of *zakah*. These *fukara* and *miskin* might include unemployed wage earners and labourers, and those who are forced to leave their own countries due to one reason or other and the persons who are physically disabled and crippled by old age.
3. **Collectors of *zakah*:** These are those that the authority in question employs to collect *zakah*. They may be engaged in various works, including collecting, recording, guarding, dividing and distributing *zakah*. The authority may pay their remuneration out of the funds collected on this head.
4. **The converted person:** *Zakah* can be used for reconciling the hearts of those who have been converted to Islam. It is often seen that the people who embrace Islam are forced out of their families and are sometimes unable to earn an income. These people should have the right to accept *zakah* to safeguard themselves from any harm due to being poor, and in order for them to practice their faith. Also, Islamic scholars agree that *zakah* funds can be used to appeal to the hearts of those who are motivated to turn towards Islam.
5. **Freeing slaves:** *Zakah* funds can be used to buy a bondsman or bondswoman and then free him/her (this point was developed previously, when the slave trade still existed). It was expected that when the slaves became free, they would be able to worship Allah and would eventually become useful members in the community.

6. **The debtors:** These people are burdened by debts because of family or personal needs. They have borrowed money but do not have money to repay the debt. They are living hand to mouth. Islamic jurists also opined that if anybody borrowed money for social requirements, such as expenses for an orphan, reconciliation between Muslims, or reconditioning a school or mosque, and became unable to repay, this debt could also be paid out of *zakah* funds. This holds even if the person is wealthy.

7. **The wayfarers:** Finally, *zakah* can be used for those who need financial aid to complete their journey. The 'wayfarer' is sometimes defined as a traveller stuck in a distant land and requires money in order to attain his or her objective or to return to his/her country. This person can accept *zakah*, provided, of course, that the purpose of their journey is lawful. God warns us, "Benefit one another in piety and righteousness, but do not extend help one another in sin" (*Qur'an* 5:21). Some Islamic economists have even suggested that under this head, the *zakah* funds can be used for repairing roads, buildings, and so on, for the convenience of travellers.

Principles of the distribution of zakah funds

Islam not only specifies the recipients of *zakah*, as discussed above, but also provides the principles of its distribution. Some of the important principles of distribution are as follows:

1. *Zakah* funds should be distributed among the recipients as specified in the *Qur'an* (9:60).
2. *Zakah* proceeds must be distributed as soon as they are collected. This is because the recipients of *zakah* are badly in need of it, as they are very poor.
3. It is desirable to spend *zakah* in the area from which it has been collected. This act is expected to strengthen the bond of brotherhood and create a healthy atmosphere of mutual co-operation within the community.
4. During a period of inflationary pressure, a greater portion of the proceeds of *zakah* should be circulated in the form of producer goods and during a period of depression, preference should be given to cash or consumer goods.
5. *Zakah* must be distributed in such a way so as to maximize the social and economic benefit of the recipients. This should not only help the recipients to move out of poverty but also help to increase their living standards so that they ultimately become *zakah*-payers rather than remain as *zakah*-receivers.

In order to implement the last principle, it would be necessary to categorize the poor beneficiaries into 'working poor' and 'non-working poor'. The non-working poor are those who are basically unemployed, and have nothing to do. They can be treated as 'wage-labourers'. Considering poor people's socio-economic status, *zakah* funds will have to be given to them through transfer payments. This type of help would, in turn, help them buy some goods and services.

The working poor, on the other hand, may be defined as those who are engaged in some activity, say, production of agricultural commodities, handicrafts, small shops, small businesses, etc. Because of one reason or another, these people are not in a position to make any headway in their professions. These people need help – a special type of help, so that they can increase their productivity at their respective professions.

Role of zakah

The key role of *zakah* is to uplift the spirit of a human being above a practical achievement. Consequently, zakah is due on all monetary wealth for corporations and for individuals, who always desire cleansing and purification of wealth, both materially and spiritually. *Zakah*, when paid out of the submission to the order of God, is a way of cleansing the soul of a Muslim from miserliness and greed. The immoralities of greed and selfishness can essentially be controlled in order for human beings to uplift their spirits, to flourish in their social connections in their life, and get rewards from God.

Objectives of zakah

Therefore, the socio-economic objectives of *zakah* may be stated as:

1. To help the rich Muslims get rid of their lust for wealth and purify it;
2. To help redistribution of income and help alleviate poverty;
3. To achieve social justice; and
4. To create effective demand, which, in turn, helps to boost the economic conditions of the poor.

Socio-economic impact of zakah

Zakah, if properly administered, can produce a significant impact on the socio-economic aspects of the economy. Some of the important impacts are discussed below.

Alleviation of poverty

It is generally believed that, compared to tax, since the *nisab* for the levy of *zakah* is low and the base for the levy is fairly wide, *zakah* has the potential for mobilizing substantial resources for the alleviation of poverty. But in the countries where poverty is wide-spread, *zakah* alone will not be sufficient to eliminate poverty. Available empirical evidence shows that it has not been possible to mobilize more than one-half percentage of GDP as *zakah* to those Muslim countries where it is administered by the state on compulsory basis. After all, *zakah* is a redeployment measure whereas the roots of economic poverty in most Muslim countries lie in output and level of economic development (Kahf 1992, 1999).

Impact on distribution

By definition, *zakah* means transfer of income from the haves to the have-nots. Islamic economists are in complete agreement in that if *zakah* (along with other institutional mechanisms) is faithfully handled, it would play a major role in the elimination of gross inequalities of income and wealth as found in most countries of the present world, irrespective of their stages of development. Abdullah al-Tahir made an estimate of *zakah* income in eighteen Muslim countries (eight of them oil-producing), basing it on United Nations income statistics from 1980, of these countries (Kahf 1999). This study was done to see the effects of *zakah* on the income gap between the poor and the rich over a ten-year period and concluded that, under his assumptions, this gap will reduce from nine to six and a half times. Again quoting the study of al-Zarqa, Kahf (1992) ascertains that *zakah* doubles the income of the poorest 10 per cent of the society every year since most of it is collected from the rich and distributed to the poor. In view of these evidences it can be stated that *zakah* helps stop the concentration of wealth in a few hands (*Qur'an* 59:7). Therefore, the distributive role of *zakah* involves an assigned role, as the *zakah* funds are mostly used for essential goods and services. This indicates that factors of production will be diverted from the production of luxuries to the production of necessaries.

Impact on free loan

Zakah has eight categories of recipients. One of these is the debtor. If the debtor has incurred the debt for a lawful cause and is unable to pay it back, then *zakah* funds can be used for helping him/her to repay it. Al-Zarka (1992, p. 154) quoted from al-Qaradawi's interesting comment on the impact of *zakah* in the following words:

> If society provides extra protection for the creditor it means people will be more willing to finance interest *Qard Hasan* (interest-free loans) because of the knowledge that *Zakah* is liable to reimburse the lender if the debt was incurred in good faith.

Impact on consumption

There are many studies in the economic literature which shows that the Marginal Propensity to Consume (MPC) is comparatively very high for the poor people when compared to the rich. Will the final outcome be a higher or lower aggregate propensity to consume (APC) in an Islamic economy? In this matter, one opinion is that the poor people constitute the bulk of the population of the developing countries. Since *zakah* involves transfer of income to the poor who have high MPC, this implies that the aggregate consumption expenditure of the economy would increase. Given the deficiency of effective demand in these economies, higher consumption would certainly serve as a favourable factor for growth and employment.

The other opinion is that it is difficult to determine the direction of the aggregate consumption after *zakah* is effected: it may either be neutral or at best unstipulated because of inconsistent effects on income of the rich and the poor (Kahf 1999).

Impact on savings and investment

Ceteris paribus, *zakah* will have negative effects on savings. In other words, private savings above *nisab* will reduce if no effort is made to invest it. This rather punitive nature of *zakah* should encourage one to invest one's idle savings. Thus *zakah*, by imposing a penalty for keeping resources idle, actually helps push resources into productive sectors and hence produce a positive, rather than a negative, impact on savings.

It is necessary to emphasize that Islam urges the people not to keep their savings idle. The Prophet (peace be upon him) was aware of this rather unacceptable value and therefore

> urged those accountable for the management of wealth belonging to orphans to invest it so that it should not show a gradual loss due to *zakah*. This saying of the Prophet (peace be upon him) teaches Muslims to make *zakah* payments from the earnings generated from one's wealth rather than from idle wealth itself.
>
> *Nik Hassan 1991, pp. 214–215*

It is mentioned that *zakah* collection and delivery increases employment through two ways: (i) generating new jobs for those managing *zakah* itself, and (ii) transferring some sections of beneficiaries into productive workers by means of deliveries in the form of rehabilitation, capital goods and training. That is why the *Qur'an* says, "But will give increase for deeds of charity" (2:276).

Impact on stabilization

If sufficient funds are available, a portion can be used as a counter-cyclical device. That is, if during a period of inflation some *zakah* proceeds are kept in reserve and then released during a depressed period, this would produce a positive impact on stabilization of the economy. *Zakah* as an anti-inflationary device can be more successfully implemented through appropriate disbursement policy. According to some Islamic scholars, during inflationary pressure, attempts should be made to distribute a greater portion of the proceeds of *zakah* in the form of producer goods and during depression, preference should be given to cash or consumer goods.

Impact of product-mix

In the welfare point of view, sometimes it is required to bring about a change in the product-mix. *Zakah* has a role to play in this regard. It brings about a transfer of purchasing power from more affluent sections of the population to the poorer sections. As the latter would have more demand for essentials, it is highly probable that the product-mix of the country will get changed.

State-administered zakah

In the very limited Muslim countries *zakah* has been administered by the state. Amongst the countries where *zakah* is administered by the state, prominent examples are: Pakistan (from 1981), Malaysia, Sudan, Yemen (from 1951), and Saudi Arabia (from 1981) (Kuran 1993; Kahf 1999). Some experiences from these countries are noted here.

First, *zakah* systems vary from one country to another in terms of yield. In Pakistan it exceeded 0.35 per cent of the GDP, as indicated in the statistical year book. Of this only 8 per cent of *zakah* is derived from agriculture. This unexpectedly low contribution from agriculture is said to be due mainly to the difficulty of compelling rich and influential landlords to pay their dues. In Saudi Arabia, this percentage was only between 0.4 per cent and 0.6 per cent from 1991 to 1996. This implies that there must have been restrictive coverage and large-scale evasion in both these countries. Incidentally, evasion takes a variety of forms, including disguising or under-reporting one's crops, or giving adulterated grain to the *zakah* collector. In Sudan, *zakah* proceeds range between 0.3 per cent and 0.5 per cent of GDP.

Second, the rates and coverage of *zakah* items are quite diverse. Both Pakistan and Saudi Arabia have extended the obligation to companies in respect of collection of *zakah*. In addition, these countries have collected a flat levy on certain types of bank deposits. Saudi Arabia levies *zakah* on imported goods at a varying rate from commodity to commodity. On the other hand, Pakistan allows farmers to subtract their expenditures on insecticides and fertilizers. The rate is 5 per cent on all farm output, irrespective of the technology deployed in irrigation. It successfully relieves industrial workers, businessmen, shopkeepers and businessman as well as the growers of coconut, rubber and other cash crops.

Third, there are also variations in terms of distributive mechanisms. In Pakistan, *zakah* revenues are channelled by the *Zakah* Administration to thousands of local committees. These committees ultimately decide whom to support with the funds. The funds are assigned among the agencies roughly according to the population they signify. This implies that comparatively poor communities generally accept more than their contribution to the *zakah* funds. According to official statistics, during 1980–1988, 58 per cent of the *zakah* funds were used as maintenance allowance to allow people to work, including orphans, widows and the handicapped. However, the grants, as one should assume for developing countries like Pakistan, were still too small to make a substantial difference in the living standards of such groups. During the 1980s, when an individual required an estimated US$22 a month just to survive, most *zakah* payments ranged between US$4 and US$8 per individual, in some cases much less. The system covers about one million recipients, which represents about 10 per cent of the total people thought to be living below the country's poverty level.

An important finding of *zakah* administration of Pakistan is that about 20 per cent of its fund was been allocated to rehabilitation during 1980–1988. Under this scheme many poor women received sewing machines. But because of lack of training and materials on the part of the recipients this good scheme is not implemented properly.

In Malaysia, its federal set-up assigns the administration of *zakah* to an office at national level. Collected funds are passed on to the *zakah* office in each state for distribution. It may be interesting to refer to the *zakah* office in Alor Setar (the capital of Kedah) for an example. In 1970, out of total proceeds, 53 per cent was allotted to commendable measures (generally religious education), 6 per cent to people making a pilgrimage to Mecca, 2 per cent to converts, and 22 per cent as commissions to the *zakah* collectors and central administration, leaving 15 per cent for the poor. Figures for the early 1980s show that the disbursement of *zakah* to the poor ranged between 11 and 13 per cent. Those included in the list of beneficiaries received between US$3 and US$19 a year (Nik Hassan 1991). In 1993, out of the total *zakah* distributed (RM 29.28m), 11 per cent was allotted for *al-fukara* and *miskin* and as much as 76 per cent was for *fi sabil Allah* (in the path of Allah). Later, in 1997, this distribution pattern changed substantially: *al-fukara* and *miskin* received 24 per cent and *fi sabil Allah* was reduced to 64 per cent. On the other hand, a key difference between the Malaysian and Pakistani *zakah* systems lies in the source of payment for *zakah* administration officials. In Malaysia, officials are salaried out of *zakah* revenue as per the instruction of the *Qu'ran*. In Pakistan, *zakah* collectors are paid out of general government funds.

Fourth, one more interesting experience of *zakah* administration in Pakistan is in the case of Shiite Muslims. Since objections made by the Shiite community of Pakistan, they are exempt from contributing to the government-administered *zakah* fund. In Malaysia, some individuals feel that obligatory payments are not adequate to fulfil their religious obligations. Accordingly, they make additional payments to people of their choice. Payments to the government are often referred to as '*zakah raja*' (means 'ruler's *zakah*') and the voluntary payments are called '*zakah peribadi*' or personal *zakah*. Also, additional payment is made by the rich in Pakistan. This implies that transfer of *zakah* of more wealth to the poor people than shown by the official records has been different from country to country.

Fifth, *zakah* can produce substantial impact on employment through its collection and distribution. Both theory and practice put something on the proportion of *zakah* proceedings that may be used up on employment in the *zakah* organization. According to the suggestion of the scholars of the Shafi'i school of thought, a limit may be set of 12.5 per cent of the total proceeds for labour compensation in the *zakah* organization. In practice, Sudan limits it to 10 per cent while Saudi Arabia and Pakistan keep this portion keep intact for distribution to other categories, particularly the needy and poor.

Sixth, there have been severe problems in collecting *zakah* on cash and current account balances held by individuals in Sudan, Saudi Arabia and Yemen. In Pakistan, it was possible to deduct *zakah* on current accounts at the source, but it was found difficult to collect *zakah* on trade inventories and on cash balances held by both individuals and companies.

Conclusion

One of the significant aims of fiscal policy is the effectual distribution of resources so that people may gain overall benefit. A well-organized distribution of resources can be well-defined as the one that creates an equilibrium between economic imperatives and morality. Moral desires will be mostly satisfied by the voluntary sector, while economic needs would be typically provided through the market. However, it does not mean that the role of the private sector in satisfying moral requirements would be non-existent. While the private sector, enthused by the profit motive, will struggle for the attainment of economic aims and contentment of economic needs, the voluntary sector will attempt to rectify the gaps left by the private sector. The public sector will not only provide help to rationalize the operation of the private and voluntary sectors but also will ensure that their purposes are satisfied.

In an Islamic economy, *zakah*, *sadaqah*, *waqf*, etc. will play a vital part in the fair distribution of wealth. *Zakah* especially will perform as an in-built fiscal stabilizer as well as an optional extra fiscal stabilizer in the economy. The *Qur'an* mentions eight types of expenditure of the *zakah* fund. Six of these types are directly connected to the poor and low-income groups. Thus, *zakah* money streams from the rich to the poor. *Zakah* therefore plays a significant part in producing the distribution of wealth in an equitable and just way.

Payment of *zakah* is compulsory on capital investment in merchandise, business, hoarded money, gold, silver holdings and agricultural production. Islam condemn hoarding of wealth. At the same time it levies *zakah* on hoarded wealth at the rate of 2.5 per cent per annum. These actions resulted in decrease of hoarded wealth year by year. That is why Islam condemns craving to accumulate wealth and lays stress on the movement of wealth or investment in business. One of the important reasons not to keep wealth unused or stored is the yearly decrease of its amount due to the payment of *zakah*. Islam commands that even the wealth of the orphans must be invested in business otherwise it will be subject to the yearly levy of *zakah* (Mahmoud 1974). On the other hand, the owner, by investing his/her money in business, could save himself/herself from the sin of hoarding as well as earn profit. Furthermore, by spending all excess income, after meeting his/her wants, to assist the poor, the owner of this capital will gain rewards in the Hereafter. Also Islam discourages less productive and non-productive activities, so people must invest their money in very productive ventures. This will result in growth and development of economy. Another anxiety is that compulsory payment of *zakah* on capital investment will discourage investment because payment of *zakah* will lessen the marginal efficiency of capital. If we think more carefully, this fear is baseless. The Islamic economics system is based on an interest-free system whereas conventional economics is interest-based (*riba*). In an interest-based conventional economy, it is interest which deters investment. In the Keynesian theory of assets, a zero interest rate inspires a high level of investment. Therefore, as a result of a zero interest rate and the prevention of the accumulation of wealth, the level of investment in an Islamic economy will be higher than in an interest-based economy.

In the matter of savings, Islam prohibits luxury and lavish display; luxury goods and expenditure on lawful things will reduce the level of unusable expenditure. This will result in more increase than decrease in the volume of savings. It is a fact that as savings is also the results of income, that is S=f(y), the level of savings will increase in the Islamic economy. However, these savings may be assigned to investment rather than accrued in a sluggish reserve fund.

In view of the above argument, it is clear that in an Islamic economy the aggregate demand and aggregate financing (investment) will be larger than in a capitalistic economy. The question arises: Does *zakah* provide an inducement to save or does it discourage savings? The question may be answered as follows:

1. Muslims purify their wealth by giving *zakah* on it.
2. Muslim believers thereby fulfil the right of the economically poor to their wealth.

Review questions

1. Define *zakah*. What are the principles of *zakah* policy?
2. Distinguish between *zakah*, tax and *sadaqa*.
3. Discuss the principles of *zakah* distribution in an Islamic economy.
4. Discuss the socio-economic impact of *zakah* with reference to a Muslim country.

References

Al-Zarka, A. (1992). Distributive justice in Islam, in *Lectures on Islamic Economics*, eds. Ahmad, A. & Awan, K.R., Jeddah: IRTI(IDB).

Hameed, M.A. (2009). *Islamic Economics: An Introductory Analysis*, Rajshahi: Padma Residential.

Islamic Relief Worldwide (n.d.). Online *Zakah* calculation link. Available at: www.islamic-relief.org/zakat/zakat-calculator/.

Kahf, M. (1992). A contribution to the theory of consumer behaviour in an Islamic society, in *Studies in Islamic Economics*, ed. Ahmad, K., Leicester: Islamic Foundation.

Kahf, M. (1999). The performance of the institution of *zakah* in theory and practice, Malaysia: IIUM International Conference, Kuala Lumpur.

Kuran, T. (1993). The economic impact of Islamic fundamentalism, in *Fundamentalisms and the State: Remaking Polities, Economics and Militancy*, eds. Marty, M. & Appleby, R.S., Chicago: University of Chicago Press.

Mahmoud, M. (1974). Fictions, power rationing and *al-zakah*, in *Association of Muslim Social Scientists' Proceedings*, Third National Seminar, Gray (Indiana).

Nik Hassan, M.N. (1991). Zakat in Malaysia: Present and future status, in *Development and Finance in Islam*, eds. Sadeq, A.H., Pramanik, A.H., & Hassan, N.H. B. Hj N., Kuala Lumpur: IIUM.

12

THEORY OF TAXATION IN ISLAMIC ECONOMY

LEARNING OBJECTIVES

The chapter starts with an overview of the fundamentals of taxation in Islam and aims to:

*   discuss in detail the principles of taxation in Islam
*   Provide the students with a good understanding of *infaq*, *sadaqa* and *zakah*.

During the period of the four Caliphs – Abu Bakr, Umar, Usman and Ali – there was no formal taxation system except the import duty. This duty was first imposed in the reign of Caliph Umar. This duty was levied at the rate of 2.5 per cent on Muslims, 5 per cent on the *Dhimmis* (non-Muslims living in an Islamic state) and 10 per cent on merchants from foreign countries. Even this duty was imposed only because in foreign countries the authorities used to collect import duty from Muslim traders on every consignment (Duri 1974).

Another instance is that of collection of *kharaj* (tax on the produce of the land). During the time of the Caliph Umar, after the request of the rulers of Iraq and Syria, Umar decreed that the land, instead of being distributed among the soldiers, should be left in possession of the local owners on whom a rate of *kharaj* was imposed. *Kharaj* then became a source of revenue for the Muslim government and an asset for future generations. The rate of *kharaj* was subject to change at the discretion of the ruler of the Muslim government. It may be noted here that there is no trace of any discussion on taxation in writings of the early Muslim jurists because an abundance of non-tax resources precluded any need for imposing taxes (Nasr 2001). However, Kahf (1983) states that when the conventional sources of revenue were exhausted and financial needs, especially expenditure on defence, became enormous, the Islamic jurists began to give serious thought to taxation in order to meet the expenses of the Muslim government. Further, eminent Islamic jurist Ibn Hazr was in favour of a tax system for the Muslim government (Rahman 1979). According to Rahman (1979), Ibn Hazr held the view that taxes should be imposed only when the *zakah* fund became inadequate to meet the needs of the poor.

As a source of public revenue, tax plays a very dominant role in the contemporary economy. It alone accounts for some four-fifths of the total revenue income and covers around one-third of the total national income of most Muslim countries. In an Islamic economy, however, the role and scope of taxation as a means of mobilizing resources is not straightforward. Its objectives and structures are quite different from those of a conventional economy. This chapter, therefore, attempts to show the justification, objectives and the structural design of the taxation system from an Islamic perspective.

Justification of taxation in an Islamic economy

Levy system during the early days of Islam

In the literature, there is a lack of agreement among Islamic economists regarding the place of taxation in an Islamic economy as a source of government revenue. This arises simply because the *Qur'an*, the most important source of Islamic knowledge, says nothing specific about taxation, either for good or for bad. It mentions only two compulsory levies: *zakah* on Muslims (*Qur'an* 9:103) and *jizya* on protected non-Muslims (*Qur'an* 9:291). The Prophet Muhammad (peace be upon him) and his first Caliph Abu Bakr confined themselves to these two levies and used others (e.g., one-fifth of booty) as a supplementary source only. Some ad hoc funds were of course collected through donations and other measures.

However, as time passed, these sources were found to be inadequate to meet the expenditure of an expanding economy. It was the second Caliph, Umar, who started imposing additional levies in the form of *kharaj* (land tax) and *ushr* (a 10 per cent tax on merchandise imported from states that taxed the Muslims on their agricultural produce). Caliph Umar ibn Al-Khattāb was the first Muslim ruler to levy *ushr* on trade (Fauzia 2014). A one-off tax on excess income and wealth of government officers and a tax on horses were also imposed. The historians have described these as an extension of *zakah*. Revenues derived from these sources were abundant enough to render any additional sources unnecessary. In other words, in the strict sense of the term, a taxation system such as we find today did not exist; the need for such taxes was not felt either (Cizakca 2011).

Although there is nothing specific about tax in the *Qur'an* in the sense we use the term in modern economics, Hassanuz Zaman (1993) has shown that the Islamic approach to taxation can be determined under the guidance of such *Qur'anic* words as '*infaq*' (spending charity) and '*sadaqa*' (optional and voluntary charity) The meaning of these concepts are explained below. It is also important to relate these concepts to *zakah*.

Some relevant concepts

Meaning of infaq and sadaqa

Infaq literally means spending. It refers to any spending whether for good or for bad. Note that in the *Qur'an* spending by unbelievers for opposing the religion is also termed *infaq* (8:361). It can be made of anything to any extent at any time and the spender may legally expect moral, material or social benefits out of it. *Sadaqa*, on the other hand, refers to spending (i.e., *infaq*) for Allah's pleasure only. In other words, *sadaqa* and *infaq* become interchangeable only when the latter also refers to spending for Allah's pleasure only. This also implies that *infaq* is a broader term and encompasses *sadaqa*. It should be pointed out that *sadaqa* not only refers to spending in monetary terms but may also refer simply to a gesture, a word spoken, or a service rendered. "The best *sadaqa* is to learn a point of knowledge (*ilim*) and teach it to your Muslim brothers" (Ibn Majah, quoted in Rahman 1976). In this sense, the scope of *sadaqa* would appear to be broader than that of *infaq*. It is, therefore, not at all surprising that *sadaqa* has been made compulsory for all Muslims irrespective of their socio-economic circumstances.

Conditions under which infaq and sadaqa become indistinguishable

If *infaq* is to be qualified as *sadaqa*, in addition to Allah's pleasure it has to fulfil other conditions as implied in the *Qur'an*. Some of these are:

- It is to be made from one's own earnings (*Qur'an* 2:1951).
- It should be done scrupulously without any desire for publicity (*Qur'an* 4:38).
- Its amount should be determined by the capacity of the spender (*Qur'an* 65:7).
- The amount should be such that it is neither extravagant nor miserly (*Qur'an* 25:671).
- When given, the giver should not expect any reward from the receiver: such *infaq/sadaqa* is termed *qard hasan* (*Qur'an* 2:245).

This does not mean that everybody should always spend the entire balance that remains after normal daily expenditure and repayment of loans. In this regards some quotations from the sayings of the Prophet seem relevant:

- It is better for you to retain something than giving the entire surplus as *sadaqa* (*Bukhari*).
- The best *sadaqa* is one that leaves you well-to-do (*Bukhari*).

The scopes of infaq, sadaqa, and zakah

The *Qur'an* is specific about the heads of expenditure of *zakah* funds (*Qur'an* 9:60). Insofar as these are concerned, *sadaqa* becomes indistinguishable from *zakah*. However, *sadaqa* has additional beneficiaries including parents, other near relations, orphans, neighbours, and fellow workers (*Qur'an* 2:177 and 4:36).

An interesting feature of *infaq/sadaqa* is that the financial standing of its beneficiaries is ignored. As one *hadith* says, "Beggar has a right even though he visits you on a horse back" (*Abu Daud*). All these imply that there are no restrictions in the list of beneficiaries of *infaq/sadaqa* in so far as the *Qur'an* and the *Sunnah* (sayings of the Prophet) are concerned.

Moreover, *zakah* is treated as obligatory. The question may be raised: can *infaq/sadaqa* be regarded as obligatory? Or is it merely permissible or desirable? The rich reward in the Hereafter that is associated with *infaq* and *sadaqa* and the condign punishment that is forewarned on non-observance of these acts, suggests that they are more than desirable. They should rather be regarded as obligatory as noted in the *Qur'an*. For instance, "Spend your wealth for the cause of God…" (*Qu'ran* 2:1951) or "Spend out of (the bounties) We have provided for you, before the Day comes …" (*Qur'an* 2:254). Therefore, it can be stated that payments of *infaq/sadaqa* are obligatory, although the details are not given as for *zakah*. The details would certainly vary from person to person according to income, size of agricultural holdings, liabilities, and social and professional requirements. In effect, "fixity of the nature of wealth and amount or rate have been skipped in favour of honest personal judgment on the individuals" (Hassanuz Zaman 1993, p.18).

It may be argued that the scope of *sadaqa* is the widest, since it can be given both in monetary and non-monetary terms. The non-monetary expenditure is expected to exceed the unholy expenditure as implied by *infaq*. The scope of *infaq* is narrower than *sadaqa* but wider than *zakah*. *Zakah* is paid only in terms of money (or wealth that is tangible). Its scope is naturally the narrowest.

Thus *sadaqa* encompasses both *infaq* and *zakah*. Moreover, of the three words, *infaq* is the most frequently used in the *Qur'an* (more or less sixty times) and the other two words, *sadaqa* and *zakah*, are used less frequently (more or less fifteen and thirty times, respectively). Although *sadaqa* is less frequently used in the *Qur'an*, it is most frequently used in the Hadith (Hassanuz Zaman 1993).

The road from infaq/sadaqa to taxation

From the above discussion, a number of conclusions can be drawn:

- The acts of *infaq* and *sadaqa* are as obligatory as *zakah* (and even prayer or *salat*);
- Although the heads of expenditure for *zakah* is specified, those of *infaq/sadaqa* are almost open-ended;
- Since the rates, limits, etc. are not specified for *infaq* and *sadaqa*, the authority in question can handle them in accordance with the prevailing circumstances;
- The rulers in the early days of Islam made no attempt to institutionalize the acts of *infaq* and *sadaqa* simply because the nature and scope of state activities did not warrant them. That is, the revenues collected from compulsory heads such as *zakah*, *ushr*, *kharaj* and voluntary contributions obtained through *sadaqa* and others were sufficient to meet the extended state expenditures of those days.

The last point needs further elaboration. Although the act of *infaq/sadaqa* was not institutionalized, Rahman (1976), quoting several Hadiths, arrives at the following conclusions:

- In some cases a job was assigned to those who volunteered to perform it.
- In some other cases a group of persons was nominated to perform the job.
- On another occasion the entire population was required to contribute to the maximum extent without any exemption or excuse.

All these imply that in order to finance various expenditures, in addition to the voluntary contributions, the government may resort either to nominate a group of persons having the capacity to bear the burden or it may make the entire population to share it.

It may be noted that these ideas have gradually died out because of the absence of that magical hand, or more essentially because of lack of institution. In the early days, the need for a formal institution to materialize those ideas was not felt, because during those days the advice of the Prophet (peace be upon him) was taken as obligatory.

> Thus the task of removing shortage of water, or playing host to some tribal delegations, or supporting the slaves who deserted enemy ranks or even the financing of the Prophet's biggest campaign of journey to Tabuk were all managed through *Sadaqa* or *Infaq*.
>
> *Hassanuz Zaman 1993, p. 24*

Unfortunately, this scenario will not find its application in the current leadership. The socio-economic circumstances of the population, including those of the Muslims, have undergone fundamental changes. Hassanuz Zaman (1993, p. 27) has rightly portrayed it as follows:

> Quite contrary to the conditions of early Islamic society the contemporary Muslims unfortunately lack in every merit. Aberration, materialism and absence of socio-mindedness speak against relying on their fine conscience. Unprecedented increase in the population of the Muslim Ummah with scarce resources has led to innumerable social and economic problems which cannot be solved through actions. Free-riders far out-numbered sincere volunteers and social service organizations to frustrate any serious effort of socio-economic up-liftment. As a result the law abiding persons content themselves with conferring their contributions mostly to their nearest ones… and feel as if they have complied with the injunctions of doing *Infaq*.

All these imply that the act of *infaq* should be regulated and institutionalized so that all can contribute towards social and economic development. This can be possible only if this compulsory contribution is introduced in the form of tax. Hence, it can be concluded that the tax system which is found in the modern days can be traced back to words of the *Qur'an* such as *infaq* and *sadaqa*, the latter with, of course, an Islamic approach.

Justification of taxation in Islam

According to Chapra (1992, pp. 295–299), an Islamic country has a 'right' to tax in addition to *zakah*; and the Muslims are also under 'obligation' to pay taxes as well to *zakah*. These have been fortified by many jurists representing all Schools of Islamic thought, such as Hanafi, Shafi, Maliki and Hanbali; although the term 'taxes' has not been used, terms used include *duraib*, *wazaif*, *kharaj*, and *nawaib*. All these terms imply more or less the same thing as taxes. Detailed explanations are given below.

The 'right' to impose tax

- Perhaps the most important justification for the imposition of tax, in addition to *zakah*, is that the purposes for which these are to be used, from the *Shari'ah* point of view, are not necessarily the same. By the injunction of the *Qur'an*, *zakah* funds cannot be used for purposes other than those specified in the *Qur'an* (9:60). It may be noted that the expenditure needed for the general well-being of the people is not mentioned in that list. Therefore, for meeting the obligation required by the *Shari'ah*, the government will need to impose taxes.
- The government of an Islamic country is under obligation to help in removing the hardship and sufferings of the people, such as starvation, illiteracy, homeless and lack of health. Since it is not in most cases possible to perform this function with *zakah* funds, there, the government should have the right to impose taxes.
- The example of the first Islamic society, Medina, is very indicative in this regard. It was a society that depended on raising production along with voluntary contributions through *infaq* much more than obligatory *zakah*. That is why *zakah* alone may not meet all social welfare responsibility towards the needy.

The 'obligation' to pay tax

- The obligation to pay taxes can be derived from one Hadith which says, "in your capital there are duties beyond the *zakah*".
- Muslims are obliged to help the state, by way of taxes and other contributions, to perform the functions of a modern Islamic state effectively.
- The people get services, either directly or indirectly, from the government, including external and internal security, roads and transport, airports, seaports, water supply, sewage system and street cleaning. For these services, it is required that Muslims must pay taxes to the government.
- In support of taxes in the Muslim society, Chapra (1992, p. 298) argues that,

Since taxes signify mostly payment for services enjoyed indirectly or directly by the taxpayers, therefore, the effort to dodge taxes in a Muslim social order is not only a legal offense but also a moral fault to be punishable by God in the Hereafter.

• The model of the first Islamic state established in Medina is also very relevant in this regard. This state depended on nurturing production along with voluntary charities through *awqaf, sadaqa, infaq* and *fi-sabil-Allah* (for the cause of God), for more than the mandatory *zakah* itself.

Taxes do not cancel out *zakah* or substitute it, because the *zakah* must be spent in definite manners and to defined recipients. There are distinct requirements and conditions in collecting the *zakah*, its rate, and who would pay it.

Purposes of taxation plan in Islam

Most Muslim economists have tried to suggest some of the purposes of a taxation plan and policy from an Islamic perspective. The following are suggested objectives of taxation policy for an Islamic economy:

• To supplement government revenue;
• To maintain justice and equity in society;
• To allow every Muslim citizen to contribute to society irrespective of their socio-economic circumstances; and
• To curb unemployment and inflation and thereby promote economic growth.

Planning an Islamic tax structure

The purposes of a tax structure in an Islamic economy would be quite different from that of the capitalistic system. Here, an attempt is made to construct a design for a tax system under an Islamic economy.

Tax as additional government revenue

Islam gives proper emphasis to the development of the private sector. Accordingly, it is suggested that a country should make great efforts to eschew taking on those activities that can better be performed by the private sector. Kahf (1983, p. 29) argues that taxes should be imposed only after exhausting all other resources. In fact he recommends four measures to be undertaken by an Islamic economy before resorting to taxation. These are:

1. Imposing taxes should not finance expenditure cutting;
2. Financing development undertakings by means of private participation, i.e., the development projects, which can be designed on a profit basis and financed by private persons, should not be financed by the state;

3. Selling public goods for fair prices, or fees; and
4. Voluntary and forced public borrowing should also be explored before resorting to taxation.

Other Islamic scholars, however, appear to have made no such rigid conditions for taxation as a source of revenue in an Islamic economy. For instance, Chapra (2000) in one of his arguments very clearly says that "in view of the aims of social justice and rightful distribution of income, an enlightened tax system appears to be rightly in line with the social goals of Islam" (Chapra 2000, p. 161). Against this background, it may be concluded that in an Islamic economy, tax should be regarded as an important supplementary source of government revenue.

Purpose of tax

In an Islamic economy, the purpose for which the tax is to be imposed is crucial. The purposes of an Islamic state may be divided into two broad categories: subsistence welfare and desired welfare. Subsistence welfare functions of a state include those activities necessary for meeting the primary wants of the people: i.e., food, shelter, clothing, health, education, and sanitation. Islamic economists are in complete agreement in that the state will be fully authorized to raise necessary resources through additional taxation in order to reach a subsistence standard for the people in the society. However, opinions differ regarding the latter. Kahf (1983) categorically states that "a country under Islamic economy is authorized to resort to taxation only for meeting what he calls "obligatory functions of the Islamic state" and the desired functions can only be undertaken if there are sufficient non-tax resources available to the state" (pp. 33–34).

However, Iqbal and Molyneux (2005) argue that "a majority of Islamic scholars believe that the state should also attempt to promote an egalitarian economic and social order. A state has the ultimate responsibility of protecting the collective interests of the society and is authorized to take direct action whenever necessary" (p. 109).

The arguments given above, although apparently in contradiction, do show that an Islamic economy may use tax proceeds for any development activities but it is not allowed to make any wasteful expenditure, as Islam very strongly condemns 'extravagance and wasteful spending'.

Tax must be just

Many prominent Islamic scholars, like Al-Ghazali, Ibn Taymiyya and Mawardi, suggest that justice in the distribution of the burden of tax must be maintained. It may be noted that imposing taxes on the poor contradicts the principle of *zakah* itself as well as guaranteeing a minimum standard of living. Most of the burden should fall on those who have the capacity to bear: the ability-to-pay principle of the contemporary tax system. It is also suggested that the taxation policy should be such that it brings about a more equitable circulation of wealth and income within the society.

Not to extinguish inducements

In designing the tax structure in an Islamic economy, it is necessary to ensure that it does not discourage investment and that the incentive/disincentive effects of taxation policy do not run counter to the goals of Islam. For instance, it has been observed that high corporate profit tax acts counter to the introduction of a profit-sharing system of financing. High taxes on profit encourage businesses to under-declare their profits in the case of *mudaraba* (trust financing) arrangements. In fact, high rates of taxation are now being lowered even in Western countries because of their adverse effects on private sector activity. The tax rate should, therefore, be such that it does not penalize honesty and create the un-Islamic tendency of evading taxes. Islamic scholars have, however, suggested that tax on the total capital employed may be considered as an alternative to the taxes on income and wealth.

Mix of direct and indirect taxes

The composition of tax system is very important in designing the tax structure in an Islamic system. Direct tax is recommended because it falls more on the rich than on the poor. But absolute reliance on this system will be undesirable since it would be too unwieldy, unmanageable and expensive. It would also give way to evasion by a large segment of the population. Indirect tax is also recommended because it allows all people to contribute something towards the socio-economic development of the country. This is what is demanded by the institution of *infaq*. However, its scope should be limited in an Islamic country because of the fact that it is regressive in character and hence would be inequitable to low income groups. Therefore, a mixture of direct and indirect taxes would appear to be the best principle of taxation for an Islamic economy.

The indirect tax would fulfil the universal obligation of *infaq* and a direct tax on higher income groups to effect equity and distributive justice. On the whole, direct tax is to be preferred to indirect tax. It may be noted that each member of the society is needed to contribute in funding for social needs as per their capabilities and resources, which may be in terms of financial or physical work.

Defence tax

Since in a number of Muslim countries a substantial portion of public expenditure goes to defence, it may be necessary to impose a defence tax on a per head basis. However, it is desirable that this tax is imposed as an additional tax without any changes in personal taxes.

Linking the tax system with zakah and subsidy

In designing the tax structure in an Islamic economic system, one should consider not only the distribution of tax burden of the tax payers but also its link with the distribution of such funds as *zakah* and subsidy. In a sense, this is the most important and the most intricate aspect of the Islamic tax structure. Besides *zakah*, extra tax needs to be imposed in the society; a taxation system based on the total contemplation of the capabilities of the tax payers – an ability that consists of the relative levels of both income and wealth. In Islamic economics, proper attention is given on the distributive justice. From this viewpoint, people may be grouped into three categories: people living below the poverty line; those living below subsistence, but above the poverty line; and well-to-do people. Islam demands that in distributing the tax burden and the distribution of *zakah* and subsidy as justice (*adl*) and kindness (*ihsan*) will have to be maintained. The issue is discussed further in the following paragraphs.

Below the poverty line

Those people who cannot afford to meet their basic necessities are said to be living below the poverty line. These people are unable to consume the minimum 2332 calories per day as recommended by the Food and Agriculture Organization (FAO). In Islamic terminology, they are called the '*zakah*-deserving people'. Since they are to pay indirect taxes, this negative, or more technically, regressive effect should be compensated through *zakah* and other funds meant for the poor.

Subsistence level

Those people who live above the poverty line but at the subsistence level do not qualify under the condition stated by the *Qur'an*: i.e., "They ask thee what to spend; say whatever remains surplus" (*Qur'an* 2:219). That is, they do not possess any surplus income after meeting their basic necessities. Notably, these people are not *zakah*-deserving since the value of their total assets may be somewhat above or near the *sahib nisab*, in the strict sense of the term. The circumstances have been nicely described by Hassanuz Zaman (1993, p. 29) in the following way:

> This happens due to holding indispensable valuables like jewelry, house, or consumer durables. It is very difficult to convince a destitute widow to sell a portion of 125-gram gold jewelry, which makes her *sahib nisab* and thus disqualifies her to receive assistance from *Zakah* fund. An owner of a house valuing 10,000 Islamic Dinar would not agree to exchange his ancestral house with an ordinary low cost tenement and utilizes the balance of revenue for his needs. It would not be advisable to line up such asset owners with *Zakah* deserving destitute who diffuse the *Zakah* budget which may generally be limited.

This type of people should be financed through other means from general budget. Assistance may be given in the form of various subsidies. These people should not be brought under direct taxation under any circumstances.

Well-to-do people

It is presumed that well-to-do people have income above the subsistence level and have the capacity to pay direct tax even at the progressive rate. However, it should be borne in mind that the tax rate should be such that it allows the payees a comfortable margin above the subsistence level. No extra levies on collective or personal incomes are forced on those whose personal incomes decrease below the *nisab* specified in *zakah*. Double or multiple calculation of the same base would not be made in the same specified period as in *zakah*.

Review questions

1. Show the justification of taxation in an Islamic economy.
2. Discuss the factors that you would consider in designing an Islamic tax structure.
3. What are the objectives of taxation policy in Islam?
4. Discuss the implication of linking the tax system with *zakah*.
5. Write short notes on: (i) a mixed system of direct and indirect tax; (ii) a just tax system.

References

Abdel-Haleem, M. (2010). *Understanding the* Qur'an: *Themes and Style*, London: I.B. Tauris & Co Ltd.

Chapra, M.U. (1982). *Islamic and Economics Challenge*, Verdon (USA) and Leicester (UK): IIIT & The Islamic Foundation.

Chapra, M.U. (2000). *The Future of Economics: An Islamic Perspective*, Leicester, UK: The Islamic Foundation.

Cizakça, M. (2011). *Islamic Capitalism and Finance: Origins, Evolution and the Future*. Cheltenham: Edward Elgar Publishing.

Duri, A.A. (1974). Notes on taxation, *Journal of Economics and Social History of Orient*, 17(2): 136–144.

Fauzia, A. (2014). *Faith and the State: A History of Islamic Philanthropy in Indonesia*. BRILL, p. 78. Available at: https://aseas.univie.ac.at/index.php/aseas/article/viewFile/184/78.

Hassanuz Zaman, S.M. (1993). Comments on the paper of M.Y.M. Siddiqui's Role of Booty in the Economy During Prophet's Time, *JKAU: Islamic Economics*, 5: 83–66.

Iqbal, M. & Molyneux, P. (2005). *Thirty Years of Islamic Banking: History Performance and Prospects*, New York: Palgrave Macmillan.

Kahf, M. (1983). Taxation policy in Islamic economy in *Fiscal Policy and Resource Allocation in Islam*, ed. Ziauddin Ahmad et al., Islamabad: Institute of Policy Studies.

Nasr, Seyyed Vali Reza (2001). *Islamic Leviathan: Islam and the Making of State Power*, Oxford: Oxford University Press.

Nienhaus, V. (2006). Zakat, taxes and public finance in Islam, in *Islam and the Everyday World: Public Policy Dilemmas*, eds. Behdad, S. & Nomani, F., London: Routledge.

Rahman, A. (1976). *Economic Doctrines of Islam*, Vol. III, Lahore: Islamic Publications.

13

PUBLIC FINANCE IN ISLAM

LEARNING OBJECTIVES

This chapter starts with the overview of the principles of public finance in Islam and aims to:

- provide the students with a fair base for understanding the concepts of public revenues and expenditure from an Islamic perspective
- provide a brief account on the sources of revenue and heads of expenditure of both the early Islamic state and the contemporary Islamic economy.

Public finance is concerned with the income and expenditure of the government. It has assumed a very important position in the modern economy. Apart from maintaining internal peace and discipline and protecting the country from external aggression, the modern government must also perform various other functions, including enhancing economic development. This chapter deals with the nature and extent of public expenditure and public revenues in the early Islamic period and in the modern-day Islamic economy. These are followed by Islamic principles of public finance as discussed below.

Principles of Islamic public finance

To begin with, let us see what guidance we have from the *Qur'an* and the *Sunnah* for making public finance in an Islamic perspective; this guidance constitutes the Islamic principles of public finance. There are three special characteristics as described in the first three principles: namely, *zakah* as an integral part of public finance; prohibition of *riba*; and special emphasis put on the prioritization of public expenditure. The details are given below.

Collection and disbursement of zakah

Zakah is the third pillar of Islam and is regarded as a financial form of worship. Its collection and disbursement forms an integral part of Islamic public finance. This principle owes its origin to the *Qu'ran*: "Establish *salah* (prayer) and pay *zakah*" (2:43).

Permission of trade and prohibition of riba

One of the fundamental principles of Islamic public finance is to avoid *riba* in all its transactions. This principle also originates in the *Qur'an*: "God has permitted trade and forbidden usury" (2:275). According to this dictate, trade is permitted.

Prioritization of public expenditure

In Islamic public finance, it is essential to allocate the available resources according to priority. Islamic jurists have classified public expenditure into three categories (Ahmad 1992) in order of priority as shown below:

1. the necessary (*daruriat*)
2. the needed (*hajiat*)
3. the commendable (*tahsaniat*).

According to Al-Shatibi (2013), a famous Islamic jurist, 'the necessary' (*daruriat*) comprises the following items:

1. religion (*din*)
2. life or self (*nafs*)
3. family or progeny (*nasi*)
4. property (*mal*)
5. intellect or reason (*aqeel*).

Other Islamic scholars like al-Ghazali and al-Amidi also support protection of these five items. 'Needed' expenditures come next. These are necessary in order to reinforce the necessity. Commendable expenditures are encouraged only after the first two categories are satisfied.

Entitlement of return and the liability of loss

This principle implies that ownership cannot be separated from the liabilities related to such ownership. This principle ultimately leads to profit-and-loss sharing business.

Respect for contractual obligations

Islam demands that all contractual obligations must be written down and be respected with utmost care. The relevant *Qur'anic* instruction is: "Ye who believe!

When ye deal with each other, in transactions involving future obligations in a fixed period of time, reduce them to writing …" (2:821). To safeguard the rights of parties to contracts, no ambiguities must be left: the terms and conditions must be clear.

Condemnation of extravagance (israf)

Un-restricted expenditure (*israf*) on the part of the government (also on the part of individuals) is condemned in Islam. As the *Qur'an* says, "…Lo! the squanderers were ever brothers of the devils…" (17:26–27). The government must use the hard-earned money of the citizens of the country with utmost economy for the welfare of the people.

Establishment of justice to the poor

A very important principle of public finance in an Islamic perspective is to establish justice to the poor and needy. This principle also directly owes its origin to the *Qur'an* which states, "Those who, if We give them power in the land, establish worship and pay the poor due and enjoining the right and forbidding the wrong. And with God rests the final outcome of all events" (22:41).

Establishment of democracy

Islam demands that the power of the state in the matters of earning and spending money should be exercised in a democratic manner, i.e., allocation of money for those activities – particularly for those which are not clearly specified in the *Qur'an* and the *Sunnah* (although they should not contravene the *Shari'ah*) – relating to public interest are to be decided in consultation with the people, or in parliament. According to the *Qur'an*, "… and consult with them upon the conduct of affairs" (42:38)

Prevention of concentration of wealth

"In order that it (wealth) may not (merely) make a circuit between the wealthy among you" (59:71). This *Qur'anic* dictate implies that while raising resources from *zakah* and taxes, mobilizing savings from the public, and spending the money for various purposes, the state must see that wealth is transferred from the rich to the poor so that the rich do not get richer and the poor poorer.

Public expenditures and sources of public revenue in the early Islamic period

This section shows the nature and extent of public expenditure and public revenues in the early Islamic period. We begin with the heads of public expenditure.

Heads of public expenditure

The important heads of public expenditures during the life time of the Prophet Muhammad (peace be upon him) and the caliphs were as follows:

1. Procurement of horses and arms for the holy war (*jihad*);
2. Buying the freedom of the Muslim slaves;
3. Provision of money to newly converted Muslims and also non-Muslims, for reconciling their hearts;
4. Paying off the debts of the deceased poor;
5. Meeting of the basic needs of the poorer sections of the society; and
6. Payment of pensions.

These heads of expenditure continued to remain important during the period of the Caliphs. Later, however, other functions such as development works and welfare activities were included.

Sources of public revenues

In order to meet the expenses of the activities specified above, the following were the sources for public revenues in an early Islamic period.

Zakah: This was perhaps the most important source of public revenue in the early Islamic state. In effect, it occupied the lion's share of the public revenue in those days. It is a compulsory payment due to the *Qur'anic* dictate: "Establish *Salah* (prayer) and pay *Zakah*" (2:431). The rate of *zakah* is 2.5 per cent of income. *Nisab* or exemption limit of *zakah* on gold and silver are 7.5 and 52.5 *tolas*, respectively. For other commodities, the rates of *zakah* are obtainable from the Hadith.

Kharaj: In order of importance, *kharaj*, or land tax, was next. During the early period of Islam, for the purpose of this type of tax, land was classified into two categories: *ushr* land and *kharaj* land (Abu Usuf 1979). The former implies a land tax of 10 per cent of the total produce (provided the produce reaches the *nisab*); this was for the lands falling within Arabia. For the latter, on the other hand, the rate was not fixed. It was imposed on lands outside Arabia, i.e., located in the countries conquered by Muslims.

Jizya: This was a kind of poll tax levied on all 'able-bodied' non-Muslims during the early days. This was treated as a tax, for not taking part in the defence of the country. In return, non-Muslims were given the same amenities and protection as their Muslim counterparts.

Ghanimah or khums: *Ghanimah* refers to spoils of war and *khums* to the proportion (one-fifth) of the spoils to be used by the state. According to the Hadiths of the Prophet, the remaining four-fifths were normally distributed among the soldiers participating in the war.

Fay: This includes all properties received either from the enemy without actual fighting or from the properties left without an heir or 'lost and found' without a claim from the owners. In the early days of Islam, this was also an important source of revenue of the government.

Customs duties: This type of duties was first imposed during the time of the second Caliph Umar in response to similar taxes imposed by other states, which affected Muslim businessmen.

Taxes on mines and treasure troves: There was a levy of 20 per cent on the receipts from mines and treasure troves in the early Islamic period.

Linkages between sources of revenues and heads of expenditures on the basis of the Qur'an

Before we proceed further, it would be interesting to see the linkages between the sources of public revenues and heads of public expenditures on the basis of the *Qur'an* and the *Sunnah*. The following are the findings.

Zakah: The Islamic state has no option but to use the funds collected as *zakah* according to the instructions given in the *Qur'an*. It says,

> The alms are only for the poor and the needy, and those who collect them, and those whose hearts are to be reconciled, and to free the captives and the debtors, and for the cause of God, and (for) the wayfarers; a duty imposed by God.
>
> *9:60*

The eight heads specified here are: (1) the poor, (2) the needy, (3) the collector, (4) the newly converted Muslims, (5) freeing the captives, (6) the debtors, (7) the cause of God, and (8) the wayfarers.

Ghanimah or khums: The heads of expenditure of the revenues obtained through this source is also been specified in the *Qur'an*:

> And know that whatever ye take as spoils of war (*ghanimah*), lo! a fifth thereof is for God and for the messenger (i.e., for the state) and for the kinship (who hath need) orphans and the needy and the wayfarers, if ye believe in God…
>
> *8:41*

Thus by compulsion, one-fifth of the receipts of the spoils of war needs to be spent on state activities including the kinship, orphans, the needy and the wayfarers. How the remaining four-fifths is to be spent is not specified in the *Qur'an*. However, as said above, this portion was normally used for helping the soldiers who actually participated in the war.

Fay: In verses 6 to 10 of *Sura Hashr* of the *Qur'an*, the heads of expenditure of the revenues collected by *fay* are categorically specified. These heads are more or less similar to those specified for *zakah* or *sadaqa*. Basically the amount of *fay* collection will have to be spent for the general benefit of the people living in an Islamic state.

Public finance in a contemporary Islamic state

Functions of the contemporary Islamic state

The nature and extent of the public revenue and public expenditures of a modern Islamic state is determined by the nature and extent of the functions it has to perform. Siddiqi (1992) has mentioned three types of functions of an Islamic state. These are:

1. Functions assigned by the *Shari'ah* on permanent basis;
2. Functions derived from *Shari'ah* on the basis of *ijtihad* (research) for the present situation; and
3. Functions assigned to the state at any time and place by the people through the process of *shura* (consultation).

The first category of functions is derived directly from the *Qur'an* and the *Sunnah*. These are permanent responsibilities of Islamic states. This includes such activities as defence and law and order.

The second category of functions includes those functions not directly derived from the *Shari'ah* but derived on the basis of *qias* (analytical reasoning), or arguments based on *masalah* (public interest). They are necessary for realizing the objectives of *Shari'ah* as mentioned in category (1) above. This category is quite flexible and depends upon time and place. At the present time, this may include such activities as the protection of environment and scientific research.

The functions that are not covered by the above two categories but are on public demand are included in the third category. The necessary condition is that the decision to perform any function under this category must be decided in a democratic manner, i.e. through mutual consultation (*shura*). This may include any function such as generation and supply of electricity and collection of *kharaj* revenue. Thus the list of this category of functions is open-ended.

The first category of functions is directly derived from the *Qur'an* and the *Sunnah*. The second category of functions is derived through *qias* and *ijtihad*. In the third category of functions, according to Kahf (1998a), the Islamic state is not necessarily free to set the economic and political priorities nor is it free to impose a pattern of government spending that may violate the freedom and rights given to individuals by God. He states that there are clear and strong texts in the *Qur'an* and the *Sunnah* that protect private property from 'any act of aggression' whether by the state or by the individuals.

Kahf (1998a) is right in his own way of interpreting the *Qur'anic* dictates. The opinion given by Siddiqi (1992) has support from the early Islamic traditions. He himself, in support of his viewpoint, refers to a passage from Abu Yusuf's (1979) *Kitab al-Kharaj* dating back to the second century after *Hijra* in which he advised the ruler of the time to undertake certain public works like cleaning of ancient canals and land reclamation, because people of that time wanted the state to undertake this type of activity.

Principles of public expenditure

There are well-defined principles of public expenditures in the Islamic economics literature. The following principles have been derived by Chapra (1995, p. 289) from the articles of *Majallah*.

Principle 1: The principal criterion for all expenditure allocations should be the well-being of the people: This principle implies that an Islamic government will not make any spending arbitrarily. It must have a purpose. The overall purpose of government spending is human welfare. This welfare, of course, includes both material welfare and spiritual welfare. Expenditures on infrastructure (including rural infrastructure and agricultural extension services, education, character building, health, safe water supply, sanitation and malnutrition, housing and public transport system) are some illustrative examples.

Principle 2: The removal of hardship and injury must take precedence over the provision of comforts (and luxury): This means that public spending should first be directed to meet the basic needs of the society. In other words, according to this principle, preference should be given to projects that help to remove the hardship and sufferings caused by the prevalence of malnutrition, illiteracy, homelessness and epidemics, and lack of medical facilities, safe water supply and sewage disposal.

Principle 3: The larger interest of the majority should take precedence over the narrower interest of a minority: This principle implies that if there is a choice between the import of cars and buses, for the greater interest of the majority, the government should opt for the latter as the majority of the population uses buses/cycles rather than cars in the developing countries. This also implies that in the developing countries, since the majority of the people lives in rural areas, rural development programmes should be given priority in the development agenda of the government.

Principle 4: A private sacrifice or loss may be inflicted to save a public sacrifice or loss, and a greater sacrifice or loss may be averted by imposing a smaller sacrifice or loss: It may be pointed out that cars definitely provide comforts to the urban people. This transport is more convenient than the buses. On the other hand, buses are less convenient but are used by the majority of the people because buses are cheaper. A ban or reduction on the import of cars would bring inconvenience to some people, but that should be sacrificed for the greater interest of the majority of the urban population, who are poor.

Principle 5: Whoever receives the benefits must bear the cost: This is a very important principle. This means that if the benefit of a particular project (say, construction of a small dam in a remote locality) is to be financed, its cost should be borne by the beneficiaries (that is, by those persons who directly derive the benefit of the project. Toll collection from the vehicles crossing a bridge is another example in point.

Principle 6: Something without which an obligation cannot be fulfilled is also obligatory: Suppose the *Shari'ah* categorically demands that inequalities of income and wealth must be reduced, but it says nothing specifically about the development of cottage industries. If it happens that without developing the cottage industries, it becomes impossible to raise the income of the poor and hence reduce the gaps between the rich and the poor, it becomes an obligation on the part of the government to take all necessary measures in order to develop cottage industries.

Heads of public expenditure

Siddiqi (1992) has identified the heads of expenditures of a modern Islamic state based on three classifications, namely, permanent heads, heads based on present circumstances and heads based on people's demand. These are discussed below.

Permanent expenditure

The heads of expenditure are called permanent because they are all derived directly from the *Qur'an* and the *Sunnah* and the Muslims have no alternative but to obey.

Defence: To defend the motherland from external aggression is the foremost duty of a modern Islamic state. God dictates that "Against them make ready your strength to the utmost of power, including steeds of war, to strike terror into (the hearts of) the enemies of God and your enemies, and others besides, whom ye may not, but God doth know" (8:601). Therefore, the *Qur'anic* injunction of defending the motherland is absolutely clear and hence would represent an important head of public expenditure.

Law and order: Maintenance of internal security has been regarded as one of the most crucial duties of the state since the early days of Islam. Of necessity, this should represent an important head of public expenditure in any state. Ibn Tahir al-Baghdadi, has a very appropriate example: "the *Shari'ah* has a number of laws that cannot be implemented except by the ruler or one who governs on behalf of the ruler, such as implementing hudud (penal laws) on free persons" (World Heritage Encyclopedia n.d.).

Justice: It is a well-known duty of the Islamic government to obey the *Qur'anic* instruction: "God commands justice (*adl*) and doing good (*ihsan*) and liberating kith and kin…" (16:901). A good proportion of government funds would therefore be necessary to act upon this divine instruction.

Need fulfilment: The Prophet, after establishing *Baitul Maal*, declared, "If anybody dies leaving property that belongs to his heirs, and if anybody dies leaving orphans and widows empty handed, then I am their heir". In effect, according to Islamic principles the state remains responsible for meeting the basic needs of its people. These include food, clothing, shelter, education, health, etc. Given the nature of activities under need fulfilment, it would perhaps be one of the most significant heads of public expenditures in modern days.

Dawah **(invitation):** The need for this specific head of expenditure, along with other heads, is found in the *Qur'an* in several places; for instance, "Let there arise out of you a band of people inviting to all that is good, enjoining what is right, and forbidding what is wrong: they are the ones to attain felicity" (3:1041). Thus in an Islamic state, *dawah* (i.e., communicating the message of God to all mankind) forms an important head of public expenditure.

Civil administration: By definition, the government will have to allocate some money for administering the activities narrated above. This head of expenditure is quite popular among the students of general economics.

Fard *kifayah* (social obligation): In an Islamic state, this is also an important head of public expenditure. This duty is not compulsory for all individuals but is addressed to the society or community as a whole. The condition is that it must be performed or the whole society will be condemned. From an Islamic economic point of view, this includes functions arising out of natural calamities. Islamic jurists have even gone to the extent of including all "productivities on which fulfilment of basic needs such as food, clothing and shelter depends." (Siddiqi 1991, p. 80). What is important to remember in this case is that these should generally relate to public goods and that the failure of the individuals to act upon them would become the responsibility of the state.

Expenditure based on present circumstances

It should be recognised that Islam is a dynamic religion and its dictates are both inflexible (i.e., binding under all circumstances, *ceteris paribus*) and flexible (i.e., changeable in given circumstances). The following heads of expenditure are derived from the *Shari'ah* with reference to present circumstances.

Protection of the environment

Protection of the environment has now become more crucial than at any time before. This is a public good, the benefit of which is enjoyed by all individuals without causing any harm to anybody. Because of the huge costs involved in such activities as keeping the air pure, saving the water from pollution, and preserving wildlife, individuals may not come forward to perform these activities. It is, therefore, natural that protection of environment accounts for some portion of public expenditure of any modern state.

Scientific research

It is widely said that developing Muslim countries have become more dependent on the more advanced countries simply because they do not give due importance to scientific research. This type of research is necessary particularly for economic development, which is an important objective of a modern Islamic state. Viewed in this way, scientific research would call for huge expenditure on the part of the government in modern times.

Capital formation and economic development

This head of expenditure does not find explicit mention either in the *Qur'an* or in the *Sunnah*. Nevertheless, it is extremely important, according to the precepts of the Islamic jurists like Ibn Taymiyah, al-Qurtubi and al-Amidi. The universally accepted principle in this regard is that 'whatever is necessary for discharging a duty is itself a duty'. If the government is to perform such duties as need fulfilment and continued improvement of standard of living, the need for capital formation and economic development cannot be ignored. If the state desires its people to become *zakah*-givers rather than *zakah*-takers, it must make great efforts towards capital formation and economic development.

Subsidies

In the modern Islamic state, private persons are encouraged to share a large burden in the matters of need for fulfilment not only for themselves but also for their society, in terms of *dawah* activities and scientific research. These activities require huge expenditure, without, in most cases, any tangible direct benefit. It is desirable, therefore, that the Islamic state should give subsidies to those individuals who are associated with these types of activities.

Stabilization policies

Prevention of wide fluctuation in the levels of economic activities, price level, etc., is necessary to ensure *adl* and *ihsan* in the society and pave the way for economic development. For the Islamic government, this would serve as an important head of expenditure.

Expenditure on activities assigned by the people

Islam supports democracy. God loves those "who (conduct) their affairs by mutual consultation" (*Qur'an* 42:381). Those activities which are not included in the above lists but are demanded by the people (or by the parliament of an Islamic State) call for state action and hence form an important head of expenditure. In support of this viewpoint, Siddiqi (1991) refers to a passage from Abu Yusuf's *Kitab al Kharaj*, dating back to the second century: *Iijarah* (leasing) in which he advised the ruler of that time to undertake certain public works such as cleaning of ancient canals and land reclamation because people of that time demanded that the state undertake that type of activity. The government may charge the local people to the extent the benefits accrue to them.

Sources of revenues of a modern Islamic state

The above is an account of sources of public revenue of the early Islamic period. All these sources are applicable in the modern days too; however, given the wider scope of the government activities, they may not be adequate. Moreover, some of these sources might not be applicable in the present time. *Ghanimah* or *khums, jizya*, and *fay* may be cited as some examples here. On the other hand, in the present day, the sources that are used for revenues may not be permitted in so far as the principles of *Shari'ah* are concerned. This necessitates an examination of sources of revenues of the modern state from an Islamic perspective. There are basically two sources of revenues of a modern Islamic state: internal and external. Both these sources are discussed now.

Internal sources

Zakah: For an Islamic state, *zakah* represents the most important source of revenue. Its application is universal. It is a compulsory levy on income and wealth, 2.5 per cent of the total, if that income exceeds a certain minimum level, called the *nisab*. While it is the religious duty of a Muslim to pay *zakah*, the Islamic state is required to make administrative arrangement for its collection and distribution. According to Kahf (1998b), *zakah* may provide up to 5 per cent of the total GDP generated in the public sector of Muslim countries. It is also regarded as a source of revenue, which helps achieve a just distribution of income and wealth in the society. Some Islamic states like Pakistan, Sudan and Iran have already established a system of collecting and distributing *zakah*.

Given the nature and extent of state functions in the modem age, the revenue collected through this head, even when properly administered, will not be sufficient to meet the needed expenditure. Other sources of revenue will, therefore, have to be explored.

Taxation: Taxation, as a source of public revenue, occupies a crucial position in the theory of public finance as developed by Western economists. This source naturally provides the lion's share of government revenue in all modern states including the Muslim ones. It not only helps mobilize resources for meeting government expenditure but also serves as a significant policy instrument for maintaining monetary stability and reducing inequalities in income and wealth. The vital question is: Can an Islamic state use taxation as a source of revenue in the presence of *zakah* without any qualification? In the following paragraphs an attempt is made to seek an answer to this question.

Islamic economists are in fact divided on the question of taxation as a source of revenue in the Islamic state. Those who are against taxation argue that the *Qur'an* and Hadiths say nothing specifically about taxation on income. Even the early jurists made no reference to this (Kahf 1998b, p. 32). Kahf, referring to the writings of early Islamic jurists, categorically states that Islam does not support the active tax policy in order to bring about substantial reduction of income inequalities

(Kahf 1998a). Those who are in favour of this are of the opinion that although the *Qur'an* is not specific about taxation, there are clear hints in it which gives clues to this type of extra income. Zaman shows by detailed analysis that the word *infaq* (i.e., spending, referred so frequently in the *Qur'an*) actually gives rise to this type of revenue (Zaman 1999). Chapra categorically states that "in view of the goals of social justice and equitable distribution of income, a progressive tax system seems to be perfectly in harmony with the goals of Islam" (Chapra 1985, pp. 42–43). Kahf actually does not appear to be wholly against taxation when he says, "...there was simply no need for taxes at times of abundant non-tax sources" (1998b, p. 32). This implies that if the *zakah* revenues are not sufficient to meet the needed expenditure of the government, it may resort to taxation. However, in spite of the differences of opinion regarding the place of taxation in the modern Islamic state, it is accepted that it should be kept within reasonable limits.

Borrowing: In modern days, borrowing is regarded as an indispensable source of public revenue. Questions have been raised in Islamic economics literature as to whether borrowing is at all permissible in the eye of Islam. In this regard, the view expressed by Siddiqi, one of the best known Islamic economists, is of significance. He says,

> No injunction in the *Qur'an* nor in the *Sunnah* prohibits it nor have researchers discovered any rules that might require such a prohibition. On the contrary, there are examples in the *Shari'ah* of practical steps to be taken for obtaining loans, and scholars of Islam have clarified the situation by stating that circumstances can arise where the Islamic states will need loans.
>
> *Siddiqi 1983, p. 130–131*

It is also known from the history of the early Islamic period that loans were contracted by the state though in most cases this was done to meet emergencies (Zaman 1999).

The most common form of borrowing is from the central bank of the country. In economics, this is popularly known as deficit financing. This is a permissible source of finance in Islam, provided of course that it is not interest bearing. It should, however be borne in mind that large-scale financing through this may lead to inflation, which is regarded as un-Islamic by the Islamic jurists (Ibn Taymiyah 1983). Therefore, this source should be used only under compelling circumstances.

Human resources: The last, but not necessarily the least in order of importance, domestic source of financing economic development of a modern Islamic state is the under- and un-utilized human resources. Many Muslim countries including Bangladesh have huge populations. In the past, little attention has been given to them on the grounds that they are poor, illiterate, assetless and, and above all, culturally backward. However, some institutions like the Grameen Bank (although not necessarily in an Islamic way) have proved beyond doubt that if the poor can be properly organized and are given sincerely and efficiently supervised financial help they can be economic assets and can contribute significantly towards economic development of the country. If labour does have zero productivity in agriculture, it can be withdrawn and put to work on investment projects like construction, irrigation works, road buildings, etc. without any adverse impact on the production of agriculture. As most of the additional wages will be directed towards foodstuffs, agricultural income will rise. The higher income can easily be taxed. When the investment projects are completed there will be an increase in output, and some of this increase in income can be captured through taxes.

External sources

There are two purposes for which external sources are used: to supplement domestic resources available for capital formation, and to fill the foreign exchange gap. The following three external heads are used as sources of revenues of the modern state. These are discussed with reference to the principles of Islam.

External borrowing: For developing countries, external borrowing is treated as a very important source of financing their development expenditures. Generally loans are available on the basis of interest only, which is strictly prohibited in Islam. The amount of loan that is available from such institutions as 1DB is utterly negligible. Thus, although the Muslim countries very badly need external loans they cannot use interest-bearing loans. However, on the basis of the doctrine of necessity, a temporary exception is sometimes allowed by Islamic jurists. For example, the Council of Islamic Ideology in Pakistan (1973) has given the ruling that "For the time being, external borrowings (i.e. state to state borrowings) will have to be continued on the basis of interest". However, attempts should be made to gradually eschew all interest-bearing borrowings.

Foreign aid: Although the net contribution made by the large inflow of foreign aid in the developing countries appears to be controversial, its necessity cannot be denied. There are Muslim countries which still heavily depend upon foreign aid for financing development expenditure. This is not undesirable from the viewpoint of Islam, provided there are no anti-Islamic constraints attached to it. There are a large number of Muslim countries which have sufficient surplus funds, and these can hopefully be utilized for financing the needed expenditure of the poor brothers of other Muslim countries.

Foreign direct investment: Foreign direct investment (FDI) is presently being considered as a very promising source of revenue for both developing and less developed countries. There is keen competition among them for attracting FDI. This is advantageous for both the investors and the host countries. For the investors, overseas investments can offer very attractive opportunities in the form of lower wage costs, access to cheap raw materials, possibility of securing foreign markets, exploiting economies of scale and above all various attractive incentives by the host countries. On the other end, for the host countries, this source of finance provides a unique combination of long-term finance, transfer of technology, training, managerial expertise and marketing experience and above all the contract in international markets. From an Islamic standpoint, this source has special merit:

it provides an opportunity to switch dependence from interest-based foreign financing to equity-based financing. The 1DB can play a very dominant role in popularizing joint venture-type projects using such *Shari'ah*-permitted instruments as *mudaraba* and *musharaka*.

In conclusion, it may be added that, to meet the basic needs of the people, God has given abundant resources, natural and human. As the *Qur'an* says, "It is We who have placed you with authority on earth and provided you therein with means for the fulfilment of your life" (7:101). What is required is to make all-out efforts to exploit the available natural and human resources for the benefit of mankind.

Review questions

1. What do you understand about Public Finance in Islam?
2. Discuss the main components of public expenditure deduced from the *Qur'an* and *Sunnah*.
3. Give an account of traditional sources of revenues of an early Islamic state. Which of the sources can still be used when the present structure of economies and public finance have massively changed?

References

Ahmad, Z. (1992). Public finance and physical policy in Islamic perspective, in *Lessons on Islamic Economics*, Jeddah: IRTI-IDB.

Al-Shatibi, Imam. (2013). *Theory of Higher Objectives and Intent of Islamic Law*, trans. Al-Raysuni, A., London: IIIT.

Chapra, M.U. (1985). *Towards a Just Monetary System*, Leicester: The Islamic Foundation.

Chapra, M.U. (1995). *Islam and the Economic Challenge*, Markfield and Verdon: The Islamic Foundation and IIIT.

Council of Islamic Ideology of Pakistan (1973). *Islamic Rulings*, Karachi: Ministry of Law.

Ibn Taymiyah. (1983). *Public Finance in Islam: The Institution of Hisbah*, trans. Holland, M., Leicester: The Islamic Foundation.

Kahf, M. (1998a). Public finance and physical policy in Islam, in *Lessons in Islamic Economics*, Vol. 2, Jeddah: IRTI-IDB.

Kahf, M. (1998b). Zakah and obligatory expenditure, in *Lessons in Islamic Economics*, Vol. 2, Jeddah: IRTI-IDB.

Siddiqi, M.N. (1983). *Banking Without Interest*, Leicester: The Islamic Foundation.

Siddiqi, M.N. (1991). History in Islamic economic thought, in *Lectures in Islamic Economics*, Jeddah: IRTI-IDB.

Siddiqi, M.N. (1992). Teaching Islamic economics in an Islamic perspective, in *Reading in Macroeconomics: An Islamic Perspective*, Kuala Lumpur: Longman Malaysia.

World Heritage Encyclopedia (n.d.). Ibn Tahir al-Baghdadi, Gutenberg: Self Publishing Press.

Yusuf, A. (1979). *Kitab-al-Kharaj*, trans. Ali, A.A. and Siddiqi, A.H., Lahore: Islamic Book Centre.

Zaman, H. (1999). *Economic Guidelines in the Qur'an* (compiled), Islamabad: IIIT.

14

MOBILIZATION OF RESOURCES FOR ISLAMIC ECONOMIC DEVELOPMENT

LEARNING OBJECTIVES

This chapter explains the concept of development from Islamic points of view. Students should:

- realize the importance of the resources mobilization for economic development in an Islamic economy
- understand the need for economic development
- get detailed ideas in respect of the Islamic approach to financial resources and human resources mobilization.

The mobilization of economic resources and their transformation into wealth is critical for economic stability. This chapter provides an overview of the resources mobilization for economic development from Islamic perspectives. It covers the issues pertaining to the availability and mobilization of both financial resources and human resources for economic development of the Muslim countries in general and under-developed Muslim countries in particular. It discusses deficit financing; saving; borrowing; foreign direct investment without involvement of *riba* for mobilizing of financial resources; and emphasis for employment in formal and informal sector for human resources mobilization.

Goals of Islamic economic development

There are well-defined goals of Islamic economic development. Some of the crucial goals of socio-economic development under an Islamic system are discussed here.

Improvement of quality of life

The overall goal of Islamic economic development is to improve the quality of life of the people living in the country. This quality of life refers to both material and moral aspects of life. The emphasis is on the balanced development of the material and spiritual aspects, which distinguishes it from the traditional capitalistic system. Being the viceregent of God (Allah), the *homo-islamicus* (Islamic economic men) cannot but aim at materializing this goal as a top priority.

This goal calls for a high priority in these three areas:

- Employment creation, with particular emphasis on self-employment;
- An effective and broad-based system of social security, assuring the basic necessities of life to all those who are unable to undertake gainful employment; and
- Equitable distribution of income and wealth. There should be an active income policy directed towards raising the income level of the lowest income groups and reducing the disparity between the haves and have-nots.

Fulfilment of basic needs

For material development of the people, fulfilment of basic needs is very important. These include food, clothing, shelter, medical care, and education for all humans. In an Islamic society, if individual households become unable to meet their basic needs, it then becomes the responsibility of the state to help them, either through transfer payments or through other means.

Questions may be raised about the exact number of different things that constitute the 'basic needs' or 'essentials'. It should be absolutely clear that in Islamic economics no attempt is made to quantify this. It depends upon the level of development, the physical environment and a host of other circumstances. It may be of some interest to have some practical ideas from the Prophet Muhammad's sayings. In one occasion, one well-known companion of the Prophet asked the Prophet as to when and under what circumstances he can ask for help. The Prophet replied by saying that

> one can ask for help under three circumstances only. First, if one has incurred debt on behalf of other people. Second, when a person has fallen victim to a calamity which destroys his wealth. Third, when a person is so poor that three persons from his own neighbourhood say that he deserves help.
>
> *Hadith*

In the current situation it is actually the responsibility of the society or the government to define, given the time and place and the prevailing circumstances, the level of poverty which permits a person to ask for help.

Full utilization of all resources

There is another important goal of economic development in Islam. This is because in Islam, by *Qur'anic* injunction, all resources between the earth and the heaven belong to God and as viceregents of God, men have no authority either to under-utilize or to misutilize any of His resource. Therefore, the basic aim of the Islamic economic development is to utilize fully and efficiently all the God-gifted resources.

Islamic economic development puts a very high priority on the development of human resource. This includes the inculcation of correct attitudes and aspirations, development of character and personality, education and training producing skills needed for different activities, promotion of knowledge and research, etc.

Justice and equitable distribution

In contrast to conventional economic development, Islam puts the highest emphasis on socio-economic justice and equitable distribution of income and wealth. There are numerous injunctions in the *Qur'an* and the Hadiths to materialise this goal. It may be noted that attempts are made by the traditional governments to do justice and reduce inequalities of income between the rich and the poor, but these attempts are only temporary and suffers from the lack of sustainability. In Islam, there are built-in mechanisms through which this can be materialised. Examples include *zakah* and *sadaqa*.

Control of inflation

Inflation is a situation 'when too much money chases too few goods'. This is a symptom of disequilibrium and is not compatible with Islamic economic development. As Chapra has very nicely pointed out,

> Inflation implies that money is unable to serve as a just and honest unit of account. It makes money an inequitable standard of deferred payments and an untrustworthy store of value. It tends to pervert values, rewarding speculation (discouraged by Islam) and intensifying inequalities of income (condemned in Islam).
>
> *Chapra 1985, pp. 37–38*

It is, therefore, considered obligatory on the part of the Islamic government to keep the rate of inflation under full control and resort to healthy monetary, fiscal and income policies.

The availability and mobilization of resources is a *sine qua non* for real capital formation and, hence, economic development of a country. Real development can only be achieved if resources are efficiently mobilized and transformed into productive activities. The development of an efficient Islamic financial system in providing the vital link between savings and investment is thus important. Not only must there be coordination of different agencies within and among levels of governments, there must also be coordination between the public and private sectors, and among the various components of the private sector. Whatever the level of domestic savings and however large or small the net transfer of foreign direct investments (FDIs), there is legitimate concern to ensure that those savings are allocated to investment in developing Muslim countries in a manner that is efficient and desirable in the social, political and developmental aspects. Islam encourages economic development. Its urgency can be realized from the prevailing conditions of poverty, malnutrition, illiteracy and unemployment of the under-developed Muslim countries. Resources are needed for the production of physical assets, which, in turn, are required for the generation of income. Physical assets include machinery, industrial plants and other related projects. The main purpose of this paper is to provide an in-depth analysis of the resources of mobilization for economic development from Islamic perspectives.

Traditionally, financial resources are regarded as the basic determinants of economic development and great efforts need to be made to mobilize them. In Islamic economics, apart from these financial resources, human resources are given equal importance. In this chapter, the following are considered as major sources of finance for Islamic economic development:

1. Financial resources, and
2. Human resources.

Financial resources

Financial resources can be grouped into two broad categories namely, domestic and external. These two sources are now discussed.

Domestic sources

There are four sources of domestic finance: voluntary savings, taxation, deficit-financing, and equity participation.

Voluntary savings

Voluntary savings play a very important role in economic development. According to Lewis (1954), one of the prominent growth specialists of the conventional economic arena,

> the central problem in the theory of economic development is to understand the process by which the people maintains saving and investing 4 or 5 per cent of its national income and converts itself into an economy where voluntary saving is running at about 12 to 15 per cent of national income or more. This creates a big problem because the crucial fact of economic development is rapid capital accumulation
>
> *Lewis 1954*

Savings is usually defined as:

$$S - Y - C,$$

where

S = savings
Y = income, and
C = consumption.

Naturally by definition, if consumption in any society is lower, *ceteris paribus*, voluntary savings would be higher, and vice-versa.

It may be argued that in an Islamic society, savings rate should be lower and investment in the real sector would be the main objective because of two main reasons. First, savings are a function of interest (*riba*). In Islam this interest is not allowed. Therefore, there will be no or little savings. Second, in the Islamic economy, there is a provision for transfer of income from the rich to the poor through such means as *zakah* (levy on assets at the rate of 2.5 per cent calculated each lunar year and distributed to the poor) and *sadaqa* (charity). '

Keynes (1972) argues that saving is not necessarily a function of interest; it is a function of income. Moreover, there are plenty of empirical results in the literature to demonstrate that people save money not merely for earning interest but for safe custody and for the unforeseen future. The second argument is subject to empirical verification. It is possible to put counter arguments too. When income is transferred from the rich to the poor, the economic well-being of the poor is improved which, in turn, produces positive impact on their health which, again, in turn, will help increase their labour productivity. There would also be an increase in effective demand. All these are expected to promote savings, rather than decrease them. Interestingly Keynes (1972) has visualized the situation in a different way. He says that the higher Marginal Propensity to Consume (i.e., lower Marginal Propensity to Save) is essentially an advantage, rather than disadvantage, because it will lead to a higher level of output through multiplier effect.

Moreover, in an Islamic economy, the consumption behaviour of the people is guided by Islamic ethics and values, which demand, among other things, moderation in consumption. As the *Qur'an* says, "And let not thy hand be chained to thy neck nor open it with a complete opening, lest thou sit down rebuked, denuded" (*Qur'an* 17:291). This injunction for the moderation of consumption implies that the rich will not maintain a high propensity to consume; rather, by being moderate in their consumption behaviour, they are likely to save more, and not less as often believed. Again, in Islam, the people are discouraged to hoard their wealth: "And there are those who bury gold and silver and spend it not in the way of God: announce unto them a most grievous penalty" (*Qur'an* 9:34). This verse encourages the people to make full use of their resources so that more income is generated, not only for themselves but also for the society at large to which they belong to, otherwise they are liable to punishment in the Hereafter.

Moreover, the system of *zakah* provides an indirect incentive to use these surplus funds for productive purposes. If they do not do so, then 2.5 per cent *zakah* will ultimately erode their savings. In Muslim societies, there exists great scope for increasing domestic savings, as is clear from the information given in Table 14.1. It can also be seen that the scope for increasing the rate of savings in the selected Muslim countries is quite high. However, the gross domestic savings in Bangladesh, Malaysia, Morocco, Pakistan, Saudi Arabia, Sudan and Turkey increased their GDB in several times between the years 1900 to 2016. Incidentally, the gross domestic savings of Algeria, Brunei, Darussalam, Indonesia, Kazakhstan, Iran, Indonesia, Malaysia, Morocco, Qatar, Saudi Arabia and Turkey varied between 20.9 per cent and 51.1 per cent in 2016 (Heritage Foundation 2016).

TABLE 14.1 Gross domestic savings of some Muslim countries (1960 and 2016)

Country	Gross domestic savings (as % of GDP)	
	1960	2016
Afghanistan	13.2	−24.4
Albania	–	10.2
Algeria	14.1	40.0
Azerbaijan	–	27.7
Bangladesh	7.6	25.0
Brunei Darussalam	–	43.3
Egypt	–	5.8
Indonesia	6.8	35.1
I.R. Iran	21.6	–
Iraq	–	11.8
Kazakhstan	–	31.9
Lebanon	–	15.7
Malaysia	33.0	32.5
Mali	–	10.9
Morocco	11.1	20.9
Pakistan	6	8.1
Qatar	–	51.1
Saudi Arabia	-	31.5
Sudan	12.2	16.9
Tunisia	–	8.8
Turkey	8.4	25.7

Source: World Development Report 2017 (compiled by the author)

Taxation

Most Muslim countries are developing and have low incomes, low savings, and low investments. Due to these limitations, governments of low-income countries cannot avoid forced savings, that is, taxation. Emphasizing the need for such measures, Kaldor (1963) opines that the "taxes and other compulsory levies provide the most important instrument for increasing ... domestic resources" (p. 7).

In Islamic economics, the role of taxation is recognized with carefulness. Its merit actually depends upon the objective the state wants to achieve with it. If the objective is to meet subsistence welfare of the people, imposition of taxes is said to be not only permissible but also necessary because the amount of *zakah* and voluntary sources are insufficient to meet these expenses. However, the objective of this measure is to improve the living standard of the people beyond the subsistence level. According to Kahf (1999), truly the imposition of taxes may not be desirable from the Islamic perspective. However, Iqbal (1991) argues that the majority of Islamic scholars believe that the Islamic state should also attempt to reduce 'relative' poverty by reducing income inequalities and promoting an egalitarian economic and social order. In order to implement this type of social policy, there is necessary for the government to impose tax.

In some Muslim countries, there exists great scope for increasing tax revenues. This may be ascertained by comparing tax as percentage of total GDP ratio in selected Muslim countries (please see Table 14.2).

Deficit financing

The phrase 'deficit financing' actually means borrowing money from the central bank. Since this method of financing is intimately related to inflation, this is also called 'inflationary finance'. Alternatives to deficit financing in undeveloped countries are generally prompted by the inability of the governments to raise enough revenue by taxation and other means to meet the necessary development expenditure. In some situations it is regarded as an indispensable source of public revenue. According to Keynes (1972), inflation due to deficit financing may promote economic development in two ways. First, it helps redistribution of income from workers to capitalist entrepreneurs. Second, it causes the nominal rate of return on investment to rise in relation to the rate of interest, and hence promotes investment.

Several Islamic economists have raised the question as to whether borrowing (particularly during the period of inflation) is permissible or not. In this regard, Chapra (1985, p. 37) argues that, in Islamic economy, inflation is unacceptable. He gave the following reasons:

> ...inflation implies that money is unable to serve as a just and honest unit of account. It makes money an unquotable standard of deferred payments and an untrusty store of value. It enables some people to be unfair to others, even though unknowingly, by stealthily eroding the purchasing power of monetary

TABLE 14.2 Tax revenue as percentage of GDP ratio of selected Muslim countries

Country	Tax revenues to GDP ratio
	Sept 2015
Afghanistan	6.4
Albania	22.9
Algeria	7.7
Azerbaijan	17.8
Bahrain	4.8
Bangladesh	8.5
Egypt	15.8
Indonesia	12.0
IR of Iran	6.1
Jordan	21.1
Kazakhstan	26.1
Lebanon	14.4
Malaysia	15.5
Oman	16.8
Qatar	2.2
Saudi Arabia	5.3
Sudan	6.3
Tunisia	14.9
Turkey	24.9
UAE	1.4

(Data compiled based on the Heritage Foundation (2015))

assets. It impairs the efficiency of the monetary system and imposes a cost on the society. It raises consumption and reduces savings. It worsens the climate of uncertainty in which economic decisions are taken, discourages capital formation and leads to a misapplication of resources.

Further, the view expressed by Siddiqi (1983) on inflation is of significance. He argues that there is no injunction in the *Qur'an* nor in the *Sunnah* that prohibits it, nor have Islamic economists discovered any rules that might require such a prohibition. On the contrary, there are examples in the *Shari'ah* of practical steps to be taken for obtaining loans, and some Islamic economists have clarified the situation by stating that circumstances can arise where the Islamic states will need loans (Siddiqi 1983). It is also known from the history of the early Islamic period that loans were contracted by the state, though in most cases this was done to meet emergencies (Çizakça 2011).

In view of the above, it can be concluded that although borrowing from the central bank may be a permissible source of finance in Islamic economy, a large amount of financing through this means may lead to inflation which is regarded as un-Islamic by the Islamic jurists. Therefore, this source should he used only under compelling circumstances.

Equity participation

Borrowing from the banking sources as a basis of development finance has its uses, but it inevitably leads to problems if it is used as a means of financing risky projects which are long-term in nature. From this perspective, equity finance can play an important role in financing. Equity finance means that it is the provider of capital who takes on the risk. This also gives investors a voice in how the business is run, although day-to-day decision making is in the hands of the managers themselves. There are several methods through which equity participation can be materialized.

1. *Small or medium private company:* This may be formed with several unequal shareholders. This type of company is appropriate for medium-sized businesses. There is greater flexibility than a partnership business. In a country where the stock market is not well developed, this could be used as an appropriate form of development finance.
2. *Partnership:* This form of business is appropriate where the businesses are relatively small. If a partnership is created, it will be necessary to have trust from all sides. These are once formed, tough to terminate, and there is also limited flexibility in bringing new partners.
3. *Ordinary shares:* This has now become a very popular method of raising capital required for economic development. In this event, the investors need not be guaranteed a return, as they do in the case of bank borrowing. The risk-seeking investor knows the return is uncertain but provides funding in the expectation that their judgment will be proved correct, and the risk will be rewarded. It can be used as a source of long-term financing.
4. *Co-operative form:* This type of business organization has merit which can help to widen business participation and cross-conception of ideas in decision making. This can be a vehicle for risk sharing and the spreading of responsibility.

External sources

There are two purposes for which external sources funding are used. These are: to supplement domestic resources available for capital formation, and to fill the foreign exchange gap. The following three sources may be used for attaining financial resources for economic development in an Islamic economy.

External borrowing

In the developing countries, external borrowing is treated as a very important source of financing for their development expenditures. Generally loans are available on the basis of interest only, which is strictly prohibited in Islam. From the Islamic viewpoint, the amount of funds available from the International Islamic financial institutions is utterly insignificant (Ahmad 1984). Although many Muslim countries need external loans, they cannot because of the lack of availability of interest-free loans. Hence, under-developed Muslim countries use interest-bearing loans from the World Bank or IMF.

Foreign direct investment

Foreign direct investment (FDI) is presently being considered as a very promising source of development finance for both developing and less developed countries. There is keen competition among them for attracting FDI. There are some advantages for both the investors and the host countries in the FDI. On the investors' side, overseas investments can offer very attractive opportunities in the form of lower wage costs, access to cheap raw materials, exploiting economies of scale, possibility to secure foreign markets etc. Nonetheless, there are various attractive incentives by the host countries. On the other hand, for the host countries, this source of financing provides a unique combination of long-term finance, transfer of technology, training, managerial expertise and marketing experience etc. From the Islamic viewpoint, this source has special merit because it provides an opportunity to switch dependence from interest-based foreign financing to equity-based financing.

Moreover, it will be required that developing countries should make a clear and congenial investment environment in their countries where FDI could step in. It is necessary to provide adequate information about investment opportunities,, legal status and the procedural aspects. It will also be required to ensure compliance to local as well as international agreements and should proclaim the readiness of the host country to protect the parties in these agreements on an equal basis without any discrimination.

In order to facilitate FDI in an Islamic way, the emerging economies of the Muslim countries are required to restructure existing laws, to make them *Shari'ah*-compliant, so as to recognize the various formats of contracts according to the *Shari'ah* and determination of the legal position for parties to these contracts. In this regard, the 1DB can play a very dominant role in popularizing the 'joint venture' type projects using *Shari'ah*-based instruments such as *mudaraba* and *musharakah*. It can also take the responsibility of collection, verification and analysis of information concerning investment opportunities in Muslim countries, as well as legal and procedural forms in these countries. The 1DB quite understandably can demand some fees for providing this information.

Foreign aid

Although the net contribution made by the large inflow of foreign aid in the developing countries appears to be contentious, its necessity cannot be repudiated. There are Muslim countries that still heavily depend upon foreign aid for financing their development expenditures. This is not undesirable from the viewpoint of Islam, provided that there are no anti-Islamic constraints attached to it. There are a large number of Muslim countries which have sufficient surplus funds and these can hopefully be utilized for financing the required expenditure of the economically poor people of the other Muslim countries.

In summary, it may be pointed out that, in order to meet the basic needs of the people and the state, God has given abundant resources both natural and human. As the *Qur'an* says, "It is We who have placed you with authority on earth and provided you therein with means for the fulfillment of your life" (7:101). What is required is to make intense efforts to exploit the available natural and human resources for the benefit of mankind.

Human resources

One of the drawback of the domestic sources of financing in the economic development of a contemporary Islamic state is the under- and unutilized human resources. Many Muslim countries (such as Bangladesh, Indonesia and Pakistan) have huge populations. In the past, very little attention has been given to them, on the grounds that they are poor, illiterate, asset-less and socially regressive. Nevertheless, some Islamic financial institutions operating in various underdeveloped Muslim countries have proved beyond doubt that if the people can be properly organized and are given sincere and efficiently supervised financial help through poverty alleviation schemes such as Islamic microfinance, cooperative social capital, etc; they can be turned into assets and can contribute significantly towards economic development in the country. An alternative approach of mechanism of human resource mobilization is elaborated below:

Human resource mobilization programme from an Islamic perspective

The human resources mobilization programme from an Islamic viewpoint has two specific targets namely:

1. Mobilizing idle human resources (the unemployed and those outside the labour market) to make them economically active; and
2. Mobilizing those who are already the so-called employed to enable them to improve their living standards.

Strategies of the programme

Small versus large

The literature in economics shows the disagreement regarding the choice between 'small' and 'large' economic countries; for an economically underdeveloped country, the choice appears to be tilted towards the 'small'. The highlighting of small as opposed to large is based on a number of factors. First, about 90 per cent of Muslim countries are 'small' (Ahmad 1987). Second, the strategy for giving more emphasis to the 'small' is justified by the fact that the Islamic financial system has a built-in mechanism to motivate and support the 'small'. Third, the amount of investment required for mobilizing human resources in the developing Muslim countries is comparatively very small. It is anticipated that this programme may not affect the existing programmes for industrialization and technological progress. Also, a proper integration of the small sector with the medium and large scale sectors of the economy and adequate assistance to the small sector to adopt new technology would, in fact, accelerate the industrialization and technological progress.

Self-employment versus paid jobs

This is a crucial choice in connection with the mobilization of the under- and un-utilized human resources for the poor of the developing Muslim countries. While many organizations appear to prefer waged jobs, the experiences of NGO-activities in many countries show that the best strategy for mobilizing human resources is to create self-employment rather than provide low-paid jobs. This is for several reasons.

First, a self-employed person has more motivation and incentive to save as he or she has an opportunity to use their savings for the expansion of his/her business and hence improve their economic status. This is not possible in the case of waged jobs, as the person concerned can utilize his or her savings only by giving them to someone else, an individual or bank, which may give him or her only marginal returns.

Second, a self-employed person is in a position to make the decision to expand his enterprise and, therefore, his income making capacity. A waged employee lacks this decision-making power.

Third, a self-employed person has control over two of his or her productive abilities: the ability to work hard, and the ability to make decisions. In the case of waged jobs, a person can exercise the former but not the latter.

Fourth, a self-employed person has the opportunity to utilize the maximum time available. This opportunity and option is not available for a wage-paid job. In the case of a government job, the person may not have any control whatsoever over either the availability of time or the wages paid for the overtime. If the job is in the private sector, the person may enjoy no such benefit at all.

Fifth, a self-employed or family-operated enterprise can engage the women of working age in Muslim countries; the income of women from the enterprise also supplements the family income.

Formal versus informal sectors

In respect of the overall economic development of any country, the contributions of both the formal and informal sectors cannot be denied. However, keeping in view the poverty of the under-developed countries, emphasis is now given to the informal sectors. The reasons are as follows:

First, the formal urban sector is in a better position to take care of itself. It is the informal and rural sectors which are more in need of a push.

Second, more human resources can be mobilized with a certain amount of investment in the informal and rural sectors in comparison to the urban formal sector.

Third, the promotion of the urban formal sector may help to employ those people who are willing to work. But in the urban informal and rural sectors, there are good numbers of people who are not actually willing to work. For example, women labour forces come under this category. To bring them under the self-employment programme, it will be necessary to mobilize them in non-traditional ways such as Islamic microfinance.

Fourth, in most developing Muslim countries, people migrate in large numbers from the rural to urban areas in search of jobs every year. The numbers living in slum areas are on the increase. Emphasis on the informal urban and rural sectors will certainly help stop this unwanted migration and also help bridge the economic disparity between the rural and urban sectors.

Fifth, the emphasis on the informal sector's mobilization will provide competition to the formal sector with respect to the hiring of labour. It may be noted that the formal sector has to depend upon the informal sector for the supply of cheap labour. This type of competition will help to raise the wages of the labourers and hence will improve incomes in the informal sector.

Supplementary programme

When the self-employed programme is substantially promoted, a follow-up supplementary programme will be needed. This would require at least two action plans. First, an attempt should be made to identify those successful self-employing enterprises which have potential for further growth. These enterprises will be required to be helped so that they can expand their scope of activities by employing labour from outside. Second, if the chosen enterprises show the potential for further growth, they should be helped to integrate with the formal sectors. In this regard, Khan (1992, pp. 28–29) argues:

> Motivate and enable all such human resources that are either not working and contributing anything to family income that are earning (or are living on) an income less than that of market wage of comparable skills, to take self-employing economic activity that can ensure at least an income equal to the formal market wage. As these self-employed human resources gain experience and expertise, motivate and enable them to increase the size of their

enterprise to employ more non-family members, As self-employed activities grow into small enterprises, efforts are made to enable them to integrate with the formal sector so that they ultimately are recognized as a part of the formal sector and are no longer a part of the informal sector.

Areas of interventions

It is expected that the above-mentioned strategies will provide motivation; the ability of the economically inactive or less active human resources to take up self-employment will be the most crucial. Implementation of this strategy will depend upon three factors: (i) ability to produce some goods and services in demand locally; (ii) ability to market the goods or services; and (iii) access to required capital at the right time, at the right amount and at the right place. In brief, these three factors are discussed below:

Ability to produce

Those target people discussed here are basically illiterate and lack the required skills for most activities in the modern world. Given the experiences of some of the Islamic microfinance institutions, this is not being regarded as a major constraint. Islamic microfinance groups generally identify poor and unskilled village people who are involved in activities like rickshaw- or cartwheel-repairing, wheel-making for horse-, buffalo-, or bullock-driven carts, making and repairing fishing nets, sewing, carpentry, running small shops, etc. If any of these people need any extra skills, these can easily be acquired at their own initiative with very little cost, provided there is sufficient motivation to do so. Therefore, it can be presumed that implementation of this stage would require little formal intervention.

Ability to market

The second area identified is the ability of self-employed persons to market their goods produced. It can be presumed that since in the first stage the persons concerned will produce mainly those goods and services which are in local demand, not much intervention may be needed at this stage. However, the matter may not be as negligible as assumed by Khan (1992). He argues that: "The goods, being a part of the bare minimum needs of the local population and, hence, essential are not likely to face a marketing problem" (p. 30). Practically speaking, in order to develop the human resources, necessary intervention may be required and this would of course depend upon the nature of the product.

Access to finance

The financial arrangement is perhaps the most crucial area that will need substantial intervention. The target population we are concerned with lacks capital and these people will be required to initiate self-employment activities. There are two dimensions to this intervention. One relates to generating the supply of the required amount of capital at the right time; the other relates to creating demand for available capital. The supplier of capital will face at least four constraints. First, the target people have nothing to offer as collateral except their bodies and souls. The supplier must be ready to offer finance without any collateral. Sometimes, personal guarantee should be used as collateral. If this is not available, the institution concerned should be willing to provide capital to potential clients purely on the basis of their reputation and good character. Second, at the very initial stage it may not be possible to earn any positive income out of the activity. This fact of life should be acceptable to the provider of capital. In other words, they should be prepared to accept partial or total loss at the initial stage. Third, the amount of capital demanded will be very small compared to the urban formal sector. This implies that the suppliers should be very careful about cost of distribution of funds among too many clients. Lastly, the fundamental one, that is, the capital will have to be provided without interest by using instruments like *mudaraba* or *musharakah*.

However, the demand for the required capital is likely to be constrained by the lack of motivation of the clients. Because of one reason or other the clients may be afraid of taking money from the formal institutions. He or she may consider new technology to be very risky. In that case, the two major areas of interventions would be required:

1. Guarantee of minimum needs of the population through some formal system of social security; and
2. Capital market.

The capital market is the most crucial area where intervention will be required. One important reason of intervention in the capital market is to correct the elements that create bias against self-employed entrepreneurial activities and in favour of fixed wage-paying job opportunities. The corrections would relate to elimination of the need for collateral and linking the return on capital with the performance and outcome of the enterprise where money has been invested.

Conclusion

In Islamic economics, the concept of development is value-loaded. This implies that if economic development involves production of those goods and services that affect human welfare positively, that can only be regarded as development. Also, development means development of human beings' moral, spiritual and material aspects to fulfil the *maqasid al-shari'ah*. Therefore, all types of resources, including financial and human resources, should be mobilized to achieve the objectives of *Shari'ah*. This chapter discusses that financial and human resources are the major sources of finance for economic development from an Islamic perspective. *Shari'ah*-based market discipline should be the main tool for both financial and human resources. Encouraging exchanges of experiences within and across developing

Muslim countries will foster the adaptation and redesign of Islamic models of reform and turns them into reforms which can be utilized by the domestic establishment. Needless to say, mobilizing *Shari'ah*-compliant resources is essential in Muslim countries where the methods of financing may evolve through time. Further, they need to generate and mobilize domestic savings with foreign investment supplements effectively without involving *riba*.

In fragile and stagnant countries, the state has to play an important role to help mobilize financial and human resources. This will strengthen its foundation, the business community and ultimately the state's ability to provide public goods. However, the greatest challenge of strengthening underdeveloped Muslim countries is to not only to rescue them from fragility but to allow them to move from stability towards development. This study argues that economic resource mobilization is critical and can offer important lessons, particularly from within the industrial and the agriculture sectors because of the following:

First, without the cooperation of national stakeholders (economic and political), a country cannot generate sufficient internal and external resources. Without these, a country cannot be built, nor is there the possibility of development.

Second, without special attention to the economic foundations of the Muslim countries, legal entities may call the states bankrupt and un-governable. Since underdeveloped Muslim countries have only very few resources and low productivity, special attention has to be paid to how to transform these potential into actual wealth, which is the basis on which a country rests, and with it the ability to provide public goods.

References

Ahmad, A. (1987). *Income Determination in an Islamic Economy*, Jeddah: ICRIE, KAU.

Ahmad, K. (1984). *Islamic Approach to Development: Some Policy Implications*, Islamabad: Institute of Policy Studies.

Chapra, M.U. (1985). *Towards a Just Monetary System*, Leicester, UK: The Islamic Foundation.

Cizakça, M. (2011). *Islamic Capitalism and Finance: Origins, Evolution and the Future*, Cheltenham: Edward Elgar Publishing.

Heritage Foundation. (2016). 2016 macroeconomic data.

Iqbal, M. (1991). Financing economic development, in *Development and Finance in Islam*, eds. Sadeq, A.H., Paramanik, A.H., & Hassan, N.M.B.H., Kuala Lumpur: IIUM.

Kahf, M. (1999). Conference paper: The performance of the institution of *zakah* in theory and practice, Kuala Lumpur: IIUM.

Kaldor, N. (1963). Taxation for economic development, *Journal of Modern African Studies*, 1(1): 18–39.

Keynes, J.M. (1972). *The Collected Writings of John Maynard Keynes*, London: Macmillan.

Khan, M.F. (1992). *Human Resources Mobilization Through the Profit-Loss Sharing Based Financial System*, Research Paper No. 17, Jeddah: IDB-IRTI.

Lewis, A. (1954). *Economic Development with Unlimited Supplies of Labour*, Manchester: The Manchester School.

Siddiqi, M.N. (1983). *Banking Without Interest*, Leicester: The Islamic Foundation.

World Bank. (2017). *World Development Report 2017*, Washington DC: World Bank.

15

DEVELOPMENT GOALS AND STRATEGIES IN ISLAMIC ECONOMY

LEARNING OBJECTIVES

This chapter explains goals and strategies in respect of development in an Islamic economy. The objective is that students may:

* understand the goals and strategies of economic development from an Islamic perspective
* realize the importance of distribute justice in Islam.

The main objectives of the development that can be defined from a study of the *Qur'an* and *Sunnah* may be stated in terms of individual freedom, human welfare and peace and tranquillity in society. Islam has emphasized all the ingredients of human well-being including the human self, intellect, posterity and wealth along with their corollaries, not just wealth. Concentration on only material progress with the neglect of other requisites for realizing development as per the Islamic vision may enable Islamic countries to have a relatively higher rate of growth in the short term. However, it may be difficult to sustain this growth in the long-run because of rise of inequalities, family disintegration, crime and social unrest, etc. Islam stands for efforts, struggle, movement and reconstruction. Further, economic development is an integral part of the wider human development. Therefore, the Islamic model of development goals and strategies is dynamic. Having discussed these conceptual issues relating to economic development, this chapter attempts to elaborate the development goals and strategies from an Islamic perspective.

Goals of Islamic economic development

There are well-defined goals of Islamic economic development. At first sight, one may find these goals similar to those of the modern traditional economies; there are, however, genuine differences. These differences actually lie in the emphasis. Some of the crucial goals of socio-economic development under an Islamic system are discussed here.

Improvement of quality of life

The overall goal of Islamic economic development is to improve the quality of life of the people living in the country. This quality of life refers to both material and moral aspects of life. The emphasis is on the balanced development of the material and spiritual aspects as distinguished from the traditional capitalistic system. Being the vicegerent of God, the Islamic economic men cannot but aim at materializing this goal on top priority basis.

This goal calls for a high priority for at least the following three areas:

1. Employment creation, with particular emphasis on self-employment;
2. An effective and broad-based system of social security, assuring the basic necessities of life to all those who are unable to undertake gainful employment; and
3. Equitable distribution of income and wealth. There should be an active income policy directed towards raising the income level of the lowest income groups, and reducing the disparity between the haves and have-nots.

Fulfilment of basic needs

For material development of the people, fulfilment of basic needs is very important. These include food, clothing, shelter, medical care, and education for all. In an Islamic society, if the individual households become unable to meet their basic needs, then it becomes the responsibility of the state to help them either through transfer payments or through other means.

Questions may be raised about the exact number of different things needed individually which would constitute the 'basic needs' or 'essentials'. There is an example that can be given from the *Hadith*. On one occasion, one well-known companion asked the Prophet as to when and under what circumstances a person can ask for help. The Prophet replied by saying that one can ask for help under three circumstances only. First, if one has incurred debt on behalf of other people. Second, when a person has fallen victim to a calamity which destroys his wealth. Third, when a person is so poor that three persons from his own neighbourhood say that he deserves help. It is actually the responsibility of the society or the government to define, given the time and place and the prevailing circumstances, the level of poverty which permits a person to ask for help.

Full utilization of all resources

This is another important goal of economic development in Islam. This is because in Islam, by *Qur'anic* injunction, all resources between the earth and the heaven belong to God, and as His viceregents men have no authority to under-utilize or to misuse any of His resources. Therefore, the basic aim of the Islamic economic development is to utilize fully and efficiently all the resources which God has gifted to us.

Also, Islamic economic development puts a very high priority on the development of human resources. This includes the inculcation of correct attitudes and aspirations, development of character and personality, education and training producing skills needed for different activities, promotion of knowledge and research, etc.

Justice and equitable distribution

In contrast to conventional economic development, Islam puts the highest emphasis on the socio-economic justice and equitable distribution of income and wealth. There are numerous injunctions in the *Qur'an* and the Hadith to materialize this goal. It may be noted that attempts are made by traditional governments to perform justice and reduce inequalities of income between the rich and the poor, but these attempts are only temporary and suffers from a lack of sustainability. In Islam, there are built-in mechanisms through which this can be materialized and in this regard, examples include *zakah* and *sadaqah*.

Control of inflation

Inflation is a situation 'when too much money chases too few goods.' This is a symptom of disequilibrium and is not compatible with Islamic economic development. As Chapra (1985, pp. 37–38) has pointed out,

> Inflation implies that money is unable to serve as a just and honest unit of account. It makes money an inequitable standard of deferred payments and an untrustworthy store of value. It tends to pervert values, rewarding speculation and intensifying inequalities of income (condemned in Islam).

It is, therefore, considered obligatory on the part of the Islamic government to keep the rate of inflation under full control and resort to healthy monetary, fiscal and income policies.

Development strategies in Islam

These goals discussed above cannot be realized without appropriate strategy. In this regard, Islam has a clear advantage over both the capitalist and the socialist system. Some of the important strategies are discussed below.

Emphasis on moral uplift

> Do not acquire wealth from each other wrongfully…
>
> *Qur'an 2:188*

> Earning a lawful livelihood is obligatory upon every Muslim.
>
> *Hadith*

Perhaps the most important strategy for attaining the goals of Islamic economic development as discussed above is the integration of material and spiritual aspects of life in order to bring about moral uplift of the human being and the society in which the person lives. In effect, Islam does not make any distinction between these two aspects of life. Interestingly, all worldly activities may automatically bring out the heavenly benefits provided these are performed in accordance with the tenets of Islam. Chapra has very nicely described this issue as:

> All human effort whether for 'economic', 'social', 'educational', or 'scientific', goals is spiritual in character as long as it conforms to the value system of Islam. Working hard for the material well-being of one's own self, family and society is as spiritual as the offering of prayers, provided that the material effort is guided by spiritual values.
>
> *Chapra 1985, p. 46*

Emphasis on the brotherhood of mankind

One of the goals of Islamic economic development is the equitable distribution of income and wealth as described in the *Qur'an*, "And those in whose wealth is a recognized right for the (needy) who asks him and who is prevented" (70:241–251). This type of objective cannot be fully realized unless and until we recognize the universal brotherhood of mankind so much emphasized in Islam. Therefore, a belief in the brotherhood of mankind is regarded as one of the fundamental strategies of economic development in Islam. This will come about when human beings believe in the Oneness of God to Whom we are all accountable in the Day of Judgment.

Emphasis on total human development

Islam emphasizes human development in its totality, not only material development but also moral and spiritual development (Ahmad 1981). The Islamic pattern of development is conditioned by the extent of the appropriateness of investment in human capital. According to Mannan (1970, p. 401), education output is a complex social product. It may be considered as an investment for:

- raising productivity of labour;
- providing personal satisfaction for both parents and children;

- promoting national identity and forming an informed electorate;
- transforming of a rural society into an egalitarian society; and,
- influencing attitudes, norms and values or economic behaviour of the people.

This composite nature of educational product aiming at total human development for preparation of life is hardly reflected in the emphasis of the educational system in Islamic countries. Mannan maintains that the schools become irrelevant in most cases as "It induces alienation and de-Islamisation, making one foreigner within one's own country and culture" (1970, p. 402). Therefore, the existing education system needs reform and change. The following suggestions have been made:

First, there should be equitable distribution of educational resources. In the developing Islamic countries, this would mean a greater allocation of resources to mass literacy, primary education and adult education programmes.

Second, formal schooling may be considered rather costly in the developing countries for many years to come. It would, therefore, be advisable to give more emphasis to non-formal education.

Third, it is highly necessary that the curriculums should be modified and re-organized at all educational levels. Emphasis should be put on the closer link between the informal sector and its orientation towards rural development and self-employment.

Fourth, the labour market should be reoriented so that it becomes possible to create employment through non-formal education and on-the-job training. This would obviously de-emphasize the importance of higher education.

Fifth, it will be necessary to review the aims and objectives of education from an Islamic perspective.

Emphasis on consultation

Emphasis on consultation (*Shura*) directly owes its origin to the *Qur'an* (42:38). According to some Islamic jurists (such as Ibn Taymiyyah), this Islamic development strategy is not an option, but an obligation. Chapra opines that the consultation required is not of the "cosmetic kind, to rubber-stamp decisions made by the rulers". There should be a free, unhindered and fearless discussion of development issues related to economic well-being within the framework of the *Shari'ah* (Chapra 1995, p. 243).

Emphasis on balanced development

This strategy owes its origin to the *Qur'an*. It says, "And in the earth We have spread out (like a carpet); set thereon mountains firm and immovable; and produced therein all kinds of things in due balance" (15:191). This strategy refers to balanced and harmonious development of different regions within a country and of the different sectors of society and the economy. Decentralization of the economy and balanced development of the entire country without discrimination is not only a demand for justice, but is also essential for rapid economic development of the country concerned. This strategy when implemented would not only remedy economic dualism from which most Islamic countries suffer but would also lead to greater integration within each country.

Emphasis on useful production

While meeting the demand of the societies, Islamic economic development will be concerned about the correct product-mix. Production would not mean production of anything or everything that may have a demand or that the rich might be able to buy. Production would be concerned with things that are useful for man in accordance with the norms of Islam. The *Qur'an* states: "Not equal are things that are bad and things that are good, even though the abundance of the bad may dazzle thee" (5:100). The three priority areas for production would be as follows:

1. Abundant production and supply of food and basic items of necessity (including construction materials) at reasonably cheap prices;
2. Defence requirements of the Islamic world; and
3. Self-sufficiency in the production of capital goods.

Emphasis on distribution as the basis for resource allocation

Conventional economists tend to treat development and distribution separately. Normally, this conflict is resolved by saying that Islam encourages development with social justice. Mannan adds a new dimension to it. According to him,

> The key thrust of economic development in Islam lies not in the integration of development and social justice via distribution, nor in viewing development with social justice as an adjustment, but in treating distributive consideration as the fundamental basis for allocation of resources — both human and non-human, their use and maintenance.
>
> *Mannan 1970*

This emphasis is crucial in understanding the concept of Islamic economic development.

Emphasis on export substitution

One of the development strategies in most of the developing countries is to emphasize import substitution industries. This is based on the belief that if the goods that are imported can be produced at home, this would save foreign exchange which can be used for some other purposes for which no substitution is possible. However, if the amount of foreign exchange expenditure required for importing the capital goods needed for the production of import substitution industries exceeds the foreign exchange saved due to the reduction of the quantity of the imported goods, then this type of industry will have a negative impact on the earning of foreign exchange.

Apart from this purely economic argument against import substitution industries, there is another argument for this from the viewpoint of Islamic economics. Islam emphasizes the equitable distribution of income. If import substitution industries are accepted as a strategy, then it is apprehended that the distribution principle will get affected. The explanation is simple: poor countries normally import non-agricultural goods, and export agricultural goods. If import substitution industries are established this automatically mean that the country is emphasizing foreign goods at the cost of the agricultural sector. If, on the other hand, export substitution industries are established this would mean that more and more agricultural and agro-based industrial goods would be produced. This would lead to increase in employment and income of the rural people and hence the income disparity that exists between rural and urban sectors would tend to decline.

The above-mentioned strategy would of course, among other things, require a package of supportive policies including changes in the pattern of allocation of resources, imposition of appropriate productive tariff and taxation, introduction of sound wages, income and pricing policies and manipulation of monetary policies.

Emphasis on rural development

Islam's emphasis on equitable distribution of income and wealth should be given priority for development in the rural areas. Emphasis should particularly be placed on the development of infrastructure in rural areas and on the building up of agriculturally based industries so that migration from the rural areas to urban areas can be reversed.

Emphasis on group

The *Qur'an* says, "Help ye one another in righteousness and pious duty" (5:2). One economic implication of this *Qur'anic* dictate is that "stress is to be given on the use of the technique of 'cooperative forces' in achieving equilibrium in different sectors of the economy" (Mannan 1970, p. 36). Stated in another way, cooperation or group approach should be treated as an important strategy of socio-economic development in an Islamic society.

Emphasis on women

Islam is a universal religion. The *Qur'an* says, "Their reward according to the best of their actions. Whoever works righteousness, man or woman, and has Faith, verily to him will We give a new life, a life that is good and pure." (16:971).

The World Development Report (1981) shows that a great majority of the world's illiterate population is female. This is more so in Third World countries.

Islamic countries are no exception. In these countries the education bias towards men is most pronounced. The World Bank also suggests that educating girls may be one of the best investments a country can make in future economic growth and welfare. Even if the girls never enter the labour force, they can make tremendous contributions to the socio-economic development of a country in question. For example, in nutrition, household surveys made in Brazil show that for any given level of income, families were better fed when their mothers have higher education.

Islam fully recognizes the role of women in the family and in the society. The *Qur'an* categorically declares that "To men is allotted what they earn and to women what they earn" (4:321). This means that women will be held responsible for their deeds as much as their male counterparts. Therefore, if women are to make their contributions to national development, access to quality education is essential; and, hence, one of the development strategies of the Islamic countries should be to discard the bias towards men and allocate larger resources for women's education programmes.

Emphasis on the role of state

The last strategy, not necessarily the least in terms of importance, is the great emphasis given to the role of the state in Islamic economic development. While Islam recognizes individual freedom, it does not give any sanctity to the market forces. The state must play the decisive role in guiding and regulating the economy to ensure that Islamic socio-economic goals are realized. The role of a state should not, however, be confused with 'state intervention' as found in a capitalist economy. In an Islamic economy, "It is the obligation of the Islamic state to play an active role for the fulfilment of the goals of the Islamic system without either unduly sacrificing individual freedom or compromising social welfare" (Chapra 1985, p. 48). He also points out that the strategy should be to bring about a healthy balance between the interests of the individual and the society in accordance with one of the fundamental teachings of the Prophet: "Let no one harm others or be harmed by others".

It is the responsibility of an Islamic state to secure the proper environment for producers, investors and consumers. This would require, among others, prohibition of all types of illegitimate goods and services, prohibitive monopolies, elimination of *riba* in all forms, quality control of all goods and services, and adherence to announced specifications. Commitment from the government is also needed to undertake direct investment in areas where individuals are not able or willing to step in.

Distributive justice in Islam

Conceptual

The issue of distributive justice has been referred to both as one of the goals and has one of the strategies of Islamic economic development. Distribution of income among different productive factors of production in the form of wages, rent and profit is a very important part of an Islamic economy. This distribution is technically called 'functional distribution'. In connection with economic development, there is another type of distribution, i.e. 'distribution of personal income'. This section shows how income is distributed among different individuals in a society, regardless of how it has been received (rent or profit or any other means). A distinction is also sometimes made between distributive and redistributive schemes. When income distribution takes place through mutually agreed transactions among individuals through the market, it is referred to simply as distribution. On the other hand, when income distribution is effected through special market or non-market forces, it is called redistribution.

Goals

In Islamic economics, distributive justice has specific goals; some are economic and some are ideological. Economic goals are: to guarantee the fulfilment of basic needs (or essentials) of all people living in the society, irrespective of their age, sex, sect or region; and to reduce inequalities of income and wealth. The ideological goals are: to purify the donor's inner-self and their wealth; and to generate good will among the people (Ahmad 1981).

Tools and schemes

In Islamic economics, there are a large number of tools and schemes for achieving the distributive justice in the society. Some schemes are traditional and some are in-built into the Islamic system. Some measures are voluntary and some are mandatory, involving institutional arrangements. A few examples are given below.

Replacement of interest by PLS system

The traditional banks operate their transactions on the basis of a fixed return system, i.e. interest. This system has been found to be largely responsible for the maldistribution of income and wealth in the society. First, it helps widen the income gap between the rich and the poor. Funds collected from millions of poor and rich persons are loaned out to only the rich and relatively rich persons. The poor can provide neither the necessary collateral nor the assurance of repayments as the rich can do. Second, it widens regional gaps. Funds collected from the rural and urban areas are loaned out mostly to urban people.

The PLS system, on the other hand, involves sharing of profit and loss. The financier needs to examine the economic viability of the project. Whether the client is rich or poor is immaterial to Islamic banks. If the projects submitted by the poor appear to be more profitable than those of the rich, Islamic banks would give priority to the former. Therefore, under the PLS system the poor have a better chance of getting finance compared to the interest-based system. If implemented, this Islamic financial instrument can help redistribute income and wealth in the society.

Prohibition of harmful monopoly

Monopolies may be of two types, natural and artificial. Islamic economics is not necessarily against monopolies. Because of peculiarities in the process of certain commodities (such as electricity and gas), a certain degree of monopoly will have to be tolerated. However, Islamic economics does not support that form of monopoly that always strives to keep the price artificially higher and extracts excessive profits, causing hardship to the masses. This type of monopoly is responsible for the concentration of wealth and income in a few hands. Islamic economics demands that the government should intervene and control the prices of products (particularly if they are essential in nature) of the monopolists. Thus, prohibition of harmful monopoly can help redistribution of income and wealth in the society.

Access of natural resources to all

Islam prohibits concentration of many natural resources in few hands. One Hadith states: "The Muslims are partners of three things, in water, pastures and fires." Details of the Hadith can be seen in the *fiqh* literature. By analogy (*qiyas*), many items have been added under the category of natural resources. These include salt, sulphur and naphtha. Islamic economics demands that natural wealth should be easily accessible to all people, including non-Muslims living in an Islamic country, and that these should not be too costly for the common people. By implication, access by the common people to basic education is also included in the above list. By providing more equal access for all to natural resources, Islamic economics can help to improve the distribution of income and wealth.

Invigorating zakah *and* fitr

Of the redistributive schemes which are built into Islam, the institutions of *zakah* and *fitr* are the most important. *Zakah* is a compulsory payment by the rich to the poor. It is generally the responsibility of the state to collect *zakah* and distribute it according to the *Qur'anic* principles. As mentioned in the text, if properly administered, it can contribute 3–4 per cent of the GDP of the Islamic countries.

According to the majority of Islamic jurists, *fitr* is also obligatory on each Muslim, irrespective of age and sex. In other words, each individual pays it for themselves and for all their dependants "as long as they have more than one day's food for themselves and their dependants on the night of *Eidul Fitr*" (Zarqa 1981). Thus, this is paid by even the poor Muslims to those who are poorer, the beggars and the *miskins*.

Law of inheritance

Islam has a well-defined law of inheritance. This system leads to the redistribution of the wealth of the deceased. A large number of heirs are recognized. It does not concede a bequest in excess of one- third or bequest for any of the heirs, its impact on the dispersion of wealth is well known.

The system of marriage interacts to a great extent with the system of inheritance in generating distributive effects. Zarqa (1981) shows that if the coefficient of correlation between the levels of wealth of husband and wife is weak, the impact on the redistribution of wealth increases for the system of inheritance with all the children inheriting. On the other hand, if the rich marry only the rich and the poor marry only the poor (i.e. the correlation is high between the wealth of the spouses), the impact of inheritance on latent redistribution is weakened.

Awqaf *(charitable trusts)*

The *waqf* or charitable trust can also be considered as another important distributive scheme in Islamic economics. Throughout Islamic history, the institution of *waqf* has done tremendous service in the Muslim community. This perhaps owes its origin to the Hadith: "A man's works ends upon his death except for three things: (a) contribution to knowledge, (b) ongoing charity, and (c) faithful child." *Waqf* represents one form of 'ongoing' charity (*sadaqa jariah*).

Review questions

1.   Discuss and critically evaluate the concept of development strategies from an Islamic perspective
2.   What are the goals of economic development in an Islamic economy?
3.   Discuss distributive justice in Islam.

References

Ahmad, K. (1981). Introduction, in *Studies in Islamic Economics*, Leicester: The Islamic Foundation.
Chapra, M.U. (1985). *Towards a Just Monetary System*, Leicester: The Islamic Foundation.
Chapra, M.U. (1995). *Islam and the Economic Challenge*, Markfield and Verdon: The Islamic Foundation and IIIT.
Mannan, M.A. (1970). *Islamic Economics: Theory and Practice*, Lahore: Sheikh Muhammad Ashraf.
World Bank (1981). *World Bank Development Report*, Washington DC: World Bank.
Zarqa, A. (1981). Islamic economics: An approach to human welfare, in *Studies in Islamic Economics*, Leicester: The Islamic Foundation.

16

CONCLUSION

WHAT HAVE WE LEARNT? *QUO VADIS?*

LEARNING OBJECTIVES

This chapter is aimed at both students and tutors and addresses the concluding question: what have we learned? The objective is that students may:

- realize the essence of evolutionary learning in Islamic economics as an academic discipline in the eyes of the Islamic methodological worldview of Islamic unity of knowledge from the perspective of analytical universality
- critically discuss mainstream economic reasoning
- understand how Islamic economics is different from existing conventional economics
- appreciate the *Qur'anic* point of view on the extension of the economic and social phenomena from the earth to the heavens according to the law of *Tawhid* and understand how the *maqasid al-shari'ah* may be extended to study problems that extend beyond the narrow domain of economic matters.

The objective of this book accomplished: teaching the thoughtful student and the awakened Islamic scholar the Islamic methodological worldview of Islamic economics

This book began with the objective of the search and discovery of the epistemic methodology of Islamic scientific thought in general. The particularity of this generalized domain is the field of economics and society. This search and discovery was accomplished in the premise of the ultimate truth of unity of being and becoming. The underlying methodology for formalizing and applying this episteme of unity of knowledge could not be found in any other area of intellection but monotheistic consilience, in order to explain everything. This encompasses the conclusively universal explanation of the nature of truth versus falsehood; that is, oneness versus dichotomous differentiation; discursive holism to embrace collective resolution versus methodological individualism; and formalize the organic inter-relationship between all the good things of life as determined by the law of oneness versus rationalistic speculations on goodness.

The nature of Islamic socio-scientific order in its universal entirety is inextricably premised on the monotheistic consilience of unity of knowledge in everything. This methodology is conclusively contrary to the epistemology of rationalism. Rationalism neither has the methodology to reach out for the ultimate consilience of unity of knowledge nor does it give due attention to the theme of Islamic epistemic unity of knowledge and its induction and explanation of the generality and particularity of the world-system. This problem of heteronomy is the obstruction inside all of reality. Any episteme that does not decipher it and remove it from intel-lection does not attain the sure reality of the socio-scientific order.[1]

Neither Western scientific intellection nor the study of mainstream economics has been able to unravel the theory of consilience that remains intrinsic in sure reality. The nature and discovery of this final truth and the beginning of science and reality though does not mean the unravelling of any arbitrary new reality. Contrarily, it is to explain what reality truly is always, everywhere, and in every-thing; that is, over the entirety of knowledge, space, and time.

This book has accomplished the epistemic and logical basis of *Tawhid* (oneness) as a dynamic organic unity of relations that spreads its wings as the invincible law. *Tawhid* as *Qur'anic* monotheism is reality that is ingrained in belief and in the order of reality. It is also the methodology of how formally and in applicative ways of discovering the nature of that everlasting consilience of being and becoming. *Tawhid* as law thereby, spans everything; and it constructs upon this understanding the incessant evolutionary processes of knowing oneness through the discursive intellectual process. Indeed, the *Qur'an* (81:26–29) declares in respect of the finality, power, and logical basis of explanation, the phrase – *Quo vadis:* "Then whither go ye? Verily this is no less than a Message to (all) the Worlds: (With profit) to who-ever among ye wills to go straight: But ye shall not will except as God wills, – the Cherisher of the Worlds."

The guidance of this book arising from the *Qur'an* is to know how the socio-scientific universality needs to be learnt, formalized, and applied with great con-structive inferences. These goals should be achieved through the implementation of the principles of Islamic economics in participatory and complementary relations. The manifestation comprises complementary wholeness. This is the summation of emergent Islamic economics. In the substantively analytical form of the nature and essence of evolutionary learning in Islamic economics, there is a resemblance to mathematical 'knot theory': The evolutionary loops stretch out like elastic from one to the next evolutionary phase of the learning universe and so on, across the dimensions of knowledge, space, and time until the Hereafter.[2]

Teaching and learning the nature of *Tawhid* as the law of oneness ingrained in and unravelled by the signs of God in the order and scheme of reality is therefore neither too difficult nor too easy for the reflective mind. The demand of evolutionary learning to fathom the universe of Islamic organic oneness is to keep up advancing from the beginning to the end. This is the Islamic methodological worldview to which students and academics must be introduced in order to begin to understand the ultimate originality and end of being and becoming. This book has kept this foundational methodology of evolutionary learning in view while introducing its originality in terms of the epistemology of *Tawhid* and carrying it through in detail over many economic topics and comparative critical perspectives. However, the end is not near.

The universe is the science of the Signs of God in a generalized manifestation of *Tawhid*

The endless evolutionary 'mathematical knots' as continuous loops of evolutionary learning in the dimensions of knowledge, space, and time explain the universality of mind–matter interplay in the nexus that appears and enlarges. This nexus forms the conceptual and manifest signs of God in the order and scheme of everything. Within such vastly comprehensible complexity, Islamic economics becomes the study of the economic universe that specifically applies *Tawhid* as the law of monotheistic oneness in organic inter-causality of being and becoming.

Indeed, the *Qur'anic* design of the universe is a prolific ecological completeness. Within such a domain, all things exchange by discourse, complements and participation to form their organic unity of being.[3] The signs of God are reflective of the cause and effect of this organic explanation of the evolutionary learning universe of the Islamic unity of knowledge and its induction of everything. These elements can be good or the opposite, false ones. Yet they are uniformly explained and analysed by the self-same method that arises from the methodology of Islamic unity of knowledge. This book has developed this perspective of analytical universality in a thoroughly methodical way, while also being critically comparative of mainstream economic reasoning.

Thus the coterminous problems of economics and society taken together, and along with the diversity of specific ones centring on the objective criterion of well-being as substantively defined in this book, form the totality of the *Qur'anic* world-system. As an example, economic meaning abides even in the distant cosmology of the universe, when we interpret economic science as we have done in this book, as a holistic socio-scientific study centring on the objective of the multidimensional concept of well-being (*maslaha*). That is how the *maqasid al-shari'ah* may be extended to study problems beyond the narrow domain of commercial matters (*muamalat*) (Choudhury 2015).

This book has shown that this design of the learning universe reflected in the world-system cannot be dissociated from the divine law (law of *Tawhid*). If it were so, then contrary to the *Qur'anic* worldview of unity, the world-system would express the belief: "Give unto God what is God's; and unto Caesar what is Caesar's." That would be contrary to Islamic belief. In this regard Mohammad Marmaduke Pickthall (2005, p. 22) comments:

Islam is a worldly religion which considers first the worldly affairs of humanity, then the Hereafter that is an eternal continuation of the worldly life. It is difficult to believe that man can be saved in the Hereafter without being saved in this world. To be saved in the Hereafter without being saved in this world is simply unthinkable. The sensible approach is to follow the way shown to us by Prophet Muhammad. When his wife, Aishah, was asked by a Companion about the Prophet's daily conduct, Aishah replied that the conduct of the Prophet was the *Qur'an*, which is the guidance from God and for which Muhammad was given authority by God to interpret. That is why his conduct was the most exemplary expression of human conduct.

Economic science is a particular characterization of *Tawhid* as the law of consilience

The *Qur'an* points to the extension of the economic and social phenomena from the earth to the heavens according to the same law of *Tawhid*. In this regard we note the *Qur'anic* verse (14:24–27):

> Seest thou not how God sets forth a parable? – A goodly word like a goodly tree, whose root is firmly fixed, and its branches (reach) to the heavens, of its Lord. So God sets forth parables for men, in order that they may receive admonition.
>
> It brings forth its fruit at all times, by the leave of its Lord. So God sets forth parables for men, in order that they may receive admonition.
>
> And the parable of an evil Word is that of an evil tree: It is torn up by the root from the surface of the earth: it has no stability.
>
> God will establish in strength those who believe, with the word that stands firm, in this world and in the Hereafter; but God will leave, to stray, those who do wrong: God doeth what He willeth.

The tree of knowledge and its fecundity, and its opposite as the dying tree, can be interpreted through the moral productivity of resource abundance and its contrariness. In this book we have treated the topic of continuity of resource regeneration as a central issue of rejecting the postulates of mainstream economics. Knowledge makes the difference for the tree of abundance and its contrariety in resource scarcity of the dying tree. The latter comprises the central issue of mainstream economics, contrary to the first attribute that characterizes resource abundance in Islamic economics. The *Qur'an* thus extends the economic and social scenario by inducing the episteme of unity of knowledge in it as the only life-sustaining possibility and vice-versa. This book has extensively studied the *Qur'anic* explanation of knowledge induction and its opposite through the economic and social picture, which spans the universe.

Economics and science are not separated in the eyes of the Islamic methodological worldview. We have therefore developed the scientific version of Islamic economics without leaving out the pervasive relevance of the Islamic episteme of unity of knowledge inducing all things in both generality and details. The extension of economics and society in the broader meaning of complementarities between these disciplines is not simply restricted to the effect of technology and innovation that economics quantifies to make policy prescriptions. Rather, on the methodological scale of understanding, we have invoked formalism and applications that remain universal between economics and science so that these disciplines can intermingle to be inter-causal and organically tied. This book has implicated the meaning of the science of the signs of God in this sense of its universality. Economics is the intermingling field that remains universal when embedded with science and multi-disciplines in this sense of knowledge-induction.

This book has established the fact that, for the universality of a specific scientific worldview to overarch all the socio-scientific disciplines, two foundational premises must be satisfied. These are: first, that the conceptual and formal arguments must self-reference by means of the methodology and methods that are used; and second, that the method of addressing the objective criterion of the problem must be unique in all domains both by generality and particulars. Such a comprehensive model must be applicable both in the domains of truth and falsehood to establish the inherent objective. In the Islamic *methodological* worldview we have established this unique and universal groundwork to lie on the objective criterion of simulation of the well-being function (*maslaha*), subject to the system of circular causation relations between the representative variables of *maqasid*-choices. The true and the false domains of investigation produce their own opposite results. This work has established this case with many examples, exercises, and comparative critiques.

According to the *Qur'an,* the universe of the known (the knowable) and the unknown (the un-knowable) comprise an extended economic venue

The universality of the Islamic worldview is across all existence, encompassing mind, matter, and the extensive domain of the unseen that may not be fathomed. But despite this hidden quality of the core of things resting on Islamic unity of knowledge, the unseen has its own effect in reality; however, it is never known by a reverse causality from the material world-system to the unseen domain (*ghayb*). Such an exogenous one-directional influence of *ghayb* on materiality is essential in impressing unity of knowledge in everything. The obvious example of such exogeneity is of *Tawhid* in relation to the world-system. *Tawhid* establishes the nature of the world-system in both truth and falsehood. But the world-system cannot attain the completeness of the supercardinal domain of *Tawhid*. The evolutionary learning of the world-system as the interactive, integrative, and evolutionary (IIE) learning processes intra-system and inter-system, as the characterization of Islamic methodology of learning in this book, develops consciousness of the Islamic law into higher planes of knowledge. It simultaneously unravels the details of the world-system in greater depth. This book has derived this process of characterization from the *Qur'an* as the starting point of the ensuing circular causation of unity of knowledge and of its opposites that lie in falsehood.

Both of these realities, truth and falsehood, are essential to know well in order to guide reality in the directions of moral/ethical and social reconstruction. In this regard this book has explained that well-established knowledge of trade and *riba* is necessary to understand the inverse nature of inter-causal relations between them and thereby the nature of their inverse dynamics and the underlying cultures and institutionalism. Such analytical understanding can lead the *ummah* to its moral/ethical reconstruction away from *riba* and into an increasingly integrated and sustainable social economy.

The entire *Qur'an* is simply the endless study of *Tawhid* comprising its belief, and its influence on the organization of the generality and particularity of the world-system encompassing mind, matter, the seen and discoverable; and the unseen and unfathomable. This book has been a study of the *Qur'anic* reconstructive methodology along such ultimate epistemic foundations of organic unity.

Here is one such foundational characterization of the dynamics of *Tawhid* derived from the *Qur'an*. It reflects the IIE-learning process underlying the Islamic episteme of unity of knowledge and its induction of unity in the world-system:

See they not how God Originates creation, then Repeats it: truly that Is easy for God. (*Qur'an* 29:19)	Say: Travel through the earth And see how God did Originate creation; so will *Allah* produce a later creation: For God has power Over all things (*Qur'an* 29:20)	Not on earth nor in heaven Will ye be able (fleeing) To frustrate (His Plan), Nor have ye, besides God, Any protector or helper (*Qur'an* 29:22)
The reorigination process as of evolutionary learning is in the design of *Tawhid* (God). It reflects the design of divine law.	Continuity of the divine characterization of the evolutionary learning reality. This characterization is unravelled in the small experiences of life and is established in the final 'Closure' of the Great Event, The Hereafter. Thus *Tawhid*, the world-system, and *Akhira* together establish the sure reality. This comprises the socio-scientific methodology of Islamic phenomenology.	The Divine Law is the overwhelming truth as the core of everything. Thus the entire world-system of mind and matter including the Islamic world must turn to the Islamic centre and nowhere else. Besides *Tawhid* there is no other ontological source to guide to and explain the sure reality.

The double arrows establish the confirmation of the conscious truth of *Tawhid* and the world-system. This book has emphasized that the critical nature of Islamic methodology is continuous in knowledge, space, and time. Such is the socio-scientific study in which economics shares, spreading across the design of the universe according to the Islamic episteme of organic unity of knowledge. This is referred to in this book as *continuity* across *continuums*.

Socio-scientific thought is disabled in the absence of Islamic episteme of unity of knowledge

While the world of learning is always in search of a new episteme to ascertain socio-scientific reality, Islamic economists and scientists today must realize that they are faced with the challenge to host Islamic methodology at the heart of this endless field of inquiry (Iqbal 2012).[4] Failing to undertake this great task is to both deny truth that remains embedded in reality, and to fail in offering a substantially revolutionary methodological worldview to the world of learning at large so as to abide for all times. This book has presented this challenge to the young and reflective minds at this juncture of the world of learning. There is no religious and ritualistic partitioning in this study. According to the *Qur'an* there is an overwhelmingly great intellectual undertaking with the abiding truth in it for all.[5]

Now when we realize that the *Qur'an* has bestowed the entire universe on mankind as a field of socio-scientific inquiry of the signs of God, then the question to be faced squarely is: How has the study of science and economics been engulfed in the error of heteronomy? This book has explained this problem in which Muslims today have been caught. Islamic economics is the revolutionary new outlook of the sure reality in a garb of methodology of unity of knowledge. Islamic economics is conceptual, applied, and explains the real issues of collective market-institutional interrelations, and the interdisciplinary moral/ethical embedding.

In this sense of its socio-scientific inclusion, Islamic economics represents the totality of conscious transactions according to the good things of life (*hallal attayyabah, maqasid al-shari'ah*). Islamic economics is also based conceptually and in applied and inferential ways on the analytics of the well-being criterion (*maslaha*) linked with *maqasid*-choices. Islamic economics is also based on the avoidance of the choices that are opposed to or are not recommended by *maqasid al-shari'ah*. In all such determinations, Islamic economics undertakes the *Qur'anic* discursive approach (*shura*) to differentiate between truth and falsehood, good and evil (*Qur'an* 3:104):

> Let there arise out of you a group of people inviting to all that is good (Islam), enjoining *al-ma'roof* (i.e. Islamic monotheism and all that Islam recommends) and forbidding *al-munkar* (polytheism and disbelief and all that Islam has forbidden). And it is they who are the successful.

In the universal socio-scientific transactional understanding of Islamic economics the answer is now offered to those who ask: Why is it necessary to invoke the Islamic epistemology to establish the field of Islamic economics as the only true way to understand the sure reality? Why is it that without this foundational methodological worldview there cannot be and there has not been any such field of authenticity as Islamic economics as it stands today?

These questions can be answered by first understanding the exegesis of the *Qur'anic* verses. Second, we examine the analytical truth of these *Qur'anic* verses. We apply the exegeses to the great watershed of Islamic economics in the meaning of the universal socio-scientific transactions. Why is the present-day idea of Islamic economics untenable in the light of the *Qur'an*? How do these verses address the validity of Islamic economics above all others?

The *Qur'anic* verses we consider are the following, with their exegeses made by Choudhury (2003): "Such is God your Lord, the Creator of all things, there is no god but He: Then how ye are deluded away from the Truth!" (40:62). Delusion is to be away from the singular truth of *Tawhid* in belief, thought, and action. There is no other sure reality than *Tawhid* because of its central theme of unity of knowledge and the absoluteness of knowledge with God and in His law that differentiates the good things from the bad things of life. This cardinal law is reflected in the universe by the signs of God. When man has been given the revelation through the prophet then it must be considered for its truth in everything. This does not mean compulsion of belief. It means the credibility of this singular ground of truth that is premised in epistemic unity of being and becoming. Thus we find Hawking's words in regards to the failure and challenge of science to recognize this foundational objective of unity of science. Or else this concept is distorted to give it simply the meaning in physicalism without God in it as the divine One; and His law as the law of epistemic unity in explaining everything. Thus Muslims in particular and the world of learning overall ought to build upon the Islamic methodological worldview. There is no excuse.

The *Qur'an* denies the place of truth to the rationalists and their speculative philosophy. Thus *Tawhid* stands single, universal, and unique by its episteme of unity of knowledge and the world-system against the doctrine of rationalism. The *Qur'an* (51:10–11) says in this regard: "Woe to the falsehood-mongers, – Those who (flounder) heedless in a flood of confusion."

Hawking (1988, pp. 10–11) writes about his own emphasis on the need for unity of science:

> The eventual goal of science is to provide a single theory that describes the whole universe. However, the approach most scientists actually follow is to separate the problem into two parts. First, there are the laws that will tell us how the universe changes with time… Second, there is the question of the initial state of the universe. Some people feel that science should be concerned with only the first part; they regard the question of the initial situation as a matter for metaphysics or religion. They would say that God, being omnipotent, could have started the universe off any way he wanted. That may be so, but in that case he also could have made it develop in a

completely arbitrary way. Yet it appears that he chose to make it evolve in a very regular way according to certain laws. It therefore seems equally reasonable to suppose that there are also laws governing the initial state.

The problems of science are steeply buried in rationalism along with its ultimate premise on human claim of supremacy of reason above God. Economics reflects this overweening problem of self and individualism (O'Donnell 1989; Buchanan 1999), as does science by its heteronomy. Thereby, the extension of science of the signs of God in which Islamic economics, not mainstream economics, resides as the great beacon of universality, has been laid aside. This book has brought out many of the errors in economic reasoning in the face of Islamic economics.

On rationalism the *Qur'an* (24:35) declares:

> God is the Light of the heavens and the earth. The example of His Light is like a niche within which is a lamp, the lamp is within a glass, the glass as if it were a pearly [white] star lit from [the oil of] a blessed olive tree, neither of the east nor of the west, whose oil would almost glow even if untouched by fire. Light upon light. God guides to His light whom He wills. And God presents examples for the people, and God is knowing of all things.

The *Qur'an* (24:40) continues to explain the nature of rationalist inclinations:

> Or (the Unbelievers' state) is like the depths of darkness in a vast deep ocean, overwhelmed with billow topped by billow, topped by (dark) clouds: depths of darkness, one above another: if a man stretches out his hands, he can hardly see it! For any to whom God gives not light, there is no light!

The contrast of the ultimate truth of *Tawhid* in the sure reality with the rationalism of the non-Islamic world-system continues in these two uncompromising opposites. The challenge of the whole socio-scientific project is to believe, discover, formalize, and apply the Islamic methodology as a carrier of the divine light against the darkness of the rationalist and heteronomous world-system in entirety. One cannot discover truth out of darkness. Yet one can decipher falsehood and explain it in contrariness to truth by the divine law, which is complete and governs over the domains of truth and falsehood to establish the distinction between them in every sphere of experience.

Such a rise of consciousness in intellection as also in belief is the duty of Islamic scholarship to boldly and clearly unravel in the highest frontiers of knowledge. Indeed, God and the *Qur'an* (*Tawhid*) form the ultimate absoluteness of knowledge. The *Qur'an* (96:1–5) declares in this regard: "Read, in the name of your Lord Who created; created man from a clot of blood. Read! Your Lord is endlessly generous, Who taught by the pen, taught man what he did not know." Not to be able to present this declaration in the best of ways is to hide truth, and to be ignorant. Through such intellectual negligence, the Muslim world has failed.

The exhortation of the *Qur'an* (2:42) on the indispensable belief and practice of *Tawhid* is this: "And cover not *Truth* with *falsehood*, nor conceal the *Truth* when ye know (what it is)." While the universe that God has bestowed for the benefit of mankind is the playground for experiencing the blessings out of the functional nature of consciousness of *Tawhid* in the order and scheme of things, *Tawhid* by itself remains complete and productive. The Islamic worldview does not need to be mixed with the rationalist origin of non-Islamic episteme. In this verse, the *Qur'an* asks for restraint from mixing truth with falsehood. This is the same as mixing monotheistic oneness with rationalism in belief and intellection.

The foundational ontology is based on the domain of methodology – *Tawhid* versus rationalism. On the other hand, the diversity of methods and formalism that arises in compliance with the Islamic methodology is an acceptable venue of action. However, not all methods comply with the Islamic methodology. This book has shown that all the postulates of mainstream microeconomics and macroeconomics are contrary to Islamic economics. Thereby, the method of maximization objective of neoclassical economics in microeconomics and its prototype in macroeconomics and all different fields of science and economics are contrary to the Islamic methodological worldview of the Islamic economics – process-oriented learning methods. Islamic economics cannot accept methods that depart from the Islamic axiomatic reality. Yet all fields of criticism must be studied deeply. This book has thus been comparatively critical in nature to nurture the young and the thoughtful minds.

To teach and apply: how is Islamic economics different from existing conventional economics?

The field of Islamic economics is multidisciplinary in nature. Its study goes through stages of teaching and comprehension that are no different from the way that other thoughtful and useful subjects are taught and studied for the good of the learning world and academia. Even though students and scholars will begin from soft launching pads of the study of Islamic economics, the field will prepare them for critical investigation at advanced levels of multi-disciplinarity. These approaches entail the following directions; none of them is isolated from the rest. Without this holistic study, Islamic economics will not be understood and will fail to be beneficial to the world of learning, for students, scholars, and progeny.

1.   The methodology of Islamic economics must be strictly in accordance with the *Qur'an* and the *Sunnah* while treating human contributions in this area as subject to critical discourse (*shura* and *ijtihad*). While *fiqh* as jurisprudential interpretation is to be treated as a necessary way of understanding the law, rules, and circumstances, the practice of the *fiqhi* approach must be in continuous reference to the *Qur'an* and the *Sunnah* along with the discursive venue of *shura* and *ijtihad* in addressing emergent issues and problem of every kind. Exception must be made for matters of *aqidah* (Islamic faith), which are practices linked with Islamic belief and practices directly derived from

the *Qur'an* and the *Sunnah*. In the case of socio-scientific investigations, this approach remains most vivid. But since the socio-scientific universe is the universal world-system expression of *Tawhid* as law, therefore, the method of *fiqh al-Qur'an wal-Sunnah* along with discourse remains permanently continuous in generality and particulars. Continuity over the systemic continuums of knowledge, space, and time is an essential characteristic of the interactive, integrative, and evolutionary learning processes (IIE) in the theory and application of Islamic economics to all issues and problems in generality and particulars.

2. The derived exegeses of the *Qur'an* and the *Sunnah* in respect of the Islamic centrepiece of methodology must be made to yield its relevant formal and explanatory structure. This discovery of the socio-scientific permanence of the *Qur'an* and the *Sunnah* must result in a unique and universal formalism of 'everything'. The method that thus results can be diverse, but on the basis of critical examination such methods must comply with the nature of the Islamic methodology in respect of issues and problems under investigation.

   The universal and unique formal method in this book has been mathematized. It is a simulation of the well-being function (*maslaha*), subject to circular causation variables. The methodology along with the derived method extends the legitimate bounds of the *maqasid al-shari'ah* to all socio-scientific subtleties. Such a model is equally applicable in investigating the potential of moral/ethical reconstruction out of the temporary imperfections caused by non-*maqasid* variables. Such a model and method can also critically investigate the nature of relations of the un-Islamic cases.

3. The formal model of Islamic economics is always of a systematic and cybernetic type because of the organic nature of Islamic methodology of unity of knowledge and its induction of the diversity of issues and problems. These may be of the purely *maqasid*-type, purely non-*maqasid* type, or a mix of these. The end goal is interpretation of the existing state of the inter-variable relations and the inferences so derived for moral/ethical reconstruction in accordance with the Islamic worldview.

   The analytical properties of the formal model and its extensions must be studied in the most rigorous of ways. Such an approach will bring out the truly socio-scientific and analytical nature of Islamic economics while purifying the socio-scientific inquiry from pseudo-science or polemics.

4. Islamic methodology and the formal and explanatory methods, the analytical design, knowledge of the comprehensive mathematical properties, and the institutional discursive practices along with knowledge of the real world phenomena must be combined in methodical and applied approaches. These will take the form of empirical models and/or institutional discourse models determined on the basis of the nature of Islamic economic methodology and analytics. But at the same time, there is no need to tally explanation of Islamic economics concept, formalism, and empirical results with mainstream economic interpretations. We have thus followed the approach that McCloskey (1985) has suggested in regards to using common-sense realistic explanation of

results as opposed to stylized conceptual entrapping of mainstream economic theory. Almost all the time such theories have proved erroneous and unpredicted. The neoclassical economic theory has no empirical bearing.

5.   There is good reason to exemplify all Islamic economic conceptual points with real-life examples. The chapters of this book have followed such a direction. There are several exercises and examples that bring out the contrast of Islamic economics with mainstream economic theory and applications.

It is highly recommended that students and teachers bring and use the *Qur'an* in class lectures in order to refer to relevant *Qur'anic* verses for their exegeses on various topics of Islamic economics. It is necessary for teachers of Islamic economics to master this field of economic heterodoxy even as they are teaching. There are also many concepts mentioned for both mainstream economics and Islamic economics that are not elaborated upon. The teacher of Islamic economics would be required to explain such concepts and details to students. In every case the use of diagrams, examples and exercises, several of which are given in this text, should be used by the teacher. PowerPoints can be prepared from this text as a separate tool for presentation to students. This text covers enough material for a six-credit course.

One of the tests of the versatility of Islamic economics is its application to the study of mainstream methodological problems from the critical viewpoint. This is how Islamic economics assumes its growing universality and uniqueness. No wonder this has proven itself in the case of a wide coverage of issues and problems of modern nature in the critical light of Islamic methodology and its derived methods. Yet Islamic methodology and its derived methods remain in a different category. This book has examined a number of such issues and problems, contrasting Islamic economics with the mainstream economic approach. Many more problems and issues can be inquired into, that bring out the distinctive nature of Islamic economics and Islamic methodology, and its derived analytical and discursive methods.

The comprehensive example that we will finally wind up with is an Islamic economics orientation to complement the issues of poverty alleviation with human resource development, microenterprise development, and sustainable development. Over this is the understanding of justice as balance (*al-wasatiyyah*). In mainstream economic approaches to these issues, the argument made is that governments ought to lead the way to spend to alleviate poverty. It is also argued that human capital development ought to be the way towards the goal of poverty alleviation via productive employment. The goal of sustainable development focuses on the study of intergenerational conservation of environment, avoidance of waste, and reformation of consumption habits. Population growth is seen as a menace to sustainable development and to good standards of life. The idea of sustainability as the role of complementarities as balance between the good things of life and the overarching organic interrelationships between the good things of life is subjected to humanistic decisions. Humanism too is a form of ethical rationalism.

For instance, government spending to avert poverty is not the way to raise moral and ethical consciousness in concert with individual, institutions, and society by extended participatory development (Bordo 1998). There is theoretical impossibility in moving an interior 'starvation point' to the production possibility surface by policy measures, as has been theorized by Amartya Sen (1986). Human capital theory is a neoclassical concept. It focuses on labour market efficiency out of the mainstream concept of efficiency and productivity. Yet the intergeneration effect of human capital theory can result in utter inequality (Bowles & Gintis 1975). The concept of social justice in the framework of the social welfare function poised between social justice and economic efficiency is a competition and conflict model based on resource scarcity.

EXERCISE 16.1

Make a critical assessment, using the Islamic methodological worldview of Islamic economics, of the outcry being raised in Western circles on the issue of 'Man and Machine' for use in warfare, such as in future robotics and today's drone warfare technology. The West and its academic mind-set are promoting the use of robots in war machinery to replace soldiers on the ground. The arguments made are that fewer soldiers would be lost in battle, and more destruction at less cost will be inflicted on the enemy. This efficient form of warfare will be conducive to winning. The proponents call this a robotic approach to war moral and ethical.

How would you raise a critique on the theme of 'Humanity and Machine' in the light of the Islamic methodological worldview in Islamic economics regarding the Western mind-set of warfare efficiency, social cost evaluation, and the consequential objective of optimization of the war output?

At the end

This book has argued against such a futile moral and ethical concept that cannot be embedded in ethico-economic theory. This book has argued against every such concept of mainstream economic theory. Instead, the idea of sustainability was translated in terms of the balance (al-wasatiyyah) of sustainability by way of extensive complementarities reflecting Islamic unity of knowledge induced in and between the maqasid-choices in the well-being function (maslaha).

It is noteworthy to understand the following approach suggested by the World Bank (2000, p. 6) in poverty alleviation by means of factors of extensive complementarities:

> The choice and implementation of public actions that are responsive to the needs of poor people depend on the interaction of political, social, and other institutional processes. Access to market opportunities and to public sector services is often strongly influenced by state and social institutions, which must be responsive and accountable to poor people. Achieving access,

responsibility, and accountability is intrinsically political and requires active collaboration among poor people, the middle class, and other groups in society. Active collaboration can be greatly facilitated by changes in governance that make public administration, legal institutions, and public service delivery more efficient and accountable to all citizens – and by strengthening the participation of poor people in political processes and local decision making. Also important is removing the social and institutional barriers that result from distinctions of gender, ethnicity, and social status. Sound and responsive institutions are not only important to benefit the poor but also fundamental to the overall growth.

EXAMPLE 16.1: FAILURE OF STUDYING SOCIAL JUSTICE IN MAINSTREAM ECONOMICS AND THE ALTERNATIVE IN ISLAMIC ECONOMICS

Here is another example concerning the concept of justice in the *Qur'an* that points out the economic and scientific relevance in such a study of social justice. Muslims have not been able to offer a *theory of justice* out of the *Qur'an*. What has been done is a personal thought regarding certain *attributes of justice* (Kamali 2002). Yet personally felt enumeration and discussion of attributes are polemics. They cannot convey the true universal picture. For the universal *theory* of justice, it is necessary to derive it from the Islamic worldview arising from the *Qur'an* regarding a *theory of justice*. Bayrakli (1992) writes regarding Al-Farabi's understanding of justice in the *Qur'an* as balance. And in the vastness of knowledge, space, and time the precept of balance (*al-wasatiyyah*) spans the heavens and the earth in the divine law. Thus if the life-fulfilling regime of development that has been studied in this book is the direction to contain the *maslaha*-complementarities for poverty alleviation, then there ought to be an organic balance of inter-causal relations between poverty alleviation and the other factors of *muamalat* and the cosmological issues to sustain such regimes of participatory development *res extensa* and *res cogitans*. A theory of justice according to the Islamic worldview must therefore arise from the inter-causal relationships between *Tawhid, al-wasatiyyah*, and *maqasid al-shari'ah* according to the principle of balance (*mizan*) in the *Qur'an*. This book has treated such a holistic organically linked approach to the *maslaha* of *zakah*, trade by exchange and inversion of *riba* in the economy-wide context.

The call on Islamic thinkers

Islamic thinkers and students must rise to the challenge and intellectualize the Islamic methodological worldview as in the economic science of Islamic economics. This is the way to render the revolutionary originality of the new way of thinking and constructing moral and ethical reality inside the socio-scientific order with science and economics progressing the entire way. All it needs is the will, organization of thought, and bold conduct of *Qur'anic* intellection and its application in everything across the world of learning.

Shall we then rhyme together with conviction?

> The long day wanes: the slow moon climbs: the deep
> Moans round with many voices. Come, my friends,
> 'T is not too late to seek a newer world.
> Push off, and sitting well in order smite
> The sounding furrows; for my purpose holds
> To sail beyond the sunset, and the baths
> Of all the western stars, until I die.

Alfred Lord Tennyson, Ulysses

Notes

1 *Qur'an* (69:1–3): "The Sure Reality! What is the Sure Reality? And what will make thee realise what the Sure Reality is?"

2 Rovelli (1993) defines a mathematical knot as follows: "One starts with a loop – a closed smooth curve – in space. The loop must never intersect itself. Then two closed loops represent the same knot if one of them can be deformed continuously into the other without ever introducing self-intersections. Equivalently, one may think of space as superstretchable rubber; two closed loops represent the same knot if one can stretch, bend, and shrink the space until one curve takes the position of the other... A knot is a link formed by a single loop."

3 We have pointed out in Chapter 4 that the *Qur'an* explains the complete order of creation as the domain of exchange. Such exchange is not only in respect of the material artefacts. In fact, wherever there is the concept of everlasting learning equilibriums, and not steady state terminal equilibrium, there is the reality of balance and exchange. Equally there is the contrariness to these principles, as in the case of disequilibrium of exchange caused by the choices of the forbidden things in the concept of total valuation. Consider the following verse of the *Qur'an* (24:38) in respect of the reward in heaven: "That God may reward them [according to] the best of what they did and increase them from His bounty. And God gives provision to whom He wills without account." One finds similar universal importance given to trade in the sayings of the Prophet Muhammad, for instance in this Hadith (385, Narrated: Abu Said Al-Khudri): "God's Apostle said, "Do not sell gold for gold unless equivalent in weight, and do not sell less amount for greater amount or vice versa; and do not sell silver for silver unless equivalent in weight, and do not sell less amount for greater amount or vice versa and do not sell gold or silver that is not present at the moment of exchange for gold or silver that is present."

Here is another saying of the Prophet Muhammad (Hadith 511, Narrated: Abu Said Al-Khudri): "Once Bilal brought Barni (i.e., a kind of dates) to the Prophet (peace be upon him) and the Prophet (PBUH) asked him, "From where have you brought these?" Bilal replied, "I had some inferior type of dates and exchanged two *Sas* of it for one Sa of Barni dates in order to give it to the Prophet (SAW) to eat." Thereupon the Prophet (SAW) said,

"Beware! Beware! This is definitely *riba* (usury)! This is definitely *riba* (usury)! Don't do so, but if you want to buy (a superior kind of dates) sell the inferior dates for money and then buy the superior kind of dates with that money."

There is also the message of the central role of exchange as reward between God and his beloved ones in heaven: "The Messenger said, "When the inhabitants of Paradise enter Paradise, God will say to them, 'Do you want Me to give you anything more?' They will reply, 'Have You not made our faces bright? Have You not brought us into Paradise and moved us from Hell?' God will then remove the Veil and they will feel that they have not been awarded anything dearer to them than looking at their Lord.'"

4 Allama Mohammad Iqbal wrote (1958): "The not-yet of man does mean does mean pursuit and may mean failure; the 'not-yet' of God means unfailing realization of the infinite creative possibilities of His being which retains its wholeness throughout the entire process:

> In the endless self-repeating,
> For evermore flows the Same,
> Myriad arches springing, meeting,
> Hold at rest the mighty frame.
> Streams from all things love of living,
> Grandest star and humblest cold
> All the straining, all the striving,
> Is eternal peace in God.

Goethe

5 *Qur'an* (38:87): "It (the *Qur'an*) is indeed a message to the worlds."

References

Bayrakli, B. (1992). The concept of justice (*Adl*) in the philosophy of Al-Farabi, *Hamdard Islamicus*, 5: 3.

Bordo, O.F. (ed.) (1998). *People's Participation: Challenges Ahead*, pp. 43–62, New York: Apex Press.

Bowles, S. & Gintis, H. (1975). The problem with human capital theory: a Marxian critique, *American Economic Review*, May.

Buchanan, J.M. (1999). The domain of constitutional economics, in his *The Logical Foundations of Constitutional Liberty*, Indianapolis, IN: Liberty Fund,.

Choudhury, M.A. (2003). *Explaining the Qur'an, a Socio-Scientific Inquiry*, 2 volumes, Lewiston, NY: Edwin Mellen Press.

Choudhury, M.A. (2015). *Res extensa et res cogitans de maqasid as-shari'ah*, International Journal of Law and Management, 57(3).

Hawking, S.W. (1988). *A Brief History of Time, From the Big Bang to Black Holes*, New York: Bantam Books, Inc.

Iqbal, M. (1958). *The Reconstruction of Religious Thought in Islam*, Lahore, Pakistan: Ashraf Printing Press.

Iqbal, M. (ed.). (2012). *Studies in the Islam and Science Nexus*, Volume I, Farnham, UK: Ashgate.

Kamali, H. (2002). *Freedom, Equality, and Justice in Islam*, London: Islamic Texts Society.

McCloskey, D.N. (1985). *The Rhetoric of Economics*, Wisconsin, MN: The University of Wisconsin Press.

O'Donnell, R.M. (1989). *Keynes: Philosophy, Economics and Politics*, London: Macmillan.

Pickthall, M.M. (2005). *The Quran Translated: Message for Humanity*, Washington DC: International Committee for the Support of the Final Prophet.

Rovelli, C. (1993). *Knot theory and space-time: Yearbook of Science and the Future*, Chicago, IL: Encyclopaedia Britannica, Inc.

Sen, A. (1986). Exchange entitlement, in his *Poverty and Famines: An Essay on Entitlement and Deprivation*, pp. 167–73, Oxford: Clarendon Press.

World Bank. (2000). *World Development Report 2000–2001*. New York: Oxford University Press.

INDEX

Printed in the United States
by Baker & Taylor Publisher Services

Printed in the United States
by Baker & Taylor Publisher Services

Printed in the United States
by Baker & Taylor Publisher Services